ARTFUL CRAFTS

ARTFUL CRAFTS

Ancient Greek Silverware and Pottery

Michael Vickers and David Gill

CLARENDON PRESS · OXFORD

Oxford University Press, Walton Street, Oxford OX2 6DP
Oxford   New York
Athens Auckland Bangkok Bombay
Calcutta Cape Town Dar es Salaam Delhi
Florence Hong Kong Istanbul Karachi
Kuala Lumpur Madras Madrid Melbourne
Mexico City Nairobi Paris Singapore
Taipei Tokyo Toronto
and associated companies in
Berlin Ibadan

Oxford is a trade mark of Oxford University Press

Published in the United States
by Oxford University Press Inc., New York

© Michael Vickers and David Gill 1994
First issued in paperback 1996

British Library Cataloguing in Publication Data
Data available

Library of Congress Cataloging in Publication Data
  Artful crafts : ancient Greek silverware and pottery
Michael Vickers and David Gill.
  Includes bibliographical references.
  1. Pottery, Greek. 2. Vase-painting, Greek. 3. Silverwork,
Ancient—Greece—Influence. 4. Goldwork, Ancient—Greece—
Influence. I. Gill, David (David William John), 1961– . II. Title.
NK3840.V53 1994   738.3'0938—dc20   93–49462

  ISBN 0–19–813226–3   ISBN 0–19–815070–9 in paperback

10 9 8 7 6 5 4 3 2 1

Printed in Great Britain on acid-free paper by
St. Edmundsbury Press Ltd., Bury St. Edmunds

Preface to New Edition

'Nor is ignorance the reason why we do not allow our potters to repose on couches, and feast by the fireside, passing round the glittering bowl, while their wheel is conveniently at hand, and working at pottery as much as they like and no more . . . for if we listen to you . . . the potter will cease to be a potter' (Plato, *Republic* 420f–421a). We wish that we had been aware at an earlier stage of this statement by an Athenian who, for all his faults, was in a position to know how social and artisanal life was conducted in classical Greece. Similarly, Aristotle's observation that 'some objects change their colour and assume a variety of hues when polished by rubbing or other means, like silver, gold, copper and iron, when they are polished' (*de Coloribus* 793[a]), should have been known sooner. Between them, these quotations vindicate the case we have made in *Artful Crafts* for the low status of workers in clay in classical Athens, and for the tolerance of oxidized silver in Greek antiquity. We are grateful to kind friends for having drawn them to our attention, and to generous reviewers for having pointed out minor errors which have been corrected in this reprint.

January 1996   M.V.
                                                                                  D.G.

Preface

J U S T recently, a piece of decorated Greek pottery was sold at Sotheby's for more than £2m. Such a transaction says a great deal about the perception of 'Art' (and the aspirations of its collectors) in twentieth-century Europe and America. But what relevance has this to antiquity? It is a commonplace to assume that the values which prevail today in some sense reflect the esteem in which such products were held in classical Athens; that the undoubted skills which are reflected in 'Greek vases' must have commanded equal respect—and monetary value—among the contemporaries of Pericles or Demosthenes. Yet this equation is illusory. It is a myth that has grown up because of the nature of what has survived the passage of two and a half thousand years, a myth which the writings of those specializing in such remains has done little to dispel. Because pottery survives in such quantity (often in tombs), and is the most abundant medium to carry traces of the rich artistic life of the period, it has been assiduously collected by modern bourgeois Europeans and Americans to represent the achievement of Greek artists in a formative phase of European culture. Through an unexamined (and sometimes actively promoted) assumption that such surviving materials are truly representative of the entire output of ancient craftsmen, pottery has come to be seen as an 'Art' in its own right: created for itself and desirable as a commodity. Ancient Greeks were imagined as dining off pottery, and patronising potters much as Renaissance princes patronised artists and craftsmen. The reconstructions, like the museum displays, were entirely ceramocentric.

The literary and epigraphic record of the period, however, presents a different picture. We read of temple treasuries containing thousands of vessels in precious metal; rich townsmen flaunting their possession of silver drinking-sets, misers begrudging their loan. Such equipment is now long gone: lost to the melting pot, or turned, when times became hard, into coin to purchase necessities, or to hire military help. Such pieces were literally worth their weight in gold or silver; the prices paid for them were fully comparable with the sums now paid for pots at Sotheby's. But what of the pots themselves? Surviving inscriptions record prices that were trivial fractions of the cost of a single silver cup—just one of which would have paid for hundreds of kilograms of finely painted pottery. In the course of the last three centuries of collecting, however, ancient values have been turned upside-down. How reliable, therefore, are the conclusions of an art history based on a fraction of the original output of an ancient society—and that limited to the cheaper and more disposable products which have differentially survived to dominate twentieth-century museum collections? Is it not more likely that pottery as a medium was part of a collectivity of craft skills, influenced in its design not just by other pottery and pot-painters but by metalsmiths, textile workers, and painters in other media? It is the pottery itself which can help to answer such questions. A tradition of Oxford scholarship that has included such distinguished figures as Sir John Myres and Sir Arthur Evans has consistently pointed to the analogies between pottery design and that of contemporary metalwork: metalwork which, as a more precious and valuable medium preferred by those able to afford it, would inevitably have set the tone for craftsmen working in humbler materials. Fortunately, not all the products of craftsmanship in precious metal have disappeared. In the barbarian lands on the fringes of the Greek world, imported pieces were put into the tombs of native chieftains whose prestige was ensured by their ostentatious burials. Comparing such pieces with the more abundant pottery, it is clear that there are many similarities between them; and moreover, that ceramic products echo features which clearly have their origins in the designs appropriate to other media.

This book is a summary of work that began in the early 1980s, and of research that has been published in several places. It also attempts to clarify our thinking, which has evolved over time as we have listened to our critics and discussed our position with colleagues. It has also benefited from our curatorship of major collections of classical antiquities: MV in the Ashmolean Museum at Oxford and DG in the Fitzwilliam Museum at Cambridge. It includes new material that we feel strengthens our general argument. To some extent our case rests here; but at the same time, we hope that this book will stimulate further debate and discussion. In particular, we hope that readings of Greek imagery will be enriched once it is realized that the images in question were for the most part originally intended to be viewed as gold on silver or silver on bronze.

We have tried to separate our discussion of plate and its relationship to pottery from two other somewhat controversial areas; from first, our view that the absolute chronology of the archaic and early classical periods is in need of revision, and second, from our ideas concerning the role of pottery in ancient maritime trade. We can but touch on these issues here (and our case is in any case independent of them). Nor is this book about Sir John Beazley, whose special contribution to the study of Greek ceramics is well known. We have, however, consciously departed from his methodology and questioned some of his values. We realize that some of our colleagues see any criticism of the status of Greek pottery as an attack on the man, but we do not agree. Beazley raised important issues that need to be answered. We concur with Dr Johnson, who said that for the shuttlecock to remain in the air, it must needs be hit from both ends of the room. We appreciate that those who have formed private collections of Greek pottery—often on the advice of scholars—may not be especially comfortable with our conclusions and may feel that they have been ill-advised. But that is not our problem.

We should especially like to thank John Boardman, who first introduced us, and without whom this book might not perhaps have been written. We have also gained a great deal from the scholarly criticisms of Martin Robertson and Robert Cook. Similar, and other, debts are owed to: James Allan, Cesare Ampolo, Ernst Badian, Keith Bennett, Henry Blyth, Dietrich von Bothmer, Hugh Bowden, E. L. Bowie, Sidney Brandes, Ann Brown, Kevin Butcher, Ted Buttrey, Christopher Chippindale, Maria Čičikova, Graham Clark, Derek Content, Brian Cook, Jim Coulton, Stephanie Dalley, Nancy de Grummond, Richard Edgcumbe, Murray Eiland, Clive Foss, the late E. D. Francis, Michael Fulford, Philippa Glanville, Jasper Griffin, Gareth Harris, Francis Haskell, the late Richard Hattatt, Denys and Sybille Haynes, William Heckscher, Herbert Hoffmann, Nicholas Horsfall, Simon Hornblower, Seymour Howard, Oliver Impey, Michael Inwood, Ian Jenkins, John Ellis Jones, Richard Jones, J. Kathirithamby-Wells, Jerry and Suzanne Labiner, Viviane Lacroix, D. M. Lewis, Tullia Linders, François Lissarague, Arthur MacGregor, Cyril and Marlia Mango, Jody Maxmin, Christopher Mee, Peter Meech, Dieter Metzler, Gwyn Miles, Paul Millett, Terence Mitchell, the late Warren Moon, P. R. S. Moorey, Oleg Neverov, Peter Northover, John Oakley, Andrew Oliver Jr, Robin Osborne, Martin Ostwald, Kenneth Painter, Peter Parsons, Alain Pasquier, Carlos Picón, Maurice Pope, Dan Quillen, Julian Raby, Jessica Rawson, A. E. Raubitschek, John Rea, Ellen Reeder, Colin Renfrew, Christoph Reusser, Ellen Rice, Nicholas and Jenny Richardson, Sally R. Roberts, Joseph Rykwert, Irena Saverkina, Diana Scarisbrick, Alain Schnapp, Gertrud Seidmann, Michael Sharpston, Andrew and Susan Sherratt, George Sines, R. R. R. Smith, Anthony Snodgrass, Christiane Sourvinou-Inwood, A. J. S. Spawforth, Ian Spence, Andrew Stewart, Zofya Stos-Gale, Gerald Taylor, Tim Taylor, Dorothy Thompson, Jacques Tréheux, Gocha Tsetskhladze, Louis Valensi, Fanny Vitto, Andrew Wallace-Hadrill, Thomas Weber, Helen Whitehouse, Tim Wilson, Florence Wolsky, and Paul Woudhuysen. MV would like to acknowledge a grant for Research in Design History from the Guild of St George, and DG the tenure of a James Knott Research Fellowship at the University of Newcastle upon Tyne. The Jowett Copyright Trustees made a timely contribution towards publication costs.

We cannot adequately thank the staff of the Clarendon Press. They have handled this book with friendly patience and understanding; we owe particular debts to Hilary O'Shea, Lucy Gasson, and Elizabeth Stratford.

We must also thank our respective wives, Susan Vickers and Caroline Gill, for their forbearance. This book is dedicated to Brian Shefton, to whose friendship and instruction we owe much, and who, we hope, will come to see the merits of our case.

Oxford   MICHAEL VICKERS
Swansea   DAVID GILL

Contents

List of Illustrations

Abbreviations

AA	*Archäologischer Anzeiger*
AB	*Art Bulletin*
ADelt.	*Archaiologikon Deltion*
AJA	*American Journal of Archaeology*
AJ	*Antiquaries Journal*
AK	*Antike Kunst*
AR	*Archaeological Reports*
BABesch.	*Bulletin van de Vereeniging tot Bevordering der Kennis van Antieke Beschaving*
BICS	*Bulletin of the Institute of Classical Studies*
BMMA	*Bulletin of the Metropolitan Museum of Art*
BSA	*Annual of the British School at Athens*
CVA	*Corpus Vasorum Antiquorum*
FdD	*Fouilles de Delphes* (Paris, 1909–)
FGH	F. Jacoby, *Fragmente der griechischen Historiker* (Berlin and Leiden, 1923–58)
GR	*Greece and Rome*
HSCP	*Harvard Studies in Classical Philology*
IDélos	*Inscriptions de Délos* (Paris, 1926–)
IG	*Inscriptiones Graecae* (Berlin, 1873–)
JdI	*Jahrbuch des deutschen archäologischen Instituts*
JHS	*Journal of Hellenic Studies*
JRS	*Journal of Roman Studies*
NC	*Numismatic Chronicle*
OJA	*Oxford Journal of Archaeology*
PBA	*Proceedings of the British Academy*
PCG	R. Kassel and C. Austin (eds.), *Poetae Comici Graeci* (Berlin/New York, 1983–).
PdP	*Parola del Passato*
RA	*Revue archéologique*
REA	*Revue des études anciennes*
ZPE	*Zeitschrift für Papyrologie und Epigraphik*

1 Value and Simplicity: A Historical Case Study

I T is widely believed that Greek pottery was an especially valuable commodity in antiquity; the view is also widespread that pots with simple decoration are somehow more worthy than those which are ornate. The fact that many scholars in the field of classical archaeology have for long taken these ideas for granted should not obscure the reality that they are concepts of relatively recent date and that they have little to do with the values or aesthetic judgements of antiquity. It will be necessary to examine these questions before discussing what ancient Greeks did set a value on, and before reflecting upon the consequences for the interpretation of the ceramic record. This chapter begins by noting the concepts of 'value' and 'simplicity' expressed in a highly respected work of nineteenth-century scholarship, then shows how they are still widespread, and then examines how and when they started.

George Dennis's *Cities and Cemeteries of Etruria*, first published in 1848,[1] has been praised in recent years for its continuing 'charm and value'.[2] Indeed, 1985 saw the publication of an abridged version of the second edition of Dennis's influential work.[3] While the charm of his book remains undimmed, its 'value', at least as regards his assessment of painted pots, is open to serious question. The fact is that although *Cities and Cemeteries* may well contain an 'unrivalled wealth of accurate detail',[4] its author has confused the remains of antiquity with the totality of the ancient world, and as a consequence his view of the past is somewhat flawed.

Dennis's views with regard to the high value of ancient ceramics occur throughout his writings, but they are expressed in their most telling form in the account of 'painted vases' in his introduction to *Cities and Cemeteries*:

There can be little doubt, whatever purpose they originally served, that these vases were placed in the tomb by the ashes of the deceased, together with his armour and jewellery, as being among the articles which he most prized in life. That these vases are found in such multitudes in Etruria is the more astonishing when we remember that almost all the tombs which contain them bear manifest proof of having been rifled in bygone times. It is extremely rare to find a virgin sepulchre. At Vulci, where the painted vases are most abundant, not more than one tomb in a hundred proves

---

[1] Dennis (1848); (1878); (1883); (1907).
[2] R. Bloch, cited in Rhodes (1973), 12.
[3] Dennis (1985).
[4] Rhodes (1973), 56.

to be intact. It is obvious that those who in past ages violated these sepulchres were either ignorant of the value of the vases, or left them from superstitious motives—most probably the former, for they are often found broken to pieces, as though they had been dashed wantonly to the earth in search for the precious metals.[5]

The possibility that ceramic vessels may have been of negligible value both at the time of burial and when the tombs were violated has clearly been overlooked.[6]

The virtue of simplicity is another theme which frequently recurs in Dennis's work; a single example will suffice to give the flavour. Dennis is speaking of the earliest Attic red-figure style:

No one can casually view the best works of this style without delight; and a more intimate acquaintance with them begets in the man of taste an unbounded admiration. . . . The dignity of the conception and force of expression, not unfrequently rising to the sublime, the purity and chasteness of taste, the truth and simplicity of the design, the delicacy of the execution, well entitle the best vases of this style to the appellation of 'Perfect'.[7]

This attitude is made all the clearer when we read a few lines later of how Dennis regarded South Italian Greek pottery:

The vases are often of enormous size and exaggerated proportions. The multitude of the figures introduced, the complexity of the composition, the general inferiority and carelessness of the design, the flourish and lavishment of decoration—in a word, the absence of that chasteness and purity which gives the Perfect style its chief charm, indicate these vases to belong, if not always to the period of decadence, at least to the verge of it, when art was beginning to trick herself out in meretricious embellishments, and to forget her sublime and godlike simplicity.[8]

An example of South Italian ware is shown in Fig. 1.1.

There would be little reason for drawing attention to such views were it not for the fact that they are still central to the way in which classical archaeology is conducted in some quarters even today. J. D. Beazley was a leading figure in the study of Greek ceramics in the twentieth century. In discussing two pots which appeared to him to have enjoyed a long life above ground before being buried in a Campanian cemetery, he claimed that they

must have been treasured for many years before they were placed in the grave. Treasured it may be by more than one owner—father and son, father and daughter's husband. Treasured as wonders . . . of art pure and simple: not πάγχρυσα . . . but peak of possessions, κορυφὰ κτεάνων.[9]

---

[5] Dennis (1848), p. lxxxiii; (1907), 63–4; cf. (1878) and (1883), p. xcvi.

[6] See further, pp. 85–6, below.

[7] Dennis (1848), p. lxxxii; (1907), 62; cf. (1878) and (1883), pp. xciv–xcv.

[8] Dennis (1848), p. lxxxiii; (1907), 62; cf. (1878) and (1883), p. xcv.

[9] Beazley (1945), 158.

FIG. 1.1 Apulian red-figure pottery *pelike*. Bride at her *toilette*. Oxford, Ashmolean Museum AN G.269 (V.550).

Behind the charm of Beazley's prose, there lies a disturbing naïvety. The allusion to *panchrusa* and *korupha kteanon* is clearly a reference to Pindar's Seventh *Olympian Ode*, where the poet speaks of 'a solid gold bowl, the peak of possessions'.[10] But judging by the fees which Pindar and other poets could command,[11] or by such statements as 'one man is gladdened by honours and crowns won by wind-swift steeds; other men by living in chambers rich with gold'[12] or 'gold gleameth more brightly than all other lordly wealth',[13] it is unlikely that Pindar—or any other ancient Greek—would have understood the point that Beazley was trying to make.[14] This aspect of Greek material values will be explored more fully in the next chapter.

It would be invidious to assemble all the references in scholarly literature which have tended to the view that Greek pots possessed great value in the eyes of contemporary consumers, and that the pottery trade was synonymous with the 'luxury trade'.[15] An index of the degree to which this was, until recently, the prevalent view is provided by a statement in an influential work by a writer whose main interests lie outside the field of Greek ceramics: 'Most of the Greek painted pottery now on show in museums has been found in graves, which indicates that it was highly prized and regarded. Painted pottery was valued both for the amount of work and skill such painting entailed and for the nature of the scenes depicted.'[16] Another indication is provided by the title of the catalogue of a recent exhibition in the United States, namely *Wealth of the Ancient World* (Fort Worth, 1983), where pride of place is given to 'The Vases of Nelson Bunker Hunt', with, however, no reference to the now well-known but comparatively little-publicized fact that the prices recorded in antiquity for Greek pottery, painted or otherwise, are very low indeed.[17]

J. D. Beazley attributed many decorated Athenian pots to the hands of

---

[10] Pind. *Ol.* 7. 1–4.

[11] Cf. the 10,000 dr. (= 43 kg. of silver) given to Pindar by the Athenians in the 470s (Isocr. 15. 166), or the gold cup given to Euripides by King Archelaus of Macedonia later in the fifth century (Plut. *Mor.* 177a).

[12] Pind. *Fr.* 221. 1–3 (Snell–Maehler); cf. Bacch. *Enc.* 20a. 13–16 (Snell–Maehler).

[13] Pind. *Ol.* 1. 1 f.

[14] For other modern reversals of ancient values, see Wycherley (1976), 755: 'For Homer Rhodes was already old in story (*Il.* 2. 653–70), with three notable cities, "Lindos, Ialyssos and shining Kameiros" (the epithet is arginoeis in our text, but one wonders whether in fact Homer said argiloeis, with reference to the clay used for pottery'; the emendation χυτρεῖα ('potteries') proposed for χρυσεῖα ('goldsmiths' workshops') or χρυσία ('gold products') in Strabo's description of the reasons why Euboeans had once prospered on Pithecusae (5. 4. 9): for accounts of the problem,

see Mureddu (1972); Ridgway (1973), 21–2 n. 1; Buchner (1979), 135–6.

[15] A few examples must suffice: 'In the pottery line Athens enjoyed a complete monopoly . . . goods of the highest quality were being imported, presumably for the use of Persian court circles which would naturally demand the best': Woolley (1953), 185 (in fact, clay vessels were given to those the Persian king wished to dishonour (Ath. 11. 464a)); 'The ancient Etruscans collected Greek pottery (though not systematically) which they prized highly, imitated, and buried with their dead': Moon (1979), p. xvii; 'Athens was already beginning to challenge in both the eastern and western markets . . . with her fine black-figure vases which must certainly have been carried for their intrinsic value': Boardman (1980a), 17 (but contrast now Boardman (1988a), 28, and cf. Gill and Vickers (1990), 28 n. 212).

[16] Cooper (1981), 29.

[17] Johnston (1979), 35, and pp. 85–6, below.

individual artisans; among these his favourite, we are told,[18] was his 'Berlin Painter', a craftsman whose work frequently consists of a single figure silhouetted against a black background: the 'simplicity' of Dennis's 'Perfect' style taken to extremes. Likewise, Beazley's view of South Italian pottery echoed Dennis's: 'When we turn to the big Apulian vases of the second half of this century, we note the slickness of hand, and we can put up with a square inch or so here and there: but it is really time that vase-painting ceased.'[19] It is probably the case that more books and articles have been devoted to Beazley's 'Berlin Painter' in the past few decades than to any other decorator of Greek pots,[20] and although South Italian is beginning to gain favour[21] and emerge from 'neglect, except by a few specialists',[22] it is still widely felt that 'strong stomachs'[23] are necessary to appreciate it.

The cult of simplicity has its roots in an earlier generation than Dennis's (see below, p. 27). Dennis, as we have seen, gave expression to it in 1848. A year later, we find Dennis's friend Emil Braun, secretary of the Istituto di Corrispondenza Archeologica at Rome, preferring the archaic style of the newly discovered François vase even to that of 'many vases painted in red-figure of the so-called perfect style', making adverse comments the while about the degeneracy of both the Baroque style and South Italian pottery.[24] In the same year, John Ruskin made a moral issue of the nature of ornament, declaring that: 'Nobody wants ornaments in this world, but everybody wants integrity . . . ornament is an extravagant and inessential thing.'[25] Not many of his contemporaries heeded him, but 'simplicity' was nevertheless a recurrent theme among *bien pensants*. In this century, the Modern Movement 'eschewed ornament with the greatest acerbity'.[26] In 1908, Adolf Loos, 'the arch-enemy of all ornament',[27] published his influential *Ornament and Crime*,[28] in which he declared: 'I have had the following perception and presented it to the world: evolution of culture is synonymous with the removal of ornament from objects in everyday use.'[29] It was Loos, moreover, who in 1898 wrote that 'Greek vases are as beautiful as a machine, as beautiful as a bicycle.'[30] He was presumably thinking of the 'simple' kind.

[18] Ashmole (1970), 454.

[19] J. D. Beazley, in Beazley and Ashmole (1932), 64.

[20] Four books and monographs and seventeen articles during the period 1952–87. On low prices in antiquity for pots attributed to Beazley's 'Berlin Painter', see p. 86, below.

[21] Cf. Mayo (1982); Stähler (1985).

[22] R. M. Cook (1972), 191. Noteworthy among these specialists is A. D. Trendall, who has written many of the standard works on South Italian painted pottery.

[23] Ibid.

[24] 'molti dipinti vasculari a figure rosse del cosi detto stile perfetto': E. Braun, in François and Braun (1849); (Marzi (1981*a*), 82).

[25] Ruskin (1903–12), 8. 83.

[26] J. Rykwert, 'Ornament is No Crime', in Rykwert (1982), 94.

[27] J. Rykwert, 'Adolf Loos: The New Vision', ibid. 71.

[28] A. Loos, 'Ornament und Verbrechen', in Loos (1962), 276–88. One of the few ornaments Loos allowed himself was the use of the Doric Order: cf. the façade of his Villa Karma at Clarens: Behalova (1970), 13, fig. 6; or his *Project for the Chicago Tribune Tower* of 1923: Rykwert (1982), 66; Schachel (1970), 8, fig. 4.

[29] Loos, 'Ornament und Verbrechen'.

[30] A. Loos, 'Glas und Ton', in Loos (1962), 57: 'Die griechischen Vasen sind schön, so schön wie eine Maschine, so schön wie ein Bicycle.'

Even today, we find that arbiter of contemporary elegance Sir Terence Conran declaring that 'to be simple in decoration is always to be in good taste',[31] which, however true it may have been back in the 1960s, is patently not 'always' the case.[32] Admiration of the simplest kind of Greek vase decoration and active dislike of the most ornate seems to be due to a largely unconscious modernism on the part of the *cognoscenti*.[33]

VALUE

The origin of the notion that Greek pots were valuable, and its persistence, lie in the close relationship which most scholars who have studied Greek vases have had with the art market.[34] The first major sale of Greek pots in modern times was made by Sir William Hamilton in 1774 when he persuaded the British Museum to pay 8,000 guineas for his collection. The sale was only achieved after a long campaign, the most prominent, and lasting, element of which was the sumptuous publication (Fig. 1.2) of pots in his own and other large collections in the Kingdom of the Two Sicilies.[35] When the first two of what were eventually four volumes were published in Naples in 1767 and 1770,[36] it was uncertain quite who would buy the goods on offer, and so they were targeted at two possible audiences: the collection, it was said, was 'equally proper for the compleating of well understood Collections of Prints and designs, or to furnish in a manner not only agreable but useful and instructive, the Cabinet of a Man of Taste and letters'.[37] The writing of the text was put in the hands of Pierre d'Hancarville, a remarkable personality who was well acquainted with J. J. Winckelmann and who clearly shared many of his liberal views (Fig. 1.3).[38]

D'Hancarville performed a highly astute marketing job on Hamilton's vases,[39] but it is only by paying close attention to the composition of the text, and the order in which the volumes were published, that it is possible for us to see how really clever he was. Volume 1 was published in 1767 (not 1766 as stated on the title page), and volume 2 in 1770. This may have been a matter of policy: to whet the public's appetite with a foretaste and then

---

[31] Quoted in *The Times* (London), Saturday section, 19–25 May 1984.

[32] For an evocation of 1960s' 'simplicity', see Priestley (1965), 120: 'a non-profit-making shop for handknitteds, woodcarvings, sealskin articles and handwoven materials, all in flawless taste'.

[33] And perhaps not so unconscious: cf. Robertson (1989*a*), 319.

[34] See Hoffmann (1979). Note too Beard (1986): 'No one would suggest that he exploited his position . . . But others profited from Beazley's work, for he provided that most saleable of commodities, artists' names.'

[35] On the Neapolitan antecedents of Hamilton's collecting activities, see Lyons (1992).

[36] Loose sheets were available by April 1767: Rykwert (1980), 403; cf. Ramage (1991); bound volumes were not issued until later in 1767 (Ramage (1991)) or early 1768: Rykwert (1980), 403–4.

[37] D'Hancarville (1766[1767]–76), 1. 168. On the importance of 'audience targeting', see Vestergaard and Schroder (1985), 71–3.

[38] For d'Hancarville, see Lamberg (1774), 116–18; Haskell (1987); Ramage (1991); Schnapp (1991); Griener (1992). For Winckelmann's political outlook, see Metzler (1983–4), 7–17.

[39] See further Ramage (1987) (on the care that went into the composition even of the initial letters of the publication); Ramage (1990*a*) (on Hamilton's salesmanship in general).

FIG. 1.2   Dedication of P.
d'Hancarville, *Hamilton
Collection*, 1 (Naples, 1766
[1768]).

to follow through with what was intended to be the main offering (in fact the plates for volumes 3 and 4 were pawned by d'Hancarville in 1770 and were only published in 1776). This arrangement necessitated holding over to volume 2 part of the introductory matter said to have been originally intended for volume 1. D'Hancarville put the matter thus:

It is to answer the Expectations of the Public and the wishes of our subscribers that we now give them the first Volume, if we had in this Volume placed the dissertations only without the Plates, they would have had just cause to complain, but on the other hand it being impossible to give the Plates and their Explanations at the same time, without swelling the first Volume into an enormous size, we have

FIG. 1.3   A fanciful 'Tomb of Winckelmann': P. d'Hancarville, *Hamilton Collection*, 2 (Naples, 1770), 3–4.

been obliged as much as possible to keep a just medium between these two inconveniences.[40]

It is unlikely that either d'Hancarville or Hamilton can have been quite as disingenuous as this, for the essay in which the status in antiquity of the pottery on offer was discussed was one of the pieces held over. The arguments presented there are very weak, as we shall see; had they appeared in 1766 (or 1767) a possibly sceptical world might have seen through them. As it was, the world had to make do with learned, but largely irrelevant treatises: 'Of the Origin of the Etruscans and their letters', 'Of the history of Etruscans and what we know of their customs', and 'Of Architecture, Antiquity and the Tuscan Order'. These were especially irrelevant as one of the major, and valid, arguments d'Hancarville presented elsewhere in the

[40] D'Hancarville (1766[1767]–76), 1. 168–70.

FIG. 1.4 Corinthian pottery column-crater. Huntsmen. P. d'Hancarville, *Hamilton Collection*, 1 (Naples, 1766 [1768]), 152, pl. 1.

work was that the pottery in question was not Etruscan but Greek, albeit as yet Campanian Greek.

A treatise towards the end of volume 1 entitled 'Of Sculpture and Painting' deals with the literary sources for these arts in antiquity, but does not yet speak of painted pottery. This topic is broached only near the very end, when two pots, a Corinthian column-crater (Fig. 1.4) and an Attic red-figure hydria, are discussed in some depth. The former, whose 'ornaments . . . are of the most ancient stile' was said to be 'one of the most ancient monuments of the painting and writing of the Greeks',[41] the latter (Fig. 1.5) to be 'not . . . unworthy of Raphael himself'.[42] Winckelmann is cited as saying much the same about classical pottery: 'The painted clay vases are all the same the marvel of ancient art.'[43] The only value which is adduced for Hamilton's vases at this stage is educational:

[41] Ibid. 1. 164.   [42] Ibid. 1. 166.   [43] Ibid. 1. 168.

FIG. 1.5 Attic red-figure pottery decoration. Women. P. d'Hancarville, *Hamilton Collection*, 1 (Naples, 1766 [1768]), 164, pl. 5.

such is the value of the singular Collection which we present to the Public, that of all the Collections that can possibly be made either of marbles, Bronzes, Medals or engraved Stones, this alone is capable of indicating the successful progress of Painting and design; and as in a Gallery of Pictures one endeavours to unite those of the Master from Ghiotto and Cimabue down to our time, so in this Collection, one may see the stiles of the different periods in the Arts of the Ancients.[44]

Any suggestion that they may have been valuable in monetary terms is held over until volume 2, and then only after a further disquisition.

The first fifty-five pages of volume 2 are taken up with a 'Preliminary discourse' in which d'Hancarville elaborates on his perception of the role of the artist in society. Artists in antiquity apparently had an enviable existence: 'Born free, they scarcely worked for any but their Equals, and had not the mortification of employing, in order to gain protectors, a time which they

[44] Ibid. 1. 168.

must have taken from their study's.'[45] All nonsense, of course, but these lines are probably responsible for the conspicuous lack of interest on the part of most classical archaeologists in questions of patronage,[46] and for the ease with which they see pot-painters at play with the idle rich.[47] 'Painting', moreover,

was not intended for the decoration of a private habitation, but was consecrated to the decoration of City's; A good Painter was then the property of the whole Earth; by this means the masterpiece of an Artist, buried in an appartment was not only known to the friends of the person who possessed it, and who took to himself, for having given his protection to that Artist, the praises due to his talent, but it was the publick that decided, that compared these works, that set the value on their merit . . . and as Athens esteemed talent more than riches, the Artist, to acquire them, had need only of cultivating the Art which made him shine and ranked him among the Citizens of the greatest credit in the Republick. Being the work for the Publick only, who is seldom in a hurry to enjoy, because it is sure to exist for ever, he was at liberty to employ as much time as he pleased in his composition; he could see, learn, examine, and did not lose his reputation and his time in executing slowly, but in executing ill: hence painting fewer pieces, the Artist did not exhaust his spirit on a multitude of different works, but employed his whole strength upon a small number: he did less but he did better.[48]

D'Hancarville was attempting to create artificial classical *exempla* in order to improve the status of the artist in his own world. He was also attempting to enhance the status of the painters of the pots which Hamilton was trying to sell, as well as the status of the pots themselves.[49]

It is only on page 56 that there begins the chapter entitled '[1] Of the General Uses the Ancients made of their Vases. 2. Where, When, and by whom, they were made. 3. How they are found. 4. Of the manner of painting them.' Even though the ancients made vessels from precious materials, these scarcely exist any more (p. 60), and in any case metal vases copied the clay ones (p. 62: the source of another myth which dies hard).[50] Then comes the first deliberate sleight of hand: 'It follows then from this great affinity between the Vases of precious materials, with those of bronze, and

[45] Ibid. 2. 48.

[46] Notable exceptions: Webster (1972); Schneider (1975); Stewart (1979).

[47] e.g. Boardman (1975), 30; Gollan (1982), 5–6.

[48] D'Hancarville (1766[1767]–76), 2. 48–50.

[49] The degree to which he succeeded may be judged by the fact that Cooper (1981), 29 appears to believe that 'The State' was a major patron of painted pottery in classical Greece. Little state-owned pottery was decorated (cf. Thompson and Wycherley (1972), 89; Sparkes and Talcott (1970), 78; for the problematic amphora in Munich, see p. 98, below), and there is only one epigraphically attested record of any public body in Greece order-ing a ceramic vessel: a 'bowl for the sacred figs' bespoken by the authorities of the Eleusinion in 408/7 (*IG* l[3] 386, lines 163–4). This was a time, however, which was remarkable for extremely detailed record-keeping: cf. nos. 474–6 (the documents relating to the completion of the Erechtheum); for Panathenaic amphoras, see n. 77 below. On ceremonial occasions, the Athenian state would employ gold and silver vessels: [Andoc.] 4. 29; Plut. *Alc.* 13. 3; Diod. 12. 40. 2.

[50] For a defence of the view expressed by d'Hancarville, see Hill (1947); for another inter-pretation of the evidence: Vickers (1985*a*); Gill (1986*a*); Vickers, Impey, and Allan (1986); Gill and Vickers (1990); see Ch. 5.

of these again with the Vases of Earthen Ware, that, what has been said by the Ancients relative to the uses of one, may be equally applied to the others.'[51] In other words, any account in an ancient writer alluding to a vessel in precious metal may be taken to apply equally well to one made in ceramic. Licence having thus been granted, the very few ancient references to pottery vessels, whether in 'Sacred, . . . Publick,' or 'Domestick' contexts are mingled with many others which either refer explicitly to gold, silver, or bronze or are non-committal.

A point which d'Hancarville is eager to make is the very high value placed in the Roman world on 'Murrhine vases'. These were vessels made from a semiprecious stone and were truly of very great value. The assumption is made that the 'Barberini vase', a vessel subsequently known as the 'Portland vase' and which already enjoyed a high reputation,[52] was made from Murrhine ware; it is referred to by d'Hancarville as a cinerary vase 'of very precious material' (in fact, as Josiah Wedgwood was to discover in 1786, it is only glass).[53] It might seem that reference to this vessel was made almost in passing; in reality, however, there can be little doubt that it was done with the utmost care. It was extremely important for d'Hancarville's argument to demonstrate that the Romans placed a high value on Murrhine vases, for his one piece of 'hard' evidence (though, as we shall see, it was not hard at all) depended on this fact having been absorbed. The trick is played in a passage on the 'Buffets of the Ancients':

it was upon these Buffets that the ancients used to place their richest Vases, and there is no doubt, but those of St Denys, Capo di Monte, and the fine Emerald Cup, which I have had in my hands, have been employed for this purpose; they placed upon them also, Vases of Earthen Ware, for they were not less precious than the others, and Pliny assures us, that, the Earthen Ware, sold still dearer than the Murrhine Vases.[54]

Pliny does indeed make the statement 'quoniam eo pervenit luxuria, ut etiam fictilia pluris constent quam Murrhina' (since luxury has reached a point where even earthenware costs more than vessels of Murrhine ware),[55] but the context in which it occurs cannot be made to bear the weight which d'Hancarville places on it. The statement occurs in the middle of a diatribe against the Emperor Vitellius, the full context of which is as follows:

Vitellius when emperor had a dish made that cost 1,000,000 sesterces, and to make which a special kiln was constructed in open country, since luxury has reached a point where even earthenware costs more than vessels of Murrhine ware. It was

[51] D'Hancarville (1766[1767]–76), 62.
[52] Cf. de Montfaucon (1719–24), vol. 5, bk. 2, ch. 6; Ridgway (1989), 213.
[53] Wedgwood (1790), 10; Meteyard (1865–6), 2. 581.

[54] D'Hancarville (1766[1767]–76), 2. 80–2. The use of 'Buffets', or sideboards intended to exhibit silver (but not pottery) is described in Greek Sicily by Cicero during the first century BC: *Verr.* 2. 4. 15; 4. 16, 20, 23, 27.
[55] Pliny, *NH* 35. 162 (46).

owing to this dish that Mucianus in his second consulship, in a protest which he delivered, reproached the memory of Vitellius for dishes as broad as marshes.[56]

The pottery vessel in question was clearly exceptional and most of its scandalously high cost will doubtless have been taken up by the building expenses of a new kiln. The fact that on this single occasion ceramic cost more than Murrhine ware does not allow the conclusion that Romans regularly paid extraordinarily high prices for pottery vessels. Yet this is precisely what d'Hancarville assures his readers did occur.

In the next few pages he makes a show of great learning and apparent honesty in wondering which could have been the

manufactures, that produced those Earthen Vases, which according to Pliny were dearer even than the Murrhine Vases; that which Petronius broke before he died, to prevent it falling into the hands of Nero, had cost three hundred talents; one may judge by the greatness of the sum, that, these Vases and those of Earthen Ware compared to them, could not have borne so high a price, had they not been extremely scarce.[57]

Pliny cannot possibly have meant any of the fourteen potteries he mentions, for the products of some of them were said by contemporaries to be extremely cheap; 'it is certain, that Pliny means to speak of Earthen Ware Vases, much more ancient than those of his time; but as their Antiquity alone would not have been sufficient to have raised them to so exhorbitant a price',[58] various possibilities are canvassed only to be dismissed, before:

we are obliged to admit what he assures, as facts happened in his own time, that Vases of a material resembling that made use of by the above mentioned Manufactures, were in still greater estimation than those of the most precious materials, and conclude that they were Earthen Vases, like those we now publish, that he speaks of in his book: the difficulty is to know, what extraordinary circumstance could give them so great a value, and how it is credible, that, they could ever have become so rare, that it was scarce possible to procure them.[59]

Already the vases Hamilton has for sale have become the vases which in antiquity sold for vast sums. Hamilton's vases were painted; Pliny's silence with regard to painted pottery is now by a brilliant, but transparent, move adduced as further evidence for their undoubted value:

Pliny says not a single word of the Ceramick or Painting on Earth; which shews sufficiently that it was not known in the Age he wrote. Perhaps the secret was lost in the time of the Romans, as it is in ours, which was the reason, that nobody could imitate them, and that those they had at that time, were undoubtedly looked upon as Ancient Vases, where rarity was irreparable, which must have raised their value.[60]

---

[56] Ibid. In Pliny's day a sestertius was an artificial unit of account, of which there were four to the denarius, a silver coin which weighed about 3.20 g.

[57] D'Hancarville (1766[1767]–76), 2. 86; a talent of silver weighed 25.86 kg. (Lang (1970)).
[58] D'Hancarville (1766[1767]–76), 2. 86.
[59] Ibid. 2. 90.
[60] Ibid. 2. 92.

D'Hancarville's last piece of evidence is one which in his view 'leaves nothing further to wish for upon this subject'. This is the testimony of Suetonius, who mentions the fact that the new inhabitants of a colony established by Julius Caesar at Capua were spurred on in their work by the discovery of 'a number of vases of ancient workmanship' in 'very old tombs' which they disturbed in their building operations.[61] D'Hancarville spends five pages squeezing every imaginable nuance from Suetonius' words, concluding: 'After all this, I leave the Publick to judge whether one may conclude, that the Vases found there at present, are the same, as those which were sought after, anciently.'[62] It is in fact more likely than not that Caesar's veterans did find similar pottery, and it is even possible that they sold it to antiquarians. It is a clever debating ploy to conclude a tendentious argument with an incontrovertible point, and this is what d'Hancarville seems to have done here. It is not, however, legitimate to conclude with him that immense sums were paid for the pots from Capua.

Hamilton was not the only collector of Greek pots at Naples. Vivant Denon (who was later to be instrumental in the creation of the Musée Napoléon) was counsellor at the French embassy from 1778 to 1782, and for the next three years was *chef de mission* awaiting the appointment of a new ambassador.[63] Intrigues at the court of Ferdinand IV and his queen Maria Carolina, the elder sister of Marie Antoinette, occupied his professional energies. At leisure, he was an avid collector of paintings and antiquities, and was thus in direct competition with Hamilton: 'As soon as he learnt that painted vases of beautiful shapes had been found in tombs at Nola or some other town of Campania, he would hurry to the spot to buy them, to the great regret of the English minister Hamilton who also collected vases from all parts.'[64] A letter of 4 June 1785, written just before Denon's departure for home, states that he was bringing with him 'a very considerable collection of Etruscan vases, and perhaps the most complete in existence for the forms'.[65] This collection consisted of 520 pieces,[66] which Denon is said to have sold to Louis XVI for 40,000 *livres*.[67]

We shall return later to this acquisition by the French court; for the moment Denon holds our attention because of his association with the Abbé de Saint-Non, the author of *Voyage pittoresque ou description des Royaumes de Naples et de Sicile*,[68] a work of a splendour comparable to that of the four

[61] Suet. *Iul.* 18.

[62] D'Hancarville (1766[1767]–76), 2. 104.

[63] Amaury-Duval (1829); Massoul (1934), pp. xi–xiv; Lelièvre (1942); Nowinski (1970); Chatelain (1973); Rodinis (1977).

[64] Amaury-Duval (1829), 4.

[65] Lelièvre (1942), 20.

[66] Ibid.

[67] Massoul (1934), p. xi.

[68] Saint-Non (1781–86). Denon's notes had

been used anonymously by Saint-Non, but the parts dealing with the island of Sicily were published by him under his own name in de Non (1788), which is as charming a work as Goethe (1817 (1964)), which it might well have influenced. Denon's account of the mainland was published in the French edition of a work by Henry Swinburne (1785–7). The relationship between Denon and Saint-Non ('an erudite writer of a more rigidly scientific temperament') is well summarized by Rodinis (1977), 21.

FIG. 1.6 The excavation of a tomb near Naples, *c.*1790: Sir William Hamilton, *Collection of Engravings from Ancient Vases*, 1 (Naples, 1790), frontispiece.

volumes in which Hamilton's collection was marketed. Saint-Non made use of notes made by Denon when they travelled together in 1778, and it is clear that both men accepted uncritically the points which d'Hancarville had made regarding the extraordinarily high value the Romans were supposed to have placed on Greek painted pottery. In an appendix Saint-Non discusses 'Some Campanian Vases Commonly Called Etruscan Vases'.[69] D'Hancarville is cited as the authority on the subject, and the text is little more than an abbreviated summary of his views.[70]

Saint-Non's massive work was dedicated to Queen Marie Antoinette. Within a few years of the publication of the first volume, her husband paid 77 *livres*

[69] Saint-Non (1781–86), 2. 276–83.   [70] Ibid. 277.

apiece for Denon's Campanian vases. Once again the influence of the market on the reception of Greek pottery can be seen to have operated, and what is perhaps more important still, d'Hancarville's erroneous conclusions were disseminated to a wider public.[71] In 1789 and 1790, Sir William Hamilton formed another collection which he published in 1791 in a further series of folio volumes (Fig. 1.7). This time the presentation was slightly less opulent; perhaps it was no longer an uncertain business to sell Greek pots, or perhaps Hamilton was sincere in his stated aim of making the purchase of his publication 'easy for young artists' that they might 'reap the desired profit from such excellent models as are now offered to them'. There is certainly not the same sense as before of a 'hard sell' in Hamilton's brief and thoughtful text. 'Much has been written upon the subject of these sort of vases,' he writes, 'but the most rational account of them is to be found in the Works of Mr d'Hancarville, and the Abbé Winckelmann. . . .' He repeats the essence of d'Hancarville's argument with regard to value, but does so in terms which have ceased to relate closely to the relevant sources, attributing all the elements in what had come from Suetonius and Pliny to Suetonius alone.[72] Hamilton's second collection went into several editions, and appeared in Germany in 1797–1800.[73]

Germany had been the original source of a revival of interest in Greek culture, less perhaps for any intrinsic merit on the part of the ancient Greeks than because an enlightened interest in the Hellenic tradition was a highly effective way of challenging a traditional establishment which reckoned its own descent from the Trojans. German intellectuals in the middle decades of the eighteenth century were 'ignorant of the Greeks, but ready to believe the best of them'.[74] It was with a view to capturing something of the Greek spirit that Goethe visited Southern Italy and Sicily in the spring of 1787. In Rome earlier in the year he acquired Winckelmann's *Geschichte der Kunst des Altertums*, a work with which he was already acquainted, but which he began to study in earnest for the first time.[75] Here he will have learnt something of Winckelmann's views of Campanian Greek pottery, which had in any case probably influenced d'Hancarville's account (Winckelmann was in close contact with both Hamilton and d'Hancarville).[76] Goethe will not have learnt of the argument for the value in antiquity of Greek pots based on Pliny from Winckelmann, nor, surprisingly about Suetonius and Julius Caesar's veterans at Capua. He will, however, have read Winckelmann's flimsy arguments for the ancient Greeks having competed for painted pots

[71] A greatly reduced version of d'Hancarville (1766[1767]–76) was printed at Paris in 1787: d'Hancarville (1785–8).

[72] Hamilton (1791–5), 1. 26. On the significance of the use of 'simple outline' by W. Tischbein, Hamilton's engraver, see Rykwert (1980), 368–9; cf. Howard (1985).

[73] Böttiger (1797–1800). Italian editions were also produced: Hamilton (1800–3); de Sanctis (1814).

[74] Trevelyan (1941), 14.

[75] Goethe (1817 (1964)), 11. 614.

[76] For Winckelmann's friendship with Hamilton, see Constantine (1984), 112.

FIG. 1.7 A 'First Day' Wedgwood 'encaustic' ware vase decorated with a scene from one of the vases in d'Hancarville, *Hamilton Collection*. Wedgwood Museum, Barlaston.

at public games,[77] as well as his paean of praise for volume 1 of the publication of Hamilton's collection, which concluded with the following high estimation of the two pots chosen for special treatment: 'The worthy owner of this collection is the proud possessor of two vessels which are respectively one of the earliest monuments of Greek art and one of the most utterly perfect in drawing and beauty.'[78]

When Goethe reached Naples in March 1787, he met Hamilton at the latter's hunting lodge at Caserta, where Emma Hart was the main attraction.[79] He had already observed the high prices being paid for Greek pots: 'One now pays a lot of money for Etruscan vases, and certainly one finds beautiful and exquisite pieces among them. Every traveller wants one. People do not value their money so highly as at home, I was afraid that I should be tempted myself.'[80] By the time Goethe arrived in Sicily in April, he was conditioned to write in glowing terms of an Attic red-figure column-crater in the cathedral at Agrigento: 'We were taken back into earlier epochs by inspecting a precious vase of considerable size and perfect preservation (*einer kostlichen Vase von bedeutender Grosse und vollkommender Erhaltung*).'[81] Goethe's *Italian Journey* has long been regarded as one of the most successful pieces of German prose,[82] and will thus have influenced a wider audience than might have been anticipated from its content. Goethe's report of high prices being paid for Greek pots, reprinted innumerable times since 1817, will only have assisted the acceptance of d'Hancarville's tendentious views by his nineteenth- (and twentieth-)[83] century readers.

Why should eighteenth-century *cognoscenti* have been so ready to accept

[77] Winckelmann (1764), vol. 1, bk. 3, ch. 4, sect. 31: 'Not less known is the use made of such vessels in the games of Greece, where already in the earliest times a mere earthen vessel was a prize of victory.' But the vessel mentioned at *Il.* 23. 259 (one of the prizes at the funeral games of Patroclus) was far more likely to have been bronze, rather than earthenware; there is no way of telling whether vessels shown on coins of Tralles or Athens, or on gems, were of metal or clay; Callimachus (*Fr.* 122) does not specify the material from which Athenian prize hydriai placed on a temple roof were made; Pindar uses a poetical periphrasis at *Nem.* 10. 68 ff. to describe the pottery containers of the prize oil at the Panathenaic games. A victorious charioteer could take away 140 Panathenaic amphoras filled with oil (Amyx (1958), 178–86); he competed for the oil, not the pots (as the relevant inscription (*IG* 2² 2311) indicates at every entry). It is therefore sad to see Cooper (1981), 29 repeating, in essence, Winckelmann's assertion: 'The careful and highly sophisticated painted pottery was as highly regarded as any other art form [in Greece] and was used at various times . . . as prizes for athletic prowess'; cf. Gollan (1982), 6: 'the special

amphoras awarded as prizes in the contests staged at festivals'.

[78] Winckelmann (1764), vol. 1, bk. 3, ch. 4, sect. 20.

[79] Goethe (1817 (1964)), 209. Goethe only saw Hamilton's antiquities (which he also admired) on his return from Sicily in May 1787: pp. 330–2.

[80] Noted on 9 March 1787: Goethe (1817 (1964)), 197. For the Greek pots Goethe actually owned, see Schuchardt (1848), 2. 329–30 (nos. 43–51).

[81] Goethe (1817 (1964)), 274. Winckelmann had already seen and praised this pot: Winckelmann (1764), vol. 1, bk. 3, ch. 4, sect. 24. Another early traveller who refers to it is Vivant Denon, who saw it in 1778: de Non (1788), 123. The pot in question is illustrated by Wegner (1944), fig. 37 (cf. p. 113). For the admiration of a 'fine Etruscan vase' in Agrigento in 1752, see Gill (1990), 227.

[82] Cf. Michea (1933), 112 (citing Erich Schmidt and Thomas Mann).

[83] Herbert Hoffman kindly informs us: 'I myself carried a copy [of *Italienische Reise*] in my knapsack on my first trip to Italy, in 1948, and remember reading the relevant passage in front of the vase in the cathedral at Agrigento.'

Greek pottery as a valuable commodity? The reasons are many and complex, and seem to have been different on the Continent and in England. Holland apart, Continental Europe was relatively poorer than England for much of the eighteenth century. The need to keep up appearances on the part of those in power was often achieved by means of artifice: the creation of an illusion of pomp and magnificence with relatively little expenditure. One material with which Continental rulers adorned their surroundings was porcelain, the manufacture of which they actively encouraged.[84]

The first porcelain in Europe was imported from China at great expense. It was often mounted in precious metal, and was highly prized. Many unsuccessful attempts were made to imitate its hard, white qualities as well as its attractive, superposed colours, but it was only in the early eighteenth century that the process of making hard-paste porcelain was discovered, at Dresden. The nearby factory at Meissen, under the direct control of the Elector of Saxony, was the first to produce the new ware. The secret of manufacture, the *arcanum*, was known to only a few, the arcanists. Although in theory these men learned what they knew under binding oaths, in practice 'the highways were populated with wandering arcanists, men knowing something or claiming to know something, of how to make porcelain, and peddling their claims to the porcelain-hungry courts of Europe.'[85] Factories were established, frequently by rulers, in Mainz, Brunswick, and Prussia, at Vincennes and later at Sèvres, and in Denmark and Naples and elsewhere. Their products catered both for the taste of the courts—much of the imagery of porcelain decoration is aristocratic[86]—and for that of the emerging middle class. The popularity of porcelain was aided by the new fashion for drinking hot liquids such as tea, coffee, and cocoa, and as this consumption increased, so did that of porcelain. Porcelain might be used for diplomatic gifts, and although prices varied according to the degree of elaboration, they could be high.[87] Individual painters gained prominence in the various royal factories: Herold at Meissen between 1720 and 1765, for example, or Gottlieb Friedrich Riedel, who worked successively at Höchst, Frankenthal, Meissen, Ludwigsburg, and Augsburg. Porcelain production constituted a major element in some states' economies: when Frederick the Great forbade the transport of Meissen across Prussian territory, he inflicted considerable damage on Saxony. Porcelain was, moreover, produced at the very epicentre of the eighteenth century's rediscovery of Greek pottery: the Capo di Monte factory was active from 1743 to 1759 before its craftsmen

---

[84] Much of the next paragraph is derived from Charles (1964).

[85] Ibid. 25.

[86] Cf. the observation of the Duke Karl Eugen, the owner of the Ludwigsburg factory: porcelain was 'a necessary appanage of lustre and prestige', cited in Finer and Savage (1965), 20.

[87] Louis XVI paid 77 *livres* each for the Greek pots he acquired from Vivant Denon in 1785; this was rather more than the average cost of the pieces in a Sèvres *service ordinaire*: the Comte de Durfort paid 4704 *livres* for 145 pieces of Sèvres in 1762, an average cost of 32.44 *livres*, or 60.73 if the 96 plates at 18 *livres* are omitted: Charles (1964), 140.

were moved to Spain on Charles III's succession; its successor was established at Portici in 1771 before being moved to buildings adjoining the royal palace in 1773.[88]

Already in the middle of the eighteenth century, the Count de Caylus had convinced himself that Greek pottery found in Etruria was made with as much care as porcelain; 'One could even, regardless of their antiquity, regard them as being as precious.'[89] It is easy to see why the pots found in tombs around Naples in the second half of the eighteenth century should have found a ready market on the Continent, and we can understand why writers such as Caylus, Winckelmann, d'Hancarville, and Hamilton should have devoted such attention to the techniques employed in making Greek pottery. For d'Hancarville, the very fact that the secret was lost was one of the reasons for exalting the value of the wares he was selling.[90] In a world where the potter and the painter could be persons of some prominence, it was easy to imagine that they were equally important in antiquity, and to overlook the evidence to the contrary.

In England, too, there were successful porcelain factories, but they did not have the same intimate relationship with the court as those on the Continent. It is true that Josiah Wedgwood was glad to style himself 'Potter to the Queen' and to have a line of creamware called Queensware, but his political inclinations lay in another direction. In many ways he personifies the 'Age of Improvement' and the role played by nonconformist Midlands manufacturers in the course of the Industrial Revolution.[91] His business acumen led him successfully to meet a growing demand for less expensive wares than porcelain. He catered for both aristocratic[92] and middle-class[93] markets; production techniques which were originally aimed at increasing quality and quality control led eventually to mass-production and lower prices. He was aware at a relatively early date of the potential importance of classical Greek models. Acquaintance with the works of Caylus led him to see what was still thought of as Etruscan ware as a suitable source of inspiration,[94] and by 1768 he was already making red-on-black 'Etruscan' ware at

---

[88] On Naples, see further Gonzalez-Palacios (1984).

[89] Caylus (1752–67), 1. 88–9; he also (p. 89) states that he did not know of anything so perfect in terracotta, 'and that they employed to execute it the hands of the most famous artists' the first time, but not the last, that such an opinion was expressed. For material from Caylus's collection subsequently appearing in England, see Gill (1990), 227.

[90] D'Hancarville (1766[1767]–76), 2. 92.

[91] Meteyard (1865–6); Farrar (1973); Finer and Savage (1965); Westhoff-Krummacher (1980); McKendrick, Brewer, and Plumb (1982); Berghaus *et al.* (1983).

[92] Cf. an observation made by Wedgwood to his partner Thomas Bentley in a letter of September 1767: 'if a Royal or Noble introduction be as necessary to the sale of an article of *Luxury*, as real Elegance and beauty, then the Manufacturer, if he consults his own interest will bestow as much pains, and expence too if necessary, in gaining the former of these advantages, as he would in bestowing the latter' (Finer and Savage (1965), 58–9).

[93] Cf. Westhoff-Krummacher (1980).

[94] Wedgwood was lent part of Caylus's *Recueil d'antiquités* in 1767 (Meteyard (1865–6), 1. 480; Farrar (1973), 1. 177. He and Bentley acquired their own copy in 1769. For the appeal of the neoclassical style to industrialists intent on simpler (and less costly) modes of production, see Irwin (1972); (1976).

FIG. 1.8 The Lamberg collection: A. de La Borde, *Collection de vases grecs de Mr le Comte de Lamberg*, 1 (Paris, 1813).

his Burslem factory. On 13 June 1769 Messrs Wedgwood and Bentley opened their new Ornamental Works at the appropriately named Etruria in the English Potteries. Six black pots were thrown by Wedgwood at the opening (Fig. 1.7), with his partner Thomas Bentley turning the wheel. These vessels were subsequently decorated in London with red 'encaustic' enamel with a scene from one of the red-figure pots in Hamilton's plates.[95] (See Fig. 1.5.) These had been acquired from Wedgwood's friend and patron Lord Cathcart who, like Winckelmann, had received proof copies.[96] Wedgwood immediately saw commercial possibilities in decorating blackware with scenes taken from such an eminent source. His confidence was not misplaced; in 1770, a correspondent could write to him: 'When Roman luxury increas'd, Etruscan ware gave place to Plate; but when English luxury seems at the height, your elegant taste has put to flight Gold & Silver vessels, & banished them from our Tables.'[97] We should overlook the

[95] Best illustrated in Finer and Savage (1965), pl. 2; for a full bibliography, see Borsi (1985), 78–9.

[96] Ramage (1990*b*).
[97] Quoted in Farrar (1973), 1. 364.

implication that Greek pottery 'gave place to Plate' in antiquity, but the contemporary success of Wedgwood's venture is clear.

The prices of the encaustic Etruscan wares varied greatly according to size. Small pieces cost 6 or 7 shillings, but large vessels with figure decoration might sell for 30 guineas or more.[98] Horace Walpole records in 1770, as an example of contemporary 'luxury and extravagance' that 'we have Etruscan vases, made of earthenware, in Staffordshire, from two to five guineas'.[99] A letter from Bentley to a retailer shows how prices were enhanced by means of clever salesmanship:

We have at length got some Etruscan Vases in great forwardness, & shall send you several sets by the next Carrier. If any of your Friends wonder why you have not got more & oftener, please to give them to understand that it is very difficult to make fine and perfect things of any kind. How often does our great Mistress Nature Fail, even in the finest Order of her Productions! The angelic Sex themselves are not all perfectly straight, delicate and beautiful, no more than our Vases; and you may contrive to edge in the *Natural Inference* that *every good Thing* deserves *a good Price*.[100]

Wedgwood's patent for 'encaustic' was infringed by another manufacturer, an occurrence which made him write to Bentley:

May not this affair furnish us with a good excuse for advertising away at a great rate? ... And in this advertisement could you not weave in Count Caylus' lamentation that no artists had then been able to imitate the ancient Etruscan Vases ... at this time such a publication might answer more purposes than one to us.[101]

Wedgwood did not know of d'Hancarville's text to Hamilton's plates, but like him realized that if the public was made aware that the technique involved in the manufacture of black-and-red pottery was difficult, then the value of their own wares might be increased. A combination of d'Hancarville's and Wedgwood's wholly distinct kinds of entrepreneurship was a major factor in the decision to buy Hamilton's vases for the British Museum in 1772, and it was in no one's interest to dispel the notion that Greek vases were valuable in antiquity.

By the end of the eighteenth century, large collections of Greek pottery had been formed throughout much of Europe. Thus, in 1808, A. L. Millin could state: 'Today governments have formed collections of this kind for the improvement of industry (*pour le perfectionnement des manufactures*)'; and there are some in all the capitals of Europe where the arts are respected.'[102]

---

[98] Meteyard (1865–6), 2. 148.
[99] Letter to Sir Horace Mann, 6 May 1770: Toynbee (1903–5), 7. 380.
[100] Meteyard (1865–6), 2. 98–9; see too McKendrick, 'Josiah Wedgwood and the Commercialization of the Potteries' (McKendrick, Brewer, and Plumb (1982), 105–8), on Wedgwood's policy of charging for his pottery 'not ... at

what it was worth ... but at what the nobility would pay for it'.
[101] Farrar (1973), 1. 378, letter to Bentley, 13 Oct. 1770.
[102] Millin (1808–10), 1, pp. xvii–xviii. For some Continental manufacturers' responses to the fashion for vases *à l'étrusque*, see Berghaus *et al.* (1983), 62–5.

Large sums had been expended on their acquisition. Although part of
Hamilton's second collection had gone down in HMS *Colossus*, it was, in
its owner's words, the 'worst' part;[103] the rest were sold to Thomas Hope
for £4,724, about £25 a pot.[104] Another English collector, E. J. Edwards,
paid 1,000 guineas in 1790 for a single vessel, which he considered to be
so precious that he actually kept it in a glass case in his library.[105] With this
extraordinarily high price life imitated art, for the 'Barberini vase' d'Hancarville
thought of as Murrhine ware had been bought in at the Portland House
sale in 1786 for £1,029.[106] In France, the taste for Greek pots survived the
Revolution. Millin's *édition de luxe* was dedicated to the Empress-Queen
Josephine, and the Musée Napoléon provided temporary lodging for many
pieces from the Vatican.[107] In Austria, there was the collection of Count
Lamberg (Fig. 1.8), formed in 1783–4 when he was ambassador at Naples,
and published, in imperial folio, between 1813 and 1828.[108] The only part
of Europe in which Greek pots were in comparatively short supply was
Germany,[109] but this deficiency was overcome when great numbers were
found in 1828 and 1829 on the Tuscan estates of the Prince de Canino,
'Napoleon's slippery brother, Lucien'.[110] At first they were looted without
Canino's knowledge,[111] but he quickly became a successful dealer in his own
right. His wife is said to have reaped two harvests from her land, grain in
summer and pots in winter.[112]

Many of these vessels went to Munich and Berlin.[113] It was, moreover, the
interest expressed by the King of Prussia which persuaded the otherwise
indifferent Grand Duke of Tuscany to pay 500 sequins for the François
vase in 1845.[114] But the main interest in Greek ceramics came from middle-
class collectors: individuals such as Thomas Hope (whose collection was
used to adorn his house in Duchess Street, London),[115] or John Disney, who
in 1828 found Vulci to be 'the very hot-bed of fictilia antiqua'; pots seemed
'to grow there like truffles underground'.[116] Greek vases might even serve as

[103] Fothergill (1969), 402.

[104] Reitlinger (1961–70), 2. 369. This represents
an increase over the prices of either 10 + or 23 +
guineas per pot achieved for the first Hamilton
collection (Dyfri Williams kindly reports that 'The
question [as to how many Hamilton vases were
acquired by the British Museum in 1774] is not so
easily answered. Smith in his unpublished introduction to a vase catalogue says 347, but the register lists numbers up to 747. Of these, there are
only about 300 descriptions.')

[105] Millin (1808–10), 1, p. xviii.

[106] Reitlinger (1961–70), 2. 362.

[107] Cf. Chamberlin (1983), 123–48.

[108] La Borde (1813–28).

[109] There were a few Greek pots in Berlin at an
early date: Beger (1699), 391 (a red-figure bell-
crater), 396 (a Corinthian alabastron), 463 (a South
Italian amphora).

[110] Hoffmann (1979), 62.

[111] Cf. Canino (1831), 260.

[112] Dennis (1848), 1. 409; (1873) and (1883),
1. 450; (1907), 1. 431. For bibliographical details,
see Jahn (1854), p. xvi.

[113] Ibid.

[114] Cf. Marzi (1981b), 27–50, esp. 28 and 47.

[115] Watkin (1968), 106–8.

[116] Disney (1849), p. ix; cf. Gill (1990a), 229.
Disney, like most writers before the later nineteenth
century, wrote of 'fictile' vases, alluding to the
material from which they were made (Lat. *fictilis*:
'earthenware, clay'). There was still an awareness
that 'vases' without qualification implied something
grander than clay. For information on many more
early nineteenth-century English collectors, see
Jenkins (1988), 456–7.

4	Grande terrine	
4	Pieds de Vache	
4	Pots à anses Teste de chevres	
4	a	Pots à anses relevé	
2	b	Jattes écuelle	
4	c	Jattes à anses Etrusques	
2	d	Jattes à Bandeau	
8	e	Gobelets cornets	
6	f	Gobelets à anses relevés avec Sa Soucoupe	
8	g	Gobelets à anses Etrusques	
6	h	Gobelets à bandeau	
4	i	Letons avec Son pied à teste de chevre	
4	k	Sucriers	

props in paintings, almost as guarantees of the sitters' respectability, and certainly as attestations to their tastes.[117] By the 1860s, the Syndics of the Fitzwilliam Museum in Cambridge were conscious of a need to acquire Greek ceramics.[118] Oxford was a late starter in the Greek pottery stakes: in 1884, 'Fine specimens of the "perfect style" of Greek vase-painting' were lacking in the Ashmolean.[119] Arthur Evans filled the gap by buying pots on the museum's behalf in Sicily (though for himself he bought coins and gems).[120] American collecting activity began later still, in the 1890s.[121]

Hamilton's lavish volumes had set standards which were hard to emulate, but they established an ideal for the publication of Greek pots for decades to come. A rich collector would spend large sums of money on the acquisition of these fashionable objects; he would spend more money on having them engraved, and even more on employing a learned man to write the text. Few under such circumstances would have dared to downgrade the objects they had been invited to 'expertize'. Instead, the learned men preferred to praise their patron for his good taste, and to say what a splendid collection he owned. The same pattern occurred even on a small scale; witness the title of a pamphlet published in Palermo in 1826: *Illustration of the Painting of a Greco-Sicilian Vase Representing Nemesis Found in Ancient Agrigentum in April 1825 and Acquired by H.E. the Marchese delle Favare, Secretary of State, Lieutenant-General in Sicily, Written, and Dedicated to the Same by Raffaello Politi Syracusan Painter, and Architect.*[122] Only James Millingen came close to letting the cat out of the bag when he wrote:

the vases, of which the origin is supposed to be so mysterious, are no others than the common pottery intended for the various purposes of ordinary life, and for ornament, like the China and Staffordshire ware of the present day . . . All those which served for common use, experienced the common fate of such fragile objects, and accordingly great quantities of fragments are usually found in the neighbourhood of ancient Greek cities. At Tarentum, the sea is continually washing on shore innumerable remains of similar vases, which were probably thrown into it, with other rubbish belonging to the ancient inhabitants of the city.[123]

Most writers, however, preferred to stress the value of their material in antiquity. A. de La Borde writes of Count Lamberg's 'precious vases of

---

[117] Greifenhagen (1978); Jenkins (1988).
[118] Fitzwilliam Management Syndicate Papers, 11 February 1864, 3. Thanks are due to Paul Woudhuysen for providing this reference.
[119] Evans (1884), 19; Vickers (1983c), 276.
[120] Vickers (1983c); (forthcoming).

[121] Mayo (1983), 33; cf. von Bothmer (1983).
[122] Politi (1826).
[123] Millingen (1822–6), 1, p. vi (a work dedicated to the Egyptologist W. R. Hamilton, on whom see Chamberlin (1983), 144–5). For a more recent, realistic view of the material evidence, see Childe (1944), 86 (quoted below, p. 71).

FIG. 1.9 (*Opposite*) J.-J. Lagrenée, 'Vases étrusques' for Queen Marie-Antoinette's dairy at Rambouillet. Archives, Manufacture Nationale de Sèvres.

clay',[124] and Millin even makes the claim, wholly unsupported by any ancient evidence, that '[the Greeks] often preferred, to vases of precious metal, vases of baked clay of good workmanship'.[125] The most common argument, however, was to repeat and expand Winckelmann's erroneous view that pots might be used as prizes at Greek athletic events. Thus E. Q. Visconti: 'These kinds of vases . . . became . . . on some occasions the prizes at games';[126] or L. Politi: 'The greater part of the fictile vases were destined to be prizes for the victors at the games'.[127]

D'Hancarville's views on pots were still generally held in high regard, although his other researches came in for criticism. Millingen, writing in 1817, could state; 'The introduction of the collection of vases of the Chevalier Hamilton had a great influence on public taste in England. The account of it given to Europe by the publication of M. d'Hancarville had elsewhere the same happy effect.'[128] It is thus scarcely surprising to find d'Hancarville's argument based on Murrhine ware still being alluded to in the introduction to the publication of Count Lamberg's collection in 1813: 'at the time of the Romans these vases were so rare that they were more highly estimated than Murrhine vases'.[129]

What is surprising is that the same argument should be repeated in successive editions of G. Dennis's *Cities and Cemeteries of Etruria*—in 1848, in 1878, in 1883, and in 1907:

Pliny states that in his time fictile vases, by which he probably means those that were painted, fetched more money than the celebrated Murrhine vases, the cost of which he records (XXXV.46; XXXVII.7); . . . That these painted vases were very rare in his day is confirmed by the fact that not one has been discovered among the ruins of Pompeii or Herculaneum.[130]

It is ironic, and amusing, that Dennis, whose chief aim was 'truth and accuracy',[131] should have been duped by d'Hancarville, who 'only wanted common honesty to make a brilliant figure'.[132] It is ironic too that the consequences of d'Hancarville's deception lie at the heart of classical archaeology as it is studied and taught today. Although no one would use the argument from Pliny nowadays, it has never been formally rebutted, and the

---

[124] La Borde (1813–28), 1. 1.

[125] Millin (1808–10), 1. 1–2.

[126] E. Q. Visconti (writing in 1804), in Panofka (1834), 3.

[127] Politi (1826), 20 n. 24; cf. Gargiulo (1843), 7. The only ceramic prize known to us from antiquity is the cup given as a prize for woolworking at Tarentum: Milne (1945). More recently,—as Ian Lowe kindly informs us—du Paquier porcelain was offered as prizes in archery contests in eighteenth-century Vienna: Hayward (1952), 14–15.

[128] Millingen (1817), p. ii.

[129] La Borde (1813–28), 1, p. xii.

[130] Dennis (1848), 1, p. lxxxv; (1878) and (1883), 1, p. xcvii; (1907), 1, 64.

[131] Dennis (1848), 1, p. ix; (1878) and (1883), 1, p. vii; (1907), 1, p. xv.

[132] Quoted by Haskell (1987), 38, Sir Horace Mann in a letter to Horace Walpole, 30 Jan. 1773. Even Winckelmann considered d'Hancarville to be a rogue ('einer grösten Avanturiers'): Diepolder and Rehm (1952–7), 3. 366, as did—eventually—Hamilton: Ramage (1991), 35 (quoting a letter written in 1773).

notion that the ceramic vessels in our museums were extremely precious in antiquity is still widespread.[133]

SIMPLICITY

And do you really think that we may make a *complete conquest* of France? Conquer France in Burslem? My blood moves quicker, I feel my strength increase for the conquest. Assist me my friend & the victorie is our own. We will make them . . . our Porcelain after their own hearts, & captivate them with Elegance and simplicity of the Ancients. But do they love simplicity? Are you certain the French Nation will be pleased with simplicity in their Vessells? Either I have been greatly deceiv'd, or a wonderfull reformation has taken place amongst them. *French & Frippery* have jingled together so long in my ideas, that I scarcely know how to separate them, & much of their work which I have seen cover'd over with ornament, had confirmed me in the opinion.[134]

Wedgwood's letter, written in 1769, reveals a conventional view of France, but one which was apparently dispelled by his partner, to whom he replied: 'I am fully satisfyed with your reasons for the Virtuosi of France being fond of *Elegant Simplicity*, & shall, more than ever make that idea a leading principle in my usefull, as well as in our Ornamental works.'[135] There had indeed been important changes in France, 'a revolution in the minds of men', as Voltaire put it in 1767, which had taken place during the previous fifteen years.[136] Rousseau's ideas in favour of simplicity in art and in life had taken the Republic of Letters by storm. His *Discours sur les sciences et les arts* published in 1750 attacked luxury,[137] and in *Émile: ou de l'éducation* (1762) an ideal existence is described which was greatly at variance with prevailing civilized standards: 'On the slope of some pleasant well shaded hill, I would have a small country cottage, a white cottage with green shutters.' Although it was ordered that *Émile* should be burnt by the public hangman in Paris, its underlying philosophy came to be accepted by the highest in the land: witness, for example, the visit paid by Marie-Antoinette to Rousseau's grave at Ermenonville and her pastoral experiments at the dairy built for her by Louis XVI at Rambouillet.

The Comte de Caylus was more directly instrumental in bringing about the change in French taste Wedgwood looked forward to exploiting. He was

[133] See n. 15, above.

[134] Wedgwood to Bentley, undated, but written between February and September 1769: Farrar (1973), 1. 301–2.

[135] Wedgwood to Bentley, 17 September 1769: Farrar (1973), 1. 273.

[136] Quoted in Richter and Ricardo (1980), 143. On Voltaire and his belief in the *simplicité* of Greek literature, see Mat-Hasquin (1981), 139 (kindly brought to our attention by Haydn Mason). Ear-

lier, 'simplicity' had been a pejorative word; cf. Salter (1982), 496: 'The Bible gives us a splendid view of English in the 17th century. In every single occurrence of the word *simplicity* the meaning is negative. It is taken to be the antonym of wisdom and subtlety . . . (see *Proverbs* 1.4 and 22).'

[137] Havens (1946). The related topic of Utopianism in the context of the study of Greek ceramics is discussed elsewhere: Vickers (1985a); (1990c); cf. Raby and Vickers (1986); see Ch. 4.

not only the author of what was, before Winckelmann, the standard work on Greek, Etruscan, and Roman antiquities,[138] but he was highly regarded by most of his contemporaries as an authority on art in general and ancient art in particular. He was a member of the Académie and gave lectures in which he advised young artists to employ classical themes and models. Many gave heed, and Caylus's influence can be detected, for example, in early neoclassical furniture. Sébastien Mercier wrote of him: 'Count Caylus has revived Greek taste amongst us and we have at last renounced our Gothic [i.e. rococo] forms.'[139] Not everyone admired him, however. Diderot is supposed to have composed the following epitaph when Caylus died in 1765:

> Here lies an antiquary peevish and rude.
> How suitably lodged he is in this Etruscan urn![140]

Diderot preferred Winckelmann, 'this charming enthusiast',[141] perhaps because the latter did not care much for Caylus either. It little mattered that Winckelmann's immortal words regarding the simplicity of Greek art and literature: 'noble simplicity and quiet Grandeur' ('Edle Einfalt und stille Grosse') were applied to the Laocoön,[142] now thought to be Roman work, and to reflect the tastes of either Augustus or Tiberius.[143] Winckelmann thought that he was characterizing Greek art of the age of the best period of Greek literature, 'of the writings of the school of Socrates',[144] and so did his audience.

Caylus had already, in 1752, written of some Greek pots in his collection that 'the elegance and simplicity of their shapes merits attention',[145] and by the time d'Hancarville was preparing Hamilton's vases for publication, Winckelmann had shown that the pots found near Naples were painted by Greeks. Simplicity was one of the qualities Hamilton's vases were supposed to possess: 'The Elegance of the outline . . . the Character of their distinguishing simplicity'.[146] Later, the fact that the forms of ceramic vases are 'much less rich, and less ornamented' than bronze is a point in their favour.[147] D'Hancarville speaks too of 'the taste of simplicity the Artists sought for in their figures',[148] and elsewhere of 'the grace, the simplicity, the expression

---

[138] Caylus (1752–67). There is an excellent biographical sketch of Caylus in Eriksen (1974), 160–3; see too Gaborit (1984), 481.

[139] Quoted by Eriksen (1974), 162.

[140] 'Ci-gist un antiquaire acariâtre et brusque. / Ah! qu'il est bien logé dans cette cruche étrusque' (quoted and translated by Eriksen (1974), 163). In 1772 there was talk of Wedgwood's making a portrait medallion of Caylus as a companion piece to one of Hamilton, but it came to nothing (Ramage (1990*b*), 75). The frontispiece of d'Hancarville (1766[1767]–76) 4, however, includes such a medallion (Ramage (1990*b*), 86, fig. 7; cf. Griener (1992) 80, fig. 22).

[141] Diderot (1875–7), 10. 417.

[142] Winckelmann (1755), 21; cf. Winckelmann (1909), 60.

[143] Rice (1986), 209 (Augustus); Stewart (1977), 76–91 (Tiberius); Pollitt (1986), 120.

[144] Winckelmann (1755), 21. Cf. Butler (1958), 81: 'The Laocoon group is an ironical symbol of the German classical movement which was tangled into painful contortions by preconceived notions of what Greek art should be.'

[145] Caylus (1752–67), 1. 41.

[146] D'Hancarville (1766[1767]–76), 2. 58.

[147] Ibid. 2. 62.

[148] Ibid. 2. 142.

and intelligence that one sees in every part' of Hamilton's pots.[149] D'Hancarville was hardly unaware of the changes in taste under way in those countries in which it was hoped Hamilton's vases might find a buyer, and thus plays on 'simplicity' for all it is worth.[150] His views on this matter, too, were repeated by Saint-Non in his volumes dedicated, as we saw, to Marie-Antoinette in 1781: 'What one can even more justly admire is the beauty, the simplicity of the shapes of a large number of these vases whose proportions, grace and elegance ought to make us the more regard them as models.'[151]

D'Hancarville does not neglect the opportunity to take a side-swipe at porcelain, a material closely identified in his day with Absolutism, and of which Winckelmann had declared: 'Porcelain is nearly always made into idiotic puppets.'[152] D'Hancarville, moreover, believed that the black colour on Hamilton's pots,

which at first appears so singular, and requires the eye's being accustom'd to it, is of all others the most proper to set off the forms and show the elegance and purity of their outline: and I have had occasion to remark that a vase of a bad form cannot bear the black colour, nor any dark colour without appearing still more ridiculous, and on the contrary that white is of all the tints the most proper to hide the defects of the composition of the forms.[153]

It was said of Denon's pots that they were acquired by Louis XVI 'to serve as models of simple and pure shapes and to change by these examples the bad direction given to the shapes of porcelain under the preceding reign'.[154] Although the Sèvres porcelain factory had been making 'Vazes antiques', 'Vazes etrusques', and 'Vazes grecs'[155] since the 1760s, the impact of the new acquisitions is clear from the forms of some of the porcelain vessels made for Marie-Antoinette's dairy, together with other 'Etruscan' pieces for which Jean-Jacques Lagrenée's design is still preserved (Fig. 1.9).[156]

J. G. Herder thought that the simplicity of ancient Greece was unattainable, and lamented in an essay in memory of Winckelmann:

---

[149] Ibid. 2. 152.

[150] 'Elegance' and 'simplicity' figure large in the correspondence between Hamilton and Wedgwood which began in 1773: Ramage (1990b), 73–4.

[151] Saint-Non (1781–86), 1. 282.

[152] Cited in Finer and Savage (1965), 2. Porcelain continued to be a marker of political inclination; see Reitlinger (1961–70), 2. 163–4: 'Both Gladstone and Disraeli found time to collect. Disraeli, a somewhat rococo figure himself, of course collected Meissen, whereas Gladstone, with his Homeric interests, favoured Wedgwood jasper ware, which had, moreover, a sound Midland Radical tradition behind it.' In 1860, G. Dennis wanted to dedicate a book on Bourbon misrule in Sicily to

Gladstone: Rhodes (1973), 68. Also relevant, perhaps, are the words of Sir Arthur 'Bomber' Harris in a letter written 29 Mar. 1945: 'The feeling over Dresden could easily be explained by any psychiatrist. It is connected with German bands and Dresden shepherdesses': Hastings (1979), 344.

[153] D'Hancarville (1766[1767]–76), 2.146. For another view of the black colour on Greek pots, see: Vickers (1985a); Gill (1986); Vickers, Impey, and Allan (1986); Gill and Vickers (1990); Ch. 5.

[154] Brongniart and Riocreux (1845), p. xiii.

[155] Cf. Eriksen (1974), 112.

[156] *Age of Neo-classicism* (1972), pl. 121a, no. 1418. See too: Grandjean (1957), 180–4; Guth (1958), 74–81, esp. 78.

Where have you vanished, childhood of the ancient world, sweet beloved simplicity, in pictures, works and words? Where are you now beloved Greece, full of beautiful, god-like and youthful forms, full of truth in illusion, and of illusion filled with sweet truth? Your day is done, and the dreams of our memory, our histories, researches and wishes will not recall you again. The foot of the traveller will not arouse you, as he treads upon you and collects your sherds.[157]

There was, though, as we have seen, a traveller from Germany who did think that he had experienced something of the Greek way of life. 'Et in Arcadia ego' was the motto of Goethe's *Italian Journey*, an allusion both to the simplicity of the way of life of the inhabitants of the Central Peloponnese, proverbial in antiquity,[158] and to the fact that in the Kingdom of the Two Sicilies he had come close to ancient Greece. Goethe found the Neapolitans wholly natural, with something elemental ('etwas Ursprüngliches der Menschengattung') about them.[159] He felt that he had come into direct contact with the simplicity of what Herder had called the 'Kindheit der alten Welt'. Although the *Italian Journey* met with severe criticism in some quarters for its lack of political or historical sense when it was first published in 1817,[160] it was regarded as a guide and inspiration by successive generations of German travellers in the South, most of whom accepted unquestioningly Goethe's anti-historicist approach to the classical past, and readily saw Italy—and especially Greece—in 'simple' terms.[161]

Goethe's exposure to a kind of Greece and its art lay behind his 'Homeric' *Hermann and Dorothea* of 1797. This poem, 'the crown of Goethe's Hellenism',[162] exemplifies 'noble simplicity'[163] and was consciously based on Goethe's acquaintance with the visual arts.[164] 'In *Hermann and Dorothea* his characters, his images, his lines, his very movements are sculptured.'[165] Goethe's bourgeois epic is relevant here in that it includes a concise and ironic account of the change in taste brought about as a consequence of the French Revolution. The apothecary of a small town on the Rhine describes

---

[157] 'Wo bist Du hin, Kindheit der alten Welt, geliebte süsse Einfalt in Bildern, Werken und Worten? Wo bist Du geliebtes Griechenland, voll schöner Götter—und Jugendgestalten, voll Wahrheit im Truge und Trug voll süsser Wahrheit?—Deiner Zeit ist dahin und der Traum unsres Andenkens, unsre Geschichten, Untersuchungen und guten Wünsche werden Dich nicht wieder erwecken, der Fuss des Reisenden Dich nicht erwecken, der auf Dich tritt und Deine Scherben sammlet': Duncker (1882), 56 (trans. Butler (1958), 77).

[158] See Gatz (1967), 162.

[159] Goethe (1817 (1964)), 206; Trevelyan (1941), 151.

[160] See especially Niebuhr (1838), 2. 288–9.

[161] Michea (1933), 106–7. For two such reactions to Greece in the 1830s, see Ross (1863) and Curtius (1903).

[162] Trevelyan (1941), 215.

[163] Spalding (1968), p. xviii.

[164] 'Alle Vortheile, deren ich mich bediente, habe ich von den bildenden Kunst gelernt': ibid., pp. xix, 131, letter to Schiller, 8 Apr. 1797. D'Hancarville may prove to have contributed to *Hermann and Dorothea*. Goethe had the idea for the poem in July 1796 and began the immediate work of composition on 11 September 1796. In July 1796 he returned d'Hancarville (1766[1767]–76), 2–4, to the Weimar Library, having had all four volumes out since 1789: Keudell and Deetjen (1931), p. 4, no. 16. D'Hancarville (1766[1767]–76), 3, is concerned with the history of Greek sculpture; pp. 163–6 contain an account of a passage in Homer, *Il.* 18ff., which is interpreted in terms of a bas-relief; the tone is reminiscent of *Hermann and Dorothea*.

[165] Butler (1958), 128.

how in the good old days his garden gnomes ('farbigen Zwergen') were famous for miles around, and that even experts were taken in by the false coral which adorned his garden grotto; the painting of fine lords and ladies ('geputzten Herren und Damen') in his parlour was much admired. Now, however,

> I go but little abroad, for vexation,
> Since fashions so greatly have changed and the burgher
> Conforms to good taste, as he styles it; no carving
> Or gilding is suffered, for all must be simple . . .
>
> Yet still I would move with the times and make changes,
> Procure me new furniture, bow to the fashion;
> But truly I fear to disturb the least trifle,
> For who can afford now the workmen's high wages?[166]

In this vignette we see how new canons of 'good taste' replaced those of the preceding age.[167] Garden gnomes, henceforth 'das klassische Kitschsymbol'[168] had simply been part of rococo garden decoration.[169] So too, 'fine lords and ladies' were the characteristic ornaments of the *ancien régime*[170] rather than of the Biedermeier style, an early manifestation of which the apothecary describes.[171] But the worst sin against 'good taste' the apothecary commits is in the description of his grotto, decorated with cheap imitations of expensive materials. In a world where 'Beauty is truth, truth beauty', this was truly unforgivable.[172]

Goethe's implied criticisms, moreover, rest on the same ethical basis as Dennis's evaluation of South Italian pottery: 'vases which belong, if not always to the period of decadence, at least to the verge of it, when art was beginning to trick herself out in meretricious embellishments, and to forget

[166] Trans. Brandon (1913). This passage is discussed by Gombrich (1979), 30–1; see too *Moderne Vergangenheit 1800–1900* (1981), 17. Goethe left his parental home in Frankfurt partly as a consequence of 'his incautious criticism of . . . some mirror frames and Chinese wallpapers in the Rococo style': Robson-Scott (1981), 30.

[167] The concept of 'good taste' began with Winckelmann, whose *Gedanken* (1755) actually begins 'Good taste [Der gute Geschmack] . . . had its first beginnings under the Greek sky.'

[168] Richter (1972), 72. The literature on garden gnomes is limited. There are a few useful pages by P. Oliver, 'The Galleon on the Front Door: Imagery of the House and Garden', in Oliver, Davies, and Bentley (1981), 189–71. Huygen and Poortvliet (1977) and Melville (1983) are rather less scholarly.

[169] For an extreme manifestation, and one to which Goethe took an intense dislike, see the Villa Pallagonia at Bagheria, near Palermo: Goethe (1817 (1964)), 242–7. Not surprisingly, G. Dennis was to take a similar view: Dennis (1864), 141. Goethe's

own deceptively simple garden ornament at Weimar is discussed by Heckscher (1962*a*); (1962*b*); both reprinted in Verheyen (1985), 189–216, 217–36.

[170] Pascal (1973), 38; cf. 294–5: 'one of the distinguishing features of the popular play and novel, the best seller, is the admiration of the aristocracy—one might say that the recommendation of obsolete values is the essence of kitsch'. P. Bourdieu usefully defines the well known distinction between '"Civilisation", marked by lightness (legerété) and superficiality' and '"Culture", defined by seriousness, depth and sincerity': Bourdieu (1979), 80.

[171] For the philosophical background to Biedermeier, see Heinrich (1985), 200–1.

[172] Pazaurek (1912) comes down very hard on those who disobey the principle of *Materialgerechtigkeit*—the view that a craftsman should be faithful to the aesthetic of the medium in which he works; cf. Ch. 5. This concept was unknown in antiquity: see Kopcke (1964), 25; Raby and Vickers (1986), and Chapters 5 and 6, below.

her sublime and godlike simplicity'. For Dennis, born in 1814, was the child of an age which saw itself as having emerged from a long period of decadence. He was also at the beginning of a tradition of scholarship which thinks of South Italian pottery in the terms in which persons of 'taste' regard garden gnomes, and for the same underlying reasons: both were originally thought to evoke the values of the *ancien régime*. In the case of South Italian pottery, this is obviously an anachronistic judgement; so too, however, is the view that ancient Greeks placed greater store by simplicity than embellishment. Like 'value', 'simplicity' is an eighteenth-century construction whose central role in modern scholarship has had its day.

In summary, the notion that fine Greek pottery—the black- and red-figure wares which fill our museums—was ever especially valuable in antiquity is based on arguments which are at best weak and at worst wholly misleading. The modern taste for Greek pots with 'simple', as opposed to ornate decoration also has its roots in the eighteenth century. Its origins lie in the growing reaction to absolutism which found its most radical expression in the Modern Movement; it is an uncertain tool for reconstructing ancient value systems, or even the history of Greek art.

2 Golden Greece: Élite Consumption and Relative Values

I F it really is the case that the value placed on ceramics is a relatively modern phenomenon, the question immediately arises as to what ancient Greeks did put a value on. After personal honour and family pride, the answer is quite simply real luxuries such as gold and silver, purple and ivory. This will have been the case at any level of society, but possession of precious metals will have been the prerogative of the rich and powerful. That there were indeed considerable differences between the material conditions of one level of Greek society and another is clear from Plato's dictum that 'In every city there are two cities: the rich and the poor.'[1] But in the case of Athens, by far the best-documented centre, there has been a tendency to look upon the city's material culture from the point of view of the poorest members of society, to consider prices and values in terms of what an artisan might earn—a drachma a day for the skilled labourer, half that for the unskilled— and to edit out of the popular image of ancient Athens the idea that the rich might have lived lives of luxury, or at least respectable gentility. The sources show that the rich at Athens conducted their business in *minae* (1 *mina* = 100 drachmas), and that among the wealthy a drachma was considered a 'trifling sum'.[2]

A tale told about Socrates well expresses the wide disparity which existed between the rich and the not-so-rich in fifth-century Athens:

When Socrates heard one of his friends remark how expensive [Athens] was, saying 'Chian wine costs a *mina*, a purple robe three *minae*, a *kotyle* [0.24 litres] of honey five drachmas', he took him by the hand and led him to the grain market. 'An obol for a *hemiekton* [3.84 litres] of grain, the city is cheap;' then to the olive market, 'a *choinix* [0.96 litres] of olives for two coppers'; then to the clothes market, 'a tunic [*exomis*] for ten drachmas! The city is cheap.'[3]

There was clearly a level of society within which it was natural to speak in terms of *minae*,[4] with silver drachmas as the small change. At the other end

[1] Pl. *Rp.* 422e.
[2] Dem. 24. 114; cf. 24. 16.
[3] Plut. *Mor.* 470f.

[4] 1 *mina* = 430 g., approximately 1 lb. of silver; 1 drachma = 4.3 g. of silver; there were 100 drachmas to the *mina*, and 60 *minae* to the talent.

of the social scale it was possible to obtain a substantial amount of grain, and hence the means of survival, for one six-hundredth of a *mina*.[5] The most expensive item here is expressed in terms of drachmas.

It might be instructive, not least to assist our understanding of the surviving remains of classical antiquity, to explore something of the value system of the upper echelons of Athenian society. There is a related question, namely, how can we express the range of levels of consumption in classical Greece in a way that we today can understand? Was A. H. M. Jones right to say in 1957 that 'Twenty *minae* is difficult to express in modern terms'?[6] Are there *any* constants between antiquity and the present which would enable us to express these figures in a manner we can grasp? Precious metal may provide such a means.

In Victorian history books, ancient prices were converted to quaint-looking figures in pounds, shillings, and pence which were, however, meaningful to the nineteenth-century reader (because they were expressed in terms that related to gold and silver.) There then came a time when Britain and America went off the gold-standard, and in 1934 the price of gold was pegged artificially at $35 per Troy ounce.[7] It became increasingly impossible to make any realistic comparisons, and so the practice of expressing ancient values in terms of current gold prices died out, and in 1957 Jones was perfectly correct to say that it was difficult to express 20 *minae* in modern terms. But since August 1971, gold has ceased to be pegged, and it may be worth while trying to use it again as a means of expressing ancient values. A problem, but not an insurmountable one, is presented by the fact that most prices in ancient Greece were expressed in denominations of silver, a metal whose value with respect to gold has fallen since antiquity. In the 430s[8] the ratio of gold to silver was in the order of 1 : 14; today it varies greatly. The Texan speculators, the Bunker Hunts, hoped—but failed—to get it to 1 : 5 in the early 1980s,[9] but at the time of writing it is 1 : 82,[10] a five-and-a-half-fold reduction since antiquity. Even though the modern prices quoted in this chapter are liable to sudden change (as are the current prices of gold and silver), they do, in that they are internally consistent, at least dramatize relative values in a way which we can recognize.[11]

$$1 \text{ talent} = 60 \text{ } minae \quad = £10,000$$
$$1 \text{ } mina = 100 \text{ drachmas} = £180$$

---

[5] There were 6 obols to the drachma.

[6] Jones (1957), 79.

[7] For a good account, see Green (1985), 1–13.

[8] Lewis (1968); (1986), 73.

[9] Green (1985), 13.

[10] In early April 1992, gold stood at £195.35 per oz. and silver at £2.36.

[11] A formula for creating modern equivalents for ancient prices expressed in silver might be:

$$x = \left\{ \left(\frac{a}{31.103} \right) \times b \right\} \times c$$

(where x = the equivalent modern price, a = the ancient silver price in grams, b = the modern price of silver per troy oz., and c = the ratio of the modern price of silver to gold divided by 14).

$$1 \text{ drachma} = 6 \text{ obols} = \pounds1.80$$
$$1 \text{ obol} \qquad\qquad = 30p^{[12]}$$

If we look at the figures in the Socratic anecdote in this fashion some interesting, if at times surprising, statistics emerge. The expensive wine works out at nearly £4 a bottle (in our terms; cheap wine could be the equivalent of less than 10p a bottle),[13] the purple robe nearly £550, and the quarter of a litre of honey £9. Even the best wine was only moderately expensive by our standards, but the purple robe was not cheap; purple dye was *isarguron*—'worth its weight in silver'.[14] It is the kind of garment we hear of Alcibiades wearing: swaggering into the Agora with his cloak trailing on the ground.[15] The honey seems extraordinarily expensive, but the price serves as a re-minder that sweetness was always a prerogative of the rich until cane sugar began to be exploited in the eighteenth century.[16]

The cheap goods work out at nearly 30p for 4 litres of flour, a litre of olives for rather less, and a tunic for nearly £18. The flour (and thus the means of subsistence) is, however, very cheap indeed, in effect subsidized by the existence of the Laurium silver mines: Pericles clearly got some good deals when he set up the pattern of Athens' grain trade. We would expect olives to be cheap in Attica, while the price of the inexpensive garment is in no way remarkable. The place of ceramic on this scale of values is discussed in Chapter 4.

At the opposite end of the scale from the cheap coat, chariot-racing, and horses in general, provide a way into the world of the well-to-do. In fourth-century Sparta, for example, the breeding of chariot-horses was considered 'a proof of wealth',[17] while at Athens the breeding of race-horses was pos-sible 'only for those most blessed by fortune'.[18] The price of horses, then as now, varied tremendously, but even when a horse had been purchased, it had to be fed, exercised, and groomed—by slaves. The ancient literary and epigraphical sources give the clear impression that 'being part of the eques-trian milieu was an expensive pastime which few citizens could afford' (Fig. 2.1).[19] It is clear, too, that prices of horses are expressed in *minae* or greater denominations; thus, in the fourth century BC 12 *minae*[20] was 'fairly standard for a high-quality horse'.[21] Another price we have from the same

---

[12] Equivalent values in 1992.

[13] Socrates' friend's wine was presumably an amphora-ful, hence 34.56 litres: 46.08 wine bot-tles at 0.75 litres. For the more usual run of prices of wine, see Boeckh (1842), 98–9.

[14] Aesch. *Ag.* 959; Theopomp. Hist. *FGH* 115 F 117.

[15] Plut. *Alc.* 16. 1.

[16] Wolf (1982), 149–51, 333–6; Mintz (1985). On model beehives in Attic and Boeotian graves, see Cherici (1991).

[17] Xen. *Ages.* 9. 2. 6.

[18] Isocr. 16. 33.

[19] Spence (1988); (forthcoming). Thanks are due to Dr Spence for allowing us to read his paper before publication.

[20] Equivalent to more than £2,150.

[21] Spence (forthcoming). The average price of horses sold at the 1991 Doncaster Lincoln Handi-cap Sale was 1,908 gns: £2,003.40 (*Horse and Hound*, 2 April 1992, 26).

FIG. 2.1 Attic red-figure pottery *stamnos*. Horsemen. Ashmolean Museum, Oxford AN 1965.121.

period occurs in a lawsuit brought against the son of Alcibiades in the 390s.[22] Back in 416,[23] Alcibiades had been so eager to win renown (for which read political and social clout at home and abroad) that he entered in his own name seven teams of horses in the chariot-race—the major event—at Olympia. Alcibiades' teams won first, second, and fourth places.[24] So elated was Alcibiades that he entertained all the spectators at the Olympic games to dinner.[25] Small wonder that Thucydides records that he was heavily in debt a few months later.[26]

[22] Isocr. 16.
[23] For the date, see Bowra (1960).
[24] Thuc. 6. 16. 2; Plut. *Alc.* 11; Ath. 1. 3e. According to Alcibiades Jr. and Euripides (from whom Alcibiades had commissioned an epinician ode), the teams came in first, second, and third: Isocr. 16. 34; Eur. 755 (Page).
[25] Ath. 1. 3e.
[26] Thuc. 6. 15. 3.

Alcibiades' inheritance may have amounted to around 100 talents (or 6,000 *minae*),[27] but he always seems to have lived beyond his means. One of the teams of horses at Olympia had belonged to a certain Teisias,[28] who thought that they were being entered in his name. There must have been a long history of unpleasantness, because the case was still being argued in the courts decades later.[29] The value placed on the team of horses was 5 talents (300 *minae*).[30] One and a quarter talents for a horse is a high, but credible figure: Alexander the Great's Bucephalus was variously valued at 13 and 16 talents (780–960 *minae*).[31]

A. H. M. Jones estimated that 'there was a heavy concentration of wealth at the extreme top of Athenian society' in a small group of some 300 families.[32] Very occasionally we hear how big some individuals' fortunes were, and Jones lists the largest. Nicias' fortune is said to have been the same size as that reported for Alcibiades.[33] Callias Laccoplutus supposedly owned property to the value of 200 talents,[34] Diphilus 160 talents,[35] and Epicrates, who sank a private mine outside the official limits at Laurium, was rumoured to have made 600 talents.[36] But that was wholly exceptional. The largest fortune for which we have firm evidence is that of Pasion the banker, who was worth between 75 and 80 talents.[37] If the equivalents in the footnotes possess any validity, some rich Athenians will have been millionaires in today's terms, but only just: not that much when we are, after all, supposed to be dealing with big money.

But everything is relative; in the case of an Athenian aristocrat, relative to a Persian grandee. It so happens that we have precise details of the wealth of the second richest man in the Persian empire in 480 BC. Pythius possessed 2,000 talents of silver and '4,000,000 golden darics less 7,000'.[38] This amounts to more than 50 tonnes of silver and 33 of gold; at the conversion rate employed here, more than £220 million. In the fifth and fourth centuries, standards of wealth and luxury were set in the Persian empire; Athenians strove to keep up.[39] Some of them succeeded up to a point, but many did not.

Compared, however, with the splendour of Eastern centres, or with the sybaritic luxury of Thurii in the West, the level of consumption in Periclean Athens was restrained. This is a fact for which we have Thucydides' Pericles'

[27] Lys. 19. 52: equivalent to just over £1m.
[28] Ostwald (1986), 311 n. 67.
[29] Isocr. 16.
[30] Isocr. 16. 46; equivalent to more than £50,000.
[31] Chares in Aul. Gell. 5. 2. 2; Pliny, *NH* 8. 154; cf. Spence (forthcoming). The value is equivalent to between £140,000 and £170,000.
[32] Jones (1957), 87. See too Davies (1971).
[33] Lys. 19. 47.

[34] Lys. 19. 48: equivalent to more than £2m.
[35] Plut. *Mor.* 843d: equivalent to nearly £1.75m.
[36] Harp. and *Suda* s.v. Ἐπικράτης: equivalent to nearly £6.5m.
[37] Dem. 36. 5 ff.: equivalent to between £800,000 and £860,000.
[38] Hdt. 7. 28.
[39] On the strains created on Athenian aristocratic society by the war, see Ostwald (1986), 344–58.

own word: 'We are lovers of the beautiful, yet simple in our tastes.'[40] Contrast Persian flamboyance with Athenian genteel restraint: at some time in the fifth century, it seems, the Persian king sent gifts to a Cretan gentleman. These included:

a silver-footed bed with its coverings, a tent with a gaily coloured canopy, a silver throne, a gilded sunshade, twenty gold *phialai* set with jewels, one hundred large silver ones and an unspecified number of silver craters. In addition one hundred concubines and a hundred slaves, six thousand pieces of gold, beside all that was given to him for his daily necessities.[41]

An Athenian state pension was considerably less than this. For all that it may have been a fourth-century fabrication, Plutarch's story that Aristides' son Lysimachus was granted a state pension of '100 silver *minae*, and as many *plethra* of planted land, and in addition an allowance of 4 drachmas a day',[42] indicates what was then considered to be a comfortable but not extravagant existence. One hundred *minae* of silver, however (nearly £18,000, at the rate we have been employing) points to a way of life which probably included the regular use of plate. The figure is the same as that received from the Athenian state by Democedes the Crotoniate physician in the sixth century,[43] and by Pindar for composing lines in praise of Athens in the 470s.[44] (Herodotus did considerably better, being granted 10 talents (600 *minae*)[45] for his recitations at Athens in the 440s.)[46]

Yet, even though the Athenian style of life was restrained compared with the Persian, the richest members of Athenian society regularly used plate at their symposia.[47] This is in any case borne out by a description of one of Alcibiades' youthful escapades—probably at some time in the 430s—when he reacted to the homosexual advances of the wealthy tanner Anytus by going to his house, where 'he looked into the room where the guests were, and seeing the tables covered with gold and silver drinking-cups, ordered his slaves to carry away half of them'.[48] While the symposium might be an opportunity for the presentation of gold and silver vessels to guests,[49] this was

---

[40] Thuc. 2. 40. The relative modesty of the goods listed in the sale of the Hermocopidae has been invoked as a reflection 'of a kind of distaste for any exhibit of private wealth' in late fifth-century Athens (Pritchett (1956), 210), but the evidence can be read otherwise. Either anything of real value had already gone (Lewis (1966), 183 n. 37); Amyx (1958), 208), or plate would not have been put up for auction in any case (see p. 51, below).

[41] Ath. 2. 48f.

[42] Plut. *Arist.* 27.

[43] Hdt. 3. 131.

[44] Isocr. 15. 166.

[45] Equivalent to over £100,000.

[46] Diyllus *apud* Plut. *Mor.* 862b; (*FGH* 73 F 3).

[47] For unanimity on the rich at Athens using gold and silver plate when entertaining guests: Vickers (1985*a*); Robertson (1985), 26; R. M. Cook (1987), 170; Boardman (1987); Gill (1988*c*); Gill and Vickers (1990). For a good expression of the older view, see Birch (1873), 354: 'The painted ware was employed chiefly for entertainments and the triclinia of the wealthy.'

[48] Plut. *Alc.* 4. 5.

[49] Plut. *Mor.* 177a (gift of a gold cup to Euripides at a banquet); Ath. 3. 126d–e; 4. 128c–130d (a wedding feast at which the guests were given many pieces of gold and silver); Ath. 11. 466b–c (a dinner at which three hundred men were each given a silver cup (*ekpoma*) weighing 4 *minae*). On the 'grammar' of gift-exchange, see Gould (1991).

taking things too far. In the fourth century, we hear of a house being cleared of its plate by interlopers, and a nurse murdered for having concealed a cup beneath her garment.[50] And if Socrates did indeed drink from a 'silver well'[51]—an expression for a large cup—at the symposium immortalized by Plato, then it is likely that the rest of the sympotic furniture used on that occasion, including the wine-cooler drained by Alcibiades at one go,[52] was also of precious metal. Private individuals must also have owned the silver craters which 'lined the whole of the circumference of the Piraeus'[53] when the Athenian fleet under the command of Alcibiades, Lamachus, and Nicias left for Sicily in 415, an occasion on which even the soldiers displayed 'the keenest rivalry in the matter of arms and personal equipment',[54] and when both officers and men poured libations 'on every deck', from gold and silver vessels,[55] and when 'an immense sum amounting to many talents was with-drawn from the city'.[56] Nicias earned more than a *mina* and a half per day from his interests in the Laurium silver mines,[57] and Thucydides, to whom we owe most of our knowledge of the Sicilian campaign, was himself the manager of Thracian gold mines.[58] One hundred and thirty-four triremes set sail from the Piraeus,[59] and so we may perhaps already envision 134 silver craters in the possession of members of Athens' upper crust, those who had paid for the construction and fitting out of the warships. Whether or not it was factually accurate,[60] Thucydides' account of the events leading up to the invasion of Sicily—the deception of the Athenian embassy into believing that the island was awash with precious metal[61]—shows what was the principal motivation of the participants. It has been well observed in the context of events at Athens of precisely this period that 'fine silver table ware . . . must have served . . . as an easily portable reserve of wealth';[62] we can be sure that great quantities of domestic plate were taken to Sicily never to return to a greatly impoverished Athens.

The Spartan occupation of Decelea between 414 and 404 was another serious blow to the Athenian economy, and by extension to the manufacturers of gold- and silverware. In 404 Athens was not actually sacked, but she was squeezed hard. Internal rather than external plunder was the order of the day. The reign of terror conducted by the Thirty Tyrants and their 300 storm-troopers[63] was directed against wealthy resident aliens. We are

[50] [Dem.] 47. 58.

[51] Ath. 5. 192a; cf. Pl. *Smp.* 223c. Socrates was also made out to have stolen an *oinochoe*, presumably a silver one: Eup. *PCG* 395; cf. Ar. *PCG* 295.

[52] Pl. *Smp.* 213e.

[53] Diod. 13. 3. 2; cf. Thuc. 6. 32. 1.

[54] Thuc. 6. 31. 3.

[55] Thuc. 6. 32. 1.

[56] Thuc. 6. 32. 5–6.

[57] Xen. *Vect.* 4. 14–15.

[58] Thuc. 4. 105. 1.

[59] Thuc. 6. 31. 3.

[60] For some reservations on this question, see Hornblower (1987), 22–3.

[61] Thuc. 6. 8. 2; 46.3–5.

[62] Amyx (1958), 208.

[63] The term employed by Ehrenberg (1973), 353.

tolerably well informed regarding the financial circumstances of one of these: Lysias, 'the richest metic in Athens'.[64] As K. J. Dover observes, the 3 talents of silver, the 400 Cyzicene staters, the 100 darics, and the four silver *phialai*[65] found in Lysias' house when it was searched on behalf of the Thirty 'would be unlikely to represent the major part of his capital'.[66] This will scarcely have been an isolated instance, but must have been typical of the further depredations made on the estates of once wealthy Athenians.

It is unfortunate that our principal written sources relating to private life in the fifth century—Aristophanes and Plato—refer to the period when Athenian wealth was in sharp decline. Nevertheless, enough evidence exists from other sources to show not only that the decades between the Persian and the Peloponnesian Wars were an age of great prosperity for Athens, but that one manifestation of such prosperity was the possession of domestic gold and silver plate. Even so, the age of austerity which lasted from the Peloponnesian War well into the fourth century seems, rather like the Utility Period in Britain, to have left its mark, and it was presumably the dining practices of a relatively impoverished Greece which impressed themselves upon the Hellenistic world. This in turn might explain how Juba of Mauretania, writing in the first century AD, could claim that pottery was regularly used for dining 'down to the Macedonian period'.[67] Athens' silver age had clearly been forgotten.

Aristophanes refers in his *Babylonians* of 426 to a drinking-vessel worth 2 *minae*. One character says 'I owe a debt of 200 drachmas. How can I pay it?' His companion replies: 'Here, take this silver cup and pay for it with that.'[68] Even without Pollux's gloss,[69] it is clear that the vessel was simply worth its weight in silver. It was in fact the norm for plate to be made up in round figures in terms of one coinage or another;[70] and when Attic, even in round figures in *minae*. Thus, Demosthenes speaks of 'gold vessels, weighing a *mina* each',[71] and a fifth-century silver *phiale* (Fig. 2.2) from Duvanli adorned with a chariot-racing scene done in gold[72] weighs exactly 1 *mina*.[73] A gold-figure *kantharos* (Frontispiece) from the same cemetery[74]

[64] *POxy.* 13. 1606, 153–5; cf. Davies (1971), 589.

[65] Lys. 12. 11.

[66] Dover (1968), 30.

[67] Ath. 6. 229c. For the tendency to see earlier periods, even classical Athens, as possessing wholesome simplicity, see Vischer (1965).

[68] Ar. *PCG* 68.

[69] Poll. 10. 85.

[70] The weights of Greek gold and silver vessels 'were usually rendered in units of a commonly used coin': Bothmer (1962–3), 155. For weighing practice, see Grayson (1975).

[71] Dem. 24. 184.

[72] Plovdiv 1515: Filow (1934), pl. 4; Strong (1966), pl. 15b; Danov and Ivanov (1980), pl. 16; Vickers (1990*b*).

[73] Gill (1988*b*), 10–12. Cf. the 1-*mina phiale* from Kozani: Strong (1966), 57; Θησαυροί (1979), 40, pl. 10, no. 45; Gill (1990*b*).

[74] Plovdiv 1634: Filow (1934), pl. 7; Danov and Ivanov (1980), pl. 9; Vickers, Impey, and Allan (1986), pl. 4b.

FIG. 2.2 Attic gold-figure silver *phiale* from the Bashova mound, Duvanli. *Apobates* race. Archaeological Museum, Plovdiv, Inv. 1515.

weighs $2\frac{1}{2}$ *minae*.[75] That the *phiale* was made at Athens is clear not simply on account of its weight, but because—at least according to Theophrastus— the *apobates* race represented on it was only practised in Attica and Boeotia.[76] We hear of silver vessels being given as prizes at games at Marathon and Sicyon, specifically silver *phialai* for horse-racing at Sicyon, perhaps *phialai* resembling the Duvanli specimen.[77]

Even silver *phialai* were, relatively speaking, cheap compared with gold ones. There were dozens of gold *phialai* in the hands of the trierarchs in 415, and we hear of Demus, son of the peacock-fancier Pyrilampes, attempting to raise a loan of 16 *minae* with a gold *phiale* which had been given to

[75] Gill (1988*b*), 10–12. The magnificent silver rhyton from Aul Uljap, in the form of the foreparts of a winged horse and now in the State Museum of Oriental Art in Moscow (Fig. 2.3) weighs '1,435.5 g. after conservation, and about 1,425 g. without conservation materials' (personal communication from a colleague who wishes to remain anonymous). This looks like 333.33 Attic drachmas (at 4.306 g. at the higher weight, and 4.275 at the lower (though one foreleg is missing))—a third of 10 *minae*.

[76] Theophr. in Harpocr. s.v. ἀποβάτης.

[77] Marathon: Pind. *Ol.* 9. 90; Sicyon: Pind. *Nem.* 9. 51.

F I G. 2.3 Attic silver-gilt *rhyton* in the form of the *protome* of a winged horse, from Aul Uljap. Museum of Oriental Art, Moscow, Inv. Uljap 82, GMINW, 37 M-IV.

him in recognition of *philia* by the Great King.[78] It has been estimated that Demus' *phiale* weighed 100 darics,[79] and this is frequently the kind of weight one finds for gold *phialai*, whether extant or mentioned in inventories.[80] At the rate we have been employing, 100 darics would work out at more than £5,000. Demus' *phiale* was clearly his principal asset, and it is not difficult to think of plate, whether of gold or silver, playing a similar role in most high-status families, whether in Greece or Etruria.

It has been estimated that Athenian silver mines produced something like 20 tonnes of silver a year,[81] much of it spent on raw materials and grain.[82] Artistry (of a kind discussed below)[83] will have both provided a means of enhancing a family's image and added to the bullion value of traded goods. Pliny's comment that 'we have made gold and silver dearer by the art of engraving'[84] perhaps hints at value-enhancement by decoration. Back at the melting-pot, however, the bottom line was purity and weight; purity was what Athenian silver was famous for,[85] and weights are frequently given in the ancient sources.

The family was not the only institution which might keep its wealth in the shape of vessels of precious metal. Sanctuaries, too, hoarded precious metal which was frequently given and kept in this form. This raises another issue which has been well outlined in a related context by C. R. Dodwell:

In descriptions of the radiant trappings of society there was no difference between Anglo-Saxon poetry and those pedestrian sources for Anglo-Saxon history—the annals, the legal wills and the chronicles. What we discover, in fact, is that the poets were not dreaming up gilded visions but delineating the tastes of the world around. It was a world which both in the religious and secular spheres savoured resplendence.[86]

We used to believe that when Aeschylus or Pindar refer to divine or mortal wealth in terms of 'gold-wrought and silver cups'[87] or a 'solid gold bowl, the peak of possessions'[88] that they may have been making poetical flights of fancy. But now that it is generally agreed that the rich used plate; now that the picture of at least Athenian society includes a level of consumption which can properly be described as luxurious, it is possible to begin to think of poetic accounts of great splendour at religious festivals as reflecting reality.

[78] Lys. 19. 25; on *philia*, see Wiesehöfer (1980), 7–21.

[79] Vickers (1984 (1988)).

[80] For example, a *phiale* in the National Historical Museum in Sofia (from Panagyurishte) weighs exactly 100 darics (Cahn (1960)), and another in the Metropolitan Museum, New York (Fig. 2.4: Bothmer (1984), 86) weighs 90 darics (Vickers (1984 (1988))); for another explanation, see Bothmer (1962–3)). Lewis (1986), 77 speaks of 'a hundred daric standard'.

[81] Conophagos (1980), 341–54.

[82] Garnsey (1988), 90, 105; Gill (1991).

[83] See ch. 5, below.

[84] Pliny, *NH* 33. 1. 4–5.

[85] e.g. Polyb. 21. 32. 8; 43. 19: 'best Attic silver'. Neutron-activation analysis of Athenian coins has showed that 'the fifth-century coinage of Athens was remarkable not only for its purity, but also for the regularity with which this was maintained, and that ancient eulogy of it was justified': (Kraay and Emeleus (1962), 16).

[86] Dodwell (1982), 30.

[87] Aesch. *Fr.* 184.

[88] Pind. *Ol.* 7. 1–4.

F I G. 2.4   Achaemenid gold *phiale* decorated with acorns and beech nuts. Metropolitan Museum, New York Rogers Fund 1962 (62.11.1).

Euripides' *Ion* provides a case in point. The Servant's speech at lines 1122 ff. describes the erection of a tent 100 feet square adorned with rich tapestries, in which the guests are entertained with wine served from gold craters in gold and 'silver inlaid' cups whose size increased as time went by. While this passage is rarely discussed in the context of Greek symposia,[89] there is no reason for not taking it as such. The square tent has the shape of the dining-rooms in which symposia were usually held.[90] The Lesche of the Cnidians at Delphi, whose walls were adorned with permanent reminders of valorous deeds in the form of Polygnotus' paintings,[91] was in the shape of a double dining-room: two squares side by side, which would have accommodated thirty or so people reclining on couches.[92] Ion's tent would have accommodated more than sixty couches, but even his festivities must have been on a small scale compared with the occasion at Olympia in 416 when Alcibiades celebrated his unprecedented success by entertaining the entire company. It was on this occasion too that 'the various states vied with one another in showing him honour. Ephesus pitched a magnificently adorned tent for his accommodation, Chios provided feed for his horses and a quantity of animals for sacrifice, and Lesbos provided wine and everything else necessary for giving lavish entertainment.'[93] If it really was then that Alcibiades purloined the official plate belonging to the Athenian delegation[94] (which people assumed belonged to him),[95] yet another dimension can be added to the resplendence of the scene. And such occasions will also have served to disseminate knowledge of latest fashions in luxury goods.[96]

Back at Delphi itself, we know that at least the huge silver wine-crater dedicated by Croesus was regularly used at a religious festival,[97] and when the sanctuary was sacked by Phocians in the fourth century, the Delphians subsequently claimed to have lost 10,000 talents.[98] Even allowing for an inflated insurance claim, this would leave plenty of room for 'big cups' of gold and silver. Another large figure that has come down to us is the booty amounting to nearly 40 tonnes of silver[99] captured from Pyrgi, the small harbour town of Etruscan Caere/Cerveteri, in 384. Etruria was, after all, a source of gold *phialai* in the fifth century,[100] and its élites were still living in comparative luxury in the first century BC, dining with 'a multitude of

---

[89] The only exception known to us: Schmitt-Pantel (1992).

[90] Tomlinson (1969); (1970).

[91] Francis (1990), 94–7.

[92] Tomlinson (1980).

[93] Plut. *Alc.* 12. 1. The archaeological record only preserves the evidence for less lavish entertainment; e.g. broken pottery cups from the sanctuary of Demeter and Kore at Corinth (Bookidis (1990)), from the South Stoa at Athens (Thompson and Wycherley (1972)), 89, or from a public dining room (Rotroff and Oakley (1992)).

[94] Plut. *Alc.* 13.

[95] [Andoc.] 4. 29.

[96] Cf. Dalley (1985), 48, on the way in which 'the mingling of equestrian nobility from far and wide with their entourages of servants and luxury furnishings' contributed to the dissemination of ivories in the Assyrian empire.

[97] The *Theophania*: Hdt. 1. 51.

[98] Diod. 16. 56; equivalent to more than £100m.

[99] 1,500 talents: 38,700 kg., equivalent to more than £15m.

[100] Critias 2. 7 (West); for an earlier Etruscan gold *phiale*, see von Hase (1974).

silver drinking-cups of every description'.[101] Although we possess few figures for Sparta, it was thought by contemporaries that there was 'more gold and silver in Lacedaemon than in all the rest of Hellas' (though much less than in Persia).[102] When Cleomenes III of Sparta, scandalized at the extravagance of third-century BC symposia, reinstituted traditional simple Spartan ways, he served his guests in silver cups from a bronze crater.[103]

NON-ATTIC WEIGHT STANDARDS

The ancients placed great emphasis on the weight (and purity) of objects made from precious metal. Whether in Old Babylonia,[104] Mosaic Israel,[105] the Mycenaean world,[106] or classical Greece, the weight of gold and silver was of paramount importance. At Athens, not only was the great chryselephantine cult-statue of Athena 'what the [Parthenon] was built to display',[107] but it was made in such a way that the gold plates could be taken off and weighed, should accusations of embezzlement be made (as they were).[108] It was thus natural for Herodotus to provide the weight of Croesus' gold wine-crater at Delphi: $8\frac{1}{2}$ talents and 12 *minae*.[109] In the light of Croesus' munificence elsewhere (and that of his forebears at Delphi),[110] the crater was presumably of solid gold.[111] Herodotus was writing in the fifth century, and was probably recording the weight in terms of a contemporary standard. But why is it such an odd weight? D. M. Lewis recently suggested that some 'peculiar Athenian weights' of gold objects on the Athenian Acropolis might be explained in terms of the Persian standard,[112] and a similar explanation may prevail here. If Herodotus was employing the Attic standard, the crater will have been potentially a 'round' figure in antiquity, being very close to 2,700 of the unit known to us as the Persian *karsha*.[113]

---

[101] Diod. 5. 40. If this was a literary *topos* (cf. Spivey (1991), 135) it only serves to emphasize the luxury traditionally enjoyed by the Etruscans.

[102] Pl. *Alc.* 1. 122, 123. Unlike Athens, most of this wealth was in the hands of a few: ibid. 121, 123. The fine with which Agis of Sparta was threatened in 418 BC was 100,000 drachmas (Thuc. 5. 63. 2). Cf. Holm (1894–7), 2.409 n. 7: 'Consequently a Spartiate might possess $16\frac{2}{3}$ talents!'

[103] Plut. *Cleom.* 13. 4.

[104] Dalley (1984), 59–62.

[105] e.g. Exod. 38. 24–27; Num. 7. 12–86; and cf. Millard (1988); (1989); Greenfield (1985), 85.

[106] Eiwanger (1989).

[107] Osborne (1987b), 101.

[108] Eddy (1977).

[109] Hdt. 1. 50.

[110] Hdt. 1. 50, 92; 6. 124. Gyges of Lydia (685–657 BC) gave six gold craters to Delphi (Hdt. 1. 14.1–2), as well as silver objects (Hdt. 1. 14. 3); Alyattes (610–560 BC) dedicated a 'large silver crater' (Hdt. 1. 25. 2).

[111] *Pace Griffith* (1988), 11–21, who believes that Croesus' dedications were of plated bronze. Contrast Linders (1987), 115.

[112] Lewis (1986), 77.

[113] At 25.86 kg. to the talent (i.e. 4.31 g. to the drachma: cf. Lang (1970)), Herodotus' weight would be equivalent to 224,982 g.; at 25.80 (4.3 g. to the drachma), 224,460. The *karsha* weighed 83.3 g. (cf. Bivar (1985), 637). 224,982 ÷ 83.3 = 2700.86; 224,460 ÷ 83.3 = 2694.60. Little is known about the pre-Achaemenid history of the *karsha*, but Herodotus' evidence perhaps points to its having been adopted from Lydia. It may be relevant that the gold bowl dedicated by Cypselids at Olympia (Boston, Fig. 3.2), discussed below (p. 65) weighs 835.8 g.: the equivalent of 10 *karsha*. (There is a widespread misapprehension that this bowl weighs the equivalent of 2 Babylonian *minae*, but this, as Ms Florence Wolsky kindly informs us, seems to have come about as the result of an incorrect transcription of the weight on to a catalogue card in 1921.)

It is probably because the Athenian sources dominate our view of ancient Greece, that when weights of plate have been examined in the past, it was usually expected that an Athenian pattern would emerge.[114] In fact, extant plate made to an Athenian standard is extremely rare and most surviving plate appears to have been made to an Achaemenid Persian or to the closely related Thraco-Macedonian standard.[115]

Perhaps the most striking instance is to be found in the Parthenon inventories,[116] where the weights of objects are given in Attic drachmas. The Table lists some of the items in the Pronaos whose weights are recorded. Some are given in round figures (e.g. (3) seven *phialai* at presumably 1 *mina* each, and (4) two *phialai* at 1 *mina* each), while others clearly are not. Among the dedications listed in the Table, 38 dr. (1), 329 dr. (5), 910 dr. (7) and especially 643 drachmas 2 obols (10) are so much out of keeping with some of the others that they invite a search for some other weight standard which might have been employed. One does not have far to look, for just as 'peculiar Athenian weights' of gold objects might be explained in terms of Persian *karsha* and darics, odd weights of silver vessels can usually be read in terms of Persian *sigloi*.[117]

This is what appears to be attested in contemporary sources. A good example is to be found in the pseudo-Demosthenic speech *Against Timotheus*, where 'two *phialai* of Lycian workmanship', among other items, were in dispute. The plaintiff's father persuaded an associate 'to accept the value of the *phialai*, as much as their weight amounted to, which was 237 drachmas'.[118] Two hundred and thirty-seven drachmas equal 180 *sigloi*,[119] and we may surmise that the *phialai* weighed 90 *sigloi* each. Elsewhere in the same speech, we hear of a request made by Timotheus for a loan of '1,351 drachmas and 2 obols; that was the exact sum he said he wanted'.[120] Thirteen hundred and fifty-one drachmas 2 obols equal 1,025 *sigloi*.[121]

Applying this principle to the weights of the silver in the Pronaos of the Parthenon[122] as listed by officials when handing over responsibility to their successors,[123] we get the results given in the Table (the drachma is assumed to have weighed 4.3 grams). Thus we get a lamp (1) weighing 30 *sigloi*,[124] a set of four *phialai* (5) weighing a total of 250 *sigloi*, seven *phialai* (7)

---

[114] e.g. Bothmer (1962–3); Oliver (1977), 15.

[115] For the possible use of the Thraco-Macedonian standard, see Vickers (1989*c*); (1991).

[116] Extrapolated from W. E. Thompson's summary in *IG* 1³, pp. 305–6, 318, 331–2; cf. Vickers (1990*a*).

[117] *Sigloi* were struck on two weight standards: an earlier one which ranged between *c.* 5.2 and 5.49 g. and a later, heavier standard of between *c.* 5.4 and 5.67 g.; the best summary is by Noe (1956), esp. 42. The precise date of the change is disputed,

opinions varying between early in the reign of Xerxes I (Bivar (1985), 618), 480–475 BC (Price and Waggoner (1975), 98), and 'some time after this date' (Kraay (1977), 194).

[118] [Dem.] 49. 32.

[119] At 5.66 g.

[120] [Dem.] 49. 7.

[121] At 5.67 g.

[122] *IG* 1³, pp. 305–6.

[123] Linders (1988).

[124] Perhaps on the earlier *siglos* standard (see n. 117, above, and Vickers (1990*b*), 622 n. 106).

TABLE *Recorded weights of silver items in the Pronaos.*

Object and date of first appearance	Weight in Attic drachmas	Weight in grams	Number of *sigloi*	Average weight of *sigloi* in grams
(1) lamp 434/3	38	163.40	30	5.45
(2) *poterion* 430/29	25			
(3) 7 *phialai* 429/8	700			
(4) 2 *phialai* 428/7	200			
(5) 4 *phialai* 427/6	329	1,414.70	250	5.66
(6) Chalcidian *poterion* 427/6	40			
(7) 7 *phialai* 426/5	920	3,956.00	700	5.65
(8) 4 *phialai* 425/4	420	1,806.00	320	5.64
(9) *poterion* 425/4	40			
(10) 7 *phialai* 424/3	643 dr. 2 obols	2,766.33	500	5.53

weighing 700 *sigloi* (probably 100 each), four *phialai* (8) weighing 320 *sigloi* (perhaps 80 each), and a set of seven *phialai* (10) weighing 500 *sigloi*. The last-mentioned figure is certainly much 'rounder' than 643 drachmas 2 obols. This pattern appears to exist throughout the rest of the Parthenon silver; it is made according to either an Attic or the Persian *siglos* standard.[125] A similar picture emerges from an examination of the weights of the gold vessels in the Parthenon inventories. These appear to have been made according to the Attic or Persian standards, either in terms of drachmas or darics. The latter point is perhaps confirmed by Mardonius' *akinake* (scimitar) an object which is listed (without its weight) in the Parthenon inventories, but which is said elsewhere to have weighed 300 darics.[126] Thus, one gold

[125] See further, Vickers (1990*b*).   [126] Dem. 24. 129.

phiale in an inventory weighs 12 *minae*, while two *chrusides* are said to weigh 293 drachmas and 3 obols,[127] equivalent to 150 darics at 8.41 grams each.[128]

The recorded weights of both the silver and gold objects in the Parthenon inventories appear to show a preponderance of material made to a Persian, as opposed to an Attic standard. This need not, however, mean that the objects were necessarily of Eastern manufacture, for there is some evidence that the Persian standard was in general use at Athens even in the thirties and twenties of the fifth century. An inventory roughly contemporary with those of the Parthenon is the list of items in the keeping of the treasurers of the Other Gods (429/8 BC),[129] which includes four *karchesia* weighing one-third of a myriad (3,333.33 *sigloi* at 5.67 grams)[130] and 'the silver of Olympian Zeus' weighing 4,500 *sigloi* (again at 5.67 grams).[131] Until recently, these figures would have been considered surprising in that they would appear to set at nought the provisions of the Coinage Decree, copies of which have in the past been dated on stylistic grounds to 450–446 BC. Now, however, that evidence has been presented to suggest that another inscription cut with three-bar sigmas and tailed rhos[132] was made in 418/7,[133] and not in 458/7 as was generally thought, the dates both of the Coinage (or Standards)[134] Decree and of many classes of archaeological material are called into question.[135] But in the present context, this is of secondary importance; the point that emerges from such figures (which are far from unusual)[136] is that plate was usually made in units either of *minae* or in hundreds (or thousands) of darics or *sigloi*. The Persian standard, like the Attic, was a guarantee of quality, for both the daric and the *siglos* were made of relatively pure metal.[137] One standard or the other was regularly used, even after the fall of the Persian empire, when darics and *sigloi* played a role akin to that of guineas today.[138]

D. M. Lewis once estimated that three gold *phialai* listed in the

[127] *IG* 1³, p. 318.

[128] See further Vickers (1990*a*).

[129] *IG* 1³ 383, 65–79; Linders (1975).

[130] Cf. the Attic rhyton from Aul Uljap weighing 333.33 drachmas (n. 75, above).

[131] Vickers (1992*a*).

[132] *IG* 1³ 11.

[133] Chambers, Gallucci, and Spanos (1990); cf. Henry (1992), who dissents.

[134] Chambers, Gallucci, and Spanos (1990), 55 n. 95.

[135] For recent discussions of the issues involved in the date of the Coinage (or Standards) Decree, see Lewis (1987); H. B. Mattingly (1987).

[136] See further Vickers (1992*a*).

[137] Darics were made of 23.25 carat gold (Schmitt (1983), 421); *sigloi* of 96–7% pure silver (Gale, Gentner, and Wagner (1980), 16–17); most

of the remainder was copper, added deliberately in order to inhibit wear. Plate can be even purer, e.g. the two silver beakers from the Thracian burial at Dalboki in Bulgaria (Prochorov (1880); Filow (1930–1); Dimitrov (1949); *Thracian Treasures* (1976), 93–5), and now in Oxford (Fig. 5.18: Ashmolean 1948.102 and 1948.103) contain respectively 98.5% and 99.4% of silver (kindly analysed by Zofya Stos-Gale by energy-dispersive X-ray fluorescence). A third beaker from the same grave group is in Leningrad (Grach (1985), 16–19, no. 8) and together they weigh 560 g. (= 100 *sigloi*; 1948.102: 183.8 g., 1948.103: 183.2 g.; Hermitage D. 1403: 193.5 g. The three together actually form a 'nesting set' (Fig. 2.5; cf. Vickers (1992*a*)).

[138] Cf. Vickers (1992*a*). It was also the case that the word 'daric' came to be used for any gold coin: Melville-Jones (1979).

FIG. 2.5   Silver beakers from a Thracian burial at Dalboki, Bulgaria (*a*) and (*b*) Ashmolean Museum, Oxford AN 1948.102 and 103; (*c*) Hermitage Museum, St Petersburg D.1403.

Hecatompedon could keep one trireme at sea for three months.[139] The known fact that many triremes were kept at sea for considerably longer suggests that even the Parthenon inventories tell us but little of the real wealth possessed either by the state or private individuals. The fact, however, that plate made on the Athenian standard was regularly made up in multiples of *minae* confirms the impression we receive from other sources that at Athens the *mina* was the denomination employed for luxury and high-cost items. For example, a visit to a high-class prostitute might cost 1 *mina*,[140] or 5,[141] or even 10.[142] A less expensive assignation might cost 1 obol, or less.[143] Eupolis speaks of a 10-*mina* gemstone as a paradigm of luxury[144]—the same price as that quoted for a brace of peacocks.[145] Alcibiades paid 70 *minae* for a hound 'of remarkable size and beauty'.[146] The median value of fourteen houses reported in the Attic orators is 20 *minae*.[147] The values of slaves given in the speeches of the orators are usually in *minae*, and vary between half a *mina* and 30 *minae*.[148] The details of Demosthenes' estate and income are given in talents and *minae*, as are business debts and loans,[149] and Demosthenes also informs us of an 80-*mina* dowry.[150]

The apparent fact that gold and silver vessels were made in round figures in terms of coinage standards perhaps provides the answer to the question which is often raised by numismatists in the face of the comparative paucity of fractional coinage, namely 'Where was the small change?' If plate served in effect as large-denomination banknotes, then even comparatively large coins would in some circles have been considered 'small change'. A drachma would indeed have been a 'trifling sum'.[151] By the same token, temples and treasuries served as the equivalent of bank vaults, in which publicly owned plate was stored.

We would also venture to suggest that the reason why plate was apparently absent from the Hermocopidae sale is that its value was already known. The purpose of an auction is to establish a price for a commodity when its value is not immediately apparent. This is why Aristotle's heirs auctioned off the seventy ceramic dishes found among his effects,[152] or why the crops, slaves, and other chattels were sold by auction in 415.[153] It has been well said that 'historically silver is a material which has always been melted down in order that it might be recreated in a new form, or even remade according to the

[139] Lewis (1986), 74, on *IG* 1³, p. 318(1).
[140] Ath. 13.583c; 584c.
[141] Ath. 13.581b.
[142] Ibid.
[143] Ath. 13.569 f.; Eup. *PCG* 247.
[144] Eup. *PCG* 202.
[145] Antiph. *Fr.* 58 Blass; Miller (1989), 8, 10 n. 40.
[146] Plut. *Alc.* 9. 1.
[147] Pritchett (1956), 275.

[148] Ibid. 277; cf. Jones (1956 (1960)), 189–90 (5–6).
[149] Dem. 33. 6–8; 34.7.
[150] Dem. 30. 20.
[151] Dem. 24. 114; cf. 24. 16. Identity tags on silver *hydriai* seem to have weighed 4 drachmas: Harris (1988), esp. 332–3.
[152] Pliny, *NH* 35. 46.
[153] The ποτή[ριον] τορ[ευτόν] (Amyx (1958), 208) will thus have been bronze, rather than silver, as Lewis (1966), 183 n. 37.

latest fashion'.[154] There would have been no point in auctioning a commodity for which there could have been only one possible bid, and that known in advance of the sale.[155]

EXTANT SILVER AND ITS IMPLICATIONS

Very few extant pieces seem to have been made on the Attic standard.[156] Some of these are decorated with gold-figure decoration of the kind that—or so we shall argue—informed the way in which pottery was decorated. Most extant plate appears to have been made according to either a Persian or a Thracian standard. The 165 pieces of silver in the Rogozen hoard (Fig. 2.6) found in 1985 and 1986,[157] *phialai* and jugs for the most part, fall into this category. Despite the fact that some of the pieces in both groups in the Rogozen hoard are badly damaged, their total weight (of 19.91 kilos) is equivalent to 3,600 silver *sigloi* (average weight 5.53 grams).[158] This 'round' overall weight implies that all the silver objects were destined for the melting-pot, the usual fate of silver through the ages from antiquity to the present day. Like most of the other Thracian hoards, the Rogozen find was hidden in an emergency which seems to have occurred between about 330 and 320 BC, perhaps the severe drought which afflicted the Aegean and surrounding areas at that time.[159] If it had not been for the unusual conditions—whatever they may have been—which prevailed in Thrace in the later fourth century, very few of the pieces we have would have survived to the present. Thanks to the accident of survival, we have a glimpse of gold and silver in Thrace at a particular moment in time. These precise conditions did not prevail in Greece proper—or in Etruria,[160] so that little or no plate of the period has survived in those places. Generally speaking, the accident of survival has brought about a concentration on the indestructible pottery; witness the developments described in Chapter 1. Conversely, the accident of disappearance has caused the comparative neglect of a well-documented aspect of ancient life, and one that was taken very seriously indeed by everyone.[161]

---

[154] Forbes, Kernan, and Wilkins (1975), 23; cf. Ch. 3 n. 3.

[155] We are grateful to Merle Langdon for discussing this point with us.

[156] Weights are not always given in modern catalogues of ancient gold and silver (honourable exceptions: Oliver (1977); Bothmer (1984); Laffineur (1986); there are still many gaps to be filled.

[157] 'Katalog' (1986); *Frakiiskii klad* (1986); *New Thracian Treasure* (1986); B. F. Cook (1989).

[158] Vickers (1989*b*).

[159] Isager and Hansen (1975), 200–8; cf. Camp (1982), 9–17; Garnsey (1988), esp. 145–6.

[160] The same considerations apply to hoards of plate as to coin hoards: 'In times of political insecurity, more hoards are stowed away, or more accurately, more hoards are not recovered by hoarders. After all, what we dig up are, rather sadly, hoarders' unrecovered savings. Their loss is our gain. . . . Paradoxically . . . we may have more coins from the very period in which most coins were withdrawn from circulation' (Hopkins (1980), 114); cf. Painter (1988), 108 n. 51 (quoted in Ch. 3 n. 190).

[161] Witness the care taken over even broken scraps of gold and silver in sanctuaries: Linders (1989–90); (1992*a*).

FIG. 2.6   The Rogozen hoard of silver and silver-gilt vessels, deposited in the later fourth century BC. National Historical Museum, Sofia, Inv. 22301–22465.

Gold and silver plate figures large in both public and private life at a certain level in ancient Greece, but it is a level at which expenditure is conducted in *minae*. It is reasonable to suppose, moreover, that in antiquity the possession of plate served as a marker of wealth and status, and that the materials used varied according to financial circumstances. This is borne out by a law of the Roman period[162] discussing the criteria to be applied to a man wanting to apply for public assistance: 'If he formerly used golden vessels, he must sell them and use silver vessels; if he used silver vessels, he must sell them and use bronze vessels; if he formerly used bronze vessels, he must sell them and use glass vessels.'[163] Ceramic is not mentioned.

[162] Goodman (1983), 10.
[163] Tosephta, *Peah* 4. 11.

The attention paid to Athens' richer citizens in this chapter should not, however, obscure the fact that Athens was probably 'a society in which, except for a small group of relatively very rich men at the top, and a larger group of casual labourers at the bottom, wealth was evenly distributed, and the graduation from the affluent to the needy very gentle'.[164] In material terms, such a society will have seen patterns of expenditure at the top end of the market determining broader changes in consumer demand.[165] Taste in most societies is created by a wealthy élite,[166] and as often as not by a small group or even an individual within that élite.[167] If this was the case at Athens, developments in silverware might have left more permanent reflections in the pottery of which we possess so much. A 'trickle-down effect'[168] whereby fashions created in expensive materials were copied in cheaper, is the most economical way to interpret such evidence as we have; this will be explored in subsequent chapters. It is, moreover, misleading in the context of a society with—even at Athens—a highly skewed income distribution, to calculate an 'average wage', still less to use such a concept as a basis for the discussion of artistic patronage or trade.[169]

When all of life is viewed through the eyes of a day labourer, or when what has survived is regarded as an adequate sample of what there was, the picture becomes distorted and the ancient world is impoverished as a result.[170] If, however, notice is taken of the range of relative values, as well as of the central and informative role of precious metal, then the picture of antiquity can be righted again—that Greece might one day still be rich.

---

[164] A. H. M. Jones (1957), 90.
[165] As in eighteenth-century England: cf. McKendrick, Brewer, and Plumb (1982).
[166] Haskell (1963).
[167] e.g. Madame de Pompadour is credited with having virtually single-handedly created the *dix-*

huitième style which is still in vogue in many parts of the world: Reitlinger (1961–70), 2. 20–1.
[168] Fallers (1967), 402–4.
[169] For a recent example, see Boardman (1988*a*).
[170] Cf. Vickers (1990*b*).

3 The Fate of Plate

ONLY a very little Greek gold and silver has survived in the archaeological record: a few hoards, and occasional finds in tombs. Temple inventories can be extremely informative,[1] but only describe a minute proportion of what there was. Some ancient writers tell us more about precious metal than others. Herodotus often mentions it, while Thucydides—for all that he had Thracian mining interests—rarely does so. Diodorus is especially communicative on the topic, often keeping score of encounters between cities in terms of talents of silver won by one side or the other. Pliny, Athenaeus, and Plutarch contain much of interest as well. This chapter is not intended to be in any way comprehensive; it is simply meant to give an idea of the vicissitudes that might befall plate,[2] and to explain how it is that so few Greek gold and silver vessels have escaped the melting-pot, the usual destination through the ages of plate that is old-fashioned or worn.[3] For obvious reasons, this chapter is less fully illustrated than some of the others.

BOOTY FROM SANCTUARIES

Sanctuaries such as Olympia, Delphi, Delos, Samothrace, or Didyma were major storehouses of gold and silver in antiquity. Temples and treasuries were well-known repositories of precious metal. Boards of officials regularly made annual inspections, and a few of the inventories they drew up on handing over their responsibilities to their successors—'memorials to scrupulous administration'[4] have survived.[5] But the most vivid account is Herodotus' description of the dedications made at Delphi by Croesus, king of Lydia, in the mid-sixth century: a huge gold shield,[6] two craters of enormous size, the gold one weighing 2,700 *karsha*,[7] and another of silver made by Theodore of Samos that could hold 600 amphoras-ful of wine;[8] four silver casks (*pithoi*)

---

[1] Lewis (1986); Vickers (1990a), (1992a), and see Ch. 2.

[2] Plate: 'silver and gold utensils', *OED* s.v. II and 15.

[3] e.g. Stone (1965), 2; Reitlinger (1961–70), 2. 14; White (1974); Forbes, Kernan, and Wilkins (1975), 23. Ancient plate could be melted down even in recent times: when the sanctuary at Idalion on Cyprus was explored in 1849, twelve gilded silver bowls were found deposited in a pot. All but two (Paris, Louvre AO.21035 and AO.20134:

Markoe (1985), 75, 169–71, Cy 1 and Cy 2) were melted down. On the effects of a silver price boom, see Boraiko and Ward (1981).

[4] Linders (1992b), 40.

[5] Lewis (1986); Linders (1987); (1992a); Knoepfler (1988); Aleshire (1989).

[6] Hdt. 1. 92. 1.

[7] See p. 46, above.

[8] Hdt. 1. 51. 1–2 (or 60, if Griffith (1988), 11–21, is correct).

and two lustral vases (*perirrhanteria*), one of gold and the other of silver;[9] a gold statue of a woman 'three cubits high'; and 'many' lathe-turned bowls of silver.[10]

But it is Herodotus' account of the most elaborate of Croesus' dedications that goes far to explain the fate of much plate from antiquity, albeit Croesus' was a ceremonial meltdown:

he offered up three thousand of every kind of sacrificial beast, and besides made a huge pile, and placed upon it couches coated with silver and gold, and golden *phialai*, and cloaks and tunics of purple. Further he ordered all the Lydians to offer whatever each of them possessed. When the sacrifice was ended, the king melted down a vast quantity of gold, and ran it into ingots, making them six palms long, three palms broad, and one palm in thickness. The number of ingots was a hundred and seventeen, four being of pure gold, in weight two talents and a half; the others of electrum, and in weight two talents. He also caused a statue of a lion to be made in pure gold, the weight of which was ten talents. At the time when the temple of Delphi was burnt to the ground, this lion fell from the ingots on which it was placed; it now stands in the Corinthian treasury, and weighs only six talents and a half, having lost three talents and a half by the fire.[11]

The loss in the fire was accidental, but the conspicuous consumption of the sacrifice was deliberate, and represented—to our eyes—the irreplaceable loss of much elaborate craftsmanship. Most (but perhaps not all)[12] of Croesus' dedications were in turn melted down for coin when Delphi was attacked by Greeks from Phocis in the 350s.

Occasionally, steps were taken by the authorities to melt down offerings at sanctuaries systematically and to replace them with larger ones.[13] Thus an inscription survives describing how in *c*.240 BC some of the offerings at the Amphiareum were 'useless, some in need of repair, or fallen from their positions' and how the inhabitants of Oropus set up a committee to repair or melt down the dedications.[14] More than a century earlier we find Nicocrates of Colonus making gold and silver libation bowls (*phialai*), water-jars (*hydriai*) and wine-jugs (*oinochoai*) for sanctuaries in Attica.[15] This Nicocrates may have been the same as the homonymous craftsman who came to Delphi in the 330s, together with two Athenian and two Corinthian citizens, to discuss the replacement of Croesus' dedications.[16] Nearly 5 talents were spent on a new silver crater.[17] Elsewhere we hear of repairs being undertaken. On a third-century inscription from Delos we learn of Aristarchus the silver-smith who had been employed to do odd jobs during the previous year: he was paid 2 drachmas for 'attaching the handle of the silver crater which

[9] Hdt. 1. 51. 2.
[10] Hdt. 1. 51. 5; cf. Gill and Vickers (1989), 299–300.
[11] Hdt. 1. 50.
[12] See below, p. 61.
[13] Lewis (1986), 72, 78–9; Linders (1989–90); (1992*a*); Tréheux (1991), 144–5.
[14] *Guide* (1929), 36–7.
[15] Harris (1988).
[16] *FdD* 3/5, 48, 23–41; Lewis (1986), 78.
[17] *FdD* 3/5, 62, 5–9; Lewis (1986), 79.

had fallen off'; the 3 obols' worth of coals, which is the next entry,[18] was presumably part of the expenditure for the same task. Later Aristarchus was paid 1 drachma $1\frac{1}{2}$ obols 'for making a cup',[19] and then paid 1 drachma for 'repairing the handle of a bronze cothon', in connection with which a drachma's worth of coals and another of wax were used.[20] But usually the craftsman's name is not given. It has been rightly said that 'we should not exaggerate the social importance of routine metalwork'.[21] The names are thus unknown of the silversmiths who, under Lycurgus, remade the equipment of the basket-carriers (*kanephoroi*) in the Panathenaic procession, equipment which was itself to be melted down to meet more pressing financial requirements in *c*.300.[22]

A few vessels from sanctuaries survive, but few if any come from their actual places of dedication. The only major dedication to survive from Delphi is a life-size silver statue of a bull made from plates of the precious metal originally laid over a wooden core. It owes its preservation to the fact that it was buried within the precincts of the sanctuary—quite why is unknown— by the authorities at some time in the second half of the fifth century.[23] A fifth-century *phiale* which had originally been dedicated to Megarian Athena was found in a fourth century tomb at Kozani in Macedonia,[24] and another from a Sarmatian tomb in the Kuban had originally been dedicated in the sanctuary of Apollo at Colchian Phasis (Fig. 3.1).[25] A hoard of the Hellenistic period now in New York includes a *pyxis* and a portable altar which were originally inscribed 'sacred to the gods' and 'from the war'.[26] A bronze hydria from a tomb at Karabournaki in Thessalonica was originally dedicated by the Athenians as spoils of war; its place of dedication is unknown.[27] A silver bowl in Dumbarton Oaks carries the inscription Διὸς Ἐπικαρπίου ('[belonging to] Zeus, bringer of fruit').[28] In view of its good state of preservation, it too was probably found in a tomb.

Some of these vessels may well have been looted; but whether or not they were, looting was the fate of many precious objects from sanctuaries—and had been from time immemorial. Gods (which were frequently gilded if not actually gold),[29] and their attendant plate, were closest to the hearts of any

[18] *IG* 11/2 161A, 102.
[19] Ibid. 107.
[20] Ibid. 111–12.
[21] Lewis (1986), 79.
[22] Koumanoudes and Miller (1971); Lewis (1986), 72.
[23] Themelis (1983), 68–9, fig. 45.
[24] Jeffery (1961), 135, 137, pl. 22, no. 2; Gill (1990).
[25] Jeffery (1961), 373 no. 72. Tsetskhladze (1994).
[26] Bothmer (1984), nos. 101 and 102.
[27] Θησαυροί, no. 334: ΑΘΗΝΑΙΟΙ ΑΘΛ[Α] ΑΠΙ ΤΩι ΕΝΤΩιΠΟΛΕΜΩ.

[28] Washington, DC, Dumbarton Oaks Collection 40.3: Oliver (1977), 84–5, no. 47.
[29] e.g. the images of Zeus and 'a man twelve cubits high, in solid gold' at Babylon (Hdt. 1. 183); the gilded Athena (the gift of Amasis) at Lindos (Blinkenberg (1941), C.29.41 ff. [on the likelihood that most Egyptian statues of deities in stone and bronze were originally overlaid in gold, see Lacau (1956)]); Amasis' statue of Athena at Cyrene (Hdt. 2. 182); the statues of Apollo at Thornax (Hdt. 1. 69. 4) and Amyclae (Paus. 3. 10. 8; the latter was 12 metres high: Paus. 3. 19. 2); the 'gilded statue of Apollo' taken from Delium by the Persians (Hdt. 6. 118. 1); the gilded wooden

FIG. 3.1   Silver *phiale* dedicated at the sanctuary of Apollo at Phasis in Colchis on the eastern shore of the Black Sea. Hermitage Museum, St Petersburg.

ancient community, and were the first things to be seized by their enemies. Thus, when the inhabitants of Phocaea moved *en bloc* to Massilia in *c*.545, they put on board their ships their wives and children, their household goods, 'and even the images of their gods from their sanctuaries, and the dedications as well', leaving behind anything that was made of 'bronze, or marble, or was painted'.[30] Had they not done so, Harpagus the Mede would

statue at Plataea (Paus. 9. 4. 1); and the chryselephantine cult images at Pellene (Paus. 7. 27. 2); Elis (Paus. 6. 25. 1); Olympia (Overbeck (1868), nos. 692–754), and Athens (Overbeck (1868), nos. 645–90; Eddy (1977)). In general, see Vermeule (1974).

[30] Hdt. 1. 164.

FIG. 3.2   Gold bowl dedicated at Olympia 'by the Cypselids from the spoils of Heracleia'. Boston, Museum of Fine Arts, Inv. 21.1843.

have taken them off instead. He would have had many precedents. To cite just two examples: in Assyria, Adad-Nirari I (911–891 BC) took from his enemy Hanigalbat 'his gold, his possessions, precious mountain stone, his gods, his chariots and teams of horses . . . golden chairs, dishes of shining gold'.[31] In 616 BC, 'the king of Akkad and his troops went upstream against the towns of Mane, Sahiru and Balihu, and took spoil from them, and carried off many of them as prisoners, and led away their gods.'[32]

Pausanias the Periegete puts his finger on the nub of the issue when discussing Augustus' removal of an ancient statue of Athena from Tegea:

Augustus does not appear to have started the looting of dedications and statues of gods from the defeated . . . what the emperor did was an established ancient tradition observed both by Greeks and barbarians.[33]

Pausanias then lists examples of looting, starting with Troy and including the pillaging of Greek sanctuaries by Xerxes. One of the rich temples sacked by the Persians was at Didyma (or Branchidae), the extramural sanctuary of Miletus. The sanctuary had attracted rich offerings from far afield;[34] some of the gifts (presumably of gold) were dedicated by Croesus, and were 'equal in weight . . . and in all respects like to those at Delphi'.[35] Following the battle

[31] Luckenbill (1926–7) 1, no. 368; cf. nos. 221 and 232.
[32] Wiseman (1956), 54–5.
[33] Paus. 8. 46. 1–5.
[34] e.g. Hdt. 2. 159: Necos of Egypt dedicated the robes in which he had defeated the Syrians.
[35] Hdt. 1. 92; cf. 1. 50–1.

of Lade during the Ionian revolt, Miletus was sacked and 'the temple (ἱρόν) at Didyma with its shrine (νηός) and place of divination (χρηστήριον) was plundered and burnt.'[36] The captive Milesians were carried off to Susa, and so, presumably, was the booty. Xerxes' men seem to have been thorough in their work; even bronze votive offerings were carried away, as is illustrated by the bronze Apollo, later restored to the sanctuary by Seleucus,[37] and the bronze knucklebone weight (originally one of a set) dedicated in the sanctuary and found at Susa.[38] Didyma was not the only East Greek sanctuary to meet this fate.[39]

During the Persian Wars, Delphi was seen as an attractive place to plunder, but the attempt was foiled. Herodotus tells the story that the oracle did not allow the sacred treasure to be buried, and that the Persian raid was repulsed by miraculous intervention.[40] He also reports a speech by Mardonius before the battle of Plataea which seems to record an oracle which foretold the destruction of the Persians should they plunder the sanctuary.[41] Both passages appear to reflect the readiness of the Persians to sack sanctuaries, and the oracle, reported by Mardonius, may reflect the realization of the relevant authorities that the sanctuary was going to be sacked. A trophy was set up recording that Zeus and Apollo 'threw their guard about the bronze-crowned shrine',[42] which implies the existence of normal security arrangements in the form of walls and fences.

Delphi was to be sacked not by barbarians but by Greeks. During the Sacred war, Philomelus the Phocian occupied Delphi. To pay for his mercenaries, he 'was compelled to lay his hands on the sacred dedications and to plunder the oracle'.[43] After the battle of Neon (354 BC) his successor, Onomarchus, continued to plunder the sanctuary, and 'prepared a great supply of weapons from the bronze and iron, and struck coinage from the silver and gold'.[44] Phayllus, Onomarchus' brother, continued to melt down the dedications to pay for his mercenaries; these included most of the dedications of Croesus. Diodorus commented that 'some of the historians say that the pillaged property was not less than the sums acquired by Alexander in the treasure chambers of the Persians.'[45] This may well be an exaggeration, for as we have already had occasion to note, the Delphians subsequently claimed to have lost 10,000 talents,[46] whereas Alexander's booty was considerably greater.[47] Be that as it may, the looting of the sanctuary amounted to a redistribution of wealth, a fact which did not go unnoticed:

---

[36] Hdt. 6. 19; cf. the stripping of the temples at Eretria in 490 before they were fired (Hdt. 6. 102), and the way the Persians 'stripped the temple of its treasures' after the capture of the Athenian Acropolis in 480 (Hdt. 8. 55).

[37] Paus. 1. 16. 3.

[38] Jeffery (1961), 334, 343, no. 30.

[39] Cf. Hdt. 6. 32.

[40] Hdt. 8. 36–9.

[41] Hdt. 9. 42.

[42] Diod. 11. 14. 4.

[43] Diod. 16. 30. 1.

[44] Diod. 16. 33. 2.

[45] Diod. 16. 56. 5–6.

[46] Diod. 16. 56; p. 45, above.

[47] de Callataÿ (1989); p. 69, below.

'After the seizure of Delphi by the Phocians, . . . gold flamed up everywhere among the Greeks, and silver also came bursting in.'[48]

Delphi was attacked by the Gauls in 279[49] but the last effective plundering (until Constantine the Great closed down all the pagan sanctuaries of the empire) was by the Roman general Sulla in 84 BC. Since he was in need of money for his war chest, he confiscated 'the sacred treasures of Greece, partly from Epidaurus, and partly from Olympia, sending for the most beautiful and most precious of the offerings there'.[50] He also wrote to the authorities at Delphi 'that it was better to have the treasures of the god sent to him, for he would either have them in safer keeping, or, if he used them, he would replace them; and he sent one of his friends, Caphis, a Phocian, instructing him to take each thing according to weight.'[51] One object, a silver cask (*pithos*) 'which was still left from the royal dedications' (presumably one of the four *pithoi* that Croesus had dedicated)[52] was so big that 'no wagon could bear it' and the Delphian authorities 'were obliged to cut it into pieces'.[53]

It was the expected thing that an enemy might make off with the dedications from a temple. At Syracuse there was a prosperous shrine of Olympian Zeus outside the city. When Hippocrates of Gela pitched his camp nearby in 491 BC, the Syracusans assumed that he would sack the temple, and consequently tried to remove to safety the gold dedications (ἀναθήματα χρυσᾶ) and the gold *himation* from the statue of Zeus. In the event, Hippocrates prevented them from doing so, but left the dedications untouched.[54] And when the Athenians were besieging Syracuse in 415, a garrison was sent to the Olympieion since the Syracusans 'were worried that the Athenians might make off with some of the treasure there'.[55] It is reasonable to suppose that the 'much booty of all kinds' and 'great quantity of spoil',[56] taken from the sanctuary of Hera at Perachora when it was sacked by Agesilaus of Sparta in 390 BC included gold and silver plate.

Only rarely is the wealth of a sanctuary quantified. The Delphians' 'insurance claim' after the Phocian sack is one example, as we have seen. Another is to be found in the context of Dionysius of Syracuse's raid on Agylle (Caere) and the port of Pyrgi in 384 BC. Under the pretence of suppressing pirates, Dionysius pillaged the sanctuary in Pyrgi, which was 'richly provided with dedications'. The booty was no less than 1,000 talents, and it was supplemented by 500 talents taken from the Caeretans after their defeat.[57]

---

[48] Ath. 6. 231b–232d.
[49] For a vivid account, see Paus. 10. 19. 4–23. 9.
[50] Plut. *Sulla* 12. 5.
[51] Ibid. 12. 6. On the possibility that Sulla regarded his confiscations as loans he meant to repay: Giovannini (1990), 135.
[52] And probably not the replacement for the silver

crater, as has been suggested: Vickers (1986*b*), 138–40.
[53] Plut. *Sulla* 12. 9.
[54] Diod. 10. 28. 1.
[55] Thuc. 6. 70.
[56] Xen. *Hell.* 4. 5. 5–6.
[57] Diod. 15. 14. 3–4; equivalent to more than £15m.

The Etruscans were notorious for piracy,[58] and if the rich pickings from Pyrgi are any guide, they must have been very rich indeed. The Etruscans' southern neighbour, Rome, was poor by comparison—but was to catch up and overtake the Etruscans by the end of the millennium. When Rome was sacked by the Gauls in 390 BC, there was only 2,000 lb of gold to be looted.[59] By 82 BC, however, the temples of Rome were much richer; when Gaius Marius the younger carried off the contents of the Capitol and other shrines to Praeneste, this included 14,000 lb of gold and 6,000 lb of silver,[60] and considerably more wealth flowed into Rome as the result of the campaigns of Pompey and Lucullus in the East and Julius Caesar in the West.

BOOTY FROM CITIES

The practice of obtaining wealth by sacking cities had timeless precedents, but the archetypal model for Greeks was the sack of Troy; in 415 Euripides presented this event as yielding 'measureless gold and Phrygian spoils' to the Greeks.[61] Herodotus gives the essence of the plundering of a city. He recounts (or invents) a conversation between Croesus and the victorious Cyrus after the capture of Sardis:

Croesus asked, 'That crowd of people, what is it they are doing so busily?' 'They are plundering,' said Cyrus, 'your city and carrying off your possessions.' 'No,' Croesus answered, 'not my city, not my possessions; for I have no longer any share of all this; it is your wealth that they are ravishing.'[62]

Diodorus records that there was 'much silver and gold' to be taken from Sardis and that it was removed by Cyrus,[63] and much the same kind of picture is given in the *Chronicle of Nabunaid*, which records the capture of Astyages the Mede in the 550s: 'Cyrus carried off the silver, gold, chattels, and possessions . . . [from] the land of Agamtanu [Agbatana], and took them off to Anshan.'[64] The cities of Ionia which revolted against Persia met a similar fate,[65] as did Athens in 480/79 BC. Although much portable wealth was taken from the city with the evacuees,[66] there was something left on the Acropolis to be plundered.[67]

Thucydides is rather less forthcoming than Herodotus regarding the taking of booty; he presumably took it for granted. A rare instance is his account of Demosthenes' activities in Aetolia in 427/6 BC. He sacked the towns of Potidania, Crocylium, and Teichium, and sent the booty back to

[58] Gras (1985), 514–22.

[59] Pliny, *NH* 33. 6. 16; equivalent to over £4m (the usual weight of the Roman pound was 327.45 g.).

[60] Pliny,. *NH* 33. 5. 16; equivalent to nearly £30m.

[61] Eur. *Tro.* 18–19.

[62] Hdt. 1. 88. 3.

[63] Diod. 9. 33. 4.

[64] J. M. Cook (1983), 27; cf. Hdt. 1. 127–30.

[65] Hdt. 5. 116, 117, 123.

[66] Cf. Plut. *Them.* 10. 4; Vickers (1985*b*), 31–2.

[67] Hdt. 8. 53. 2.

Eupalium in Locris.[68] And while Thucydides states that the revolt of Mytilene in the previous year led to the destruction of the city's fortifications, the loss of her fleet, and division of land,[69] he says nothing of the spoils of war. A Parthenon inventory of 427/6, however, records several items from Lesbos (a shield, an Illyrian helmet, and three silver *kotyloi*)[70] which might have come to Athens as a result of the suppression of Mytilene. Loyal Methymna seems to have given a gilded ivory flute-case (*sybene*).[71] Methymna herself was to be sacked and plundered of 'all her wealth' in 406 by Callicratidas of Sparta.[72]

Cities were also sacked in the West. The Carthaginians sacked Himera in 409,[73] and Acragas in 406. The booty from Acragas was especially rich: both temples and private dwellings were despoiled, and as 'great a store of plunder as one might expect a city to yield that had been occupied by two hundred thousand people, and which had been unplundered since it was founded; [a city, moreover, which] was virtually the richest Greek city of the day, and whose citizens had expressed their taste in a great wealth of all kinds of works of art (κατασκευάσματα)'[74]—which meant plate as much as anything else. At Motya in 397, Dionysius I of Syracuse gave the first man over the wall a prize of 100 *minae*,[75] and the city yielded in plunder 'much silver and not a little gold'.[76] Etruscan Veii was captured by the Romans in 393 and from a tithe of the proceeds of the sale of slaves and other booty, the city of Rome made (κατεσκεύασε) a gold crater which was sent as an offering to Delphi.[77]

Back East, the same pattern can be observed. Artaxerxes III retook Sidon in 351/0 and in the subsequent looting 'a large amount of gold and silver was taken which showed the prosperity of the householders'.[78] In 350/49 his campaign in Egypt brought in 'a vast quantity of silver and gold' from the looting of cities and shrines.[79] In Macedonia the capture of Olynthus by Philip in 348 was celebrated by a festival with magnificent sacrifices and banquets at which guests were presented with *poteria*, presumably of silver.[80] The symposium was an appropriate occasion for making such gifts, as we have already seen.[81]

We are occasionally granted a glimpse of the resistance presented to plunderers: during Alexander's sack of Thebes in 335, some Thracians broke into the house of

one Timoclea, a lady of noble birth and irreproachable character. Their leader forcibly violated her, and then demanded whether she had any gold or silver

---

[68] Thuc. 3. 96.
[69] Thuc. 3. 50.
[70] *IG* 1³, 350, 84. The vessels in question seem to have been made according to the earlier, lighter, *siglos* standard: Vickers (1990), 622.
[71] *IG* 1³, p. 332 (40).
[72] Xen. *Hell.* 1. 6. 13.
[73] Diod. 13. 62. 4.

[74] Diod. 13. 90. 3.
[75] Nearly £18,000.
[76] Diod. 14. 53. 3.
[77] Diod. 14. 93. 2–4.
[78] Diod. 16. 45. 6.
[79] Diod. 16. 51. 2.
[80] Diod. 16. 55. 1–2.
[81] See Ch. 2 n. 50, above.

concealed. She said that she had, led him alone into the garden, and, pointing to a well, told him that when the city was taken she threw her most valuable jewels into it. While the Thracian was stooping over the well trying to see down to the bottom, she came behind, pushed him in, and threw large stones upon him till he died.[82]

It was the Romans above all who despoiled Greece and indeed Greek lands in general.[83] It was through the acquisition of booty that the use of precious metal became at all widespread in Roman society—much to the disgust of the traditionally minded, who were still condemning luxury in the first century AD.[84] The Greek cities of Southern Italy and Sicily were looted first (Syracuse in 211 BC, Capua in 210, Tarentum in 209), then Greece itself (Eretria in 198, Macedon in 194, Aetolia and Ambracia in 187, Asia Minor in 186, Macedon once more in 168, Corinth in 146, Athens, Olympia, and Epidaurus in 87–85). Accounts of Roman triumphs are instructive, for they often give details of the actual weight of precious metals won during a campaign. Thus, when in 209 BC Fabius Maximus sacked Tarentum (a city which in the fourth century had been a byword for 'extravagance and greed'),[85] he took away 'the money and other wealth'.[86] Fabius' booty comprised 'a huge amount of silver, both wrought and coined, and 83,000 pounds of gold'.[87] In 167 BC Aemilius Paullus had 3,000 men carry 'coined silver in 750 vessels, each holding 3 talents[88] . . . Others brought silver craters and drinking-horns and drinking-bowls and cups, each well arranged for display, and all extraordinary for their size as well as for the thickness of their embossed work.' Also exhibited was all the gold plate that had been used at the Macedonian king's dinner-table, as well as a 'sacred bowl which Aemilius had made, weighing 10 talents of solid gold[89] and set with jewels'.[90] Not only must court goldsmiths have been captured as well, but this serves as a reminder that precious metal might easily be made up into something new.

There was one notable cache of precious metal that did not leave Greek lands. This was the 'vast treasure' found at the end of the first century AD in one of the houses acquired by the father of Herodes Atticus 'near the theatre' at Athens. This, together with an inheritance from his mother 'which was not much less', provided the basis of Herodes' fortune.[91] Herodes was so rich that he was able to underwrite expenses on an aqueduct at Troy in

[82] Plut. *Alex.* 12. 1–2 (Alexander had pity on her: 12. 6).

[83] There are useful studies by Pritchett (1971), 53–84, and Pape (1975). See too Finlay (1857), ch. 1; Vessberg (1941), 26–114; J. Griffin (1976), 91.

[84] Notably the Elder Pliny, whose *Natural History* is full of strictures against new-fangled luxury; Petronius' *Satyricon*, with its implied criticism of the Maxwellesque Trimalchio, is a work in the same spirit.

[85] Eub. *ap.* Ath. 4. 166e.

[86] Plut. *Marc.* 21. 5.

[87] Livy 27. 16.7 ff.: more than £170m for the gold alone.

[88] The coins were worth the equivalent of more than £24m.

[89] Worth the equivalent of £1.6m.

[90] Plut. *Aem.* 32–3. Other triumphs where actual weights are given include those of T. Quinctius Flamininus (194 BC): Livy 34. 52. 4–5 and L. Scipio Asiagenus (188 BC): Livy 37. 59. 3–5.

[91] Philostr. *VS* 547–8.

excess of 3 million drachmas (at a time when costs had reached 4 million, or 666.66 talents), bequeathed 1 *mina* annually to each Athenian citizen, and while he was alive would entertain the whole population of Athens to banquets.[92] The tantalizing information about one of the sources of Herodes' wealth hints not only at concealment in some emergency, but also at the great wealth in earlier times of the city which, in the words of Aeschylus' Atossa, possessed a 'fountain of silver beneath her soil';[93] this is a reference to the mines at Laurium which, as we have already seen, may have produced 20 tonnes of silver per annum for much of the fifth century BC.[94] It is a safe assumption that possession of the Athenian silver mines was high among the Persians' war aims.[95]

There is even a little extant plate that can be shown with more or less confidence to have come from plundered cities. The deep gold *phiale* in Boston found at Olympia (Fig. 3.2) is inscribed '[dedicated by the] Cypselids from the spoils of Heraclea'—wherever that may have been.[96] Then a silver-gilt bowl from Cyprus bears two sets of inscriptions which have been interpreted as indicating successive owners:[97] the first, Akestor, an otherwise unknown king of Paphos, whose name appears in syllabic script below the rim; the other stating that the bowl was the property of one Timukretes. It has been suggested that the bowl—which was part of the so-called 'Treasure of Curium'—came into the possession of its second owner after 498, when Cyprus revolted from the Persians and Paphos was besieged, taken, and sacked. All the cities, except Amathus, had joined in the revolt, but during the battle on the plain of Salamis, the tyrant of Curium deserted the Cypriot side.[98] Also in the 'Treasure of Curium' were two bracelets with inscriptions that show them to have been the property of another king of Paphos, Etevandros; another bowl which seems to be Paphian in origin carries the name of one Kyprothales.[99] It is not unreasonable to suppose that the tyrant of Curium—Stesenor by name—was rewarded for his treachery from the booty taken from defeated cities, although the possibility that the objects simply attest to the *xenia* between the aristocracy of Paphos and Curium should not be overlooked.

BOOTY WON ON THE FIELD OF BATTLE

In 339 BC, Timoleon of Corinth defeated a vast Carthaginian army at the River Cremisus in Sicily. After the battle, the victorious Greeks 'discovered

---

[92] Philostr. *VS* 548; the Trojan aqueduct represented open-ended expenditure in excess of the equivalent of £1.8m.

[93] Aesch. *Pers.* 238.

[94] Conophagos (1980); cf. p. 43, above.

[95] On the relative shortage of silver in the Achaemenid empire at the time, see Price and Waggoner (1975), 139 n. 246. For a parallel in the Roman period, see Mitchell (1983).

[96] Perhaps the Heraclea near Anactorium in Acarnania: A. R. Burn (1960), 189. On the *phiale* itself, see Ch. 2 n. 113, above.

[97] New York 74.51.4554: Mitford (1963); Bothmer (1984), 20 no. 10.

[98] Hdt. 5. 113.

[99] And two more bear inscriptions indicating that they had passed into the possession of Diveithemis and Epiorvos: Mitford (1963), 29.

the rank of the dead by the richness of their spoil; for when they collected the booty no account was taken of bronze or iron, such an abundance was there of silver and gold.' It took them three days to gather up the booty.[100] A century and a half earlier, the Persian Wars had been another occasion for the introduction of great amounts of gold and silver into the Greek world.[101] Not only were many of the troops in the Persian armies magnificently fitted out, but the king and his officers travelled in style. They brought much plate with them, and acquired more on the way to Greece.

The Persian troops leaving Sardis in 480, for example, included 2,000 spearmen with golden pomegranates on the butt-end of their spears, 1,000 spearmen with golden apples, and 9,000 with silver pomegranates.[102] The Persians were said in 499 to 'have everything, gold, silver, bronze, elaborately embroidered clothes and beasts of burden and slaves',[103] and, when they marched on Greece in 480, they 'were adorned with the greatest magnificence . . . [and] glittered all over with gold, vast quantities of which they wore about their persons'.[104] Xerxes could fling a gold *phiale* and crater into the sea at the crossing of the Hellespont,[105] and he will also have travelled with his personal supply of drinking-water taken from the River Choaspes and carried in silver vessels on 'many four-wheeled waggons drawn by mules'.[106] More plate will have been accumulated on the march through northern Greece, and much of it will inevitably have remained in central Greece in the form of booty. Cities were instructed to entertain their Persian guests as lavishly as possible; the Thasians, for example, laid on a meal on which 400 talents were spent (including the 'manufacture of drinking-cups and craters of gold and silver, and of everything that is needed to adorn the table'). When the army moved on they took any plate or portable wealth with them;[107] small wonder that 'the Greeks who received Xerxes' army and entertained the king himself were brought to the depth of misery'.[108] At a conservative estimate, the gold and silver that Xerxes' army accumulated on their march from the Hellespont to the Thermaic gulf alone will have been worth more than 5,000 talents.[109]

When a storm caught the Persian fleet unawares off Magnesia, 'a vast treasure was engulfed', and for years afterwards, a local farmer 'found the wreck of these vessels a source of great gain to him; many were the gold and silver drinking-cups, cast up long afterwards by the surf, which he gathered; while treasure chests too which had belonged to the Persians, and golden

---

[100] Plut. *Tim.* 29. 1–4.
[101] Vickers (1985*a*), 113; (1985*b*), 24–5.
[102] Hdt. 7. 41.
[103] Hdt. 5. 49. 4.
[104] Hdt. 7. 83. 2.
[105] Hdt. 7. 54.
[106] Hdt. 1. 188. Cf. the pair of silver urns, each weighing 300 kg. in which the Maharajah of Jaipur had made to carry his drinking-water from the Ganges when he went to London in 1902 for the coronation of Edward VII: Boraiko and Ward (1981), 284–5, 309.
[107] Hdt. 7. 118–19.
[108] Hdt. 7. 118.
[109] Vickers (1985*b*), 32; equivalent to more than £50m.

articles of all kinds and beyond count, came into his possession'.[110] Despite this set-back, Artabazus was able to say on the eve of the battle of Plataea 'that coined gold was plentiful in the [Persians'] camp, and uncoined gold too; they had silver moreover in great abundance, and drinking-cups. Let them not spare to take of these, and distribute them among the Greeks, especially among the leaders in the various cities . . .'.[111]

The Persian camp at Plataea was square and measured '10 stades on each side'.[112] Estimates of the number of Persians and their allies who were slaughtered here varied in antiquity between 100,000 and more than a quarter of a million.[113] The rich contents of the camp were divided amongst the members of the Hellenic League. Herodotus tells us that the camp contained

many tents richly equipped with gold and silver, many couches plated with gold and silver, and golden craters, *phialai* and other drinking-vessels. On the carriages were bags containing silver and golden water-containers; and the bodies of the slain furnished bracelets and torcs, and scimitars with golden ornaments—not to mention intricately decorated clothing, of which no one made any account.[114]

Portions were set aside for offerings at Delphi, Olympia, and the Isthmus and 'the rest of the spoil was divided among the soldiers, each of whom received less or more according to his deserts; and in this way was a distribution made of the Persian concubines, of the gold, the silver, the beasts of burden, and all the other valuables.'[115] The commander-in-chief was granted ten of each category of booty: 'women, horses, talents, camels, or whatever else there was in the spoil':[116] 'talents' implies that the plate and jewellery were simply weighed.

Writing in the first century BC, with the benefit of a good deal of hindsight, Diodorus says of the period after the Persian Wars, that 'every Greek city was filled with such abundance that everyone was amazed at the change for the better. For the next fifty years Greece enjoyed great progress towards prosperity.'[117] Fifth-century writers confirm this assessment of widespread and increasing wealth, and make a point of stressing how Athens in particular was blessed with a remarkable change in her fortunes as a consequence of victory. Ion of Chios reports the view that although Themistocles, the architect of the naval victory at Salamis, may have been backward in the social graces, 'he knew how to take a city that was small and inglorious and make it great and rich',[118] and Aristophanes reminded a fifth-century Athenian

---

[110] Hdt. 7. 190.
[111] Hdt. 9. 41.
[112] Hdt. 9. 15. 3, i.e. nearly 2km square.
[113] Diod. 11. 32; Hdt. 9. 70. 5.
[114] Hdt. 9. 80. 1–2.
[115] Hdt. 9. 81. 1.
[116] Hdt. 9. 81. 2. Not all the treasure was recovered, for 'long after these events many people in Plataea found coffers full of gold, silver, and other valuables': Hdt. 9. 83. 2.
[117] Diod. 12. 3–4.
[118] Plut. *Them.* 2. 3; cf. Frost (1980), 66–7; Plut. *Cimon* 9. 1.

audience that Themistocles had 'filled the city to the brim, though he had found her empty'.[119] Booty from the battlefield—from Salamis, Plataea, Mycale, and especially the Eurymedon (where Cimon took 'pavilions full of rich spoil')—[120] as well as the proceeds of ransom demands,[121] will have contributed much to this prosperity.

In Sicily, the defeat of the Carthaginians at Himera in 480 resulted in comparable amounts of booty (as well as manpower and ransom money). Stories of Sicilian wealth circulated in Greece, and were to be a contributory factor in the Athenian expedition of 415. In describing the preparations for what was to prove to be Athens' last imperial fling, Thucydides observed that 'if anyone had reckoned up the whole expenditure (1) of the state, (2) of individual soldiers and others . . . he would have found that an immense sum amounting to many talents was withdrawn from the city'.[122] The intention was, of course, to bring this treasure back augmented, but in the event the Sicilian expedition represented nothing other than the transfer of a vast amount of both public and private Athenian capital to the West. Some of this will have been in the form of plate, especially if the gold objects—perhaps *phialai*[123]—set up in a temple at Selinus (and mentioned in an inscription) were paid for with the proceeds of the Athenian disaster.[124] The only known relic of this event described as such was the shield of Nicias, decorated with 'purple and gold' (presumably copper and gold),[125] still to be seen in Syracuse in Plutarch's day.[126] The Carthaginians in 409–405 very nearly achieved what the Athenians had failed to do, and conquered most of Sicily. In doing so, they sacked such important cities as Selinus and Himera, Acragas[127] and Gela. Syracuse alone escaped, though at great cost. This city would have been the sole repository for any fifth-century Athenian silver in the island that still remained intact. Not many pieces will have escaped 'modernization' during the reign of Dionysius I (405–367), a tyrant whose court was noted for its wealth and luxury.[128]

Campaigns against the Persians during the fourth century continued to bring in booty. In the *Anabasis* Xenophon records that when Tiribazus' tent

[119] Ar. *Knights* 814; cf. Ath. 12. 553e, with Gulick's note ad loc.: 'in the new prosperity after the Persian Wars, in the second quarter of the fifth century'; [Arist.] *Ath. Pol.* 24.1; Ael. Arist. *Panath.* 143–4.

[120] Plut. *Cimon* 13. 2.

[121] Plut. *Cimon* 10.

[122] Thuc. 6. 32. 5–6.

[123] Ampolo (1984), 87–8.

[124] Calder (1963), esp. 61–3. If the 60 talents mentioned were really of gold, there would have been more gold than on the Athena Parthenos at Athens. Alternatively, the 60 talents may have been the cost in silver of the gold object(s): see Meiggs-Lewis (1969), 83. Solid gold would have been

equivalent to nearly £10m; silver to more than £645,000.

[125] See below, pp. 141–4.

[126] Plut. *Nic.* 28. 6. Cf. the bronze shields of the Spartiates captured at Sphacteria in 425 BC, exhibited in the Stoa Poecile at Athens (Paus. 1. 15. 4; Thompson and Wycherley (1972), 92–3, fig. 26)—preserved for their associations rather than their intrinsic value.

[127] Cf. the Acragantines' proverbial taste for luxury (e.g. Ael. *VH* 12. 29: silver *lekythoi* and solid ivory couches), and the presence there in the early fifth century of 'Athenian cups' (Pind. *Fr.* 124. 4 (Snell-Maehler)), presumably of silver: cf. Vickers (forthcoming).

[128] Stroheker (1958), 159 ff.

was captured, silver-footed couches and drinking-cups (*ekpomata*) were found.[129] During Agesilaos' campaigns in Asia Minor in 396–395, he collected 1,000 talents' worth of booty from the territory of Sardis;[130] on one occasion he captured a Persian camp, the booty from which fetched more than 70 talents.[131] But these achievements were as nothing compared with the booty Alexander captured from Persia between 333 and 331. He is said to have taken 180,000 talents; depending on the amount of gold, this would have been the equivalent of between 1.7 and 22 billion pounds sterling.[132]

CONNOISSEURSHIP

It is usually the case that whenever an aesthetic judgement is made in the sources relating to antiquity, the material of the object of admiration is of metal, and as often as not, precious metal. Thus, it was the gold throne of Midas at Delphi that 'is worthy of admiration',[133] although the object at Delphi that apparently deserved most attention was an inlaid iron salver made by the pioneering ironworker Glaucus of Chios.[134] Herodotus vouches for the attribution of Croesus' silver crater at Delphi to Theodore of Samos with the words 'it does not seem to be the kind of work one comes across every day'.[135] It was presumably the sheer size of the solid bronze manger found in Mardonius' tent at Plataea and subsequently dedicated at the temple of Athena Alea at Tegea, that made it 'well worth looking at'.[136] And it was both the size and splendour of the chryselephantine statues of Zeus and Athena at Olympia and Athens (both more than 11 metres high) that made them the most talked-about works of art in antiquity.[137] That gold was held in higher regard than silver is clear from Thucydides' remark concerning the plate in a temple at Eryx that 'most of the vessels were only of silver, and therefore they made a show quite out of proportion to their value';[138] and it was the intrinsic value of a gold Persian drinking-cup (as well as the hope of a bribe) that caused Demosthenes in 324 BC to 'admire its workmanship and appearance'—and weight.[139]

The last century of the Roman Republic was one of those rare periods in antiquity—indeed in history[140]—when there was a genuine interest in the art of the past. The objects that attracted the attention of connoisseurs were of silver plate. The bequest of Pergamum to Rome in 133 BC by its last king

---

[129] Xen. *Anab.* 4. 4. 21.
[130] Xen. *Ages.* 1. 34; equivalent to more than £10m.
[131] Xen. *Hell.* 3. 4. 24; cf. the 'great quantity of plate and other valuables' at Xen. *Hell.* 4. 1. 24.
[132] Cf. de Callataÿ (1989). For a graphic description of a highly elaborate and costly procession—though not of booty—held in Alexandria in the eighties of the first century BC, see Ath. 5. 196a–203e and Rice (1983).

[133] Hdt. 1. 14. 3.
[134] Hdt. 1. 25. 2.
[135] Hdt. 1. 51. 2–3.
[136] Hdt. 9. 70. 3.
[137] Judging by entries in Overbeck (1868).
[138] Thucydides 6. 46. 3.
[139] Plut. *Dem.* 25. 3.
[140] Alsop (1982), 28–9; Reitlinger (1961–70), 2. 9.

is said to have brought much silver to the Roman market and to have encouraged an interest in old pieces.[141] It was probably on this occasion that Gaius Gracchus (died 122 BC) acquired some silver dolphins for more than ten times their bullion value.[142] Even higher prices are recorded in the first century BC: Lucius Crassus possessed a pair of cups decorated by the Greek silversmith Mentor, active more than three centuries earlier, for which he had paid 100,000 sesterces,[143] but 'he confessed that for shame he never dared to use them'.[144] More shameless were Roman provincial governors of the period: Cotta 'appropriated untold gold and silver' from Heraclea in Bithynia,[145] while of C. Verres, propraetor of Sicily from 73 to 70 BC, it was said that 'in the whole of Sicily, in a province which is so wealthy and old, which has so many towns and so many rich family estates, that there is no silver vase, neither Corinthian nor Delian, no gem or pearl, no object of gold or ivory . . . which he has not sought out, inspected, and, if it pleased him, stolen.'[146] Verres would hold whole communities to ransom until they had handed over their plate. He was especially interested in the emblems on drinking-vessels, which he would cut out and have remounted by his palace goldsmiths.[147] It was a relatively easy matter for Verres to locate his targets, for it had been the practice in Sicily for rich men to exhibit their plate on stands (*abaci*),[148] which probably resembled Welsh dressers. The whereabouts of existing collections of plate were thus well known, and once again few pieces of antique silver will have escaped. Verres was very keen to lay hands on the works of famous artists of the past. From one inhabitant of Lilybaeum, he seized some 'exquisite examples of the silversmith's art (*perbona toreumata*)', including some 'Thericleans' made by the hand of Mentor 'with the greatest artifice';[149] from another, he stole a *hydria* 'made by the hand of Boethus, with remarkable workmanship and of great weight'. Intrinsic value was as important as artifice, even for a connoisseur like Verres.

PLATE IN TOMBS

Vases in precious metals are conspicuously absent from Greek burials of the archaic and classical periods; not, however, for reasons of general poverty, but because in Greece, as with us, capital wealth of this nature was custom-

---

[141] Pliny, *NH* 33. 148–9.
[142] Ibid. 33. 147.
[143] Equivalent to £30,000.
[144] Pliny, *NH* 33. 147.
[145] Memn. *FGH* 434 F 59.
[146] Cic. *Verr.* 2. 4. 1.
[147] Ibid. 2. 4. 24.
[148] Ibid. 2. 4. 15–16; 20; 25; 27. Cf. Russian court practice in the 16th c.: 'for goodly and rich plate we never saw the like or so much before. There dined that day in the Emperor's presence above 500 strangers and 200 Russians, and they were all served in vessels of gold, and that as much as could stand by one by one upon the tables. Besides this there were four cupboards garnished with goodly plate, both of gold and silver': Hakluyt (1904), 134. At the Field of the Cloth of Gold in 1519, there was a cupboard of seven stages 'covered with plate of gold, and no gilt plate': Pollen (1879), 136.
[149] Cic. *Verr.* 2. 4. 18. On 'Thericleans', see Gill (1986*a*), 19–20.

arily passed on to surviving heirs rather than being interred. It is a matter of historical record that gold and silver was passed on from father to son in Athens.[150] It has been wisely said in the context of Athenian burial practice: 'Large metal vases were probably prized in the rites of death as they were in the service of the living, and if few have been found in excavated Athenian graves it is probably because the living felt their need was greater.'[151]

Even the relatively modest contents of Greek graves became more modest as time went by. This was noticed years ago by V. Gordon Childe:

In the Classical world, the citizens of the still poor Greek States of the Dark Age, before 700 BC, might be buried with their arms and jewellery. In later cemeteries, both in old Greece and her colonies in Sicily and Italy, the grave-goods are poorer, though the cities were now rich; the furniture normally consists of vases, lamps, and figurines of clay, all beautiful, but actually factory-made and very cheap, less often of mirrors, strigils, gamesmen, and ornaments of very thin gold, made apparently for funerary use, exceptionally a horse or a dog or a fine metal vase—in any case a tiny fraction of the deceased's possessions. Wealth as such was not left in the tomb.[152]

Subsequent research has borne out this general picture. During the Geometric period, as the number of bronze objects buried in tombs decreased, the number of similar artefacts dedicated in sanctuaries increased.[153] Over the same period, while the number of metal artefacts in Athenian graves falls, the number of pottery vessels rises.[154] Later still, problems occur concerning the nature of the burials we actually do have. Even the large numbers (some 1,800 graves) of fifth-century BC Athenian burials—often accompanied by painted pottery, represent less than 2 per cent of the population.[155] Wealthier Athenians appear to have cremated their dead. Lucian's well-known tag: 'the Greek burnt, the Persian buried'[156] will have been a reflection of upper-class Athenian practice rather than an accurate account of 'everyman's grave'.[157] The point of Thucydides' report of the funeral pyres built at the time of the Athenian plague[158] is not, as has been suggested,[159] that it was a temporary public-health measure, but that 'the customs which had hitherto been observed at funerals were universally violated'.[160] The form this violation took was for families to use other people's pyres.

Cremation was probably effectively restricted to the landed aristocracy, the owners of private burial plots[161] and olive plantations: olive plantations because among the very few exemptions from a stringent law designed to

---

[150] Cf. the ἐκπώματα καὶ χρυσία which formed part of Demosthenes' inheritance: Dem. 27. 10.
[151] Kurtz (1975), 70.
[152] Childe (1944), 86.
[153] Snodgrass (1980), 52–4.
[154] I. Morris (1987), 141, table 9, 142, fig. 48.
[155] Ibid. 100.
[156] Lucian, *de Luctu* 21; cf. Becker (1874), 390 ff.; pp. 383–402 still constitute the soundest introduction to Athenian burial practices. One looks

in vain for an account of cremation in classical Athens in Kurtz and Boardman (1971).
[157] Cf. Browne (1658): 'with rich flames and hired tears they solemnised their Obsequies' (ch. 3).
[158] Thuc. 2. 52.
[159] Kurtz and Boardman (1971), 190.
[160] Thuc. 2. 52.
[161] [Dem.] 43. 79 (Buselids); Plut. *Mor.* 838b–c (family burial plot of Isocrates); cf. Becker (1874), 394.

protect olive trees from unnecessary felling were clauses allowing them to be cut down for official purposes or 'for the disposal of a corpse'.[162] Olive wood was highly valued in antiquity as fuel for furnaces,[163] and its fragrance[164] will have added to its suitability for use in a funeral pyre. The landed gentry were also the people who would have used plate in everyday life, and vessels of precious metal may have been placed on the funeral pyre,[165] to be retrieved during the separation of the bones from the ashes, a ritual usually conducted by close relatives.[166] Little of this would be apparent in the archaeological record, and we might, with I. Morris, compare the Athenian picture with the situation which prevailed until recently in Bali where 'the highest-ranked individuals were exposed without any subterranean disposal facilities',[167] with the result that 'only the poorest members of society would be visible to the archaeologist'.[168]

Etruscan élites did not practise cremation, but buried their dead in chamber-tombs. These tombs, it has been estimated, have produced 90 per cent of the fine Athenian pottery in our museums.[169] In antiquity, these pots will have provided the show, but not the expense, of an elaborate funeral.[170] They will have served as 'tokens and symbols' substituted for the real wealth—especially gold and silver plate—which was bequeathed to surviving heirs to enjoy above ground.[171] Sumptuary laws and fear of grave-robbers may have encouraged such precautions. A king of Sidon in Syria had the following inscription placed on his sarcophagus: 'Do not open the coffin-lid nor disturb me. No gold, no silver, no treasures lie in this box but only I.'[172]

There are, however, some notable exceptions to the general rule that plate is not placed in the tomb. In the classical period, these are to be found beyond the bounds of Greece proper, namely in Scythia, Thrace, and Macedon. It was said of the Scythians in antiquity that 'they despise gold and silver, much as other men covet them'.[173] This used to be taken to mean that the Scythians lived a simple life, free from greed and acquisitiveness (and as a consequence, precious metal).[174] The rich finds of precious metal objects from Scythian tombs in the Crimea and the Ukraine[175] indicate instead that,

---

[162] [Dem.] 43. 71. The fine for illicit felling was 100 drachmas per tree. Cf. the use of olive wood on the pyre depicted on the Attic red-figure psykter illustrated in Guy (1983), 152.

[163] Theophr. 5. 9. 6.

[164] Cf. *Encyclopedia Britannica*, 11th edn. 20 (1911), 86: 'a resinous matter called "olive gum", or Lucca gum, formed by the exuding juice in hot seasons, was anciently in medical esteem, and in modern Italy is used as perfume'; Smyth (1821), 294: 'olive wood . . . has an agreeable smell'; Browne (1658): 'the Funerall pyre consisted of sweet fuell . . . Trees perpetually verdant'.

[165] Cf. Croesus' sacrificial pyre at Delphi, p. 56, above.

[166] Isae. 4. 19; cf. Becker (1874), 393; add Eur. *Or.* 403–4.

[167] I. Morris (1987), 100.

[168] Ibid. 93–4.

[169] Hemelrijk (1985).

[170] Vickers (1985–6), 165.

[171] Hoffmann (1988), 152; cf. Kurtz (1975), 70. Even terracotta mirrors might be placed in tombs as surrogates for metal ones: Schneider-Hermann (1962).

[172] Childe (1944), 87; cf. Philostr. *VA* 7. 23.

[173] Justin. 2. 2.

[174] In the 18th c., Scythians were the archetypes of the simple life, e.g. Voltaire (1767) (new edn. by R. Niklaus in press, Voltaire Foundation, Oxford).

[175] e.g. Galanina and Grach (1986).

unlike most other peoples, the Scythians were so careless of gold and silver that they even placed vessels made from them in the grave, rather than keeping them for the use of the next generation. Stringent taboos against theft[176] will have ensured safety from grave-robbers in antiquity. Similar attitudes towards precious metals may have prevailed in Thrace and Macedon as well, for objects of gold and silver are also sometimes found in graves in these areas.[177]

LATER VICISSITUDES OF PLATE

It is impossible to estimate how much gold and silver there was in antiquity. Athens seems to have been extremely well placed in the fifth century BC, thanks both to booty and the products of her silver mines. Sparta was probably richer than most people realize. Alexander's conquest of Persia brought great quantities of precious metal westwards, to be enjoyed first by his successors, and then by the Romans who, by the second and first centuries BC, had effectively laid claim to be the heirs of the Hellenistic kings. As early as 161 BC there was a sumptuary law controlling the amount of plate that could be used at banquets at Rome. The limit, of 100 Roman pounds in weight of silver,[178] suggests how resplendent some banquets may have been. This legislation will undoubtedly have encouraged the melting-down and refashioning of older silver, for it is at precisely this period that a new technique is adopted by silversmiths, namely to make vessels in two pieces: an outer casing that carried the embossed decoration, and an inner, smooth liner.[179] The space between would be hollow, and the plate would thus look as if it was heavy and of great intrinsic value, while in reality it was not.[180] By the first century AD things had changed somewhat. The Elder Pliny's friend Pompeius Paulinus, who was governor of Germania Inferior in the mid-first century AD, is said never to have travelled without taking with him 12,000 pounds of silverware.[181] An English ambassador in the eighteenth century only needed 4,000 oz (124 kilos) to make the necessary impression on those with whom he did business.[182] Even the most apparently lavish hoards of Roman silver known to us are modest by comparison with such flamboyance, but they attest to a high degree of skill on the part of the ancient silversmith, and—what is more important in the present context— changes in fashion which will have brought about the periodic refashioning of silver.[183]

[176] Justin. 2. 2: 'No crime in their opinion is more heinous than theft; for, among people that keep their flocks and herds without fence or shelter in the woods, what would be safe, if stealing were permitted?'

[177] e.g. Filow (1934); Θησαυροί (1979); Andronicos (1984).

[178] Aul. Gell. 2.24 (= 32.745 kg.).

[179] A. Oliver (1977), 79.

[180] Cf. Vickers (1993), 23.

[181] Pliny, *NH* 33. 143 (= nearly 4 tonnes); cf. Baratte and Painter (1989), 63.

[182] Hayward (1959), 78–9.

[183] See e.g. Baratte (1986); Baratte and Painter (1989); Baratte *et al.* (1990).

When pagan temples were stripped of their possessions by Constantine the Great in AD 311,[184] the practical consequence will have been that much gold and silver plate was melted down and remade, not least on account of the pagan imagery with which much of it was decorated.[185] Not only were the rich dedications made over centuries confiscated, but cult images were stripped of their gold sheathing. Phidias' Olympian Zeus was probably reduced to its wooden armature at this time, since when it next appears in the historical record, it is described simply as 'ivory'.[186] It was now part of a collection formed in Constantinople soon after 408 (when it was enacted that 'the statues which are still in temples and honoured by pagan rites should be taken from their seats').[187]

The precious metal was required for different purposes: for imperial *largitiones*, where gold vessels, jewellery, and coins figure large in representations of imperial largesse—as does silverware;[188] for church plate, or for the domestic use of anyone rich and influential enough to own it. The relative profusion of extant late Roman and Byzantine silverware[189] should not obscure the fact that its survival is due in large part to the unsettled times in which it was made, rather than to the fact that there was necessarily more plate around then than at other times. Any hoard found today involves doubly disturbing circumstances in the past: things had to be bad enough for precious objects to be buried in the first place, and so bad that no one was able to return to dig them up.[190]

Liturgical plate figures large in both the historical sources and the surviving silver (although the latter mostly comes from village churches, rather than metropolitan centres), and we hear of lavish donations of silver revetments: to cover screens, altars, *ciboria* (free-standing shrines), doors, and thrones: 40,000 Roman pounds of silver, for example, were given to St Sophia in Constantinople by Justinian in 537.[191] (The practice survives in the way icons in Orthodox churches today are usually covered with metal.) All of this silver has gone into the melting-pot, as did the 5,000 pounds of plate belonging to the cathedral at Syracuse when that city was taken by the Saracens in 846.[192] Cheaper substitutes might begin to be used: 'Glass

---

[184] A. H. M. Jones (1964), 1. 92, 108.

[185] Cf. Vickers (1987*b*), 55.

[186] Cedrenus 1. 564 (Bonn). Mango, Vickers, and Francis (1992).

[187] A. H. M. Jones (1964), 1. 92.

[188] Delmaire (1988).

[189] e.g. Dodd (1961); *Spätantike* Catalogue (1978); Toynbee and Painter (1986); Mundell Mango (1986), (1990*a*), (1990*b*).

[190] Cf. Hopkins (1980), 114 (quoted ch. 2, n. 158, above); Painter (1988), 108 n. 51 adds a refinement: 'Because silver was important, it had to be looked after carefully. One of the main ways

available to safeguard it was burial. Burial therefore may be attributable to a datable moment of danger which can be known; but it *need* only mean that its owner was being careful. A collection of silver was part of the fabric of the owner's life and not a disposable asset. Hoards found now should not therefore be associated too readily in themselves with crises. It is non-recovery which indicates crises, not the initial burial.'

[191] Procop. *Aed.* 1. 1. 65; Mundell Mango (forthcoming), (40,000 Roman pounds = more than 13 tonnes).

[192] Gibbon (1896–1900), ch. 52.

vessels only came into use [in Coptic Egyptian churches] when the more precious vessels had been plundered or destroyed by the Muslims. Thus it is recorded that about the year 700 AD so great a spoliation of the churches took place, that glass chalices and wooden patens were substituted for the lost vessels of silver and gold.'[193]

These vicissitudes are no different from those which have afflicted objects made from precious metals in any period. It is regularly the case that written sources are full of references to precious metal, while gold and silver vessels are distinctly lacking in the archaeological record. A useful parallel for the way the poetry of archaic and classical Greece echoes reality[194] is provided by Anglo-Saxon England, as we have already seen.[195] Apart from the fact that it was 'a world which both in the religious and secular spheres savoured resplendence',[196] it is even more important to note that 'if the survival pattern of the various crafts of the Anglo-Saxons has distorted our knowledge of their arts, it has also falsified our understanding of their tastes',[197] for this is precisely what has happened in the study of the Greek world. Apart from jewellery and the gold used to illuminate manuscripts, surviving Anglo-Saxon work in precious metal could be held in one hand. In one respect, this is extraordinary, in that contemporary accounts give the impression that England was abundantly endowed with gold and silver in both churches and private houses. According to a twelfth-century report, a chalice found in the coffin of St Cuthbert at Durham had a bowl of onyx mounted on a lion 'of the purest gold';[198] at York altars were covered with gold, silver, and precious stones;[199] and at Ely there was an effigy of the Virgin 'of gold, silver and gems' which was 'priceless because of its size' and which sat on a throne 'as long as a man'.[200] It was in the expectation of rich booty that England was constantly attacked by the Danes; finally in 1066 Norman invaders came into possession of 'vessels of silver and gold, the description of whose number and beauty would strain credulity',[201] all of which have gone into the melting-pot.

This was to be a constant pattern throughout history. *Ex votos* of gold and silver, for example, 'like other forms of goldsmith's work, are always imperilled, even more than other works of art, by the intrinsic value of the precious metal, which has again and again brought destruction on them from a variety of causes—not least from religious conviction, as at the Reformation, or from ideological conviction, as at the French Revolution, not to

[193] Butler (1884), 2. 38–9.
[194] See pp. 43–5, above.
[195] See p. 43, above.
[196] Dodwell (1982), 30.
[197] Ibid. 12.
[198] Ibid. 208.
[199] Ibid. 209.
[200] Ibid. 215. For an idea of its likely appearance, compare the much smaller Carolingian reliquary statue of Ste Foy at Conques, made from sheet gold and studded with gems set *en cabuchon*: G. Clark (1986), 89, fig. 31.
[201] Guillaume de Poitiers, quoted by Dodwell (1982), 193; cf. 216–34.

mention theft, pillage, or seizure by the state in moments of desperate financial crisis'.[202] Antiquarian interest in such objects is a relatively modern development, which has had much to do with the increasingly privileged role of the artist.[203] The ancient picture was identical with that prevailing before the eighteenth century. The bottom line then was the same as in the Middle Ages and later: 'The prestige attached to the possession of a large collection of plate was fully recognised by the rulers of medieval Europe. This was not due to a more widespread appreciation of the art of the goldsmith, but to the fact that in the last resort the plate could be melted down and converted into money. A well-furnished cupboard of plate at the end of the great hall was evidence of solvency.'[204]

We have felt it necessary to dwell at some length on these issues in order to meet the objection that is sometimes made that because there is so little surviving Greek, and especially Attic, plate, there must have been commensurately little in antiquity. In the light of the evidence presented here for the perpetual reworking of precious metal, it is rather a matter for comment that there is any at all. We fully agree with D. B. Thompson's wise observation that 'our ignorance of the quality and quantity of [lost masterpieces in precious metals] has perhaps warped our judgement as to their position in the history of [the] artistic tradition.'[205] It is largely thanks to the un-Hellenic burial practices of Scythian and Thracian chieftains that we have any figured plate to provide fleeting glimpses of the kind of material that informed the work of potters in Greece, Southern Italy, and Sicily in the archaic and classical periods.

[202] Lightbown (1979), 353. For illustrations of similar, but extant, material, see Busch and Lohse (1959). On the almost total loss of English Romanesque work in precious metal, see Stratford (1984), 232, esp.: 'over and over again great works of the goldsmith's art must have been destroyed for purely economic reasons'.

[203] Cf. Reitlinger (1961–70) 2. 7–8; Haskell (1963); on d'Hancarville's role in this development, see ch. 1.
[204] Oman (1961), 1–2.
[205] D. B. Thompson (1939), 316.

4 'Born Free': The Worthy Potter

LET us take stock at this stage. We have seen how Greek ceramics only became objects of value in the eighteenth century, but that arguments were put forward to persuade potential purchasers that pots were sold for large sums in antiquity. It is at this point that Greek pots became 'vases', with a special aura of their own. We have seen that Athenian élites did their business in *minae* (units of 100 drachmas), and that their gold and silver vessels were regularly made up in either *minae* or round figures in darics or *sigloi*, as though plate served in effect as large-denomination banknotes. We have also seen why so little of the plate that existed in both public and private hands in ancient Greece has survived in its original form, having found its way to the melting-pot as the result of the looting of shrines and cities, or as a consequence of changes of fashion, or simply from the need to realize liquid capital.

It is difficult to reconcile these facts with the notions that have grown up in the name of the Enlightenment around ancient Greece: that it was a world in which 'for most of the fifth century no plate was manufactured for private domestic use',[1] a world whose wealthiest citizens ate and drank from fine pottery decorated by highly creative artists,[2] some of whom not only had an entrée to the best houses,[3] but returned such hospitality.[4] The private life of Athens, on such a view, was on a ceramic rather than a gold or silver standard, but it is a view for which it is difficult to find support in the evidence we have from antiquity. There is thus a good deal of scholarly rubble to be removed before we can begin to assess the role that pottery did play in antiquity.

UTOPIANISM

The high status of ceramic has nothing to do with the ancient world, but has come about during the past few centuries. The earliest society in which pottery rather than plate represented the peak of human acquisitiveness is a fictional one. In 1516, Thomas More's Utopians were systematically

---

[1] Strong (1966), 74.

[2] e.g. '[Attic pots were decorated by] great artists encouraged by prosperous and appreciative patrons': Shapiro (1981*a*), 137; 'The archaic age was the great age of sympotic pottery: potters and painters became rich and famous': O. Murray (1983), 264.

[3] Boardman (1975), 30, which led to Gollan (1982), 6: 'Famous potters and painters appear to have mingled socially with the leading families.'

[4] Boardman (1975), 30; Paul (1982), 72.

conditioned to despise precious metals: 'inasmuch as they eat and drink from vessels fashioned out of clay and glass which, though handsomely shaped, are nevertheless of the cheapest kinds they . . . make night jars and all kinds of squalid receptacles out of gold and silver.'[5] There had of course been a long classical moralizing tradition in which precious metals were attacked, but More's 'provisional blue-print for a perfect society'[6] (which was an oblique criticism of the opulence of the court of Henry VIII) was in the long term far more influential on both the ethical and aesthetic planes.

To assess the impact which More's subversive ideas had, we have only to look at Alciati's emblem *Those who sin against Nature* (Fig. 4.1) in which a naked man empties his bowels into a golden vessel while close by him stand an earthenware pitcher and a glass goblet. Johannes Thuilius observed in the seventeenth century: 'does a more scandalous abuse exist than to commit one's own excrements to gold, while drinking from simple glass and earthenware?'[7] Others, however, echoed More's critique of luxury. In *c*.1550, Pierre de Ronsard wrote an ode in praise of glass in conscious imitation of Pindar. Yet whereas for Pindar gold came very high in the scale of values,[8] Ronsard gives a long list of mythical quarrels which broke out over gold. He then contrasts it with the simplicity of glass and thus reverses Pindar's scale of values: 'But you, pretty glass, . . . are more pleasing than a vessel of gold, heavyweight of the table.'[9] The efforts of Ronsard's contemporary Bernard Palissy (1510–90) to perfect techniques of pottery manufacture (he even burnt his furniture to fire his kiln) became by the nineteenth century a paradigm of courage in adversity. They were confused in semi-devotional literature with his death as a Huguenot martyr in the Bastille,[10] and thus contributed in the eyes of many to an image of the essential worthiness of the potter's trade. William Morris was to create another Utopian paradise in his *News from Nowhere*. Here, there were 'Banded-workshops' in which

folk collect to do handwork in which working together is necessary or convenient; such work is often very pleasant. In there, for instance, they make pottery and glass . . . there are a good many such places, as it would be ridiculous if a man had a liking for pot-making or glass-blowing that he should have to live in one place or be obliged to forgo the work he liked . . . As to the crafts, throwing the clay must be jolly work: the glass-blowing is rather a sweltering job; but some folk like it very much indeed.[11]

[5] Trans. Heckscher (1981), 297. While there may be echoes of the Persian chamberpots at Ar. *Ach.* 82, the immediate origins of More's image lie in the New World, early reports of which held that there were societies there which 'held as nothing the wealth that we enjoy in this our Europe such as gold and jewels, pearls and other riches' (Vespucci [(1505/6)] (1893), fo. 4ᵛ); the influence such reports had on More have been well described by Slavin (1976).

[6] Turner (1965), 13.
[7] Cited by Heckscher (1981), 297.
[8] Cf. Pind. *Ol.* 1. 1–2.
[9] . . . Mais toi verre joly,
  Loin de tout meutre en te voyant poly,
  Net, beau, luisant, tu es plus agreable,
  Qu'un vaisseau d'or, lourd fardeau de la table.
                    (Ronsard (1967), 4. 346–7)
[10] e.g. Morley (1852).
[11] W. Morris (1890), in Briggs (1962), 221–2.

Emblemata.   353

Aduersus naturam peccantes.

EMBLEMA LXXX:

TVRPE quidem dictu , sed & est res improba factu,
Excipiat siquis chœnice ventris onus.
Mensuram , legisque modum hoc excedere sancta est ,
Quale sit incesto pollui adulterio.

FIG. 4.1   Emblem, *Adversus naturam peccantes*. Andrea Alciati, *Emblemata* (Padua, 1621), 353.

Gold and silver in this society were the distinctive signs of the lower orders: a waterman, a weaver, a dustman, road-menders.[12]

Already, in the eighteenth century, there had been other developments, notably a change in taste which favoured simplicity in design and a change in the perceived role of the artist. Art ceased to be simply a means by which individuals or institutions could display their wealth and influence, and came closer to art of a kind recently defined as 'a term for a vast number of ways to express yourself'.[13] These changes would have happened in any case, but the publication of the catalogue of Hamilton's first collection of Greek pots[14] will have done much to help them on their way. D'Hancarville's text, as we have seen, included what can only be described as fraudulent arguments in support of the view that Greek pots were valuable in antiquity, and was composed with a view to enhancing the status of the pots Hamilton wished to sell.

One effect of the rise in the status of ceramics and of the artist was that the act of painting pottery itself became socially acceptable, and nowhere can this be demonstrated more clearly than in the United States. It is ironic that the immediate origins of Thomas More's Utopian conceit lay in the New World, of which Amerigo Vespucci stated that there were societies there which 'held as nothing the wealth that we enjoy in this our Europe such as gold and jewels, pearls and other riches'.[15] A taste for 'art pottery' was one of the first fruits of the Arts and Crafts Movement in America, a movement whose philosophical roots were decidedly Utopian. Thus we learn that in 1872 there was 'instituted a class in china painting for socially prominent women at the Cincinnati School of Art; . . . enthusiasm for this new medium spread quickly in the city, for not only did it satisfy the ambitions of an age bent on culture' but, in the words of a contemporary observer, 'tidings of the veritable renaissance in England under the leadership of William Morris and his associates had reached [the United States]'.[16]

The activities of the ladies of Cincinnati neatly encapsulate several trends that had come together by the nineteenth century. We saw something of the eighteenth-century history of porcelain in Chapter 1.[17] Its acceptance in Europe had much to do with Utopian ideals. A Portuguese delegate at the Council of Trent in 1562, shocked at the display of gold and silver on the papal table, recommended to Pope Pius IV, 'a type of baked earthenware which is far superior to silver in elegance and neatness', called porcelain from China. 'Its lustre surpassed that of both crystal and alabaster, while its relatively low price compensated for its fragility.' The Pope duly ordered a porcelain service.[18] There was also the question of taste—literally. Ulisse

[12] Ibid. 190–1, 200, 222.
[13] Coral Gables (1980), 46.
[14] d'Hancarville 1766[1767]–76.
[15] Vespucci (1893), fo. 4ᵛ; cf. Slavin (1976).

[16] Clark (1972), esp. 119–20; cf. Naylor (1971).
[17] See pp. 19–20, above. For its early connections with Chinese silverware, see Ch. 5.
[18] Lach (1970), 41–2; Raby and Vickers (1986), 218–19.

Aldrovandi describes in his *Musaeum Metallicum* how 'many princes' had abandoned silver services in favour of foreign porcelain because food tasted better when served in ceramic rather than metal vessels.[19] This recalls a remark of Vitruvius concerning the dining practices of Augustan Rome. It comes as an aside in an account of plumbing: 'Water ought not to be conducted in lead pipes, if we want to have it wholesome. That the taste is better when it comes from clay pipes may be proved by everyday life, for although our tables are loaded with silver vessels, yet everybody uses earthenware for the sake of purity of taste.'[20] The extent to which this custom existed elsewhere is open to question, but Vitruvius' statement only reinforces the principle that silver took precedence over ceramic.

Once the secret of porcelain manufacture was discovered in the West, European courts set up their own workshops, manned by painters whose fame often extended beyond their principality: individuals such as Herold or Riedel.[21] Such painters were, however, very much obliged to their princely patrons; hence, no doubt, d'Hancarville's insistence that the painters of Greek pots were 'born free . . . and had not the mortification of employing, in order to gain protectors, a time which they must have taken from their study's'.[22] Still in princely Germany, it is as representatives of Painting that Greek vases are being held aloft by two of the *Künstler und Gelehrte* in one of the frescoes with which Ludwig I of Bavaria's Neue Pinakothek was adorned.[23]

In the second half of the nineteenth century there was a growing antiquarian interest in ceramics of all kinds,[24] and Greek pottery, hitherto prized for its antique associations and painterly qualities alone, gained a chapter to itself in numerous popular handbooks on ceramics. The most influential work of this kind was A. Jacquemart's *Histoire de la céramique* (1873) where it was stated that Greek ceramics should be studied 'with the same methods, . . . with the same impartiality that one would bring to the examination of Hindu, Egyptian or Chinese products'.[25] Jacquemart's work was soon followed by German and English equivalents, both heavily dependent on it.[26] Pottery had also, during the previous century or so, come to replace

[19] Aldrovandi (1648), 231; Raby and Vickers (1986), 219. Cf. the (exceptional) practice of drinking from clay vessels enriched with aromatics: Ath. 11. 464c–d.

[20] Vitr. 8. 6. 11.

[21] Charles (1964); and see Ch. 1.

[22] D'Hancarville, (1766[1767]–76), 2. 48; and see Ch. 1.

[23] The full title of the work (of which Wilhelm von Kaulbach's original study is still extant in the Bayerische Staatsgemäldesammlungen, Munich) is: *König Ludwig, umgeben von Künstlern und Gelehrten, steigt über die Stufen des Thrones herab, um die aus früheren Jahrhunderten stammenden und* *ihm darbrachten Werke Plastik und Malerei näher zu besehen*; discussed most recently by Mittlmeier (1977), 53, fig. 57.

[24] e.g. the great majority of titles in the bibliography to Fortnum (1873), 657–65, were published after 1850.

[25] Jacquemart (1873), 219.

[26] Jaennicke (1879); J. J. Young (1879). There was also an English translation of Jacquemart (1874), of which there was a challenging review by W. B. Scott (1874): 'Monsieur Jacquemart is one of the writers who seem to put on the official cocked-hat when he takes up the pen, and who instantly claims a paramount importance for the

silver or pewter in polite society as the normal material for drinking-vessels, largely as a result of the widespread adoption of the practice of drinking hot liquids such as tea, coffee, or cocoa (drunk from metal they would burn the mouth).[27]

It was thus quite reasonable at the end of the nineteenth century to believe that 'fine ceramics could only come from the labours of independent artists using new technical knowledge with the pure objective of making beautiful things'.[28] This was written in the context of the Arts and Crafts Movement, which was well under way in various forms in Europe and the United States by the mid-1880s. There was a related interest in the handicrafts of peasant communities throughout Europe; shortly before the Great War, *The Studio* put out several supplements on this topic, where ceramics figured large. In their Italian number of 1913, maiolica is treated in a fashion that is highly reminiscent of the way Greek pottery was beginning to be studied:

One imagines a teacher, then a second teacher with a following of pupils, forming a school, and the seeds of their teaching falling upon minds already imbued with that odd mixture of piety and fantasy, which was the salient feature of the art of the period, has resulted in a harvest of those singular productions of which many pieces have come down to us.[29]

This quotation was taken from a copy of *The Studio*'s Italian Peasant number that was bequeathed to the Ashmolean Library by J. D. Beazley, who was writing in identical terms about Greek potters and pot-painters at the time it was published. Beazley's personality and methodology came to dominate the study of Greek painted wares, but it is important to recognize that throughout his life his sympathies lay within the Utopian tradition. Beazley's intellectual heroes[30] were Lytton Strachey and J. M. Keynes, who himself wrote a Utopian tract[31] and once described gold as a 'barbarous relic'.[32] Beazley had 'learnt much about arts and crafts from his father', who was not only an interior designer but went to Brussels in 1897 'to learn glass-making techniques'.[33] And although in 1910 Beazley travelled in Sicily with C. R.

---

subject in hand. "L'histoire de la céramique, c'est l'histoire de l'humanité toute entière" is the motto on the title-page; and the opening of the book affirms at once the same superlative position. "A philosopher," he says, "seeking among the products of human industry the one which would best enable him to follow, through the course of ages, the progress of intelligence, and give him the approximate measure of the artistic tendencies of man, would select incontestably the works of the potter." We should have thought both architecture and stone-carving, or sculpture, would necessarily rank higher: pottery is indeed a division, and a humble one, being mainly applied to domestic uses and perishable materials, of the sculptor's or modeller's art.'

[27] Charles (1964), 18; Hatcher and Barker (1974), 280–1; cf. Ch. 1. According to Mathias (1959), 375, consumption of tea in England had grown from 1 oz per head to 2.3 lb between 1722 and 1833; the change in drinking habits 'favoured the potter . . . and having sold the cups [he] also supplied the matching saucers, plates and other dishes as well' (Hatcher and Barker (1974), 281).
[28] Caiger-Smith (1973), 191.
[29] Balzano (1913), 11.
[30] Ashmole (1970), 446.
[31] Keynes (1931); on Strachey and Keynes, see Levy (1979), esp. 270.
[32] T. Green (1985), 2.
[33] Ashmole (1970), 443.

Ashbee, the Arts and Crafts silver manufacturer,[34] he will not have received from him reliable insights into the traditions of working in precious metals; for Ashbee prided himself on not employing silversmiths 'with trade experience; such experience was . . . regarded rightly as rather a detriment'.[35] Beazley could be as outspoken as Ruskin in his condemnation of industrialism,[36] or of what he considered to be falsehood in art,[37] and as we saw in Chapter 1, he believed that there were individuals in antiquity who might view a painted pot in the same light as a gold *phiale*. It should be clear from the evidence discussed in Chapters 2 and 3 that no one in antiquity would have understood Beazley's point, and it is equally certain that no one outside the intellectual tradition to which Beazley belonged would agree with the underlying assumptions.

Nevertheless, by the mid-twentieth century, it could be stated with absolute confidence that 'a potter must be an artist'.[38] The Omega Workshop, Bernard Leach, Hans Coper, Lucie Rie, and even Clarice Cliff,[39] are now household names, and the concept of the 'artist potter' is firmly established.[40] Whether it existed in antiquity is, however, another matter.

Another issue which increasingly concerned critics was the concept of *Materialgerechtigkeit*—of a craftsman being faithful to the aesthetic of the medium in which he worked. It is not generally realized that this principle was unknown to the Greeks,[41] probably because of the view widespread amongst aesthetes of the earlier part of the twentieth century that 'it is an infallible symptom of decadence and jaded resource when the craftsman, ill-content with the limitations proper to his craft, seeks to supplement them by adventitious devices borrowed from extraneous arts and processes'.[42] And there is a tradition that regards a failure to respect perceived canons of craft integrity as a moral issue. The Elder Pliny's reservations concerning the taste for luxury that had overwhelmed Rome as a consequence of the Hellenistic East included objections to the use of veneer, 'of covering up one tree with another and making an outside skin for a cheaper wood out of a more expensive one'.[43] A similar view was expressed by the philosopher and

---

[34] Information from Warren Moon and R. S. Sennott.

[35] Ashbee (1909), 5.

[36] He thus objected to the concept of 'industrial art' as a 'shoddy concept': Beazley (1945), 158.

[37] Beazley wrote to Paul Jacobsthal in 1931: 'Flaxman is to me the Beast. He, Thorwaldsen and Wedgwood are the Bogus classic, as the English Pre-Raphaelites are the Bogus Gothic and early Renaissance. And nothing more.' The letter is preserved with Beazley's correspondence in the Beazley Archive in Oxford, where it may be consulted.

[38] Leach (1961), 7.

[39] Wentworth-Sheilds (1976); L. Griffin (1988); Spours (1988); H. Watson (1988).

[40] O'Reilly, Taylor, and Atterbury (1984).

[41] Kopcke (1964), 25. Cf. the story of Agathocles, who had been a potter before becoming tyrant of Syracuse, judging his success as a potter by the degree to which he was able to imitate precious metal: he boasted that he remained a potter until he could make a clay cup as good as a gold one: Diod. 19. 2 and 20. 63.

[42] Vallance (1909), 20, writing in the context of Hispano-Moresque lustre ware. Cf. Platnauer (1921), 153: 'a natural and on the whole commendable diffidence prevents our attributing to the Greeks anything that seems in the least derogatory from an artistic point of view'.

[43] Pliny, NH 16. 223.

statesman Francis Bacon in his *New Atlantis* of 1627: 'but we do hate all impostures and lies, insomuch as we have severely forbidden it to all our fellows, under pain of ignominy and fines, that they do not show any natural work adorned or swelling, but only pure as it is, and without all affectation of strangeness.'[44] 'Pure as it is' comes close to the values expressed by the Puritans, who rejected the flamboyance of Caroline England.

It was towards the end of the eighteenth century, as we have seen,[45] that a general change in taste occurred among the educated middle class. There was, however, a large public that was content—or forced by material circumstances—to accept imitation. Critics could be outspoken:

Nobody wants ornaments in this world, but everybody wants integrity. All the fair devices that ever were fancied, are not worth a lie. Leave your walls as bare as a planed board, or build them of baked mud and chopped straw if need be; do not rough-cast them with falsehood... You use that which pretends to a worth which it has not; which pretends to have cost, and to be, what it did not, and is not; it is an imposition, a vulgarity, and a sin. Down with it to the ground, grind it to powder, leave its ragged place upon the wall[46]

Or:

In a cardboard travelling-case made to imitate alligator skin, in a bakelite hairbrush made to imitate enamel, there is something dishonest. A pressed-glass bowl trying to look like crystal, a machine-made coal-scuttle trying to look hand-beaten, machine-made mouldings on furniture, a tricky device to make an electric fire look like a flickering coke fire, a metal bedstead masquerading as wood—all that is immoral. So are sham materials and sham technique.[47]

As David Watkins has amply demonstrated, such questions of taste are not moral issues at all,[48] but they have become almost inextricably entangled with the Enlightenment's concern with plagiarism and originality, which was brought to a head with Edward Young's 'Declaration of Creative Independence', his *Conjectures on Original Composition* of 1759. For Young, 'Genius *grows*, is not *made*.'[49] Out went the ancient practice of *imitatio*, of the artistic borrowing of motifs by writers and by craftsmen in the visual arts. But while Samuel Johnson counselled poets not to 'submit to the servility of imitation' of the ancients,[50] Sir Joshua Reynolds still constructed his pictures by borrowing 'here... an attitude, there an expression or a gesture, from Poussin or Van Dyck or Michelangelo'. And 'what Reynolds called "imitation", Walpole called "wit" or "quotation", Nathaniel Hone called "conjuring", and Blake called "thievery".'[51] The German Romantics' search

---

[44] Bacon (1922), 158; cf. Raby and Vickers (1986).

[45] See pp. 27–32, above.

[46] Ruskin (1903–12), 8. 83.

[47] Pevsner (1937), 11; cf. Pazaurek (1912).

[48] Watkin (1977), esp. p. 98.

[49] Heckscher (1966/7), 243; (= Verheyen (1985), 3).

[50] Johnson (1825), 2. 142–3; Lipking (1970), 333.

[51] Lipking (1970), 175–6.

for Truth and Beauty in Art then added elements to criticism which were for the most part absent in classical antiquity. The belief that the best kind of art was the repository of Truth, coupled with the belief that Greek art was the best kind of Art, meant that critics could be blind to the possibility that the clay vases we have, for all their sham rivets and sharp carinations, were made to evoke vessels made in another material. All this would be harmless enough were it not for the fact that many of these notions have been imposed on the material culture of Greek antiquity in such a way that the world of the contemporary artist and craftsman was perceived to have existed in classical Athens—and often, not even the real world, but something approaching the Utopian ideal.

PRICES OF POTTERY

Much has been said in earlier chapters on the value of plate, which was worth at least its weight in gold or silver, with the likelihood of an additional premium for artistry. But this will only have held good so long as the vessel in question was fashionable and new; thereafter, it will have reverted to its intrinsic value. The silver gold-figured *kantharos* from Duvanli, which weighed $2\frac{1}{2}$ *minae*, would thus have cost the equivalent—at the time of writing—of more than £450, and the 1-*mina* gold-figured *phiale* upwards of £180.[52] How do Athenian pots compare on the same scale of values?

To begin with, the highest recorded price for any Athenian painted pot is 3 drachmas: the equivalent of £5.40. But not only is this price exceptionally high, but the two pots which are thus inscribed are rather large: 48 cm- and 47 cm-high red-figure *hydriai* now in Syracuse (23912) and St Petersburg (St 1206).[53] *Hydriai* in any case appear to be priced more highly than other shapes, perhaps because they cost more to ship, being incapable of containing other pots. Be that as it may, it is interesting to note that a toy silver *hydria* in Oxford the size of a hen's egg (Fig. 4.2) has a bullion value of 6 drachmas and 4 obols, which is more than double that of its much larger ceramic counterparts.[54] A commercial graffito on the underside of a red-figure *pelike* (Fig. 4.3) currently in Oxford and attributed to J. D. Beazley's 'Achilles Painter' (Fig. 4.4), may be read as four items for 3.5 obols,[55]—which gives a price of 0.88 obol, or just over 26p. While this may seem extraordinarily low (and surely incompatible with the view that the work of 'the Achilles Painter' was 'highly regarded . . . in antiquity'),[56] it is higher than a price found on a *pelike* in Göttingen which is marked with a price of

[52] Cf. Ch. 1.
[53] Johnston (1979), 33, 113, and 165. Irene Saverkina kindly provided the height of the Leningrad pot.
[54] Ashmolean Museum AN 1971.894; Vickers (1983a), 36 and 44, fig. 5; (1985a), pl. vi, b.
[55] Münzen und Medaillen (1986), 75, no. 216; Vickers (1990), 616–17, figs. 3–4; Gill (1991), 32.
[56] Kurtz (1988), 146.

FIG. 4.2   Toy silver *hydria*. Ashmolean Museum, Oxford AN 1971.894, Bomford acquisition.

16.5 obols for thirty-two pieces (or just over 15p each).[57] Nor are such prices out of line with the general run, whether or not the pots are decorated by able artisans. Beazley's 'Berlin Painter' has been characterized as one of 'the . . . great pot painters of the early fifth century, arguably [one of] the . . . greatest red-figure artists whose works and careers we can judge'.[58] And yet, three vessels from Vulci bear prices which appear to suggest that the 'Berlin Painter's' work was not as highly—or differentially—valued in antiquity as it is today. An amphora attributed to him/her seems to have cost only 7 obols—equivalent to just over £2, and the same is true of a hydria said to be 'in imitation of' the painter. Another amphora 'near' the 'Berlin Painter' carries a price of 5 obols—equivalent to £1.50.[59] The highest price known for a figured bell-crater (one of the largest shapes) is 4.5 obols[60]—equivalent to £1.35. The degree of skill involved in pot-decoration had no noticeable effect on prices, and it is even the case that some black-glazed pots were more expensive than their decorated counterparts.[61]

George Dennis was the last to repeat d'Hancarville's argument concerning the immense value of Greek painted pottery in antiquity as it stood,[62] but the ground gained was defended with other arguments. Amongst these was J. W. Winckelmann's claim that pottery vessels served as prizes at games;[63] but, as we have already seen, this has no basis in historical fact.[64] In fact, the

[57] Johnston (1979), 250 n. 1, Type 26F, no. 1.
[58] Boardman (1975), 91.
[59] Johnston (1979), 159, Type 10F, no. 21, fig. 12p, nos. 23–4, fig. 9w.
[60] Ibid., Type 14F, no. 5.
[61] Ibid. 63 n. 15.

[62] Dennis (1848), p. lxxxv; (1878) and (1883), p. xcvii; (1907), 1. 64.
[63] Winckelmann (1764), vol. 1, bk. 3, ch. 4, sect. 31; cf. Birch (1858), 220; (1873), 155; Cooper (1981), 29.
[64] See ch. 1.

FIG. 4.3 Attic red-figure pottery *pelike*. Horseman. Ashmolean Museum, Oxford, Loan 399.

FIG. 4.4 Graffito on the underside of the *pelike* in Fig. 4.3. Ashmolean Museum, Oxford, Loan 399.

virtual absence of ancient references to painted pottery[65] has encouraged the creation of modern myths; just as man-made fibres can be highly durable, so too, man-made factoids regarding 'value' have been long-lasting. Thus, H. B. Walters claimed that 'great value seems to have been set upon the painted vases by their possessors'; his evidence being the fact that some were mended.[66] We might as well claim that the bucket discussed at such length by Dear Liza and Dear Henry was an object 'of great value'. And yet, 'mended therefore valuable' is a recurrent motif in works of 'vase' scholarship.[67] So too is the belief that pots were bought by contemporaries for large sums. Walters again set the tone of later assumptions (he was writing before price-inscriptions had been properly studied): 'Of the prices paid for painted vases in ancient times, no positive mention occurs in classical authorities, yet it is most probable that vases of the best class, the products of eminent painters, obtained considerable prices. For works of inferior merit only small sums were paid . . .'. His evidence this time was the fact that Greek pots in recent London sales had realized 'considerable sums'.[68]

Not only have d'Hancarville's underlying assumptions regarding the status of Greek ceramics remained unchallenged until recently, but the practice of rich collectors and dealers employing a learned hack to publish or puff their 'vases' has inevitably meant that the status of the material, and of the craftsmen who produced it, has been exaggerated and that market imperatives have resulted in the suspension of critical judgement on the part of those otherwise best equipped to discuss the question of value.[69] The bureaucratization of the study of Greek ceramics, and the mounting of 'major' exhibitions likewise encourage those involved to inflate the importance of Greek pottery in antiquity, and although most scholars have forgotten d'Hancarville's fraudulent arguments, new points have been brought forward to support his position.

TRADE

To put the question of value into perspective: it appears, on the basis of the most recent research, that in a good year Athens might have imported 190 shiploads of grain,[70] at a cost of upwards of 479 talents (at 5 drachmas per

---

[65] 'Few allusions to [painted vases] can be traced in classical literature': Walters and Birch (1905), 131. In an earlier edition, Birch had cited imaginary literary references to decorated pottery: Birch (1873), 156; cf. Richter (1923), 86–105.

[66] Walters and Birch (1905), 147; cf. Birch (1858), 220; (1873), 156.

[67] e.g. A. S. Murray (1892), 72; Johnston (1979), 65 n. 6: 'Repairs to vases were frequent and sometimes elaborate . . . it is possible that even repaired vases could fetch a worthwhile price'; ibid. 242: 'Cups were repaired more often and more elabo-

rately than other shapes, indicating their value'; Brunn (1988), 14.

[68] Walters and Birch (1905), 43; Gill (1988c), 740; cf. Reitlinger (1961–70), 2. 369–73.

[69] Cf. n. 5, above on the close links between the art market and the study of Greek ceramics. See too, Boardman (1980b), and note that Messrs Sotheby's sponsored, in part, the Beazley Centenary celebrations at Oxford; cf. AK 35 (1992), 76; Gill (1993), 455.

[70] Garnsey (1988), 105 estimates that Athens normally imported 230 kg. of grain per annum for

medimnos),[71] some 12½ tonnes of silver. If these imports were paid for with Attic red-figure bell-craters (among the largest pots) costing 4.5 obols apiece, some 2,589,189 such vessels would have been required per annum. If, moreover, we take account of those commercial graffiti found on Attic red-figure bell-craters which include lists of pots of different sizes,[72] and compare the prices given for such batches with the cost of a single ship-load of grain, the figures are even more telling. The cost per set (between fifty-eight and ninety-six pots) was approximately 5.5 drachmas. At the rate of 5 drachmas per *medimnos*, the value of a shipment of wheat (of 3,000 *medimnoi*) would have been the equivalent of *c.*3,000 sets, or up to more than a quarter of a million pots. The annual requirement at this rate would have approached 50 million—or 5 billion for the fifth century, which is unlikely.

Comparing values per cubic metre of shipped goods, wheat at 5 drachmas per *medimnos*[73] was worth 95 drachmas whereas sets of pots of the kind under discussion would have been worth only 42 drachmas. Such exchange rates between painted pots and bulk cereals do not sit happily with the view that Athenian painted pottery was an extremely valuable commodity.[74] But it is unlikely that Athenians were producing pots at such rates, and it is perhaps more realistic to think of the Athenians paying for imported raw materials with silver.

A story preserved on a papyrus of the eleventh century BC gives us a rare glimpse into Mediterranean trade at an earlier period than that with which we are principally concerned. It concerns the voyage of Wen-Amun from Egypt to Phoenicia to buy timber. One of Wen-Amun's shipmates had run away, having stolen the goods that were to be used as payment. These consisted of 'one [vessel] of gold [amounting] to 5 *deben*, four jars of silver, amounting to 20 *deben*, and a sack of 11 *deben* of silver. [Total of what] he [stole]: 5 *deben* of gold and 31 *deben* of silver.'[75] Here we have vessels of precious metal used as trading items (vessels made up, it is worth noting, in round figures in a standard weight), as well as silver bullion probably made up in the form of ingots or wire rings, used as currency before coinage.[76] At the rates of exchange employed in Chapter 2, the total value of the gold and silver was the equivalent of £4,000. If a similar pattern of trade was conducted in historical times between, say, Athens and Etruria, plate would have constituted the principal trading commodity (and such a trading pattern would account for the relative lack of coinage in North Italy until a

---

some 100,000 people (= 23,000 tonnes). A grain ship might carry 3,000 *medimnoi* (Casson (1971), 182–3) or 120 tonnes; 23,000/120 = 191.6 ships.

[71] 1 *medimnos* = 52.53 litres.
[72] Amyx (1958), 289–92; Johnston (1979), Type 14F, nos. 3–4.
[73] One of the lowest prices recorded: Pritchett (1956), 196–8.

[74] For an earlier objection to the conventional view, see R. M. Cook (1959).
[75] Pritchard (1969), 17.
[76] Dalley (1984), 67; cf. Sherratt and Sherratt (1993) on the relatively slight difference between 'pre-monetary' and 'monetary' economies in antiquity.

comparatively late date).[77] That trade was indeed carried on in this way in historical times is borne out by the stele set up at the Greek trading-post at Naucratis in 380 BC by the pharaoh Nektanebis I, who imposed a tax of 10 per cent on both 'the gold and the silver, of the timber and the worked wood, and of everything which comes from the Greek Sea' and 'the gold and silver and of all things which are produced in . . . Naukratis'.[78] The role of Naucratis in archaic times was doubtless similar.

It is being more widely recognized among archaeologists that the movement of pottery by sea was a by-product of trade in staples and other important commodities.[79] Shipwrecks suggest that maritime trade often included the long-distance movement of commodities that were of no great value in themselves but were worth transporting if more valuable goods had to travel in the same, or even opposite, direction. Thus the archaeological evidence would suggest that consignments of pottery were carried amidst the main cargo as a 'saleable ballast'.[80] The black-glaze pottery known as Campana A provides a useful parallel: 'Recent work on shipwrecks suggests that pottery of this kind was never the principal cargo, but that it could be added as ballast or simply as an extra commodity, and that therefore its distribution was essentially costless.' The widespread distribution of Campana A is seen as a visible sign of the mercantile prosperity of Campania in the first half of the second century BC, and as evidence of 'the amazing growth in production and investment' in the area at the time.[81] If 'it is of the greatest importance that the production of these forms of pottery can now so clearly be seen to be parasitic upon developed trade',[82] how much more important is it for scholars—and the public at large—to see the prolific output of Corinthian and Athenian pottery in the same light?[83]

A recent analysis of cargoes[84] has shown that pottery, other than transport amphorae, 'may not account for more than about 20 per cent of the recov-

[77] 'Evidently the Etruscans had no need for a continuous supply of coins. Rather, wealthy Etruscans, especially those engaged in sea trade, used the system of barter and exchange, trading Etruscan minerals, wood and worked bronze for foreign luxury goods': Tripp (1986), 203.
[78] Trans. Gunn (1943), 58. Xenophon, too, states that silver was regularly used for trading purposes: *Vect.* 3. 1–2. For the view that silver was not so used, being 'simply wealth', see Boardman (1988*a*), 28.
[79] e.g. Frederiksen (1984), 328–9; cf. Boardman (1987), 293; (1988*a*), 27.
[80] Using the word in the sense of 'space-filler' (cf. Hobhouse (1985), 107–8; Gill (1988*a*), 739). S. McGrail has rightly observed that no ship could in reality be ballasted with pottery (McGrail (1989)). See too Vickers (1984), 90–1; Gill (1987*b*); (1987*c*); (1988*a*); (1988*c*); (1991); cf.

Jörg (1982), 27; Pijl-Ketel (1982); A. J. Parker (1990), 342.
[81] Frederiksen (1984), 328.
[82] Ibid. 343.
[83] Talk of Athenian pottery 'ousting' Corinthian —a commonplace in discussions of Greek mercantile activity—should thus be quietly dropped. Both wares are the lasting, and indestructible, remains of 'developed trade' in more valuable commodities of a kind which brought Sostratus of Aegina so much wealth (60 talents' profit on one voyage in the sixth century): Hdt. 4. 152; Harvey (1976). Sherratt and Sherratt (1993) plausibly argue that the shift in the character of the ceramic record in Italy came about as the result of the inability of the large vessels used for grain transport to pass across the Isthmus of Corinth, and their consequent need to take the route round Cape Malea.
[84] A. J. Parker (1984).

ered cargoes'.[85] At the same time it should be remembered that pottery, because of its durable nature, is easy to detect in difficult water conditions and is thus likely to figure much more prominently in what is recovered from the sea-bed than in what sank down to it two thousand and more years ago. Pottery production may also, as we have just seen, have been stimulated by vigorous trade. Michael Fulford, looking at pottery production in this wider context of Mediterranean trade, observes:

given that the demand for surplus foodstuffs was broad-based, the best way of ensuring a widespread distribution of manufactured goods, such as pottery, was to ship them alongside foodstuffs. It is then perhaps not surprising to find the major potteries within traditionally fertile regions with access (by sea) to wide markets. In the case of Italy the most important sources of pottery—Etruria (Arretine, wine amphorae), Campania (black-glazed ware, cooking wares and wine amphorae)—correspond with the most important agricultural regions, renowned for the quality and yields of their cereals.[86]

If we take the example of pottery production at Athens, its export could be equally secondary to major export items such as oil, and especially to the shipping of silver from Laurium. Indeed, Attic pots have been found alongside a consignment of silver ingots and nuggets on the Porticello shipwreck.[87] It is important to remember that trade was two-way. An area like Etruria may have been receiving Greek pots, not because the Etruscans 'were apparently enthusiastic students of Greek mythology',[88] but because the trade mirrored in part the export from Italy of gold and bronze,[89] and of pig-iron produced on the Etruscan mainland from ore mined on Elba.[90] These commodities were presumably effectively paid for with objects of real value, not with pottery.[91]

It is salutary to reflect in this context on the figures relating to goods carried on East Indiamen during the eighteenth century. The statistics for the sales of the East India Company in London between March 1786 and

[85] Fulford (1987), 61.
[86] Ibid. 69.
[87] Eiseman (1979a); (1979b); (1980).
[88] Shapiro (1981b), 10.
[89] Crit. ap. Ath. 1.28b–c; for an Etruscan tripod at Athens: see Savignoni (1897), 277–8; for exports of Etruscan bronze vessels as far afield as Syria: Weber (1990).
[90] Vickers (1985–6), 165; Gill (1987b). For an important, more recent, parallel for this pattern, see Tognarini (1980). It is, however, highly unlikely that 'i materiali etrusco "di ritorno" per i mercanti greci fu ezzenzialmente il bucchero' (Martelli (1985), 177); still less that 'Athenian decorated pottery . . . was as valuable and profitable a trade commodity as most that any classical ship took on board' (Boardman (1988a), 33; cf. Gill (1988c); (1991)). Even a cargo of 4,000 amphoras of oil

(which cost 36 drachmas per metretes: Arist. Oec. 2. 2. 7) would have been worth 18 talents; a cargo of 3,000 medimnoi of grain (at 5 drachmas the medimnos) would have cost 2.5 talents: twice as much as the estimated value of a cargo of decorated pottery (see p. 89, above).
[91] Cf. Garnsey (1988), 110: 'the point to be stressed is the implausibility of the suggestion that fine pottery was an exchange item for grain'; Osborne (1987a), 109: 'Despite the millions of pots made in and exported from Athens . . . pottery can never have made a significant mark on the Athenian economy'; Finley (1985), 23: 'other ceramic goods—table ware, cooking vessels, lamps—also shipped in large quantities, were "parasitic" on the containers and their contents in their occupation of shipping space'; Hopkins (1983), p. xxiv: 'pots . . . were only a minor item in gross product'.

September 1789, detailing trade in textiles, wooden products, and other items, reveal not only that ceramic would have constituted the only non-perishable commodity, but that its value as a proportion of total trade would have been minimal. It does not even figure as a separate item, but is listed in a category which included 'chinaware, drugs and coffee'. The proportion of total sales represented by this category in 1786 was 1.8 per cent, in 1787, 2.6 per cent, in 1788, 2.2 per cent, and in 1789, 1.6 per cent.[92] Only the ceramics will have survived in any quantity two centuries later.

Similarly, the economic importance of the Italian maiolica industry should not be exaggerated. Although pottery production was the mainstay of a few small townships and one middle-sized city, Faenza, 'ceramics constituted a mere sliver in the overall economic pie of Renaissance Italy'.[93] Nor was pottery production a passport to high social status. Even in Faenza ceramic production was deemed a 'vile' profession, and only two potters ever made it to the ruling élite.[94] And the same picture emerges wherever one looks. Potters in general have belonged to the 'lower echelons of society';[95] it is unlikely that things were different in classical Greece.

LUXURY

In the light of such evidence, it should be clear why it is no longer possible to maintain that the trade in painted pottery was a 'luxury trade'. That such a concept existed at all is the result of a change in the meaning of the word 'luxury' since antiquity. For the ancients, τρυφή, *luxus* applied to high living, and that alone, but more recently 'luxury' has come to mean 'something desirable but not indispensable'[96] and has little to do with what the ancients regarded as luxury. Eratosthenes neatly distinguishes luxurious practice from what was not, in describing how some men had once set up a clay wine-crater to honour the gods, and 'not one made from silver, nor one set with jewels'.[97] Silver and jewels belong within the range of 'luxury' in the ancient sense, and clay clearly belongs in another category.

The question of luxury has usually been approached from the standpoint of the lowest-paid worker. Since jurymen received 3 obols per day (but only when cases were tried) this has been regarded as a subsistence wage. Accordingly, a pot which cost more than 3 obols was a 'luxury,' and so it might be in the 'recent' sense of the word. If, however, we recall what passed for

---

[92] Calculated from the figures given in Kathirithamby-Wells (1977), 220.

[93] Goldthwaite (1989), 14.

[94] Marsilli (1982), 164; Goldthwaite (1989), 14.

[95] Peacock (1982), 7; cf. Richter (1923), 105: 'Potters had, it is true, no social status'.

[96] *OED*, s.v. Luxury 5b: 'in recent use' (the

entries for L were prepared in 1900–3). It is in this sense that Hasebroek (1933), 51 employs the word in his influential work; followed by e.g. Cartledge (1983), 4, 14; Boardman (1988*a*), 28.

[97] Ath. 11. 482a–b. For peacock-raising as another example of τρυφή, see Miller (1989).

respectable gentility in classical times,[98] then painted pottery would not have figured large in popular estimation.

If this picture is broadly correct, then it would be difficult to maintain that even painted pottery was a 'luxury' or that it ever constituted a major trading item. Real luxuries, such as silver vessels decorated in gold-figure, would have been priced in *minae*. Such vessels will have influenced the infinitely cheaper red-figure pottery made at Athens, which was exported to Etruria for aristocrats to place in their tombs. But such Etruscans, as we have seen, seem not only to have used plate for dining,[99] but to have exported gold *phialai* to Athens.[100]

VALUE, AND THE STATUS OF POTTERS

D'Hancarville's position is often defended today with the dedications supposedly made by prosperous potters on the Athenian Acropolis. Thus, potters apparently had 'extra disposable income' with which they 'made dedications on the Acropolis frequently enough so that as an identifiable class of dedicators they outnumber all others'.[101] But this can only work if (1) it can be shown beyond doubt that the Acropolis dedications do refer to potters and (2) it is reasonable to expect that the only persons from the deme Kerameis to have made such dedications were potters.

It is true that several dedications bear names which also occur on Athenian pottery, apparently as craftsmen. These names have consequently been claimed as those of potters and painters.[102] But this assumption is far from secure, and Beazley was surely right in his cautious approach to the Acropolis dedications, of some of which he wrote, 'as none of the identifications are certain and some of them are improbable I relegate them to a footnote.'[103] T. B. L. Webster was similarly hesitant, as 'without the description *kerameus* it is difficult to be certain whether the dedicator is a potter or not.'[104]

Even the remaining 'certain' dedications are far from secure. Although Nearchos' dedication of a *kore* by Antenor is often quoted as the most important of the potters' dedications,[105] the crucial words ὁ κεραμεύς are not present on the extant inscription; they have been supplied because it was assumed that this was the Nearchos known from decorated pottery. A suggestion that the gap could be filled by, for example, Ἐλευθερεύς[106] was initially met with scepticism,[107] but the latest epigraphical judgement is that

[98] See pp. 38–43, above.
[99] Diod. 5. 40; cf. Vickers (1985–6), 165.
[100] Crit. *ap.* Ath. 1. 28b.; cf. what appears to be a gold *phiale* in the hand of a banqueter on a fresco in the Tomba degli Auguri at Tarquinia (Coarelli (1975), 191). See too, pp. 172–4, below.
[101] Boegehold (1985), 28; cf. Johnston (1979), 35; Paul (1982), 70; Boardman (1987), 293.
[102] For example, Raubitschek (1949).
[103] Beazley (1944), 105.
[104] Webster (1972), 5.
[105] Boardman (1974), 12; (1978), fig. 141; Boegehold (1985), 28, fig. 4.
[106] Vickers (1985a), 125 n. 162.
[107] Johnston (1985), 182, followed by Boardman (1987), 293 n. 30.

'the Nearchos base cannot be said with any conviction to be that of a potter.'[108] Any argument that potters 'must' have been wealthy is thus seriously weakened.

A further supposedly 'certain' dedication by a potter is a relief showing a seated figure holding cups dedicated as a tithe.[109] It was assumed that the cups were of clay and that the dedicator was a potter, and Beazley restored the name Pampha]ios.[110] Earlier doubts that this was a potter's dedication[111] have received support from A. W. Johnston, who considers the restored reading 'even more dubious' than that of Nearchos.[112] Other dedications, namely those of Peikon[113] and of Mnesiades and Andocides,[114] include κεραμεύς without the definite article. There is also a fragmentary dedication by a Euphronios[115] in which Raubitschek supplied ὁ to join κεραμεύς. However, the space on the preceding line could be filled instead with a patronymic,[116] and to argue that such reservations are unnecessary because a Euphronios is known in the modern literature as a potter is to come dangerously close to circularity.

Such an argument would also overlook evidence which suggests that the word κεραμεύς might identify the deme rather than the trade ('Mr X from Potters Bar', as it were, rather than 'Mr X the potter'), in which case any argument on such a basis would be futile.[117] ἐκ Κεραμέων was epigraphically interchangeable with Κεραμεύς,[118] and on ostraca the aristocratic Leagros, son of Glaukon, was described as Κεραμεύς.[119] A. W. Johnston agrees that 'there is in fact much to be said' for the argument that *kerameus* might be demotic,[120] but we disagree with his attempt to rescue something of the old view in maintaining that any individuals known from inscriptions on pottery and from the deme Kerameis must be potters. This both assumes that only one person called Mnesiades came from Kerameis, and denies the possibility that potters might have come from other demes as well (some came from Kollytos).[121] There is no unambiguous evidence even for the view

[108] Johnston (1988), 135, 140 n. 56 (where τοῦ δεῖνα ὑ]ύς is proposed).

[109] Raubitschek (1949), no. 70.

[110] Beazley (1944), 104; cf. Boardman (1978), fig. 137. Paul (1982), 70 tentatively restores 'Euphron]ios'. Boardman now accepts that the dedicator may have been a metalworker ((1988c), pl. 173).

[111] Vickers (1985a), 125.

[112] Johnston (1988), 135.

[113] Raubitschek (1949), no. 44.

[114] Ibid., no. 178. *Kerameus* is linked to [M]nesiades and need not be associated with Andocides.

[115] Ibid., no. 225.

[116] For instances of demotic or ethnic + patronymic, see ibid., no. 135).

[117] Vickers (1985), 124–5; cf. Vitelli (1992), 552–3.

[118] Thus, a certain Protonikos is described in separate inscriptions as *ek Kerameon* and *Kerameus*: (Πρωτόνικος ἐκ Κεραμέων Ἐπιχάρος: IG 1³, 278. 1; Πρωτ[όνικος] Κερ[αμε]ύς: IG 1³, 465. 123–4. In both cases it is his demotic status which is in question, not his trade.

[119] Willemsen (1968), 29; cf. Vickers (1985a), 124–5. Johnston (1988), 135 seems to be unaware of this: 'we would surely have expected the form *kerameus*... to have appeared here and there in the reasonable number of *ostraka* against Leagros of that deme'. For what can be known of the *vita* of Leagros, see Francis and Vickers (1981).

[120] Johnston (1988), 135.

[121] Raubitschek (1949), 239, under no. 209. Other 'certain' dedications (ibid., nos. 92, 150, 209) have been restored with κεραμεύς; they could equally well be restored with a demotic such as Μελιτεύς.

that 'some potters did accede to modest wealth, and that is a measure, however unsatisfactory, of the financial success, if not social status, of the members of the Athenian Kerameikos.'[122] Potters clearly made a living (compare the Yiddish proverb, 'von Dreck kann man a Leben machen'), but this is a world away from seeing 'celebrated sculptors like Endoios and Antenor receiving commissions from the great and prosperous potters'[123]— a scenario that must now be discarded.

THE WORTHY POTTER

It is a well-kept secret that the status of the craftsman in classical Greece was low, and that of the potter lower still. 'It does not necessarily follow that we esteem the workman because we are pleased with the work,' says Plutarch, having stated that 'no well-born youth, having seen the Zeus at Olympia, would wish to be a Phidias'.[124] The rise of the craftsman is a modern phenomenon: Rousseau's *Émile: ou de l'éducation* (1762) was again a seminal work, in that the well-born hero is taught by actually making something.[125] Plutarch's position is the same as that of Herodotus:

Whether the Greeks borrowed from the Egyptians their notions of trade, like so many others, I cannot say for certain. I have remarked that the Thracians, the Scyths, the Persians, the Lydians, and almost all other barbarians, hold the citizens who practise trades, and their children, in less repute than the rest, while they esteem as noble those who keep aloof from handicrafts, and especially honour such as are given wholly to war. These ideals prevail throughout the whole of Greece, particularly among the Lacedaemonians. Corinth is the place where craftsmen are least despised.[126]

Although the proverbial dismissal of the 'wealth of a potter' as something 'cracked, unsound and easily broken'[127] may well have had its origin at a period in Greek history later than the fifth century, potters seem then to have been held in generally low esteem.[128] A simple contrast serves to indicate that their products were not especially highly regarded. In discussing the nature of surpluses of various commodities, Xenophon noted that nobody ever 'had so much plate as not to desire an increase of it; and if people have a superabundance, they hoard it, and are not less delighted with doing so than with putting it to use'.[129] Aristophanes' Dicaeopolis, by

---

[122] Johnston (1988), 135–6.

[123] Beazley (1944), 107.

[124] Plut. *Per.* 2. 1.

[125] Cf. Mellor (1950).

[126] Hdt. 2. 167. Cf. Schlaifer (1936 (1960)), 175 (103): 'and if there was disdain at Corinth, there must have been contempt elsewhere'.

[127] Diogenian. 5. 97; cf. 5. 98: 'A potter: what is unsound'. For Near Eastern views, cf. Vitto (1986), 61 (citing an Egyptian source): '[The potter's] life is that of an animal. Dirt besmears him more than a pig'; Ecclesiasticus 22 : 7: 'Whoso teacheth a fool is as one that glueth potsherds together.'

[128] Ehrenberg (1951), 125; cf. Wittkower (1963), 4; Finley (1985), 136–40; de Ste Croix (1981), 274–5; Robertson (1985), 26. Contrast Boegehold (1988), 27–31; Boardman (1987), 293–4.

[129] Xen. *Vect.* 4. 7.

contrast, is unable to persuade a Theban merchant to accept pottery at all in exchange for his merchandise, and the packaging of a political informer like a pot is a vehicle for much comic humour.[130]

Then a story told by Plutarch about Agathocles, tyrant of Syracuse 317–289 BC, relates how he was the

son of a potter, but becoming the chief man of Sicily, and being made king, he was in the habit of putting drinking-cups of pottery next to those of gold, and showing them to the young men would say that 'those were what I used to make, but these are what I make now thanks to my diligence and bravery'.[131]

It would be difficult to conclude from this that the ceramic art was especially highly regarded, and impossible to do so from Justin's epitome of Pompeius Trogus:

Agathocles, tyrant of Sicily, who attained greatness equal to that of the elder Dionysius, rose to royal dignity from the lowest and meanest origin. He was born in Sicily, his father being a potter, and spent a youth not more honourable than his birth; for, being remarkable for beauty and gracefulness of person, he supported himself a considerable time by submitting to the infamous lust of others. When he had passed the years of puberty, he transferred his services from men to women.[132]

All that can be gleaned from these accounts is that to be a potter was not a praiseworthy calling—on a par with rent-boys; indeed, 'rough trade' seems to have been a step up from 'vile profession'.[133] In modern times, moreover, the ethnographic record shows that most traditional potters regard themselves as successful when they can afford to give up potting and become farmers on their own land.[134]

Nevertheless, potters and their products might occasionally be mentioned positively. Once again, however, there is insufficient evidence for the exaggerated claims for high status that are still sometimes made. Thus, Kittos and Bakchios, sons of Bakchios, have been regarded as high-status Athenian potters,[135] and are thought to have made the containers for the prize oil at the Panathenaic games.[136] They appear on a decree at Ephesus where they 'made a hydria for the goddess and black tiles [or pots] for the city', and were granted temporary citizenship.[137] While some individuals are given full citizenship, the potters are only granted citizens' rights for as long as they remain at Ephesus.[138] Bakchios and Kittos have also been seen as the sons

[130] Ar. *Ach.* 900–58.
[131] Plut. *Mor.* 176e.
[132] Justin. 22. 1.
[133] Cf. Hsch. s.v. Κεραμεικός· ἔνθα οἱ πόρνοι προεστήκεσαν/ 'The Ceramicus: where the rent-boys ply their trade'. For another view of Agathocles' career, see Boardman (1987), 293.
[134] Vitelli (1992), 552.
[135] Robertson (1985), 21–2; cf. Boardman

(1987), 293–4. For Kittos the goldsmith or gilder (χρυσοτής) and Kittos the bronzesmith (χαλκεύς): Harris (1988), 331 n.3.
[136] Frel (1973), 21–2.
[137] Engelmann (1980), nos. 1418–22, Block I.
[138] Gauthier (1985), 150–1 n. 48 *bis*, draws attention to the threat implied in this 'exemple curieux de *politeia* potentielle.'

of [Bak]ch[ios] son of [A]mphis . . . ἐκ Κεραμέων, on whose tombstone is written: 'Of those who blend earth, water, fire into one by τέχνη ('art' or 'skill'), Bakchios was judged by all Hellas first, for natural gifts; and in every contest appointed by the city he won the crown.'[139] It has been maintained that this epitaph shows that 'Bakchios was clearly not a poor man exercising a poor and despised craft',[140] but poverty is not the point at issue, and allowance should be made both for the fact that the tombstone was set up by his heirs, perhaps potters themselves, and for the likelihood that 'contests' were the usual way for a community to put out to tender orders for a particular commodity.

It goes without saying that ceramics are 'useful,' whether at the level of Winnie-the-Pooh's 'Useful Pot for Putting Things In', or of Josiah Wedgwood's 'Usefull Works', and the Athenian tyrant Critias was aware of the high quality of Athens' wares: 'And she that raised the glorious trophy at Marathon invented the potter's wheel and the child of clay and the oven, noblest pottery, useful in housekeeping (χρήσιμον οἰκονόμον).'[141] But pottery was self-evidently useful for household purposes, and it is usual to find coarse wares in quantity excavated from domestic sites. It is these 'useful' pots used for cooking, storage, and other domestic functions to which Critias may have referred,[142] for all that Athens seems to have 'imported certain cooking pots during the 6th to 4th centuries'.[143] The confiscated properties of the Hermocopidae (in whose activities Critias was implicated) included substantial quantities of coarse pottery.[144] Critias' lines therefore do not provide enough support for the high status of the Athenian ceramics industry or its practitioners; his reference a few lines earlier to an Etruscan gold *phiale*, however, does show a fifth-century Athenian aristocrat's familiarity with gold plate.[145] But, as Karen Vitelli notes, 'an acknowledged master potter may have standing among fellow potters, may even command higher prices, and still be only a potter as far as the larger society is concerned.'[146]

ARTISTIC RIVALRY

At this stage in the discussion, another influential view requires attention, namely, that potters and pot-painters engaged in artistic rivalry. The ultimate source of the idea is probably Hesiod's 'potter is jealous of potter, and carpenter of carpenter; beggar begrudges beggar, and poet poet'.[147] But the key text so far as modern scholarship is concerned in fact turns out to be illusory, and cannot bear the fanciful interpretations that have been placed

[139] *IG* 2–3², 3.2, no. 6320.
[140] Boardman (1987), 294.
[141] Crit. *ap.* Ath. 1. 28c.
[142] On which see: Sparkes and Talcott (1958); (1970).
[143] R. Jones (1986), 726.
[144] Amyx (1958), 163–307.
[145] Crit. *ap.* Ath. 1. 28b.
[146] Vitelli (1992), 552.
[147] Hes. *Op.* 25–6; Pl. *Lys.* 215c; Arist. *Rhet.* 2. 4. 21; *Polit.* 1312b; cf. Schnapp (1990), 2.

upon it. This is an inscription on the back of an amphora in Munich which has traditionally been translated as '[Painted] as Euphronios never could',[148] and (since Euphronios is also the name of a now-famous pot-painter) variously interpreted as a 'boast' and thus a 'general challenge to a rival—friendly or hostile';[149] as an indication 'that these vase-painters were consciously experimenting and innovating, that they felt themselves as pioneers and not merely as imitators of leads given in the minor arts';[150] or as an introduction 'to an atmosphere of Left Bank rivalry'[151] within an artistic milieu described as follows:

It is as though, for the first time in the history of Western art, we can here discern a conscious movement, a camaraderie of artists. Since we know no more about them than we can learn from their vases, with not a scrap of help from any ancient writer, the reconstruction of their careers, common purpose, even rivalries, can be taken as a triumph of archaeological research, though there are many archaeologists who might not recognise it as such.[152]

It has, however, now been recognized that the crucial inscription, far from continuing '*Euthymides egrapsen*' on the front, is part of a self-contained sympotic dialogue.[153] Next to the komast on the left appears: 'Leader of the komasts as never was Euphronios' (κόμαρχος ὁς οὐδέποτε Εὐφρόνιος (and thus bearing no necessary connection with a pot-painter of the same name)). Elsewhere: 'Good! It [sc. the *kantharos*] is already mine' (εὖ, ἤδη'μός) and 'You've done it! Lead! Drink!' (τελῆς, ἔγεο, πί) or 'You've done it. You are the true [sc. komarch]. So drink!' (τελεῖς, εἰ γε, ὦ πῖ). If this reading is valid, then it raises serious questions regarding the supposed artistic rivalry in the 'potters' quarter' at Athens. Potters may well have bickered, Hesiodically,[154] but that is not quite the same as a 'camaraderie of artists'; and whether or not they did, the inscription on the Munich pot is irrelevant.

THE STATUS OF METALWORKERS

We are rather better informed about the world of the metalworker in antiquity than that of the potter. Bronze was a material that had many practical uses, whether for armour or for hardware in general. During the Aegean Bronze Age, the production of sheet bronzework for vessels and armour was

---

[148] The *Euthymedes egrapsen* inscription on the front of the pot is often taken as running into the inscription on the back; e.g. Paul (1982), 39; Scheibler (1983), 110–15; Boegehold (1988), 31; Schnapp (1990), 2–3. It is sometimes even taken as continuous: 'Euthymides adds after his own signature . . . "Euphronios never did as well as this"': Wright (1923), 105.

[149] Richter (1946), 55; cf. Buschor (1914), 152; Richter (1923), 105; Beazley (1944), 107–8; Rosati (1974), 195; (1976–7), 56–7; Boegehold (1988),

31; Cohen (1991), 64, 90 n. 86; Denoyelle (1992b), 58; cf. Gollan (1982), 6.

[150] Robertson (1975), 224–5.

[151] Boardman (1975), 30.

[152] Ibid. 29.

[153] Engelmann (1987), 129–34; S. Morris (1986), 360; cf. Neumann (1977), 39–41; Linfert (1977), 19–22. For other sympotic dialogues: Lissarague (1987), 59–64, 80.

[154] Cf. Vitelli (1992), 552.

restricted to palace workshops,[155] but by the fifth century BC, we hear of entrepreneurs setting up factories at Athens: Cephalus, who was the father of Lysias the orator, was a wealthy shield-maker of Syracuse, and was persuaded to move to Athens by Pericles.[156] And a *chalkopoles* was wealthy enough to serve as a *choregus* in 403,[157] an occasion which was remarkable for the splendour of the performance.[158] 'Generally high prices'—between 30 and 80 drachmas—were paid even for second-hand bronze vessels in 415,[159] and a bronze hydria 'of great value' is mentioned in a lawsuit of the fourth century.[160] Elsewhere we hear of a bronze stand (an item of which the poor had 'one of wood; the rich of bronze or silver')[161] that was in dispute in another court case: 'I should not be so concerned about the vessel-stand itself, for it is not worth 30 drachmas,' says the speaker. But that its value was not negligible is clear from the fact that in the previous year he had 'wished to have it repaired, and sent it to the bronze foundry; for it [was] made up of different parts, as it [had] the faces of satyrs, and heads of bulls worked on it . . . [and] the same manufacturer makes many articles of furniture in the same or similar style'.[162]

The value of a bronze vessel was thus considerably greater than that of a painted pot, but a lot less than that of a silver vessel of equivalent weight. The ratio of the value of unworked bronze to silver was in the order of $100 : 1$,[163] while that of bronze to gold was greater still: in the order of $1,000 : 1$, or higher.[164] Bronze might still be placed in the grave without running the risk of major impoverishment; the metal in the Vix crater, well used at the time of disposal, was worth little more than 4 *minae*.[165] But although on one occasion we hear of body-strippers after a battle paying 'little attention to bronze or iron, so great was the abundance of silver or gold',[166] this was unusual, and scavengers would have found bronze—unlike pottery—eminently recyclable. Ancient recycling practices provide an object-lesson to our own throw-away society.[167] In Rome we hear of a trade even in glass fragments,[168] but broken pottery was usually expendable, as whole

[155] Sherratt and Taylor (1989), 107–8.
[156] Lys. 12. 4.
[157] Edmundson (1982), who estimates (50 n. 12) that the expenses could have amounted to around half a talent.
[158] Plut. *Mor.* 349f.
[159] Amyx (1958), 199.
[160] [Dem.] 47. 52.
[161] Ath. 5. 210c.
[162] Lys. *ap.* Ath. 5. 209.
[163] Price (1968).
[164] Lewis (1968).
[165] The Vix crater weighs 208.6 kg. (Joffroy (1954), 6)—almost exactly 8 Attic talents, the melt value of which would have been *c.*435 drachmas.
[166] Plut. *Tim.* 29.
[167] Scavenging is rarely discussed; for an excep-

tion, see Crow (1937), 69–70, on the reaction of the street-cleaners of Hongkew during the Japanese war in Shanghai in 1932. They refused to move to a safer part of the settlement, but 'when there was a lull in the Japanese target practice, and it appeared safe to do so, they swarmed out with their brooms and baskets to salvage the rich harvest of empty brass shells and other abandoned articles of modern warfare. This was probably the only opportunity they had ever had to sweep off the streets anything of the least possible value. Ordinarily early risers give the streets a pretty thorough going over and pick on the more important scraps of paper before the street cleaners start to work.'
[168] Pucci (1985), 583.

Mediterranean beaches consisting of ancient pottery fragments,[169] the mounds of sherds at Ostrakine in the Arabian Desert,[170] or Monte Testaccio in Rome[171] attest. The nature of the inscription on the fourth-century grave relief of Sosinas, a *chalkoptes*—(bronze-smelter), suggests that he was, like Lysias' father, a metic. The relief is also indisputable testimony of the relatively respectable status of one who earned his living from metalworking.[172]

The most illustrious metalworkers of whom we hear in the historical and epigraphic sources were artists who won renown for their invention and skilful craftsmanship. Phidias is perhaps the best known—for the huge chryselephantine statues of Zeus and Athena at Olympia and Athens. The battle between Lapiths and Centaurs on the shield of Phidias' earlier bronze Athena Promachos was made by another craftsman, named Mys (the 'Mysian'). The designer was Parrhasius, who regularly collaborated with Mys.[173] Another recorded example of their work was a huge ('Heracliot') cup decorated with the Sack of Troy. It was inscribed 'The design (γραμμά) is by Parrhasius, the work (τέχνα) by Mys.'[174] The inscription on this Heracliot cup is extremely important in that it clearly indicates a division of labour between the two men involved: the one who made the original design, and the one who carried it out. The terms employed are recognizable poetical equivalents of *egrapsen* and *epoiesen*: *gramma* is obvious, and there is but a small difference between *techne* and *poiesis*. The reason for the appearance of signatures at all will have been a combination of several factors: in part, 'the conviction of the uniqueness of artistic creation';[175] in part perhaps a desire to advertise for more custom; and in part, it has been wisely suggested, to serve as a guarantee of the purity of the metal in an age before hallmarks.[176] The silversmith would put his reputation on the line in order to assure his customers of the intrinsic value of the goods they were buying. G. M. A. Richter once observed the transmission of part at least of a silversmith's signature from metalwork to clay on a Calene black-glaze *phiale*: 'It is noteworthy that on some terracotta quadrigae the word ἐπόει appears faintly in relief between the spokes of Dionysus' chariot wheels. Presumably it was part of the signature of the original silver bowl'.[177]

Many gold- and silversmiths will have been slaves, often working for a household, fulfilling its requirements for plate: not surprising given that they were individuals whose artistry could add to the mere bullion value of

---

[169] Tocra in Cyrenaica comes to mind; and cf. Millingen (1822–6), 1, p. vi (quoted p. 25, above).
[170] Hdt. 3. 6.
[171] Rodríguez-Almeida (1984); on the evidentiary importance of Monte Testaccio, 'a monument to ancient consumerism on the grandest scale', see D. J. Mattingly (1988).
[172] Clairmont (1970), 80–2, pl. 8. Part of Demosthenes' inheritance came from sword and

bed factories; we hear of both iron and bronze in connection with the latter: Dem. 27. 9–10.
[173] Paus. 1. 28. 2.
[174] Ath. 11. 782b.
[175] Wittkower (1963), 2.
[176] Dodd (1961), 3; on hallmarks (introduced in *c*.AD 500) see now, Mundell Mango (1986), 13–15.
[177] Richter (1941), 388.

precious metal. Pliny hints at value-enhancement by means of decoration when he laments the

> prodigality of our inventiveness. In how many ways have we raised the prices of objects! The art of drawing (*picturae*) has come in addition, and we have made gold and silver dearer by the art of engraving (*caelandi*) . . . The enticements of the vices have augmented even art. It has pleased us to engrave scenes of licence upon our drinking-cups, and to drink through the midst of obscenities. Afterwards these were flung aside and began to be held of no account, when there was an excess of gold and silver.[178]

Quite what period he is alluding to is uncertain, although the account would fit very well the period before Alexander's conquests, which brought much precious metal to the Mediterranean.

The most expensive slave among the forty-five mentioned in the Hermocopid accounts was a Carian goldsmith, who fetched 360 drachmas at auction (the median price was 157 drachmas).[179] Again the high price will have reflected special skills that could help enhance his owner's public image. In an earlier chapter, we saw how a jobbing silversmith employed to mend a vessel in a shrine on Delos was paid 2 drachmas for his pains, which does not bespeak great wealth or high esteem, even for a free craftsman. And the story of Antiochus Epiphanes escaping from his administrative duties to chat with gold- and silversmiths in their workshops was told in order to illustrate his eccentricity[180] rather than to suggest that craftsmen in precious materials were especially highly honoured. They were presumably, however, higher up the social scale than potters.[181]

It is a curious fact that the relevant status of pottery and metalwork is the exact opposite today of what it was in antiquity. Nowhere is this more apparent than in their respective roles in education. Although the position is rarely expressed in print,[182] the prevalent view has been that metalwork is for the less academically able, while pottery is more suitable for fine minds. This is not the place to consider this in any detail, but it will have been a contributory factor in encouraging the view that pottery—and its study— were somehow more worthy of attention and respect than was metalwork, no matter how accomplished it may have been.

THE FINDSPOTS OF POTTERY

Thanks ultimately to d'Hancarville, it has long been assumed that possession of fine pottery, especially Corinthian or Attic, was a sign of wealth in life,

---

[178] Pliny, *NH* 33.1.4–5.
[179] Meiggs and Lewis (1969), 247.
[180] Ath. 5. 193d.
[181] Cf. Honour (1971), 20, writing in the context of medieval and later goldsmiths: 'The fact that they worked in the very materials of wealth set them apart from all other artists and craftsmen' and 'the goldsmith was the most highly honoured of all artists because he worked in the most precious materials'.
[182] *TES*, 5 July 1930, 308/1, is an exception, speaking of the 'academic limitations' of some of the teachers and pupils involved in metalwork.

as it had been assumed to be in death. It was in the belief that they were the everyday vessels of their social equivalents that '[painted Greek vases were] collected by kings and emperors, lords and ladies, scholars and poets, and business people from America, Europe and the Far East.'[183] The ancient reality was otherwise: those who had incurred the displeasure of the Persian king were made to drink from cups of clay;[184] both Greek and Etruscan aristocracies used plate for dining, as we have seen;[185] scholars were mostly mercenary, charging fees on a scale which bespeaks the use of plate;[186] the Theban neighbour appointed to look after the poet Pindar's possessions during his absence was probably the curator of a choice collection of plate;[187] businessmen did their business in talents and *minae*, and might raise loans on their plate.[188] Such people would have been mystified by an exhibition of pots and bronzes called the *Wealth of the Ancient World*[189] (though fascinated by the Hunts' attempt to corner the world market in silver in the early 1980s).[190]

The archaeological literature is full of statements based on a view of antiquity which accords a high value to painted pottery. Thus R. M. Cook (who is, paradoxically, one of the few to have questioned the supposedly important role of ceramics in trade)[191] believes that 'it should be possible to compare the prosperity of contemporary settlements and sanctuaries by the amount and quality of the pottery found in them, if the finds are representative'.[192] By this token, Delphi was twice as rich as Olympia, since sixteen attributed Attic red-figure sherds are known from the one site, and only eight from the other. Delphi may have been doubly rich, but the ceramic evidence is unlikely to be relevant. More recently, it has been supposed that 'the large quantity of Greek pottery with painted red figures' found at a Scythian site on the Dnieper, 'clearly indicates the wealth of the inhabitants, who were able to afford these costly imported objects'.[193] While such finds may well indicate trade and cultural contacts, the relatively low prices of painted pottery preclude their use as an indicator of wealth.

Similar views can be found in excavation reports of houses and farmhouses. At Athens, for example, 'even the modest dwellings on the Areopagos slope were occupied by men of moderate means, to judge by their contents, which included fine pottery';[194] and a well-fill of a house to the south-west of the Agora 'included fine pottery which shows that the occupants of this

---

[183] Moon (1979), p. xvii.

[184] Ctesias *ap.* Ath. 11. 464a.

[185] See ch. 2.

[186] e.g. Evenus of Paros charged Callias, son of Hipponicus ('a man who spent a world of money on the sophists') 5 *minae*: Pl. *Ap.* 20a–b. When Socrates was accused of stealing an *oinochoe*, we can be sure that it was of silver, not clay: Eup. *PCG* 395; cf. Ar. *PCG* 295.

[187] Pind. *Pyth.* 8. 58; Pindar earned 100 *minae*

for his *Dithyramb for Athens* in the 470s (Isocr. 15. 166).

[188] Cf. Lys. 19. 25–6; Vickers (1984 (1988)).

[189] Tompkins (1983).

[190] Boraiko and Ward (1981).

[191] R. M. Cook (1959).

[192] R. M. Cook (1972), 277.

[193] Rolle and Walls (1989), 122.

[194] Thompson and Wycherley (1972), 182.

modest house were not so poor as one might expect'.[195] In the countryside of Attica, the excavators of the Dema House suggested that the pottery tableware—which included an Attic red-figured bell-crater—indicated 'a typical prosperous Athenian family'.[196] These buildings, however, are not even likely to be complete or provide representative samples of a household's possessions, for—as well as the normal archaeological vagaries of survival and recovery—there is evidence of material being removed from domestic sites. At the Dema House most of the tiles had been taken away, and the 'small finds were scanty, and hardly representative of all the furnishings and possessions one might expect in a house of so considerable a size'.[197] This dismantling of structures is found at both rural[198] and urban[199] sites. Greek homes are often thought of as being rather bare places,[200] but this may be a misapprehension resulting from the nature of the archaeological record.

The appearance of fine decorated pottery at a site is not a simple indicator of wealth (as the old orthodoxy suggests), and this fact is of particular importance to field-survey. If we find the surface remains of structures from which most things of any value have been stripped, then how are we to interpret the remains? Indeed, if the very poor could not afford pottery (and there is evidence for the use of wooden vessels in the countryside),[201] this group will be virtually invisible in the archaeological record that reveals itself in surface-survey.[202] At the other social extreme, a wealthy class using gold, silver, or bronze instead of pottery would again not be visible archaeologically. The ceramic record of surface-survey would be a sample dominated by a social class rich enough to have pots, poor enough not to have better.

By the same token, periods noted for a low level of ceramic imports may actually reflect times of greater prosperity. Michael Fulford thus says of the finds at Carthage: 'Presumably during periods of relatively low ceramic imports of all kinds the social élite had chosen to acquire luxuries which do not register so conspicuously in the archaeological record. Metalware and glass for example, might have been more prevalent than table-ware pottery.'[203] Conversely, periods of high site-density, such as the Middle and Late Roman periods in Greece, are characterized by an increase in the amount of imported fine wares (for example, Çandarlı, African Red Slip, and Phocaean); this may not be a sign of prosperity but rather of high taxation—partly in kind—which would encourage increased exploitation of the landscape and export of staples.[204]

---

[195] Ibid. 174.

[196] J. E. Jones, Sackett, and Graham (1962), 100; cf. Osborne (1985), 190.

[197] J. E. Jones, Sackett, and Graham (1962), 83, 101 n. 26.

[198] e.g. J. E. Jones, Sackett, and Graham (1973), 360.

[199] e.g. Young (1951), 195.

[200] e.g. Pritchett (1956), 212; Wycherley (1978), 245.

[201] e.g. Ath. 11. 495a.

[202] In fact, wooden vessels only survive, exceptionally, in waterlogged conditions: Wasowicz (1966); Vaulina and Wasowicz (1974); Pinelli and Wasowicz (1986) 129–31, 139–53.

[203] Fulford (1983), 12.

[204] Mee et al. (1991).

Finally, there is, or should be, a major problem arising from the fact that 'the best' Athenian pottery is found in Italy, while that found in Attica is regarded by all as generally inferior.[205] Miss Richter once made the point unambiguously:

It is a fact which must strike the most casual observer that, speaking generally, the exported ware, now stored in foreign museums, is of higher excellence than the vessels which remained in Attica itself. The majority of the vases in the Athens Museum are of careless, swift execution, and, in this respect, compare unfavorably with the Etruscan finds, on which the Attic potter seems to have lavished all his skill and loving care. It may seem to us curious that the Greeks, who were known for their inborn good taste, should have been satisfied with inferior goods, while they sent their best work to a people who could hardly appreciate with the same fullness the exquisite beauty and finish of the articles they imported in such quantities.[206]

T. B. L. Webster made a valiant attempt to tackle the question by proposing that sets of pottery would be specially ordered for aristocratic symposia at Athens, and then sold to middlemen who would export the second-hand pots to Etruria.[207] That few have followed Webster has done nothing to remove the problem. Metalwork does, however, help to resolve it. If we can see both Etruscan and Athenian élites using fine gold- and silverware in life, and passing it on to their heirs when they died, and the pots in their tombs used simply to provide the appearance of a respectable funeral without the expense, then the problem goes away. Standards will have been set in the world of élite craftsmen working in nobler, and far more expensive, materials for the richest inhabitants of the city. Potters and pot-painters will have simply followed prevailing fashions, and in doing so will have acted as have many potters in many societies. The case for this will be argued in the following chapters.

A problem which now requires further research, but which is beyond the limits of this book, is to identify quite who at Athens might have used painted pottery. At a guess, the hoplite class might have used silver and bronze (they could, after all, afford to buy their own armour),[208] and the carelessly, swiftly, executed pots found in Attica, if used in life at all, were for the urban proletariat, and wooden bowls and platters for the very poor. Even in an industrial site such as Laurium, there was a great deal of black-gloss pottery in use,[209] though quite who may have used it—the slaves or the managers—is uncertain. Pliny observed that in his day, 'the greater part of mankind uses earthenware vases',[210] and this was also doubtless the case a few centuries earlier. This, however, is far from seeing fine pottery on the tables of the leaders of fashion.

---

[205] Hemelrijk (1985) estimates that 90% of fine Athenian pottery comes from Etruscan tombs. The only major exceptions are dedications at sanctuaries (e.g. the Acropolis and Brauron).
[206] Richter (1904–5), 237.

[207] Webster (1972), p. xiii.
[208] 'The richer citizens who had their own arms': Pope (1988), 293 n. 45.
[209] J. E. Jones (1984–5), 122.
[210] Pliny, NH 35. 46.

5 The Influence of Precious Materials on Greek Painted Pottery

THUS far, we have argued that the high status of ceramic and of its makers is a relatively modern development; that it has its roots in part in Utopian philosophies, in part in the challenge to traditional material values presented by the Enlightenment, and in part in the belief fostered by the Arts and Crafts Movement that 'a potter must be an artist'.[1] There is no evidence for any of these ideas having existed in classical Greece, and the fact that there is still a widespread belief that they did is the result of a back-projection of more recent philosophies. So too are the notions that painted pottery was a commodity of immense value in antiquity, that the fine ceramic vases found in Etruscan tombs were the objects used in aristocratic symposia—whether in Greece or in Italy—and that some of the greatest artists of the day were engaged in their decoration.[2]

What role did ceramic therefore play in antiquity? It goes without saying that it had manifold and manifest uses: for tiles, drainage pipes, storage jars, cooking-pots, for the containers used in the long-distance trade of oil, wine, honey, and other foodstuffs. The social and economic role of such items is straightforward and unambivalent. It is the social, economic—and artistic—role of the fine wares, of Attic black- and red-figure pottery, with which we are concerned in this chapter and the next. Were the shapes of Greek pottery arrived at 'through the labours of independent artists using new technical knowledge with the pure objective of making beautiful things',[3] and by craftsmen working in the medium of clay alone? Does its decoration justify the attention still paid, in some quarters, to niceties of style so that it can be said whether 'painter A' or 'painter B' held the brush?[4] Is this decoration

---

[1] Leach (1961), 7.
[2] See Chapter 6 for further discussion of some of these issues.
[3] Caiger-Smith (1973), 191.
[4] Cf. Osborne (1991), 255–6: 'The tyranny of the artist over the study of Greek painted pottery has been close to absolute, with the greatest scholarly reputation being attached to those who could most infallibly convince colleagues that their iden-
tifications of an individual hand were correct.' The study of Greek ceramics was, moreover, 'a field for the exercise of a privileged form of scholarship, from which . . . profane persons must be excluded by a kind of academic class distinction': W. B. Honey, in Lane (1963), p. ix. For Bruneau (1975), 451: 'le souci de l'attribution stérilise depuis des décennies l'étude de la céramique attique'.

the unaided product of the potter's imagination, or did real creativity lie somewhere else?

The range of shapes that occurs in the repertoire of the maker of such fine wares is predominantly sympotic—to do with the aristocratic drinking-party: wine-mixing bowls of various kinds, amphoras, jugs, and of course drinking-vessels. Another large category consists of shapes clearly intended for the boudoir: cosmetic and trinket boxes, and perfume jars. Apart from these, there are ritual vases of one kind or another, intended for funerals, weddings, or special religious ceremonies. The imagery preserved on such vessels is one which reflects the interests in war, in the palaestra, at the shrine, at the hunt, at table, or in bed, of an élite. It is this fact which has encouraged the view that because pottery vessels decorated with a high degree of skill have been found in the tombs of Etruscan aristocrats, they must have been the vessels that were used by such people in real life, as well—and especially—by their opposite numbers in Athens. These, however, are the people whom we have seen using gold and silver plate as a matter of course—vessels whose bullion value alone was measured in *minae*. Even painted pots cost but a few obols, and there is thus an uncomfortable discrepancy which has to be explained, or explained away. If, however, Greek pottery can begin to be regarded in a subsidiary role, many problems disappear.

SKEUOMORPHISM

O. G. S. Crawford once described the 'archaeological thrill' to be experienced in finding, tracing, and interpreting the remains of antiquity in the modern landscape. It is, indeed, one of the diversions of a walk in the English countryside to be able to recognize in a row of trees or a footpath the course of a road built by the Romans two thousand years ago, or to be able to see in grass-grown mounds an Iron Age earthwork or a deserted medieval village.[5] But while the totality of the past has disappeared, we can use its vestiges to reconstruct a picture of what used to exist. V. Gordon Childe put the question in these terms:

Apart from . . . exceptional cases . . . the archaeological record consists all too often of battered pieces of stone, lumps of corroded metal, fragments of indestructible pottery, shapeless banks of earth and amorphous hollows in the ground—axe-heads without handles, whorls without spindles, hinges without doors and unfurnished rooms.[6]

'And sanctuaries without dedications, and dining-rooms without plate', we might add. In similar vein, Childe wrote of 'skeuomorphism', the manufacture of vessels in one material intended to evoke the appearance of vessels regularly made in another, and has commended its study to archaeologists

[5] O. G. S. Crawford (1953).   [6] Childe (1956), 12.

since '[it] often gives us a glimpse into productive activities and artistic media of which no direct evidence survives'.[7] The ceramic record thus illustrates a constant dialectic between gourds, basketry, wood, textiles, stone, ceramic, and precious metal.

Many features of ancient Greek pottery, such as rivet-heads, strengthening bands, or sharply angled forms, are undoubtedly skeuomorphic. Another way of looking at such features is to regard them as being in a sense like footprints in snow. Even though the wayfarer may have passed on, his or her former presence can be inferred. The practice of potters imitating metal is widespread, and is to be found throughout the world, as we shall see in a later chapter. For the present, let us note its existence in the ancient Near East, Anatolia, Greece, and the Balkans.

In a letter preserved in the royal archives at Mari, on the Upper Euphrates, Mukannishum, the director of the palace workshops, ordered to be made 'Two drinking-vessels of silver in the form of a bull's head, weighing [650 grams]; eight drinking-vessels in the form of an ibex head and one drinking-vessel of red gold, weighing [nearly 3 kilos], one silver drinking-vessel in the form of a gazelle's head weighing [200 grams], weighed with the king's personal set of weights.' Although no Old Babylonian animal head in precious metal survives, there are later ceramic vessels (Fig. 5.1) which may have 'imitated roughly in pottery what the palaces enjoyed in silver and gold'.[8] We have a glimpse here of early examples of a genre of plate which was to be widespread throughout the ancient Near East and Aegean. The Mari drinking-vessels would have been used at royal banquets, displayed on elaborate silver stands themselves adorned with animal heads: lions, roebucks, and stags are mentioned in another letter. These would have been made in the palace workshops, although some vessels were imported from Tukrish, a locality north of Elam.

Silver, whether in the form of wire rings, ingots, or drinking-vessels, was the basic medium of exchange in what was still a pre-monetary society. A list from Mari includes silverware ('73 drinking-vessels [for] Hammu-shagish, two [of which are] bull's head [vessels]. 6 drinking-vessels, [for] Asqudum. 10 drinking-vessels, 2 [of which are] bull's head [vessels for] Yasim-Sumu') given to court officials either as personal payments, or for them to use in their official capacities. Banquets were often the occasion for the presentation of gifts, and plate (usually made up in any case in round figures in terms of prevailing weight standards)[9] was always an acceptable present even after the invention of coinage in the sixth century BC.

The technology which enabled gold and silver vessels to be made at all had been developed in the urban craft centres of Mesopotamia during the

---

[7] Ibid. 13–14; he attributes the term 'skeuomorph' to Sir John Myres; cf. Vickers (1989*a*).

[8] Dalley (1984), 59–61, figs. 27–9.
[9] See ch. 2.

FIG. 5.1   Ceramic drinking-vessel in the form of a bull's head, from Tell Kerab, near Carchemish. Ashmolean Museum, Oxford AN 1913.188.

fourth millennium BC. This depended in large part on the ability to make sheet metal, and the knowledge of the techniques involved gradually spread northwards and westwards, to Asia Minor, the Aegean, and beyond. This spread seems to have been accompanied by the introduction of the vine—the relationship between the consumption of alcohol by élites and the commissioning of drinking-vessels of precious metal was perennially close.[10] The dissemination of new metallurgical techniques was also accompanied by a change in the nature of pottery, and provides an early example of the principle of skeuomorphism:

It was the development of metallurgy to the stage at which vessels could be made of sheet metal that most radically transformed the shape of pottery vessels. The imitation extended to the reproduction of shapes for which clay is ill-fitted, and of details, such as rivets, which are functionless.[11]

---

[10] Sherratt and Taylor (1989).   [11] L. Scott (1954), 399; cf. Bagley (1987), 17.

An early example of the phenomenon is an Early Bronze Age silver goblet from Tell el-Far'ah near Nablus, made 'of beaten silver sheet',[12] for which ceramic parallels exist in red-slip ware,[13] where 'the potter has even copied characteristics which are typical only of metalworking, and which are entirely foreign to the potter's craft'.[14] The effects of such skeuomorphism in Europe have been compared to a series of 'metallurgical shocks'.[15] An early example is the pottery of the Baden culture in Central Europe (contemporary with the Aegean Early Bronze Age), whose shiny black surfaces, fluted decoration, and strap handles (Fig. 5.2), have been recognized as having their origins in metalwork, and ultimately in Anatolian metalwork.[16] In the Aegean, there are, as in Babylonia and Anatolia, reflections in ceramic of the forms of items made in nobler materials. Thus, 'the *Leitmotiv* of the Korakou culture is the pottery "sauceboat", and its prototype is preserved in a splendid golden find from Arcadia [and] the most famous of Troy II forms, the *depas amphikypellon*, likewise had a metal prototype of which an example in silver is preserved.'[17] In both the Levant and in the Aegean 'metal types can be inferred from the pottery but are not so far represented by finds of metal objects.'[18] Thus the pottery 'teapot' vessels of Early Minoan Crete (of a type known in silver in the Levant at a slightly later period) are suggestive of metal, and probably precious metal, prototypes,[19] and surviving parallels in both media encourage this view. Cretan Gournia has produced both a two-handled silver cup with a crinkled rim and Middle Minoan pottery of a similar character (Fig. 5.3),[20] and parallels exist in both stone and clay (Fig. 5.4) for the Middle and Late Bronze Age gold and silver cups of the 'Vapheio' type.[21] Recent experimental work has shown that the black crusts on Mycenaean pots found in a Late Bronze Age chamber-tomb at Asine in the Argolid are tin, and when the vessels were originally fired they will have looked as though they were made of gold.[22] And whatever the date of the gold drinking set (Fig. 5.5)

[12] Amiran (1984), 117.

[13] Ibid. For a possible explanation of the red slip, see pp. 179–80, below.

[14] Ibid. 117–18.

[15] Schachermeyr (1955), 154.

[16] Kalicz (1963), 57–64; esp. 57: 'Kennzeichnend für die Keramik der Péceler Kultur ist die schwarze Farbe, die glänzend polierte Oberfläche, und die allgemein üblich gewordene Kannelierung'; cf. Trachsler (1966).

[17] Renfrew (1972), 336; for gold sauceboats, see ibid., pl. 19.3; Childe (1924); Weinberg (1969); Sotheby New York, 15 June 1988, Lot 99. For the *depas amphikypellon* and a pottery analogue, see Renfrew (1972), pls. 19.1 and 2. Cf. Hood (1978), 155, on 'Minyan ware' of the Middle Bronze Age in Greece: 'with its sharply angled profiles [it] appears to be imitating metalwork'; Lloyd (1956), 211, on some of the finds from Beycesultan: 'Predominant among local vessels are "champagne-

glass" and "fruit-stand" shapes, and almost all show traces of the metal originals from which they must have been copied.'

[18] Sherratt and Taylor (1989), 109–10.

[19] Evans (1921–36), 1. 79–82; Davis (1977); Sherratt and Taylor (1989), 109–10. Amiran (1984), 116, fig. 2 illustrates a small silver spouted vessel from Uruk.

[20] Hawes (1908), 56, 60, pl. C, 1; Evans (1921–36), 1. 191–3: 'It is to the existence of these ceramic copies that we owe the best evidence of the wealth of the Minoan lords in precious metals in the palmy days of the Middle Minoan Age'; Davis (1977), esp. 89–95, and figs. 60–72; Hood (1978), 34, 154.

[21] Evans (1921–36), 1. 242, fig. 183b; 3. 178, fig. 121; Davis (1974), esp. 486; Matthäus (1985), 185–6; (1989), 87–9. Cf. in general, Walberg (1976); Foster (1989), 37.

[22] Gillis (1991–2).

FIG. 5.2   Baden culture cup from Vinča, Serbia, Ashmolean Museum, Oxford AN 1926.226.

to be found in the Vulchitrun hoard[23]—whether it was made *c.*1600–1400 BC,[24] or *c.*800 BC,[25] (or both, if it is in fact a mixture of objects from different periods), the techniques involved in the manufacture of the various pieces owe much to Aegean metalworking practice, and with their looped and strap handles, they serve to illustrate the sources for similar features on Hallstatt pottery in the Balkans, and on Geometric pottery (Fig. 5.6) in Greece.[26]

Geometric pottery with its loose forms appears more readily than most, however, to obey a ceramic aesthetic (although basketry, treen, and

[23] Sherratt and Taylor (1989), 120, fig. 3.   [25] Matthäus (1989), 104.
[24] Ibid. 127–30.   [26] Ibid. 103–4.

FIG. 5.3 Two-handled Middle Minoan silver cup and a Middle Minoan pottery vessel, from Gournia, Crete. Heraklion Museum.

FIG. 5.4 Handle of a Late Minoan pottery mug, from Knossos. Ashmolean Museum, Oxford AN AE.839.

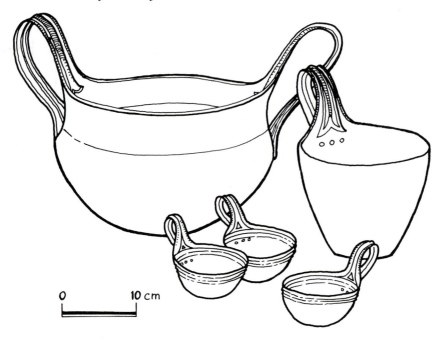

FIG. 5.5   Gold drinking set, Vulchitrun hoard (after Sherratt and Taylor (1989), 120).

weaving[27] may have played informative roles here).[28] At all events, it is generally less 'metallic' than the pottery of some other periods, and because—since Jacquemart[29] (and perhaps Darwin)[30]—Greek ceramic has tended to be studied as an autonomous 'art-form' with its own 'origins',[31] the principal roots of what is perceived to be an enclosed tradition have been sought among Geometric wares. This is to overlook the possibility that the input from metalwork may have come in phases. The development of ceramics in early modern times provides a parallel. English potteries in the sixteenth and seventeenth centuries characteristically produced slip-ware vessels whose re-lationship to metalwork was remote.[32] By the eighteenth century, however, royal silversmiths were employed to make designs (inevitably influenced by

[27] What E. A. Gardner (1897), pp. xiv–xv says about filling ornament on Corinthian pottery is, in principle, equally applicable to Geometric: 'The oriental motives are doubtless derived from imported woven fabrics; they consist mostly of animals, wild or fantastic, often in continuous friezes, and of decorative designs such as the lotus, palmette &c., usually worked into a continuous pattern; the technique of woven fabrics is especially indicated by the ornaments scattered over the field, which are due to a desire to strengthen the stuff by making the warp and woof interlace as frequently as pos-sible, instead of being stretched across large ex-panses of one colour.'

[28] On possible connections between East Medi-terranean metal prototypes and processions on Attic Geometric pottery, see Hampe and Simon (1981), 161, fig. 241; Kourou (1985), 416–7.

[29] Jacquemart (1873), and see p. 81, above.

[30] On the influence of the publication of Darwin's *Origin of Species* in 1859 on the 'search for "ori-gins" ' and on 'tracing the evolution of style', see Hoffmann (1979), 64.

[31] e.g. Semper (1863–79), 2. 4–5; Schiering (1967).

[32] See Vickers (1989a), 60, figs 11 and 12.

FIG. 5.6 Rhodian Geometric pottery drinking-vessel, from Siana. Ashmolean Museum, Oxford AN 1885.621.

a metal aesthetic) for French porcelain factories, and English manufacturers readily followed suit. No one would claim that potters had achieved these forms fortuitously, and the phenomenon in question in fact constitutes a well-documented example of 'metallurgical shock'.

The 'orientalizing' period in the Mediterranean world was by any standards another instance of 'metallurgical shock' in that the ceramic record produces material that is full of allusions to work in metal. Thus, 'it is an absolutely certain conjecture from the character of Protocorinthian and Corinthian clay vases, that metal vases were made at Corinth throughout the archaic period',[33] although it is likely that the original models for these came from the eastern Mediterranean. The Phoenicians played a major role in the dissemination of such items. This is borne out both by the ancient sources and by recent archaeological research. In the *Iliad*, which describes the material culture of Homer's own day, the eighth or seventh century BC, the first prize in the foot-race at the Funeral games of Patroclus was 'a mixing bowl (*krater*) of silver, well wrought, which only held six measures, but far surpassed

[33] Payne (1931), 210, and cf. 210–21.

FIG. 5.7   Fragment of a silver *skyphos* with fan decoration (enlarged) from Marsigliana d'Albegna (after Cristofani) (1970).

all others on earth in beauty, for skilled Sidonian craftsmen had made it well, and Phoenicians had brought it across the misty sea';[34] and the most beautiful and costly of the treasures in the house of Menelaus was a 'mixing bowl, well wrought in solid silver, with a rim of hammered gold, given . . . by the king of Sidon'.[35] No silver craters have survived, but silver vessels from sites in Italy—Palestrina (the Barberini and Bernardini Tombs), Pontecagnano (Tomb 928), and Cerveteri (the Regolini-Galassi Tomb)—provide a link between Cypriot and Phoenician metalwork on the one hand[36] and Etruscan bucchero pottery on the other. Tall silver *oinochoai* lie behind bucchero *oinochoai*, and silver *skyphoi* bearing incised fan-motifs at the rim (such as the one from the Tomb of the Ivories at Marsiliana d'Albegna (Fig. 5.7))[37] must underlie their bucchero equivalents (Fig. 5.8).[38] Scholars seem to agree that later bucchero imitates metal,[39] but the relevant metal prototypes are for

[34] Hom. *Il.* 23. 741–4.
[35] Hom. *Od.* 4. 615–18.
[36] Matthäus (1985), 238–44; cf. Cristofani (1985); Frederiksen (1979), 292.
[37] Firenze (1971), 37, pl. 9.1; Cristofani (1970), 272–3, pl. 25*b*.
[38] On which, see Rasmussen (1979) and Regter

(forthcoming). For a bucchero parallel for the hemispherical silver bowls from the Sagrona and Pelliccie tombs at Vetulonia, the Regolini-Galassi tomb at Cerveteri, and the Bernardini and Barberini tombs at Palestrina, see Vickers (1992*c*), 248, no. 39.
[39] e.g. Rasmussen (1979), *passim*; Schmidt (1982), 40; Moltesen (1991), 443.

F I G. 5.8   Etruscan bucchero *skyphos* with fan decoration. Ashmolean Museum, Oxford AN 1971.813.

the most part absent. Their absence may perhaps be accounted for if they were of precious metal. If so, transmission of both shape and decoration from oriental prototypes will have occurred among silversmiths, before being taken up by potters. A silver *kantharos* in the Louvre from Camirus[40] provides a rare example of the kind of vessel that lies behind a form of drinking-vessel common in both Athens and Etruria, but now otherwise extant only in bronze and ceramic versions.[41] The rosette in the centre of the floor has been well compared to a painted tondo.[42]

In the absence of much surviving metalwork from any period, some connections between ceramic and plate can only be hypothetical. Thus, for example, a fragmentary silver vessel from St Fiàcre en Melraud, Morbihan, Brittany[43] is one of half a dozen known examples of small cups in gold and silver, belonging to the latest phase of Bell-beakers and the Early Bronze

[40] Louvre Bj. 2165. MV is grateful to M. Alain Pasquier for allowing him to examine the piece. For bibliographical references, see Brijder (1988), 103 n. 5.

[41] Brijder (1988), although we cannot follow him in his belief that the Rhodian vessel was derived from an Etruscan pottery model: this would be to assume a 'trickle-up effect' (cf. p. 54, above), of a kind unusual before modern times. For bronze analogues of 'Ionian cups', see Guzzo (1973); Matthäus (1985), pl. 49, No. 464.

[42] Brijder (1983), 36–7; Guzzo (1973), 58.

[43] Ashmolean Museum, Oxford AN 1926.147.

FIG. 5.9   Iberian silver bowl, from Castellet de Banyoles (Tevissa, Tarragona). Museo Arqueologico, Barcelona.

Age in Western Europe, *c.*2000 BC. They include the elegant silver example from an Early Bronze Age tumulus burial at Saint-Adrien, Côtes-du-Nord, Brittany and the two gold examples, from Rillaton (Cornwall) and Eschenze (Switzerland), both unfortunately without associated finds.[44] They illustrate the kind of objects of precious metal that may lie behind the ubiquitous Beaker Ware pottery of the Early Bronze Age.[45] Similarly, the relatively crude, 'provincial' work on a silver vessel from Castellet de Banyoles (Tevissa, Tarragona) in Spain (Fig. 5.9)[46] may help us to envisage the appearance of the lost silver prototypes for the embossed work on Etruscan bucchero pottery (Fig. 5.10) of a couple of centuries earlier.

From the classical period, there is a much wider range of extant silver (and even gold) vases: cups of the conventional *kylix* form, stemless cups, cup-*skyphoi*, mugs, *kantharoi*, stemmed dishes, *askoi*, perfume pots, *pyxides*, *phialai*, and *rhyta*.[47] Several silver cups are known, some of which have gold-figure

[44] All three are illustrated in MacSween and Burgess (1984), 74–6, figs. 51–4.

[45] Thanks are due to Andrew Sherratt for this suggestion. See too, the Early Bronze Age carinated silver cup from Trialeti in Georgia: Javakliashvili and Abramishvili (1986), 9.

[46] Serra Rafols (1941), 32, pl. 16; cf. pl. 18.

[47] For something of the range, see *Thracian Treasures* (1976); *Gold der Thraker* (1979); Strong (1966); A. Oliver (1977); *Search for Alexander* (1980); Matchebeli (1983), nos. 9–11; Bothmer (1984); n. 48, below. Bronze vases are more common; cf. Weber (1983). For the pottery imitations of metal *oinochoai*, Krauskopf (1984).

FIG. 5.10 Etruscan bucchero 'Nicosthenic' amphora. Ashmolean Museum, Oxford AN 1971.937.

decoration (on which see further below). The close connections between silver and ceramic have been treated in detail elsewhere;[48] one or two examples must suffice here. In one case, the relevant pottery vessels are generally—and correctly—regarded as being dependent on silverware, but this is largely the result of the accident of survival: a precisely comparable silver vessel is known. One of the pots is an Attic ribbed 'acrocup' in Boston from

[48] Gill (1986a).

FIG. 5.11   Silver 'acrocup' from the Chemyrev mound (after Pharmakowsky (1910), cols. 219–20, fig. 18).

FIG. 5.12   Attic black-glaze pottery 'acrocup'. Ashmolean Museum, Oxford AN 1917.63.

Tanagra with a red-figure interior,[49] which was said by J. D. Beazley to be a cheap imitation, 'influenced by metal originals such as the silver cup with gold medallion from the Chemyrev grave'.[50] This cup is now lost, but it was recorded in 1910, soon after its discovery (Fig. 5.11).[51] A black-gloss cup in the Ashmolean (Fig. 5.12)[52] of 'metalloid shape'[53] is but one of several other

[49] Boston 00.354: Beazley (1963), 1516, below; Beazley (1971), 500; Caskey and Beazley (1931–63), pl. 106, 175.

[50] Ibid. 90–1.

[51] Pharmakowsky (1910), 219–20, figs. 18 and 19; Gill (1986*a*), figs. 5–6. Vickers, Impey, and Allan (1986), pl. 8b.

[52] Ashmolean Museum, Oxford AN 1917.63: *CVA* Oxford 1, pl. 48, 140, 5; Gill (1986*a*), 14, fig. 9; Vickers, Impey, and Allan (1986), pl. 8a.

[53] J. D. Beazley in *CVA* Oxford 1, text p. 39.

FIG. 5.13   South Italian pottery cup-*skyphos*, from the Lipari Islands (*left*) and a silver cup-*skyphos*, from Nymphaeum. Ashmolean Museum, Oxford AN 1945.56 and 1885.486.

ceramic versions.[54] A silver cup-*skyphos*, from Nymphaeum and now in the Ashmolean Museum (Fig. 5.13, right),[55] has a finely moulded foot and three concentric tooled ridges on the underside. These features are taken over on ceramic cups. A typical example is a black-gloss cup, probably of local manufacture, from the Lipari Islands (Fig. 5.13, left).[56] The details are cruder, but recognizably dependent on prototypes like the Nymphaeum vessel.

Mugs of so-called 'Phidias shape' are also found in silver and clay and one of the best silver examples comes from the Bashova mound at Duvanli in Thrace (Fig. 5.14).[57] It has a double-rolled handle with shouldering and a concave neck with a distinct junction where it meets the plump body. The shoulder is left undecorated but the body is decorated with narrow ribbing closed at the top by arcs. There is a clearly defined foot. In the same tumulus was found a slightly larger ceramic mug of exactly the same shape (Fig. 5.15).[58] At the junction of neck and shoulder there is a rope pattern and the vertical ribbing extends to the shoulder. So close are they that one might suspect the existence of a mixed batch of silver and clay mugs from Athens, an idea proposed by A. W. Johnston in his study of the graffito on the underside of a silver mug from Dalboki.[59] Brian Shefton has seen the kind of decoration on pottery vessels of this type as a 'conscious and intended challenge to the oriental and luxury vases in precious metal'.[60] He is surely correct in principle, but we feel that Athenian silverware is a further necessary

[54] A red-figure pottery example in New York (06.1021.186; Beazley (1963), 1516, below; Richter and Hall (1936), pls. 167, 172 and 181, 172), is said (ibid. 219) to be derived from metalwork. For the shape in black glaze: Sparkes and Talcott (1970), 94–6; Gill (1986*a*), 11–14.

[55] Ashmolean Museum, Oxford AN 1885.486: Strong (1966), pl. 17, a; Oliver (1977), 31, no. 6; Vickers (1979), 42, fig. 9 and pl. 13, a; Gill

(1986*a*), 15, 18, fig. 16; Vickers, Impey, and Allan (1986), pl. 3a.

[56] Gill (1986*a*), 15, 18, fig. 15; Vickers, Impey, and Allan (1986), pl. 3b.

[57] Plovdiv 1518: Filow (1934), 67, fig. 84; Strong (1966), 84 and pl. 17, b; Weber (1983), 451, C.II.17; Gill (1986*a*), 16, 22, fig. 20.

[58] Plovdiv 1530: Filow (1934), 78, fig. 100.

[59] Johnston (1978), 79.

[60] Shefton (1971), 110.

FIG. 5.14   Silver mug (slightly enlarged), from the Bashova mound at Duvanli, Bulgaria. Archaeological Museum, Plovdiv. (After Filow (1934), 67, fig. 84).

FIG. 5.15   Attic black-glaze pottery mug (slightly enlarged), from the Bashova mound at Duvanli, Bulgaria. Archaeological Museum, Plovdiv. (After Filow (1934), 78, fig. 100).

F I G. 5.16   Silver mug, from Dalboki, Bulgaria. Ashmolean Museum, Oxford AN 1948.104.

stage in the tradition. P. E. Corbett once made an important observation on the ribbing technique on similar pottery mugs:

the deeper segmentations of our vases involved an actual bending of the wall of the pot. Such ribbing increases the strength of a metal vase, but is a source of weakness in pottery; on many of the Agora examples the fabric has cracked the inside along the lines of division between the ribs.[61]

A silver mug from Dalboki in Thrace and now in the Ashmolean Museum (Fig. 5.16)[62] has a wall which is in a continuous curve with a slightly concave neck, out-turned rim and a single loop handle hammered on to the rim. It has a flat bottom which protrudes around the base. On the base is the

[61] Corbett (1949), 333.
[62] The silver mug is Oxford, Ashmolean AN 1948.104: Prochorov (1880); Ashmolean *Summary Guide* (1951), p. 50; Strong (1966), 85 and pl. 18, b; British Museum (1976), 95, no. 551; A. Oliver (1977), 30, no. 5; Johnston (1978), 79–80; Weber (1983), 453, C.III I; Vickers, Impey, and Allan (1986), pl. 1. Boardman (1987), 294, fig. 2; Gill and Vickers (1989), 299, fig. 1.

graffito ΣΚΥ which may mean that *skyphos* was the name for this shape in antiquity.[63] Such mugs have often been compared with its ceramic counterparts.[64] On ceramic mugs of this shape the handle is usually mounted slightly below the rim, although one from Camarina and now in Syracuse has it mounted at the rim, as on the silver example.[65]

There are many other pottery shapes for which silver parallels exist.[66] Or rather, perhaps, given the immense disparity in antiquity between the prices of silver vessels and those of ceramic,[67] as well as the almost universal tendency for the 'trickle-down' effect to operate—whereby items made from expensive materials might be copied in cheaper[68]—it may be that the far wider range of extant ceramic vessels serves as a guide to the shapes in the ancient silversmith's repertoire. They do not always provide absolutely literal translations from silver to clay, however. H. R. W. Smith once put the situation as follows: 'Sometimes the Greek potter is altogether pedantic in his imitation of metal . . . but as often his metalloid work is some easy compromise adapted to his material.'[69] The parallels now known in silverware indicate the likely immediate metallic source of pots, for no matter what the ultimate origins in earlier antiquity of various shapes of vessel may have been,[70] the makers of fine Greek ceramics followed standards set by contemporary silversmiths.

COLOUR

(*a*) *Black as Silver*

There is nothing particularly novel in suggesting that some ceramic shapes were derived from metalwork.[71] It is the proposal that norms were set in the world of the silversmith that is relatively[72] new. Until comparatively recently,

[63] Oliver (1977), 30; Johnston (1978), 79, pl. 3.

[64] e.g. Vickers, Impey, and Allen (1986), pl. 1; cf. Scribner (1937), 346, no. 6 (on a clay example in Pittsburgh): 'imitation of metalware'.

[65] Syracuse 24007, from Camarina, 1897.

[66] e.g. Vickers, Impey, and Allan (1986); Gill (1986*a*); (1987*d*); add the silver stemmed cups from Vani in Lordkipanidze (1971), 282, fig. 16; Matchebeli (1983), nos. 9 and 10.

[67] See pp. 38–43, 85–8, above.

[68] Cf. Weinberg (1988), 71 (citing D. Barag): 'The more precious material, in this case metal, probably had precedence over the baser ones; within the metals, silver most likely had precedence over bronze.'

[69] H. R. W. Smith (1944), 242; cf. Robertson (1985), 23, who speaks of the silversmith and the potter having 'like ideals'.

[70] On this issue, see Gill and Vickers (1990), 12–13.

[71] e.g. Caskey (1922), 160; Züchner (1950–1),

175; Beazley (1961), 53: 'Our kantharos is doubtless of metal, and the shape had probably a metallic origin'; B. F. Cook (1962–3), 31–6; Hoffmann (1961), 21–6, pls. 8–12; J. R. Green (1961), 73–5, pls. 6–7; Mellinghoff (1968), 56–65; Shefton (1971), 109–11, pls. 20–2; J. R. Green (1972), 1–16, pls. 1–5; Stibbe (1972), 116, 145; Kurtz (1975), 38, 70, 91, 117; Roberts (1978), 87; Moon (1979), 45; Hitzl (1982); Weber (1983), 149–50; Williams (1985), 12; Brijder (1983), 35–7; Bioul (1983–4), 8; Weber (1990), 438. By contrast, Hill (1947), 248 believed that 'although whimsical potters sometimes copied details of ornamentation from metal vases . . . the shapes in constant use had been developed by potters for pottery', and that 'in ancient times all metal was soft, and metal tools were therefore of slight importance in making metal vases'. Only Boardman (1987) has recently found merit in Miss Hill's article.

[72] Ure (1954), text to pl. 35, is exceptional among earlier scholars: 'one of the silver vases of which these little black mugs were a cheap imitation'.

it was to bronze that scholars looked when questions of metal prototypes arose. Thus, in a discussion of a black-glossed, fluted, vessel akin to the amphora illustrated in Fig. 5.17,[73] Arthur Lane assumed that its undeniably metallic appearance which it shared with mould-made Hellenistic pottery, as well as the latter's 'shiny coat of uniform black or red colouring', were characteristics of 'cheap substitutes for bronze'.[74] But this was in the days when bronze was the height of the material pecking-order in the eyes of students of the classical past.[75] As was established in earlier chapters, there was no shortage of silver- or even goldware in both public and private hands in classical antiquity, and these are much more likely than objects made from base metal to have set trends among contemporary ceramic substitutes. In any case, bronze is in general rather unlike most fine Greek painted ceramics of the classical period, whereas there are some obvious points of contact between pottery and precious metals.

To take the amphora in Fig. 5.17 as a starting-point: the flutes, and the mouldings at the rim and foot, are not the only metallic features. The shiny, reflecting surface of the glossy slip is of a kind that is often to be found on much plain and painted pottery made in Greece or Italy during the archaic and classical periods.[76] It is the same slip as that on a class of black-glossed cups—the so-called Arethusa cups—with tondo ornaments cast from silver decadrachms of Syracuse. This metallic-looking black gloss extends over both the tondo and the rest of the cup and, as A. J. Evans observed a hundred years ago, shows what a silver vessel might be expected to look like:

This interesting ceramic class, in which both the form, the central design, and the metallic lustre are imitated from silver work, presupposes the existence of a special class of silver vessels of the kind, with actual medallions . . . inserted in their central ornament. . . . The Capuan *kylikes*, in short, represented a cheap popular substitute for what was evidently a famous and highly-prized form of Syracusan plate.[77]

The metallic appearance of such glossed wares has caused some students of Greek ceramics to regard them with distaste,[78] and to apply to them epithets such as 'decadent', 'degenerate', or 'perverse'. If, however, the objective was to evoke not simply the form, but the surface appearance of silverware, the

---

[73] Oxford, Ashmolean Museum AN 1836–1868, p. 8, xiii.

[74] Lane (1963), 58.

[75] e.g. Richter (1904–5), 230 refers to the 'value' of 'articles in bronze'; but such value was relative: in reality, bronze was worth about 100 times less than silver, see Price (1968).

[76] e.g. Hayes (1984), *passim*; Noble (1988), 79; cf. A. S. Murray (1892), 96 (on the 'metallic' appearance of the glaze of black-figure); Bothmer (1962–3*a*), 2 (who speaks of 'the celebrated Greek black glaze, at its best a deeply lustrous, almost metallic black'); Cohen (1989), 73 (on the 'metal-

lic black-glaze' of red-figure). Sometimes, silver- or tin-foil was used to evoke the appearance of precious metal: for references, see Moltesen (1991).

[77] A. J. Evans (1891), 320; *CVA* Schwerin, p. 38; Vickers, Impey, and Allan (1986), pl. 14. See too, D. B. Thompson's allusion to 'silvered Italian pottery' in the context of the closely related cups adorned with casts of coins of Heraclea: Thompson (1939), 315. We do not understand Boardman (1987), 284–5.

[78] e.g. Pottier (1905), 43; Richter (1916), 64; Noble (1988), 91; R. M. Cook (1972), 212.

FIG. 5.17 South Italian black-glaze pottery amphora. Ashmolean Museum, Oxford AN 1836–1868, p. 8, xiii.

potters did a good job. Their products stand in a long tradition of wares which have often been thought of as silver look-alikes. Thus, not only does Winifred Lamb speak of 'the influence of metal prototypes' on Lesbian bucchero pottery, which 'shows itself in the plastic knobs, handles with discs, imitation rings on deinoi, ridged stems, and countless other details',[79] but John Boardman has taken the surface colour described by Miss Lamb as 'silver-grey to gun-metal,'[80] to be 'certainly influenced by . . . silver colour'.[81] J. D. Beazley once observed that the clay of some Etruscan pots 'is covered with a grey slip, which is thought to imitate silver—if so, tarnished silver'.[82] There is no difference in the role played by the 'silver-grey' slips and the shiny blue-black of much Athenian pottery, and the latter in particular is the same as that of the oxidized surface of relatively pure silver, such as the silver vessels from Dalboki as they were before cleaning (Figs. 5.16 and 5.18).[83] The high-gloss slips on archaic and classical Greek pottery are more likely to be an evocation of the appearance of the surface of much Greek silver than 'the most convenient . . . to obtain',[84] for if 'convenience' had been the prime consideration, it would have been quicker, cheaper, and easier to fire the pots red.[85] In fact, silver has a propensity to become patinated in sea air,[86] and it may not be wholly coincidental that most centres of black-glossed pottery production were situated near the sea.

While it is likely that references in Greek literature to silver-footed Thetis or Aphrodite show that silver could be, indeed ideally was, light in colour, they would not 'rule out a taste at a given time and place for tarnished vessels'.[87] We believe that there was a tolerance of patination in classical Greece and Etruria, especially in maritime centres, just as there is in some places even today.[88] There is, however, an additional reason why silver at

[79] Lamb (1932), 3.

[80] Ibid.; Lamb (1931–2), 51.

[81] Boardman (1987), 285.

[82] Beazley (1947), 282. Another ware which may fall into the same category is grey Minyan pottery:'[Grey Minyan] was once thought to be a product manufactured from a special kind of clay at a centre from which it was widely distributed. Now it is known that almost any kind of clay will do' (Blegen (1963), 141). The uniform appearance of wares with 'distinctive, largely angular shapes' (Blegen (1963), 140) throughout the Aegean world is surely due to an external factor, and recent work on silver metallurgy in the area in the Bronze Age (e.g. Gale and Stos-Gale (1981*a*); (1981*b*)) which shows how widespread silver extraction was, suggests what that factor might have been. A. H. Sayce's note to Hdt. 1. 14 may explain the existence of many black and grey wares in Anatolia: 'Silver seems to have had a special attraction for the Hittites, whose monuments in Asia Minor are usually met with in the neighbourhood of old silver mines, and their fancy for the metal may

have been communicated to the Lydians' (Sayce (1883), 9).

[83] 'Oxidized' is the term in common use with English silversmiths for darkened silver.

[84] R. M. Cook (1987), 169–70.

[85] See pp. 179–80, below.

[86] Wranglén (1985), 266–7 usefully lists the circumstances in which silver oxidizes; cf. Evans (1960), 37; (1981), 14. The late Richard Hattatt once told MV that he used to exhibit a silver electrotype of a Syracusan coin next to an Arethusa cup in his house near Bournemouth. The sea air caused it to go black within a short time of cleaning, and he eventually left it in this state.

[87] Robertson (1987), 22.

[88] The Chapel of St Januarius in the Duomo at Naples provides a good modern example of a working—and well-endowed—shrine, in which the surface colour of many of the silver *ex votos* is in the range 'gun-metal grey' to 'blue-black'. At Mentmore, Bucks, Lord Rosebery (Prime Minister 1894–5) 'set out . . . the shelves of the sideboard with a remarkable display of . . . silver. . . . [which]

FIG. 5.18   Attic black-glaze pottery stemless cup, and two silver beakers, from Dalboki, Bulgaria. Ashmolean Museum, Oxford AN 1948.105, 102, and 103.

Athens in particular may have been dusky. Bad water, adduced by Athenaeus as a reason why silver might become oxidized,[89] was a problem. Vitruvius describes how Athenian water brought in by conduits had 'a foam floating on top, like purple glass in colour' so that people only used it for washing and took drinking-water from wells.[90] This sounds like a recipe for oxidation. Fumigation too, would have had a similar effect on silver, for if Homeric precedent was followed (as it seems to have been)[91] both houses and storerooms might be cleansed by burning sulphur.[92] Both sweaty hands and flatulence would also have contributed to making silver dark, and Herodotus' surprise that Egyptians drank from bronze instead of from, presumably, silver vessels, and also that 'they all without exception scoured them clean every day'[93] suggests that fifth-century Greeks may have been indifferent to oxidation. Egyptians, moreover, were said by Pliny to 'stain silver' and 'strange

was all so tarnished that it resembled pewter. This was not due to any lack of care or an underestimation of its value on the part of the owners, but had for many years been customary with continental collectors to protect the silver from over-zealous polishing in the butler's pantry. The practice survives today only in the greatest collection of such things in the world, the two silver galleries at the Hermitage Museum in Leningrad': F. Watson (1977), pp. x–xi. Perhaps the most striking silver object in the Hermitage is the vast, coal-black, silver tomb of Alexander Nevsky, which dominates one end of the Concert Hall: *Masterpieces* (1981), 20–1. It was the policy of the V&A to leave its silver uncleaned until *c.*1920 (personal communication from Philippa Glanville). Bright English silver at the Great Exhibition of 1851 was condemned for its 'flashiness'. The foreign silver-work, by contrast was oxidized: 'The process of oxidation, as it is

termed, not only protects the silver from further tarnishing, but can convey every variety of tint from white to black, so that it is particularly well calculated to display fine modelling or chasing, which would be utterly thrown away in a dazzling white material': Wornum (1851), p. viii.

[89] Ath. 2. 46b.
[90] Vitr. 8. 3. 6.
[91] Parker (1983), 227–8.
[92] Hom. *Od.* 22. 481–2, 493. Sulphur is also used to clean a vessel of precious metal at Hom. *Il.* 16. 228. According to the Babylonian Talmud (Epstein (1938), 74), one of the activities permitted on the Sabbath was to place sulphur under silver vessels that they might 'undergo the process of sulphuring the whole day' (a reference we owe to the kindness of Jack Ogden).
[93] Hdt. 2. 37.

to relate the value of the silver is enhanced when its splendour has been sullied'.[94]

This was written from the standpoint of one who lived in a society where silver was usually kept light: witness the use by Roman silversmiths of dark *niello* inlay,[95] absent from classical Greece, where any contrast was provided by gold. Thus, for example, the writer of an Anacreontic poem creates an image of a silver cup decorated with gold stars,[96] and Athenaeus quotes extensively from a monograph, *The Cup of Nestor*, by the Hellenistic writer Asclepiades of Myrlaea, in which Homer's reference to the presence of gold studs on the legendary cup is taken to allude to stars in the night sky: 'by setting the golden studs side by side with the silver substance of the cup, he has brought out by contrast the true character of the stars and the sky in accordance with the outward appearance of their colours. For the sky is like unto silver, whereas the stars resemble gold in their fiery nature.'[97] Other literary evidence is far from clear. It is uncertain whether the vessel described by Eubulus as 'thick-lipped, rattling, black, well rounded, pointy-bottomed, glistening, reflecting'[98] was silver or ceramic, although we would favour the former alternative. Then there is the puzzling quotation made by an anonymous Roman commentator from the pre-Socratic philosopher Thrasyalces to the effect that 'silver is black'.[99] Some have taken this as an affirmation of the opposite,[100] even as 'proof' that Greek silver, like Roman, was usually kept in a brightly polished, light, condition.[101] Far better to keep the whole range of possibilities open, and agree with the anonymous Roman that 'the colour of silver is unclear'. But there may be another reason why Greeks may have been reluctant to subject their silver to frequent cleaning, for not only was silver of the period extremely pure,[102] but—as we saw in Chapter 2— most pieces of plate were made up in multiples of coins: either in terms of Attic drachmas, or of darics or *sigloi*. They were in essence the savings of a family or a community. Frequent cleaning, even of today's silver which is only 92.5 per cent pure, causes wear,[103] and it is unlikely that owners of plate in antiquity would have willingly subjected themselves to the impoverishment that the frequent removal of patina would inevitably have involved. In short, it was the effect of the shiny black sheen of pure silver which we believe potters to have attempted to evoke with their black slips.[104] In what

---

[94] Pliny, *NH* 33. 10. 56.

[95] Rosenberg (1924); La Niece (1983).

[96] West (1984), 3, no. 4i (ii and iii are not dissimilar).

[97] Ath. 11. 488b.

[98] Eub. *PCG* 56, in Ath. 11. 471d.

[99] Hughes and Parsons (1984) (= *Poxy*. 52. 3659).

[100] e.g. Robertson (1985), 22; Boardman (1987), 282.

[101] Boardman (1987), 282.

[102] e.g. the Dalboki pieces (Oxford, Ashmolean Museum AN 1947.104, 102, and 103) contain respectively 98%, 98.5%, 99.4% of silver. A cup from Nymphaeum (Ashmolean AN 1885.486) contains 98.7% silver (kindly analysed by Zofya Stos-Gale using energy-dispersive X-ray fluorescence).

[103] Olson and Thordemann (1951).

[104] Cf. Plenderleith and Werner (1971), 220: 'In silver objects there is generally a clear-cut distinction between the corrosion products derived from relatively pure silver and those from base silver alloys containing an appreciable amount of copper.' Kubaschewski and Hopkins (1962), 253: 'In practice, some copper is added to silver, and this lowers the resistance to oxidation.'

FIG. 5.19   Attic red-figure pottery cup fragment. Symposiasts. Ashmolean Museum, Oxford AN 1966.498.

is one of the very few references to the technique of pottery decoration in ancient literature, the potters of Naucratis are said to have 'baptized' their pots so as to make them resemble silver;[105] we would guess that they applied a slip which when fired turned black.

(b) Red-Figure as Gold-Figure

If the shiny black of fine Greek wares can be accounted for in terms of silver, what of the orangey-red that is used for the figure-decoration of red-figure pottery, for the undersides of many black-glaze vessels, and for bowls, jugs, and other shapes in Hellenistic and later periods down to the end of Roman antiquity? It is not the case, as is widely thought, that what is often called 'reserved' orangey-red is simply the natural colour of the clay, but it is in fact the result of the application of a separate slip.[106] This is only apparent when the black gloss is missing: on Fig. 5.19, for example, it is clear that the 'reserved' parts of the ornament are different in colour from the fabric.[107] When clay is shown as clay in red-figure (as, for example on an *oinochoe* in

[105] Ath. 11. 480e. Not mentioned by Noble (1988).

[106] Overlooked by Noble (1988); Gollan (1982), 16, but noted by Hemelrijk (1991), 242.

[107] Ashmolean AN 1966.498; *Beazley Gifts* (1966), pl. 27, no. 210.

Berlin where Athena is modelling a horse)[108] it is shown in a different colour
from the usual orange-red. There is clearly a reason for the special slip, the
explanation for which may well be found in the gold-figure scenes on silverware: the scenes which in the past were thought to be derived from decorated pottery,[109] but which must, in the light of their great cost compared
with that of ceramic vessels, have themselves been the informative influence.

The best-known examples are the four silver cups in St Petersburg and the
kantharos and *phiale* in Plovdiv.[110] The technique involved may have its origins
in an Iranian craft tradition,[111] and occurs on extant Phoenician silverware,[112]
where it generally serves as an adornment of *repoussé* work. The Athenian
innovation seems to have been to do gold-figure on the flat, rather than to
use it to adorn work in relief. In its Western manifestation, the technique has
been described as follows:

After the design was engraved in the silver, a sheet of gold of the thickness of strong
paper was laid over the whole medallion and was pressed down so hard with a blunt
instrument that all the individual lines became visible in the gold plate also and so
could be redrawn in the gold plate with a sharp instrument. Immediately after, all
those parts which did not serve to cover the figure and the surrounding band were
cut away and removed.[113]

More recently, the technique has been called 'cladding'[114] or 'diffusion
bonding',[115] but needless to say, such decoration will have been quite fragile,
which is another argument against frequent cleaning. The sizes of the surviving gold-figure vessels are small, so that comparisons with pottery are
inevitably limited.[116] Nevertheless, the simple border of the tiny tondo of the
Semibratny 'acrocup' (Fig. 5.20)[117] is similar to those of small red-figure

[108] Berlin F 2415; *CVA* Berlin 3, 27, pl. 145;
Blümel (1953), fig. 29.
[109] e.g. Strong (1966), 78; A. Oliver (1977),
29.
[110] In general: Reeder (1974), 212–31; St
Petersburg: Gorbunova (1971); Grach (1985);
Vickers, Impey, and Allan (1986), pls. 4, 5, and 7.
Gill (1987); Plovdiv: Filow (1934); Danov and
Ivanov (1980); for gold-figure from Georgia:
Lordkipanidze (1971); on Greek-influenced Iberian
gold-figure silverware: Serra Rafols (1941), esp. 34:
'la mayor parte [of the contents of the Castallet de
Banyoles hoard] son obras de arte indigenas,
inspiradas más o menos directamente en modelos
griegos'; cf. Serra Rafols (1964–5).
[111] Moorey (1988).
[112] Markoe (1985).
[113] Stephani (1881), 7, translated by H. A.
Thompson (1940), 191–2; cf. Blümner (1875–87),
4. 311. Beazley (1918), 26 actually compares the
figure decoration of some early red-figure pots to
'thin sheets of metal'.
[114] Vittori (1979), 35.

[115] It was 'in widespread use in the first millennium BC, as well as in the early Roman period', but
fell into disuse when mercury gilding began to be
developed in the 2nd c.AD': Oddy *et al.* (1981),
241; cf. Oddy (1988), 10: 'In cases where gold
leaf has been applied directly to the surface of metal,
especially when the substrate is silver, the gold can
be made to stick by rubbing it down and heating
gently to cause interdiffusion of the gold and
substrate to take place.'
[116] For a large-scale example of the genre, cf.
the gold-figure decoration of the plinth of Phidias'
chryselephantine Zeus at Olympia: Paus. 5. 11. 8.
[117] Hermitage SBr.IV.15; Schefold (1931);
Gorbunova (1971); Vickers (1983*a*), 43, fig. 3;
(1985*a*), pl. 4c; Vickers, Impey, and Allan (1986),
pl. 7; Gill (1986*a*), 11–12, fig. 3; (1987*d*). MV is
grateful to Irena Saverkina for allowing him to
examine this cup. The gilding has come away from
the right forearm of the figure, the body below the
waist, the left leg of the stool, and most of the
exergue.

cups.[118] Not only does the figure of the Nike, who sits with wings outstretched and pouring a libation, recall those painted on red-figure pottery vessels, but the treatment of details on the metal cup helps to explain the presence of various techniques used in ceramic decoration: the so-called 'relief line', whereby lines, such as those delineating the feathers on the wings of Triptolemus' chariot on a red-figure *lekythos* in Oxford (Fig. 5.21),[119] or the folds of his outer cloak are represented; or the so-called 'dilute line', used for his tunic. The deep incisions on the wings of the Semibratny Nike have the same tactile effect as the ceramic 'relief line'—'the "wiry line" which could match the true furrow bitten by the graver of the black-figure artist',[120] and perhaps provide a reason for an otherwise inexplicable phenomenon. Then finely incised lines on the Semibratny Nike's tunic occur where 'dilute lines' appear in red-figure, and again there may be a connection. The details of the head, and even the fair hair, the frills at the hems of the tunics, the zigzag borders of the cloaks (there is part of one visible over the Nike's knee), and the delineation of fingers and toes, are all part of the silversmith's repertoire, but are ably rendered by the pot-painter, whoever he or she may have been. Most would agree that both vessels were made before the mid-fifth century, and this is borne out by the fact that the silver cup appears to weigh 50 light *sigloi*,[121] the change from which to the heavier *siglos* standard seems to have occurred by then.[122] This need not, however, mean that the cup was necessarily made outside Attica, for the *siglos* standard seems to have coexisted there with the Attic over long periods.[123]

The quality of extant work in gold and silver is not as well known as it should be. The gold-figure *phiale* from Duvanli now in Plovdiv[124] is a case in point. Its 1-*mina* weight[125] suggests that it may have been made at Athens. It shows an *apobates* race,[126] and is full of finely observed characterization. One youthful charioteer is shown with his hair swept back, and the first down just visible on his receding chin (Fig. 5.22); another, more squarely built, bares his teeth in grim determination to win (Fig. 5.23). The horses are exquisitely rendered, with tossing heads and flaring nostrils, impressive musculature and flowing tails. Of similarly high quality is another gold-figure silver cup from Semibratny (Fig. 5.24),[127] in which a richly clad seated woman

[118] e.g. an 'acrocup' in Oxford: Ashmolean Museum AN 1923.73: *CVA* Oxford 1, pl. 48.5; Vickers, Allan, and Impey (1986), pl. 6b; Vickers and Gill (1990), 20, fig. 2.

[119] Ashmolean Museum AN 1891.683; *CVA* Oxford 1, pl. 33.1.

[120] Beazley (1918), 8. Hemelrijk (1991), 239–40 discusses the technique of painting relief lines, but fails to ask why they should have been there in the first instance.

[121] Wt. 270.85 g. (equivalent to 50 *sigloi* at 5.41 g.).

[122] See Ch. 2, above. We are thus unable to follow Boardman (1987), 287 in dating the Semibratny Nike cup to 'at least the end of the fifth century'.

[123] Vickers (1992*a*).

[124] Filow (1934), 63–5, fig. 80; Danov and Ivanov (1980), pl. 16; Gill and Vickers (1990), 25, figs. 4 and 5; Vickers (1990), 616, fig. 1.121.

[125] See p. 40, above.

[126] For silver *phialai* and cups as prizes at games, see p. 41, above.

[127] St Petersburg, Hermitage Museum Sbr VI–11.

FIG. 5.20   Gold-figure tondo decoration on a silver 'acrocup' from Semibratny. Seated Nike. Hermitage Museum, St Petersburg SBr. IV.15.

sits pensively, while her companion (on her feet) addresses a bearded man (also standing). Their features are exquisitely delineated, and the drapery is drawn with great skill. The 'Venus-rings' on the necks of the women are shown, as is even the hair on the naked chest of the man. The engraving of the hair of all three figures is done into the silver, and thus appears black, as in most red-figure renditions of hair. These gold-figure silver vessels are examples of craftsmanship and design of the highest order, but the surprising thing is that although the Duvanli *phiale* has been known for more than fifty years, and the Semibratny cup for more than twice as long, they never appear in histories of Greek art. It may be that since they are frequently thought to copy a ceramic technique, they overstepped the bounds of 'good taste,' that they were somehow 'kitsch'. Such considerations did not of course

FIG. 5.21 Attic red-figure
lekythos. Triptolemus.
Ashmolean Museum,
Oxford AN 1891.683
(V.315).

apply in Greek antiquity, as we have seen in an earlier chapter;[128] the boot
may, however, be on the other foot, and ceramic be the subsidiary medium.

If this is indeed the case (and the immense differences in prices between
ceramic and plate are alone sufficient to suggest that it might have been),
then other features of Greek ceramics can be seen to have their origins in
work in intrinsically more valuable materials. It is not the case that for every
painted pot there has to have been an identical piece of silverware, rather
that the norms of work in precious metals lie behind those of high-quality
pottery. In the absence of surviving examples of some of the likely techniques, any discussion of some aspects of the Greek potter's debt is inevitably speculative; but once one has been alerted to the possibilities of metallic
inspiration, there is no point at which it is reasonable to stop. Still in the

128 See ch. 4, above.

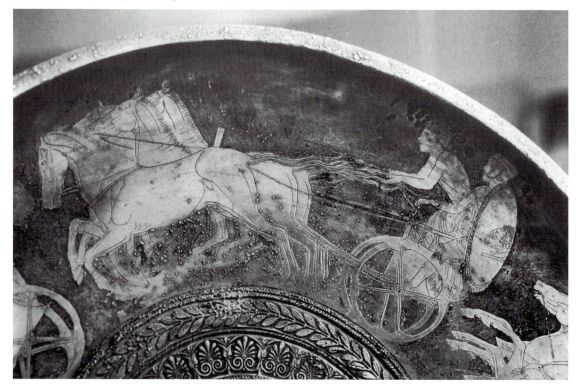

F I G. 5.22   Attic gold-figure *phiale* from the Bashova mound, Duvanli, Bulgaria. *Apobates* race, detail. Archaeological Museum, Plovdiv, Inv. 1515.

realm of gold-figure decoration, for example, it is clear that if Attic red-figure owes its conventions to the practice of applying sheet-gold cut-outs to the surface of incised silver, the same might well be true of Etruscan wares decorated with orangey-red paint applied over the surface of the black slip of the pot, and details incised. An amphora in Oxford (Fig. 5.25)[129] provides a good example of the genre. In the past, it has been the practice to describe this fabric as having been made in imitation of Attic red-figure pottery, and nothing more.[130] But given the major social and economic role of precious metal,[131] as well as the attested wealth of Etruria in classical times,[132] it is much more likely that the Etruscan 'applied red' technique was another means of rendering in clay the appearance of gold figures on silverware.[133]

    What seems to have happened in both societies is that the value of silver vessels was increased by means of artifice—or enhanced by means of art—

---

[129] Oxford, Ashmolean Museum 1988.387; Vickers (1992*c*), 248, no. 45, pl. 8, *h*.
[130] e.g. Shefton (1967).
[131] See Chapter 2, above.
[132] See pp. 61–2, above.

[133] Similarly, the 'applied red' on pots of the 'Xenon Group' (in the context of which 'metal vases [had] a role to play': E. G. D. Robinson (1990), 259) will have been another gesture in the direction of 'gold-figure'.

F I G. 5.23 Attic gold-figure *phiale* from Duvanli. *Apobates* race, detail. Archaeological Museum, Plovdiv, Inv. 1515.

by creating the appearance of something that was more precious than it really was, a phenomenon that is not unknown elsewhere.[134] Limited amounts of gold were quite literally spread extremely thinly in the form of gold-figure on silver, as a gesture in the direction of solid gold. This was the best the poorer societies of the West, who had comparatively little gold before Alexander,[135] and who were perforce 'simple in their tastes', could do to approach the flamboyant luxury of the Persian empire.[136] A more recent parallel is provided by eighteenth-century Holland and France. In Amsterdam, rich burghers might commission golden goblets;[137] in Paris and Versailles, resources were so scarce that the aristocracy were persuaded to cease using

[134] Cf. Baudrillart (1878), 1. 5: 'Riche, on voudra paraître ce qu'on est, et même un peu au delà; pauvre, on voudra paraître ce qu'on n'est pas, c'est-à-dire riche, du moins dans une certaine mesure: cela n'est pas impossible, car si la richesse ne s'emprunte pas, les signes de la richesse s'empruntent et peuvent être imités.'

[135] Ath. 6. 231f.

[136] Cf. ch. 2, pp. 37–8.

[137] de Iongh (1982), 115–31. In general, see Schama (1987).

FIG. 5.24   Gold-figure tondo decoration on a silver cup from Semibratny. Man and two women. Hermitage Museum, St Petersburg SBr. VI.11.

even silver[138] and adopt porcelain instead[139]—tantamount to admitting that the emperor had no clothes. In antiquity, gold figures on silver will have cost very little more than silver itself, but done in the Athenian manner, they will have helped convince the recipient of a vessel, whether customer, prize-winner, or guest, of the relative purity of the silver,[140] and will no doubt have added to its value.[141]

[138] For a vivid description of a transitional phase in the movement from plate to porcelain, see Norton (1967), 440; Saint-Simon (1984), 480–1. Thanks are due to Roger Moorey for bringing these references to our attention. Porcelain and ormolu snuffboxes, many made with great artifice, were simply substitutes for the gold boxes few could afford: cf. Beaucamp-Markowsky (1985), 16–17.

[139] See Ch. 1.

[140] Cf. Ch. 2 n. 85.

[141] Cf. Pliny, *NH* 33. 1. 4–5, and p. 43, above.

FIG. 5.25   Etruscan
red-figure pottery
amphora. Athletes with
halteres. Ashmolean
Museum, Oxford AN
1988.387.

(c) Black-Figure as Silver-Figure

The use of gold-figure by Greek silversmiths led, as even the few extant examples of the technique demonstrate, to highly sophisticated means of representing the human figure. The light-coloured metal seems to have lent itself to the realistic drawing of anatomical details, as well as to individual characterization. These developments are reflected in the secondary ceramic tradition which came to an abrupt halt towards the end of the fourth century.[142] Judging by its ceramic echo, the introduction of gold-figure seems to have been equally sudden. The red-figure technique in Attic pottery was preceded by black-figure: in metalworking terms, gold-figure was preceded

[142] R. M. Cook (1972), 186.

by silver-figure. The only substantial extant examples of the genre survive in the form of the silver-figure decoration on the cheek-pieces of a bronze helmet from Olympia[143] (the fashion for decorating vessels in this way will have died out before trading relations were established between Athens and the few places (such as Thrace and Scythia) where funerary practice included the burial of plate). But representation of narrative scenes in multicoloured inlaid (or overlaid) metal had a long tradition in Greece. The Shield of Heracles described in the Hesiodic *Scutum*, a work which has been associated in time with the François vase,[144] is among the most familiar. Heracles' shield is παναίολον ('multicoloured'), and 'a marvel to behold'. It was inlaid with gypsum, ivory, electrum, silver, gold. Some of the decoration is done in what we might term 'silver-figure'.[145] But 'black-figure' pottery is the nearest we can get today to the appearance of such fine metalwork. It is impossible to draw a distinction between the nature of the glaze on decorated and undecorated pots, nor is there any stage at which one can point to a qualitative change in the nature of the glaze between archaic and classical—or even Hellenistic—vessels.[146] If plain black glaze evokes oxidized silver, the same will apply to black figures on decorated wares. A gradual increase in the intrinsic value of the metal vessels in question can thus be observed over the decades. Judging by the colour of the clay, earlier black-figure will have evoked silver on bronze, while red-figure, as we have seen, was probably intended to recall gold on silver.

In between, something very interesting happens, for the transition from black-figure to red-figure perhaps reflects metalworking practices introduced when gold began to be used for the backgrounds of black-figure and for the figures of red-figure. It is a commonplace how very much more difficult it was to draw certain details in red-figure: tendrils, palmettes, or branches of trees, for instance, could be drawn in black-figure with just a few simple strokes; in red-figure they had to be painstakingly outlined with thin bands of paint alongside or around a very limited 'reserved' area.[147] In the real world it usually takes more than an interest in 'the problems of a more natural anatomy and the expression of mood' (as the change to red-figure has been epitomized)[148] to make an artisan adopt working practices that are far more difficult than those to which he is accustomed. The techniques employed in

---

[143] Kunze (1958), fig. 107, pls. 51–2: *Olympia Catalogue* (1972), pl. 2.3. A similar helmet with gold-figures on the cheek-pieces was found at Trebenischte: Vulic (1930), 285–6, figs. 11–12; Kunze (1958), fig. 108. Cf. the *argyropasta hopla* at Polyaen. 6.16, and the bronze hydria in New York (Richter (1937*a*; 1937*b*)) where 'the silver is confined to the subsidiary decoration; it is applied in narrow strips which are not *inserted* but *laid over* the bronze': H. A. Thompson (1940), 190 n. 1. Cf. the similar hydria from Aenea: Vocotopoulou (1986).

[144] R. M. Cook (1937), 204–5.
[145] e.g. Hes. *Scut.* 188, 212, 224–5, 295, 299. For an evocative discussion of the inlaid metal on the comparable Shield of Achilles and House of Alcinous, see Pater (1895), 193 ff.
[146] Cf. Rotroff (1982), 14: 'The bowls of the third century BC are covered with the black glaze familiar from Attic pottery of earlier periods.'
[147] Even letters of inscriptions might occasionally be 'reserved' (Robertson (1981), 23–5, figs. 1 and 4), and see p. 159, below.
[148] R. M. Cook (1972), 161.

'silver-figure' or 'gold-figure' would have been very similar; certainly, there would not have been the great difference in the degree of difficulty between them which prevailed in the potter's world between 'black-figure' and 'red-figure'. Potters, and the artisans employed to decorate pots, simply had to follow as best they could aesthetic norms established in another medium, if they were to do business at all.[149]

The change from black-figure to red-figure can in fact be explained in straightforward metallic terms, and a class of pots known as 'bilingual' because they have black-figure scenes on one side, and red-figure on the other,[150] provide useful clues. Many 'bilingual' vessels show the same scene on each side, the black-figure against an orangey-red background set within a frame, and the red-figure against a black background, again within a frame. An amphora now in Boston (Figs. 5.26 and 5.27)[151] provides a good example, with a scene of Heracles and the Cretan Bull done in both techniques. But let us imagine the Boston amphora in metal: the black parts in silver, the orange in gold. The 'black-figure' scene would thus consist of a silver Heracles, bull, and olive tree against a background of gold leaf; the 'red-figure' of gold-leaf figures laid on a silver background within a gold frame. If this were so, it is clear that a clever and inventive silversmith has realized that both the cut-out gold figures and their background could be used with an economy of time and effort. A related phenomenon is the proliferation of horses in 'black-figure' pottery made after the introduction of 'red-figure'.[152] If, on a metal vase, these figures were of silver and their backgrounds of gold, it would clearly be in the craftsman's financial interest to economize by causing the horses and their human or divine companions to occupy increasingly larger black spaces. Xenophon's observation (made in a military context) is perhaps relevant here: 'a horseman obstructs the view far more than a foot soldier'.[153]

The principle of the hierarchy of metals, whereby silver might be adorned with gold, and bronze with silver, but rarely the other way about,[154] suggests that much earlier black-figure, and certainly black-figure on an unframed free field, was made to evoke silver figures on bronze. The relatively light ground-colour of, for example, the François vase in Florence[155] suggests that of a tin-rich bronze,[156] and figure decoration of a metal original would have been made in silver. It is well known that in earlier Attic black-figure there is a

---

[149] Cf. Robertson (1988*b*), 39: '[The Attic black-figure] style cannot have much relation to drawing on wall or panel; its connections seem rather with metalwork', and in the case of red-figure, 'the direct influence of the potter's technique may be from metalwork rather than painting'.

[150] Cohen (1978).

[151] Boston, MFA 99.538; figs. 5.26 and 5.27 are from C. H. Smith (1899), 54–5, illustr.

[152] Good bibliography in Moore (1971).

[153] Xen. *Hipp*. 5. 14.

[154] The advice of Gerald Taylor on this topic has been invaluable.

[155] Illustrated in colour in *Materiali* (1977), pls. 2–8.

[156] For good colour photographs of tin-rich bronzes, see Fehervari and Safadi (1981), 88–91, nos. 34 and 36.

F I G. 5.26   Attic 'bilingual' pottery amphora; the black-figure side. Heracles and bull. Museum of Fine Arts, Boston (after C. H. Smith (1899), 54–5).

F I G. 5.27   Attic 'bilingual' pottery amphora; the red-figure side. Heracles and bull. Museum of Fine Arts, Boston (after C. H. Smith (1899), 54–5).

tendency for there to be extraneous figures,[157] but they are dropped with the passage of time. If on a metal vase these figures were of silver against a bronze background, the fewer the figures (and again the less the expenditure of time and precious metal), the greater the craftsman's profit. This is a reversal of what occurred after gold backgrounds were introduced, but the underlying profit motive is the same. The reason why we do not have any of the vessels concerned may be attributed to the fact that there would have been enough silver in the necks, feet, and handles to ensure both their remaining above ground and their being melted down when fashions changed or they were looted.[158] The trading relations with Thrace and Scythia which led to gold-figure vessels being deposited in graves in those areas had not yet been established, and thus the circumstances which might have led to the survival of even a few examples did not exist.

(d) Purple as Copper

Still on the question of colours, the limited repertoire of the classical Greek potter includes two more, namely purple and white. Both can be easily read as evocations of materials other than clay. Purple (frequently, though misleadingly, referred to as 'applied' or 'added red'), was probably intended to evoke copper. Copper, as everyone knows, 'is a brilliant metal of a peculiar red colour which . . . [is] purplish when the metal contains cuprous oxide. . . . It takes a brilliant polish, is in a high degree malleable and ductile, and in tenacity it only falls short of iron, exceeding in that quality both silver and gold.'[159] Purple is added to painted pots at the points where one would not be surprised to find copper on silver vessels. Purple is ubiquitous on black-figure pots, but it is progressively less frequent in red-figure.

The purity of Attic silver was famous, as we have seen:[160] 98 per cent was the norm.[161] Sterling silver, by contrast, contains only 92.5 per cent of the precious metal. The remainder is usually copper, added to make the metal harder and to withstand the wear and tear of everyday use.[162] There was a brief period at the end of the seventeenth century when the fineness of British silver was raised to 95.9 per cent, but this 'Britannia standard metal' was soon abandoned, since objects made from it had a very short active life.[163] At 98 per cent or more, Attic silver will have been very soft indeed, and it would appear that the silver vessels of which black-figure pots are the ceramic analogues were strengthened at the points at which they might have been expected to have worn most quickly, or at which extra strength was

---

[157] Called by J. D. Beazley 'Rosincrantz and Guildenstern': Beazley (1931), 258–9, and 'our Danish friends': ibid. 261.

[158] Cf. the heavy orange-yellow handles on large Etruscan red-figure vessels of the 4th c.: e.g. Beazley (1947), pls. 13a, 14, 20.1, 30.1–2, 35.5, 36.3, which were probably made in imitation of gold.

[159] Anon. (1910), 102.

[160] See p. 43, above.

[161] Kraay and Emeleus (1962), 16; cf. Ch. 2 n. 85.

[162] And also to inhibit tarnishing: cf. Kubaschewski and Hopkins (1962), 253.

[163] Cf. Craddock (1983), 132.

FIG. 5.28 Attic black-figure pottery amphora, detail of handle. Ashmolean Museum, Oxford AN 1885.668 (V.212).

required, with copper. Frequent uses to which purple is put on clay vases are on the edges of the handles of quite large amphoras (Fig. 5.28),[164] and on the rims of jugs. On silver vessels, these are points which would receive the most wear; a good reason for strengthening them with a harder and more durable substance. Purple also regularly occurs on pots at the junctions of neck and body, or of body and foot. While the individual parts of pots will usually have been thrown separately,[165] there is no compelling reason for the points of junction on ceramic vessels to have been consistently painted purple. In the case of metal vessels, however, if a strong joint were called for, copper might well have been used.[166] Yet another possible use of copper can be observed on the handle palmette on a jug in Oxford (Fig. 5.29).[167] The purple heart (a feature which is quite common on black-figure palmettes) may be

[164] Ashmolean Museum, Oxford AN 1885.668; *CVA* Oxford 2, IIIh, pls. 8.5–6, 7.9, 9.3, Vickers (1986*b*), 146, 139, fig. D.

[165] Noble (1965), 9–30.

[166] See further, Vickers (1986*b*). For earlier examples of the genre (where, however, the 'copper or bronze . . . was hidden from sight'), cf. some of the silver vessels from the shaft graves of circle A at Mycenae: one had a body 'beaten from a single sheet of silver, to which the neck and rim were added, the joint being concealed by a notched rib which was strengthened with bronze, as were the rim and the base'; another had a rim 'strengthened with a bronze band' (Hood (1978), 160, 172). For a useful list of Aegean Bronze Age silver items strengthened with copper, see Davis (1977), 337–8.

[167] The detail (though not its purpose) was first noted by A. J. Clark (1981), 45.

FIG. 5.29 Attic
black-figure pottery
oinochoe, detail of
handle junction.
Ashmolean Museum,
Oxford AN 1965.122.

intended to evoke a copper rivet of a kind employed to fasten the end of the handle to the body on a silver jug.[168] Copper rivets are famous for their strength even today, whether it be on blue jeans or on battleships,[169] and a rivet on an archaic bronze vessel in the Ashmolean Museum when analysed proved to be 98 per cent copper.[170] The phenomenon is pretty well universal on black-figure pots: purple frequently appears at the points where a need for strengthening on an analogous metal vessel might be expected.

Although the practice of using purple in what we might describe as structural contexts was carried over into red-figure, it did not survive long there. It occurs on some of the earliest red-figure, but its use on vessels made in this technique tends to be confined to lettering and subsidiary features such as streaks of blood, urine, black eyes, or cocks' combs. We might suppose that these were added in copper to silver vessels decorated in 'gold-figure'. The use of copper on vessels which had a substantial bronze component would not have affected their value, whereas its use on vessels made of precious metal had to be restrained (as it was, judging by their ceramic counterparts); for to over-use it would have been tantamount to advertising

---

[168] The feline mask in a precocious example of red-figure technique on the black-figure *oinochoe* London, British Museum B 524 (Robertson (1973)) may have been intended to evoke a gold handle-base ornament inlaid with ivory and copper.

[169] Cf. the *Hull Advertiser*, 9 July 1796, where

one may read: 'She is copper-fastened and copper-bottomed, and a remarkable fine ship.'

[170] Craddock (1977), 118. It is interesting, too, to note that the metal used in antiquity to repair Greek pots was frequently an alloy with a very high copper content: see further Vickers (1986*b*), 146 n. 56.

the fact that their value was not equal to their weight; the ancients, like their modern counterparts in the Worshipful Company of Goldsmiths, placed great store by such considerations.

Finally, a glance at the decorative, rather than a structural use of purple. Two examples will suffice to illuminate the lost world of decorative metal-work of which our black-figure pots are witnesses. A moulded jug in the Ashmolean Museum in the form of a woman's head (Fig. 5.30)[171] recalls a vessel of silver with gold decoration for the face and the volutes on the back of the head. The lips are rendered in purple, a practice which recalls the use of copper for lips and nipples on such works of sculpture as the Riace bronzes.[172] This in turn recalls the widespread practice of rendering nipples on black-figure pots in purple (Fig. 5.31). Moreover, figures in black-figure frequently have purple bands around their heads (Fig. 5.31, again). This feature can also be matched in sculpture, this time in the copper band on a roughly contemporary bronze head of a youth from the Athenian Acropolis.[173]

(e) White as Ivory

Nearly all the colours we find on Attic black- and red-figure pottery can thus be accounted for in terms of metal. Black or metallic-looking blue-grey evokes silver; orangey-red, gold or bronze; purple, copper. The only other colour found on such wares is white, which appears to have been intended to imitate sometimes alabaster, but mostly ivory. While there are extant examples of the stone vessels, ivory from classical Greece hardly survives at all. This is scarcely surprising in that ivory is notoriously subject to decay: 'The houses of ivory shall perish' said the Old Testament prophet,[174] and all of them did. If ivory *lekythoi* were oil-containers, this will, however, have helped to preserve them for a while at least, for the oil they held doubtless had a preservative effect. According to Pliny, one way to prevent an ivory statue from cracking was to pour oil through a hole in the top of its head.[175] But even the chryselephantine statue of Zeus at Olympia which was dressed with oil had to be repaired in the Hellenistic period 'when,' says Pausanias, 'its ivory was breaking away'.[176] We should not be surprised, moreover, by the fact that 'three big thrones with their backs inlaid with ivory' mentioned in an Acropolis inventory of soon after 385 were described as being in an 'unsound condition'.[177] It is not simply the difficulty of obtaining ivory nowadays which has led to its gradual disappearance from the roles it used to perform: knife handles, piano keys, billiard balls,[178] for example, but the

[171] Ashmolean Museum, Oxford AN 1920.106; *CVA* Oxford 1, pl. 44, 1–2; Vickers (1986*b*), 149, fig. M.

[172] Cf. Houser (1982), 8: 'lips and nipples are made of copper to give red colour to those areas'.

[173] Bol (1985), 152, fig. 110. For further comparanda, see Vickers (1986*b*).

[174] Amos 3. 15.

[175] Pliny, *NH* 15. 33.

[176] Paus. 4. 31. 6.

[177] *IG* 2² 1415, 11. 26–7.

[178] Cf. Maskell (1911), 93.

FIG. 5.30 Attic pottery 'head-vase'. Maenad. Ashmolean Museum, Oxford AN 1920.106.

FIG. 5.31   Attic black-figure pottery *oinochoe*, detail of figure decoration. Symposiasts. Ashmolean Museum, Oxford AN 1965.122.

fact that it is very prone to split, especially when subjected to rapid changes of temperature.[179]

It should not be necessary to dwell on the fact that ivory is attested in some quantity at Athens in the fifth century. 'Libya supplies ivory in plenty for trade', said Hermippus, the comic poet,[180] and it is surely significant that the Nile was known to the Persians as the 'Ivory River' or 'the Tusks'.[181] There will have been a substantial amount of ivory in Phidias' 11-metre high chryselephantine statue of Athena Parthenos,[182] for example, and there are references to ivory objects in temple inventories at all periods.[183] While it is

[179] Ritchie (1969), 39.
[180] Hermipp. *PCG* 63. 15, ap. Ath. 1. 27f. On the ivory trade, see Gill (1992).
[181] Kent (1950), 147 (DZc 9).
[182] Eddy (1977).
[183] e.g. *IG* 1³, p. 332, 29 (ivory lyres), 31 (table

inlaid with ivory), and 40 (a gilded ivory flute-case) (Parthenon); *IG* 2² 1388, 67–8 (an ivory and gold palladium), 80 (an ivory lyre); 1400, 22 (a sword with an ivory handle), 53–4 (a little ivory bull); 1415, 27–9 (three big thrones, unsound, with backs inlaid with ivory); 1421, 112 (a table

not the case, as has been suggested, that ivory was worth close to its weight in gold,[184] its unworked value was considerably greater than that of bronze or pottery: at a sale at Delphi in the fourth century BC, tusks cost 24.5 drachmas per *mina*,[185] or a quarter of their weight in silver. Demosthenes' inheritance included a sword factory and a bed factory, in both of which 2 *minas*' worth of ivory was used every month for sword handles and the inlay of couches.[186] Indeed, an ivory couch-ornament itself inlaid with amber—another luxury import—has been found in the Ceramicus cemetery at Athens.[187]

Ivory was also used for blazons on shields: Alcibiades thus owned 'a shield made of gold and ivory on which there was the device of Eros wielding a thunderbolt',[188] and we hear of Phocian mercenaries carrying 'gold, ivory and electrum shields'.[189] A similarly richly embellished parade shield has been found at Vergina, decorated with an ivory emblem of a Greek and an Amazon.[190] The blazons of shields on pots are frequently rendered in white; and if black, orangey-red, and purple are indeed evocations of various metals, ivory is a strong candidate for their source. White is used for many other features as well: for women's flesh, Gorgons' teeth, harness decoration, and jewellery, and it is not difficult to view these manifestations as gestures in the direction of ivory inlay in metalwork, just as the small white cones with black dots in their centres which frame the head of the maenad in Fig. 5.29 can be read as skeuomorphs of ivory pieces held in place with silver pins.

The introduction of red-figure on pottery was explained above (p. 139) in terms of changes in metalworkers' practice; a similar explanation may lie behind the existence of large white figures in otherwise red-figure scenes, a phenomenon which regularly occurs in the fourth century BC, where a white horse (Fig. 5.32),[191] a griffin, or a naked woman might dominate the centre of a composition. To argue that such a development owed its existence to a new fashion in pottery painting would be pointless, for the prices fetched by decorated pottery show it to have been far removed from the world of fashion.[192] If instead, large white figures reflected a development in the world of the silversmith, they can perhaps be explained in terms of a device

inlaid with ivory), 123–5 (a miniature helmet . . . with gold cheek-pieces and an ivory plume); 1448, 2 (a small cup inlaid with ivory); 1456, 40 ff. (little ivory animals) (Hecatompedon); Jahn and Michaelis (1901), 48 (ivory mirror-handle) (Brauronion); Michel (1900), 832, 45 (an ivory unguent container) (Samian Heraeum); *IDélos* 296B, 51 (an ivory box); 298A, 26 (handle of a fly-swatter) (Delos). In general, see Blümner (1879–87), 2. 361–75; (1905); Jacob (1892); Lorimer (1936); Barnett (1982); Masson and Pugacenova (1982); Vickers (1987c). On the properties of ivory: Penniman (1952), 15; Krzyszkowska (1990) (but cf. O'Connor (1992)).

[184] Albizzati (1916), 399.
[185] *FdD* 3/5, 2a, 5–13; Barnett (1982), 64.
[186] Dem. 32. 9–11; 30–3. The original inheritance included more than a talent's worth of ivory.
[187] Knigge and Willemsen (1964), 44, pl. 39a; Knigge (1976), 62, fig. 22, pls. 101–3.
[188] Ath. 12. 534e; Plut. *Alc.* 16. 1 (although it is possible that it only existed on the stage (Russell (1966), 45; Littmann (1970), 267–8).
[189] Plut. *Tim.* 31.
[190] *ArchRep* for 1982–3, 44; cf. Diog. Laert. 8. 5.
[191] Ashmolean Museum, Oxford AN 1970.6; Vickers (1978), 64.
[192] See above, p. 54, on the 'trickle-down effect'.

FIG. 5.32 Attic red-figure pottery *pelike*. Horse attacked by griffins. Ashmolean Museum, Oxford AN 1970.6.

which was at one and the same time eye-catching and economical, for to use an ivory inlay instead of a gold-foil figure would have led to immediate savings of gold, a commodity which was by weight some forty times more costly. Once again, artisans working in the pottery industry had to follow fashions created for another medium if they were to sell their products at all.

White occurs most frequently, of course, on white-ground *lekythoi*, cylinder-shaped vessels which were especially associated with funerary rites. For Beazley 'there was no special reason' for this shape,[193] but D. C. Kurtz has acutely associated the earliest Athenian white-ground pots with metal vases (although the only reason she gives for the existence of white-ground is that the workman 'applied the slip to set his vase somewhat apart from others').[194] If, however, the metal vases in question were luxury objects of silver, it is possible to go rather further. White-ground *lekythoi* are only white in the upper three-quarters of the body; usually the shoulder is also white, although it can be black. The handle and chimney-like neck are also black, as is the lower part of the body and the upper part of the foot. The inner part of the handle and the edge and underside of the foot are 'reserved'. The upper rim is sometimes purple on early examples of the genre. It was Oliver Impey, who tends the Ashmolean Museum's collection of Japanese antiquities, who first suggested that Attic white-ground *lekythoi* might have been intended to evoke ivory;[195] and their very shapes indicate their close dependence on vessels made from elephants' tusks. (cf. those being carried in procession on an ivory relief from Nimrud (Fig. 5.33).[196] Fig. 5.34 shows a series of white-ground *lekythoi* of different sizes laid out in such a way as to suggest their likely source. No early white-ground *lekythos* has a diameter greater than that of an elephant's tusk,[197] and if the white-ground shape known as the 'Columbus *alabastron*' is any indication, even the tip of a tusk was put to good use (Fig. 5.34, again). Ivory, it is well known, is a material which is laminated concentrically,[198] so that a large number of cylinders for silver and ivory *lekythoi* might be extracted from a single tusk. Such *lekythoi* will have consisted of an ivory cylinder and a separately turned ivory shoulder riveted together. The regular palmette decoration will have served to hide the rivets. A parallel for this may be found in the palmettes at the handles of pottery cups which, it has been suggested, were meant to refer to a means of disguising rivets on metal analogues.[199]

Both cylinder and shoulder of the kind of ivory *lekythos* envisaged would

[193] Beazley (1938), 3–4.

[194] Kurtz (1975), 11.

[195] Cf. Vickers (1985*a*), 112 n. 34.

[196] Ashmolean Museum, Oxford AN 1959.209; Mallowan and Davies (1970), 37, pl. 29, no. 100.

[197] The stoutest standard white *lekythos* known to us is one in the J. Paul Getty Museum (73.AE.41), the diameter of which is 14.46 cm at the shoulder (Mertens (1975), 27 n. 1). Many

ivory tusks and vessels are of comparable thickness; e.g. a tusk of *Loxodonta africana* in the University Museum at Oxford (no. 4004) is 14.3 cm in diameter; copies of the Medici crater in Dieppe Museum (nos. 57 and 58) are 15.8 cm in diameter.

[198] Penniman (1952), 15.

[199] Jacobsthal (1927), 39, 144; cf. Kurtz (1975), 2.

F I G. 5.33   Tribute bearers carrying ivory tusks and a tray of gold ear-rings. From Fort Shalmaneser, Nimrud. Ashmolean Museum, Oxford AN 1959.209.

F I G. 5.34   Attic white-ground pottery *lekythoi* and a 'Columbus' *alabastron*, arranged in the shape of an elephant's tusk. Ashmolean Museum, Oxford.

have been mounted in a silver setting. They would hence not have been placed *in* Athenian tombs any more than any other vessels made of precious metal. Nor is it likely that they would have been left *on* tombs either; pots may well have been,[200] but silver and ivory vessels were presumably either burnt on a funeral pyre (and the precious metal recovered together with the bones) or taken home after a funeral. A late fifth-century inscription from Iulis on Cea, indeed, stipulates that the vessels used for wine and oil should be removed once the funerary rites were over, and the fact that as much as

[200] The broken vessels on e.g. the white-ground *lekythos* Louvre G.6 certainly suggest as much.

a *mina* could be spent on the shrouds alone suggests that the vessels concerned might have been of a certain value as well.[201]

White-ground exists in shapes other than *lekythoi* of course, and it must be said that there has long been an awareness that some of these copy objects originally made in other materials. Thus J. D. Beazley rightly believed that white-ground *alabastra* 'recalled the alabastra made of the original material, alabaster', while 'white pyxides . . . recalled vases of the same shape in marble'.[202] It is more likely, however, that marble was frequently used as poor man's ivory and that stone *pyxides* too were made in a tradition established by ivory-turners.[203] There are also vessels such as craters and cups on which large expanses of white-ground are to be seen, and which are too large to be attributable to the employment of unaltered ivory tusks alone. Here the tradition of ivory-bending may come into play. The existence of this practice is known from several ancient authorities. 'Ivory-benders' appear in the list of skilled craftsmen Plutarch lists as active in Periclean Athens.[204] Pausanias actually describes the process: 'fire turns the horns of oxen and [the tusks] of elephants from round to flat, and also into other shapes',[205] and Plutarch states that ivory could be shaped and bent after being soaked in beer.[206] In modern times, eighteenth-century miniature painters are said to have made large square plates by cutting ivory cylinders down the side and flattening them out after softening them in a solution of phosphoric acid.[207] One or other of these techniques was presumably employed by the craftsmen who made the silver, gold, and ivory cups and craters of which versions still survive in clay.

It is a commonplace, and a valid one, that the way in which white-ground vessels are usually decorated probably had much in common with easel or mural painting; for example:

the technique of decoration of [white-ground] was the Greek vase-painter's closest equivalent to what we consider 'painting'. The artist was constrained neither by the inarticulable silhouette and the laborious incision of black-figure, nor by the rigid contours and black background of red-figure; he had neutral white surface on which to draw freely and apply colour, chiefly for drapery.[208]

Some of the finest classical Greek drawings we possess are those on ivory plaques found together with a golden *phiale*[209] (which shows what level of society we are dealing with) in a tomb at Kul Oba in Southern Russia.[210] The only drawings that come at all close to them in quality are those on some

[201] Sokolowski (1969), no. 97 (English translation in Kurtz and Boardman (1971), 200–1).

[202] Beazley (1938), 4.

[203] Cf. e.g. the illustrations in Plumier (1701) with those in Lunsingh Scheurleer (1926), 7–10.

[204] Plut. *Per.* 12. 6.

[205] Paus. 5. 12. 2.

[206] Plut. *Mor.* 499e; cf. Sen. *Ep.* 90. 33; Stadter (1989), 159.

[207] Williamson (1938), 12.

[208] Mertens (1975), 27.

[209] Cf. Boardman (1973), 155, 160; Galanina and Grach (1986), figs. 164–5.

[210] Peredolskaya (1945), 69–83, pls. 1–6; Artomonov (1966), pls. 258, 261.

painted clay *lekythoi* of the second half of the fifth century, and even the best of these fall short in quality of execution.[211] They serve, however, to help us reconstruct the likely furnishings of a wealthy Athenian funeral.

That ivory was regarded as a material characteristic of rich funerals is clear from the way in which Plutarch refers to the trappings of elaborate death rites. In 364, the customary 'magnificence in ivory, gold, and purple' was absent from the funeral of Pelopidas, though it was very much part of the rites accompanying the funeral of Demetrius Poliorcetes in 283.[212] It was the good will manifested by friend and enemy alike, not 'the pomp of gold, of ivory, or other expense or parade' which was the striking feature of the obsequies of Aemilius Paullus.[213] 'Hundreds' of burnt ivory fragments have been found at Vergina in a context which strongly suggests that they came from an aristocratic, if not royal, funeral pyre,[214] and the Kul Oba plaques come from a coffin.[215] It is interesting to note that in his ideal state Plato legislated against offerings of ivory at sanctuaries: 'ivory, the product of a dead body, is not a proper offering (to the gods)';[216] to take this logic one step further, ivory might have been considered a highly appropriate material from which to make vessels for the dead.

The colour on the Kul Oba plaques has disappeared, as have the fugitive colours on many of our pots. Demosthenes inherited a certain amount of oak-gall, a substance used to stain the ivory sword handles produced in his factory,[217] but this is our only direct evidence for the materials actually used to colour ivory. The poet of the *Iliad* compares the blood on a wounded hero's thigh to the red-purple dye with which a girl stains the ivory cheek-piece of a horse,[218] but the material used is uncertain. The most profitable approach here, perhaps, is to compare the colours used to decorate nine-teenth- and twentieth-century Chinese ivory vessels. This school of ivory-working which, like that of the Greeks, used ivory from African elephants,[219] could produce monodontic and straight vases of enormous proportions.[220] The range of colours employed to adorn Chinese ivory carvings is limited, but close to that used on Greek *lekythoi*. The likely ingredients, moreover, are extremely simple.[221] Some may be exotic, but scarcely unobtainable by anyone acquiring ivory in the first place. Green pigment was probably a solution of malachite; blue one of azurite; yellow of orpiment (a sulphide of arsenic). Black was either lamp black, or ivory black made by burning ivory.

---

[211] e.g. Robertson (1959), 136–45.
[212] Plut. *Pel.* 34. 1.
[213] Plut. *Aem.* 39. 4.
[214] Personal communication from Professor Andronicos.
[215] Cf. Boardman (1973), 160.
[216] Pl. *Leg.* 956a.
[217] Dem. 27. 10; 43. Cf. [Democr.] at Zos. Alch. 160b: κικίδιον, a yellow dye.
[218] Hom. *Il.* 4. 141; Barnett (1954), 677; cf.

Philostr. *Imag.* 2.7: καὶ τὸ αἷμα οἷον ἐπ' ἐλέφαντι χρῶμα; Coldstream (1968), 275 suggests that the bodies of Rhodian Late Geometric *pyxides* 'are prob-ably modelled on a Levantine ivory prototype, and their surfaces are toned with a reddish slip resem-bling the dyeing of ivory'.
[219] Cox (1946), 30.
[220] Ibid. 68, pl. 19, cf. p. 30 (illustration and discussion of an ivory vase 70.5 cm high).
[221] Ibid. 110–12.

Ivory black must have been quite costly, judging by the fact that quantities of ivory dust are recorded in temple inventories at Athens and on Delos.[222] Purple, in Greece, was in all probability some kind of purple dye, a commodity that could be spoken of in the same terms as silver.[223] Red could be either realgar (another sulphide of arsenic) or cinnabar,[224] a by-product of silver extraction said by Pliny to have been invented at Athens.[225]

Some of this chapter has been speculative; inevitably so, since some of the evidence is circumstantial. It has been argued that the fine ceramic vessels made in archaic and classical Greece, the black-figure, red-figure, and white-ground wares which fill museums from Stockholm to Sydney, and Mykonos to Malibu, are the products of highly skilled craftsmen whose special expertise lay in evoking both the shapes and decorative schemes of vessels made in more precious materials: silver, gold, bronze, copper, and ivory.[226] But if there is a possibility that most Greek pottery vases are 'mock silver', then obvious questions arise about the respect in which they (and their executants) have been held in modern times. These issues will be discussed in the next chapter.

---

[222] *IG* 2² 1412, 32–3:ἐλεφάντινα περιπρίσματα; *IDélos* 298A, 181: ἐλέφαντου παραπρισμάτων; cf. 320B, 68.

[223] Cf. Aesch. *Agam.* 959: πορφύρας ἰσάργυρων κηκῖδα.

[224] Cox (1946), 110.

[225] Pliny, *NH* 33. 37.

[226] We would not suggest that bronze or copper were especially valuable commodities, but they were worth more than ceramic.

6 Questions of Attribution, Representation, and Continuity

SO far, we have presented evidence to suggest that Greek pottery was of little consequence in antiquity and only came into its own in the eighteenth century; that the ancients placed far more store by gold and silver than ceramic; and that the fine Greek pottery we have is an evocation of the silverware on the tables of Athenian and Etruscan aristocrats. The questions discussed in this chapter are less capable of proof one way or the other; some—able scholars among them—will doubtless choose to continue to interpret the issues in the traditional way, while others may decide that they can be more easily resolved within a model where plate holds primacy of position. We are content here to try to persuade our readers by presenting them with an alternative paradigm which accounts for the phenomena, but which leaves fewer inconsistencies than the position we are questioning.

ARTISTS' SIGNATURES

It is widely believed that some Greek pots bear the signatures of the potters who made them and the painters who decorated them. In fact:

A few vases are signed, most are not. Of the unsigned vases, some can be ascribed to painters whose names are known, but most are by painters who never signed or whose signatures have not been preserved: to these painters—determinable by style—one gives conventional names, such as Villa Giulia painter, so called because his masterpiece is in the Villa Giulia.[1]

The writer was (presumably) J. D. Beazley, a scholar who spent a long career attributing thousands of extant pots to the hands of hundreds of craftsmen. It has been well said of him that 'No one would suggest that he exploited his position . . . But others profited from Beazley's work; for he provided that most saleable of commodities—artists' names.'[2] The trend towards holding exhibitions of supposedly big-name artists, such as the 'Amasis Painter' or 'Euphronios' has caused the issues involved in the nomenclature of pot-painters to be fudged. We have already had occasion to note how intrinsically

---

[1] Oxford Arts Club (1928), p. i.
[2] Beard (1986). It was presumably with a view to increasing the price that a pot was recently sold, not even with an autograph, but 'a copy of a letter written by J. D. Beazley': Sotheby Catalogue, 12 December 1988, lot 110.

unsound are some of the arguments brought forward to support the high status accorded to Beazley's 'Euphronios',[3] and there are sufficiently numerous inconsistencies in the way in which 'signatures' are commonly treated to raise questions about the role played by words on painted pottery.

Greek painted pottery is rightly regarded as a prime source for understanding how Western art evolved at an early stage in its development.[4] Since many of the surviving pots are well made and skilfully decorated, they have come to be regarded as representative of the very highest artistic output of Athens. As early as d'Hancarville, who was trying to get the best price for the wares he was trying to sell, archaic work was put on a par with 'Ghiotto and Cimabue',[5] and the equation is still made today.[6] The approach to attribution in both areas of study is very similar, and there was a time when the terminology applied to the painters of pots (the 'Master of the Berlin Amphora')[7] and Italian primitives (the 'Master of the Sforza Altarpiece')[8] was consciously identical in character.[9] The implicit assumption here has been accurately, if somewhat cruelly, characterized as follows: 'a logic that proceeds: the vases were decorated by draughtsmen who stand with Botticelli, *therefore* their pots were important and valuable, *therefore* their creators earned a good living and had considerable social standing.'[10] In reality, the products of the Athenian potteries were sold for obols, as we have seen,[11] whereas contracts relating to the commissioning of Italian Quattrocento paintings (which lay stress on the amount of gold and precious pigments to be used) mention considerable sums of money.[12]

It is the apparent presence of artists' names on some pottery vessels which has done much to perpetuate an equation between Florentine painters and the decorators of Athenian ceramics, and it has been an eagerness to foster retrospectively the role of the artist—in a way that was wholly foreign to ancient Greece—that has consistently allowed the rosiest interpretation of the evidence to hold sway at every turn. If, however, one applies even the slightest degree of scepticism, or even takes at face value Martin Robertson's frank admission that 'the signing practice on Greek pottery seems to be totally haphazard', and 'the evidence is difficult to evaluate and appears contradictory',[13] it quickly becomes clear that the conventional view regarding 'signatures' cannot hold.

---

[3] See pp. 94, 98, above.
[4] Robertson (1975), pp. xvii–xviii; (1985), 29.
[5] D'Hancarville, (1766[1768]–76), 1. 168; and see p. 10, above.
[6] Kurtz (1985); Robertson (1991), 12.
[7] Beazley (1911).
[8] Berenson (1968), 1. 256.
[9] Cf. Robertson (1976), 32–5. Beazley (1918), 41 has one pot-painter playing 'a kind of Florentine' to another's 'Sienese'.
[10] Vitelli (1992), 552.

[11] See pp. 85–8, above.
[12] e.g. the figure of 190 florins is mentioned in the context of Fra Angelico's altarpiece for the Linen-Makers' Guild at Florence, and Ghirlandaio undertook to paint the *Adoration of the Magi* for the Spedale degli Innocenti for 115 florins: Baxendall (1972), 5–14.
[13] Robertson (1972), 182, 180; cf. Beazley (1944), 115: 'Many of the best are unsigned, and some of the worst signed.'

The inscription on a small pot in the Ashmolean Museum (Fig. 6.1) will serve to illustrate some of the problems involved. It reads 'Oikopheles potted (ἐκεραμευσεν) me; Oikopheles drew (ἐγραεφσεν) me'. The pot is of a form which evokes turned wood rather than metalwork, and the carelessly painted black-figure scene lacks any programmatic unity. There is a Gorgon's head in the centre, surrounded by a sphinx, a maenad and a satyr, Heracles and a centaur, and finally a hunting scene, where boys drive a large hare into a crudely incised net. Oikopheles has been called 'the worst vase-painter whose name is known to us from antiquity',[14] and there can be little doubt that he was indeed the painter of the pot in Oxford, and that he was the potter. The question of direct imitation of precious metal does not arise here.

Oikopheles' vessel is unique in at least one respect in that it is the only known pot to bear an indisputable potter's inscription: *ekerameusen* can only mean that Oikopheles turned the clay on the wheel and saw to the firing of the pot in the kiln. It is important to recognize that *ekerameusen* occurs on no other Greek pot; and yet the study of Greek ceramics is in large part predicated on the assumption that it does. The reason lies in the occasional—and haphazard—presence of the expression 'So-and-so ἐποίησεν' inscribed on pots (usually painted in black in black-figure, and in purple in red-figure, or incised in both genres). Quite what *epoiesen* means in this context is debated: some choose to interpret the word as a synonym for 'potted' and believe that it usually indicates the name of the individual who fashioned the vessel—or at least under whose direction it was made,[15] others regard it as an indication of the name of the manager of a potters' workshop.[16] There are difficulties with both interpretations—which is perhaps why the debate is periodically reopened—and it is hard to see how the problem can be resolved so long as it is discussed solely within a ceramic frame of reference. A possible solution may lie in G. M. A. Richter's observation, already noted,[17] that the word ἐπόει visible on some black-glaze *phialai* might have been 'part of the signature of the original silver bowl'.[18] If so, it could well be that *epoiesen* inscriptions on painted pottery are also a carry-over from silver-smithing.

Quite how this might have been achieved involves a consideration of the inscriptions that are usually regarded as the autograph signatures of artists, namely those that read 'So-and-so *egrapsen*'. Sometimes these occur by themselves, sometimes together with an *epoiesen* inscription to which the name

---

[14] Payne (1931), 322; Beazley (1931–2), 21.

[15] e.g. Beazley (1944), 108–9; Robertson (1972); Bothmer (1988); Cohen (1991).

[16] R. M. Cook (1971), 137–8; Eisman (1974), 172. Charles Ricketts, an acquaintance of J. D. Beazley, wrote in his diary for 30 January 1906 his reaction to the cleaning of a cup in the possession of the dealer Ready: 'We then examined the sides, under the handle was a smear of paint which he rubbed. "By Jove!" he exclaimed. "I believe there is a signature!" This he spelt out: Hischylos epoiesen. "Hischylos? Hischylos?" I then said, "Yes, the employer or partner of Epictetos."' (C. Lewis (1939), 131) The cup is now in the Fitzwilliam Museum, Cambridge, GR.14-1937.

[17] See p. 100, above.

[18] Richter (1941), 388.

FIG. 6.1 Attic black-figure pottery standed dish, from Peristeri, Attica. Ashmolean Museum, Oxford AN G.243 (V.189).

of another individual is attached, and sometimes they state that the same person *epoiesen* and *egrapsen*. There is no hard and fast rule about the order in which these statements are given. Thus, for example, a standlet in New York bears an inscription reading Κλέτιας [ἔγρα]φσεν Ἐργότιμος ἐποίεσεν[19] while the François vase in Florence is inscribed Ἐργότιμος μὲποίεσεν Κλέτιας μὲγραφσεν.[20] Those vessels where there was an apparent division of labour bring to mind the longer verse inscription on the Heracliot cup discussed in an earlier chapter.[21] This reads: 'the design (*gramma*) is by Parrhasius, the work (*techna*) by Mys. I am the representation of lofty Ilium which the sons of Aeacus captured.'[22] Elsewhere, we learn that the metal-worker Mys and the artist Parrhasius often worked together in this way.[23] We have already noted that the inscription on the cup indicates a division of labour between the two men involved: the one who made the original design, and the one who carried it out—poetical equivalents of *egrapsen* and *epoiesen*.[24] Such a sharing of responsibility between an artist and a silversmith is well known at other periods. The drawings for the most elaborate plate by artists such as Holbein[25] or Giulio Romano[26] were made to be used by silversmiths as models for their work. Many, indeed, of Parrhasius' draw-ings—called, significantly, *graphides*—were still extant *in tabulis ac mebranis* ('on wooden tablets and parchment') in Pliny's day, from which craftsmen were said to profit.[27] Although parchment was 'costly' in the fifth century BC,[28] it would not have been a major element in the price of a piece of plate, and the design might well in any case have been shown to the client before work began.[29] For *egrapsen* can mean 'created the original design' as easily as 'drew'. There is a good example in Theocritus' poetical account of the visit of a couple of Syracusan tourists to the royal palace in Alexandria. Praxinoa and Gorgo are amazed at the fineness and elegance of a tapestry. 'Who were the weavers who worked on it? Who were the artists who de-signed (*egrapsan*) the cartoons (*grammata*)?' one of them asks. The weavers were clearly not the designers; nor should we expect them to have been.[30]

---

[19] Richter (1931), 289–90.

[20] Cohen (1991), 52.

[21] See p. 100, above.

[22] Γραμμὰ Παρρασιόιο, τέχνα Μυός: ἔμμι δὲ ἐργὸν Ἰλίου αἰπεινᾶς, ἂν ἕλον Αἰακίαδαι, Ath. 11. 782b. The date of Parrhasius' and Mys' col-laboration is disputed, but, as D. L. Page observes, there is no reason to dismiss this epigram as a late forgery: Page (1981), 495.

[23] Paus. 1. 28. 2.

[24] See p. 100, above.

[25] His (1886).

[26] Hayward (1970), 10–14; Hartt (1958), figs. 130–47.

[27] Pliny, *NH* 35. 68. For parchment before Pergamum, cf. Hdt. 5. 58.

[28] Driver (1957), 1–3.

[29] For a later example, cf. the letter written by Lancillotto de Andreasis (the Mantuan opposite number of Mukannishum at Old Babylonian Mari) to his employer Federico Gonzaga in 1483: 'I have bargained with the goldsmith Gian Marco Cavalli about making the bowls and beakers after Andrea Mantegna's design. Gian Marco asks three lire, ten soldi for the bowls and one and a half lire for the beakers . . . I am sending you the design made by Mantegna for the flask, so that you can judge the shape before it is begun': quoted by Baxendall (1972), 12.

[30] On tapestry designers, see e.g. Salet (1973), 21–3; Haverkamp-Begemann (1975); Herrero (1992), 27, 35, 55, 65, 73, 76, 81, 95.

A recent study of incised inscriptions on pots has concluded that they 'were not random graffiti but an intentionally executed feature of the design, which certainly enhanced the iconography of the representations in accord with classic Greek tradition'[31] (and much the same could be said of many painted inscriptions as well). The signing practice was related there to 'an individual potter's sense of pride in his craft', and 'perhaps [enhanced] the local market value of the vessels'.[32] There is no way to disprove these suggestions, but they are less compelling when it is recalled how infrequent are *epoiesen* and *egrapsen* inscriptions in the ceramic record: we would guess that they occur on far fewer than 1 per cent of painted pots. Had there been such 'pride', or such financial rewards attendant upon the presence of a painter's or a potter's signature on a pot, rather more claims to authorship might be expected: in a world where 'artist potters' were 'artistic rivals', more self-advertisement might be anticipated. There is a major difficulty here, and one that cannot be easily resolved without recourse to the possibility that the infrequent 'signatures' are a carry-over from work in precious metal.

Such a solution, whereby potters and pot-painters followed norms created by artists for workers in silver and gold, would account for the high quality of much of the relevant pottery, as well as for the 'haphazard' and 'contradictory' nature of the physical evidence that is usually brought into consideration. There is also some new material evidence that may bear upon the case, namely the gold-figure inscriptions reading ΑΥΓΗ and ΔΗΛΑΔΗ next to the figures on a silver-gilt *phiale* in the recently discovered Rogozen treasure.[33] This is a practice which recalls the gold letters on silver cups mentioned by Alexis ('a round, very small, old [cup], its handles terribly crushed . . . with [eleven] letters [in gold] all about it . . . dedicating it to Saviour Zeus');[34] by Athenaeus (a cup at Capua 'of silver . . . [with] the Homeric verses set upon it in letters of gold');[35] and by Achaeus (a 'lettered cup' inscribed 'Dionyso').[36] Likely ceramic equivalents of such gold letters are to be found in those inscriptions on early red-figure (or 'mock gold-figure') pots, where the letters are painstakingly outlined with thin bands of paint alongside or around a very limited 'reserved' area covered with a thin reddish slip.[37] Small silver letters inlaid in bronze, of a kind Cicero reported on a statue of Apollo by Myron,[38] or still to be seen on the Piombino Apollo

---

[31] Cohen (1991), 85.

[32] Ibid. 49.

[33] 'Katalog' (1986), 46, no. 4; *Frakiiskii klad* (1986), 32, no. 4; New Thracian Treasure (1986), 34, no. 4, colour pl. 1; *Thrakische Silberschatz* (n.d.), 67–9.

[34] Ath. 11. 466e.

[35] Ath. 11. 466e; 489c.

[36] Ath. 11. 466e–f. Cf. the inscriptions on shields done in golden letters at Aesch. *Septem* 434, 660; Plut. *Dem.* 20.

[37] Robertson (1981), 23–25, figs. 1, 4: 'The artist seems first to have reserved a billet, then filled in the glaze round the letters later'; cf. Tompkins (1983), 54–5; Bothmer (1987), 10, fig. 6. 'Yellow-red' inscriptions, of the kind noted by Beazley (1928), 12–13, will similarly have evoked gold letters.

[38] Cic. *Verr.* 2. 4. 43: 'Signum Apollonis pulcherrimum, cuius in femore litteris minutis argenteis nomen Myronis est inscriptum'.

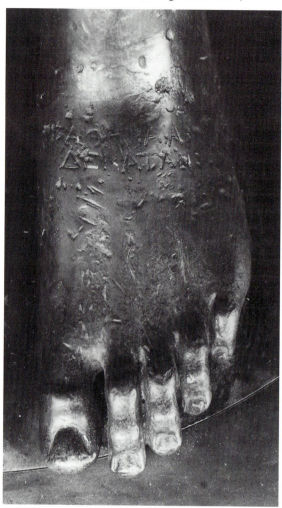

FIG. 6.2   Foot of the
bronze Piombino Apollo,
detail of silver inlaid
inscription. Louvre, Paris.

(Fig. 6.2),[39] indicate how the prototypes of letters on black-figure were achieved.

If *egrapsen* inscriptions can be seen as usually referring to the artist who made the original design for a bespoke piece of plate, and *epoiesen* inscriptions as indicating the name of a silversmith carried over from such a design, then it may be possible to explain some of the serious discrepancies which exist in the currently accepted interpretation of these expressions (where, to recapitulate, *egrapsen* is regarded as an indication of the autograph hand of the artist, and *epoiesen* variously as the 'signature' of the potter or manager).

'A typical problem', we are told, is set by a cup in Berlin which bears the inscription *Douris egraphsen*, but which is unquestionably by a different hand.

[39] B. Ridgway (1967), 65, 67, and fig. 9.

'Between the evidence of the style and the evidence of the inscription we dare not hesitate,' stated Beazley. 'The signature must give way: however its presence is to be explained.'[40] 'Ancient forgery', 'a respectful nod by the Triptolemos Painter to Douris', and 'a boast of equality',[41] are among the suggestions that have been made to get around what is a very thorny problem. None is exactly compelling, and the less so in view of the extremely low prices paid for such wares in antiquity, and in the absence of any other evidence for artistic rivalry. The existence of fragments of a second cup inscribed *Douris egraphsen*[42] but also by another hand does nothing to lessen the problem if it is viewed from a purely ceramic point of view. Far more economical to see both Beazley's 'Douris' and his 'Triptolemos Painter' having used designs made by an artist whose name we might for clarity's sake latinize and call Duris. Duris, like Parrhasius, will have worked primarily in the world of the metalworker.

There is, however, the possibility that the painters of the vessels were 'two artists of the same name': 'Douris I' and 'Douris II'.[43] On the evidence available at present this cannot be ruled out, but one of the arguments adduced in favour is itself revealing: 'We all have become used to several Polygnotoses,' states Miss Richter.[44] For 'Polygnotos' is another example of a single name apparently used as a signature by different hands: there are pots by at least three hands—possibly four—bearing the legend *Polygnotos egrapsen*. These are generally referred to as 'Polygnotos', the 'Lewis Painter', and the 'Nausicaa Painter',[45] but again it is possible that a plurality of pot-painters made use of designs originally made for another medium by a well-known artist of the day, namely Polygnotus.[46]

It should be noted that, unlike some, we are fully prepared to concur with the bulk of Beazley's attributions to individual hands of artisans, although—Oikopheles apart—we do not believe that the names of artists and craftsmen that appear on pots are necessarily those of workers in ceramic. We would thus distance ourselves somewhat from those who believe connoisseurship to be 'an expensive and ageing tart',[47] for there may well be circumstances in which it may be useful to group individual hands together (see below, p. 168). But what has tended to be obscured amid the (ultimately market-led) need to differentiate hands has been the degree to which there is an overlap of motifs between the work of one pot-painter and another. The repetition of designs—even if only of the kind to be seen on two roughly

---

[40] Beazley (1944), 123.
[41] Guy (1981), 11.
[42] Ibid. 11, 14 nn. 70–1.
[43] Mingazzini (1971), 2. 59; Richter (1965), 75–6. The argument from the supposed existence of two Epiktetoi loses force in the light of Boardman (1981).
[44] Richter (1965), 76.

[45] For the possible fourth, see Beazley (1963), 1057, no. 99; Robertson (1965), 97.
[46] For a discussion of some of the issues involved, see Padgett (1991), 24–6, who notes that like the 'Nausicaa Painter', Polygnotus depicted Odysseus and Nausicaa: Paus. 1. 22. 6.
[47] Maginnis (1990), 104.

FIG. 6.3   (*Left*) Attic red-figure pottery *stamnos*. Huntsmen. Ashmolean Museum, Oxford AN 1916.68.

FIG. 6.4   (*Right*) Attic red-figure pottery 'Nolan' amphora. Huntsmen. Ashmolean Museum, Oxford AN 1890.22.

contemporary pots in the Ashmolean (Figs. 6.3 and 6.4)[48] can best be in-terpreted against the background of silversmiths' drawings. Designs on wood or parchment would have been a minimal charge on the cost of a vessel in silver and gold, but their prohibitively high cost in the context of pottery decoration alone has contributed much to the idea that painters in ceramic worked directly on their pots without any graphic models to hand.[49] When similarities of this kind arise in the context of the transmission of manuscripts, it is normal practice to postulate a common archetype.[50] This is a perfectly acceptable procedure in the field of textual criticism, but it is not one normally applied in the study of Greek painted pottery. Only E. Hudeczek, M. Schmidt, and D. von Bothmer appear to have used it, and they postulate archetypal vases, not separate drawings.[51]

Bothmer's careful argument thus depends upon a 'genealogy of icono-graphy' of a kind we believe only to be possible if *graphides* are invoked. He postulates the 'young Euphronios' painting the Sarpedon cup formerly in Dallas,[52] and 'a few years later, on the krater now in New York, Euphronios creat[ing] his masterly scene of the body of a beardless Sarpedon lifted by Hypnos and Thanatos'. He then suggests that the 'Nikosthenes Painter' was

[48] 1890.22 (= *CVA* Oxford 1, pl. 18, 12) and 1916.68 (= ibid. pl. 29.1). And there is in the Cabinet des Médailles a *stamnos* with the same subject . . . but from a different hand'. J. D. Beazley in *CVA* Oxford 1, p. 24. For a list of sets of replicas of red-figure pots (by the same hands): see Lezzi-Hafter (1983), 112–14; for a pair of Faliscan red-figure jugs by different hands: Vickers (1992*b*), 248, no. 48, pl. 8*g*.

[49] Beazley (1944), 121; cf. Noble (1965), 50.

[50] Erbse (1961), 210.

[51] Hudeczek (1972–75); Schmidt (1980); Bothmer (1987).

[52] Robertson (1981), 23–5; Tompkins (1983), 54–5; Bothmer (1987), 10, fig. 6.

'moved by this work to paint a similar scene on [a] cup now in London', and that the 'Eucharides Painter' was similarly inspired to paint a pot now in the Louvre.[53] Bothmer, we feel, is on the right lines in principle here— in that there is creative artistry of considerable power underlying the compositions he discusses, but there is an inherent difficulty in restricting the argument to ceramic, for in practice any pottery archetype will often have been interred in an Etruscan tomb by the time its inspiration supposedly made itself felt. Similarly, it is difficult to see how an individual pot can have exerted an influence of its own, even beyond the frontiers of Attica (where the work of an Athenian decorator of pottery vases supposedly inspired a Boeotian artisan).[54] Silversmiths' designs—durable, and inherently mobile— do away with such difficulties.

On such a view, the elaborate distinctions which are sometimes drawn between a painter and a vase in his manner, and between 'manner' and following, workshop, school, circle, group, influence, kinship, and so on will prove illusory if by them is understood a creative artist working in the inexpensive medium of ceramic. The apparent existence of 'epicentres' of creative activity are perhaps shadows—in Plato's sense—of a reality that encompassed the patronage by the rich of silversmiths who employed artists such as Parrhasius, Polygnotus—or Duris, or Execias, or Euphronius—to make their designs. This is not to say that there was no independent artistry amongst pot-painters: the existence of what have been termed *pentimenti*[55] on vases, some views of potters' workshops, as well as the thousands of undeniably 'hack' pieces[56] are enough to show that a silver design does not necessarily lie behind every decorated pot. All such pot decoration, however, was done in a manner which consciously echoed the appearance of more precious objects whether of silver, gold, ivory, or bronze.

Kalos inscriptions form another distinct class on painted pots. These inscriptions apparently celebrate the beauty of certain aristocratic youths, but their precise significance is uncertain. It is unlikely that pots bearing *kalos*-inscriptions can have been intended as gifts from lovers, for even allowing for a moment that a painted cup may have cost as much as 1 drachma,[57] a present of such low value would have been regarded as an insult rather than an inducement. Since the only time when we ever hear of cups in the context

---

[53] Bothmer (1987), 10–11.

[54] e.g. the Boeotian vases discussed by Oakley (1990), 16. For the use of one designer's work in several centres of maiolica production, see Clifford and Mallet (1976), 396–9.

[55] Corbett (1965), 25.

[56] Many such pieces were found at Al Mina, and presumably formed part of batches which had not yet been distributed. A special feature was 'the constant repetition of the same design'. The excavator commented: 'Whether these duplicate vases were all painted in succession by one craftsman or whether a single one designed by a good artist was set up and copied by a number of less skilled slaves working as a team, in either case we have here proof of a system of mass-production in the *ateliers* of Athens which we had not hitherto suspected; it is a new sidelight on Attic trade': Woolley (1953), 185.

[57] Boardman (1988*b*), 373; but Gill (1991), 33. For a drachma as a 'trifling sum', see Dem. 24. 114.

of a homo-erotic encounter, they are of gold and silver,[58] it might be worth considering the possibility that *kalos*-inscriptions on pots are another carry-over from work in precious metal—from cups weighing in at a *mina* or more. If such inscriptions were placed on pots by craftsmen who were indifferent to the niceties of the genre (in a way that silversmiths could not be), this might account for the existence of such outlandish inscriptions as *Epilukosegraphsenkalos* in a series of pots inscribed *Skuthesmegraphsen* ('Skythes designed me') and *Epilukoskalos* ('Epilykos is handsome').[59] It has long been known that there are many pots on which there occur both recognizable Greek words and gibberish, long meaningless inscriptions written in Greek characters, repetitions of arbitrary assemblages of characters, and inscriptions placed by mistake against the wrong figure.[60] Although standardized orthography only came in with the invention of printing, the character of the variations in spelling made by some pot-painters bespeak ignorance if not illiteracy. It is difficult to believe that a real Phintias would spell his own name not only *Phintias*, but *Phintis*, *Phitias*, or *Philtias*,[61] or that the same individuals could write *Memnon* or *Pamphaios* as *Mnememnon*, *Memnon*, *Memmnon*, *Memnoon*, *Memnomos*, *Memon*[62] or *Pamaphios*, *Panphaios*, *Panoaios*, *Panphanos*, *Panthaios*[63] unless they were carelessly copying from another source. Such carelessness might extend to omitting parts of words: a pot in the Louvre is thus inscribed *kosthenesepoi*, said to be 'complete aft, and probably fore';[64] an original probably read *Nikosthenes epoiesen*, and it is interesting in this context to note the distinctly metallic form of the amphoras archaeologists call 'Nicosthenic'. Words without literal meaning would also explain the expression ΔΗΜΟΣΙΟΣ on a problematic amphora recently acquired by the Antikensammlung in Munich.[65]

If some of the names that come to our notice through the filter of the ceramic record are indeed those of artists and craftsmen working for and in the medium of precious metal, it may now be possible to explain some of the problems surrounding the name of 'Euphronios'. Of the Sarpedon cup mentioned above it has been said by Martin Robertson: 'The signature on the Sarpedon cup shows that the painter was Euphronios. Without it one might have thought it rather of Oltos [a name associated with slightly more archaic-looking work].' Robertson argues that it and a companion piece show '[Euphronios] at his beginning in close contact with Oltos when

---

[58] Plut. *Alc.* 4. 5.
[59] Beazley (1963), 82–6.
[60] Gerhard (1831), 170–5; Giudice (1977); cf. Beazley (1944), 122 n. 1: 'meaningless conglomeration[s] of letters'; cf. the errors in nomenclature on pots isolated by Sourvinou-Inwood (1979).
[61] Beazley (1963), 23–4.

[62] Ibid. 56–66.
[63] Ibid. 71, 124.
[64] Ibid. 161, no. 1.
[65] With a capacity 4 litres short of a *metretes*, the vessel can scarcely have been intended to serve as an official measure. We are not persuaded by Kaeser (1987), who argues that because it was too small, it was put on the second-hand vase market.

the older painter's style was beginning to mature'.[66] Perhaps; but it is easier to allow that whoever put their hands to these cups, they were using designs one of which bore the name of the silver designer we might designate Euphronius.

The subsequent career of 'Euphronios' has caused much puzzlement to scholars. Pots bearing the inscription *Euphronios egrapsen* are for the most part earlier than those inscribed *Euphronios epoiesen*, and it is generally assumed that the 'great artist' gave up painting for potting or management (depending on which explanation is adopted for *epoiesen*). Failing eyesight has been proposed as a reason why the 'painter' turned to other activities associated with his craft.[67] If, however, we view the evidence in terms of a career in silversmithing, Euphronius will have begun as a designer, before progressing to the actual execution of commissions, a task which will have required infinitely greater practical skills than drawing alone.[68] It would presumably have been a step up the financial and social ladder if he had eventually become a silversmith himself.[69] Indirect evidence that such might be the case is provided by Dietrich von Bothmer's observation that he knows of 'no vase-painter who signs as the son of a vase-painter'[70] (the names of sons of craftsmen are restricted to those known from *epoiesen* inscriptions). In the terms of the hypothesis outlined here, this would mean that 'no silversmith's designer signs as the son of a silversmith's designer', whereas there were established 'family firms' of practising silversmiths: Nearchus and his sons Tleson and Ergoteles,[71] Ergotimus and his son Eucheirus,[72] or Amasis and his son Cleophrades.[73] To go further, and to suggest that it was necessarily the silversmith Euphronius who set up an inscription on the Acropolis,[74] or whose name occurs as that of leader of the dance on the pot in Munich,[75] would be to go beyond the evidence.

On such an interpretation, the problems surrounding *epoiesen* inscriptions would disappear. While we would not for a moment suggest that the situations were necessarily similar, the working practices of more recent silversmiths bear examination in this context. No one would claim, for example, that every piece of silver bearing the mark of Paul de Lamerie was made by him personally, and the career of the distinguished Arts and Crafts silversmith

---

[66] Robertson (1981), 26.
[67] Maxmin (1972).
[68] Cf. the difficulty faced by Roger Fry's Omega Workshops: 'In one case, metalwork, the technique involved was so complex that no amount of inspiration alone would allow an artist to work in that field': Collins (1983), 6.
[69] Cf. Honour (1971), 20, quoted p. 101, n. 181 above.
[70] Bothmer (1981), 4.
[71] Beazley (1956), 162, 178–83.

[72] Beazley (1963), 26.
[73] Bothmer (1981), esp. p. 4 (but for 'potter' read 'silversmith'): 'From a commercial point of view, an established potter's workshop was valuable property, and a potter would well have wished for a son to continue in the profession, bequeathing his heir not only the equipment but also valuable trade connections.'
[74] Raubitschek (1949), no. 225.
[75] See p. 98, above.

Omar Ramsden is salutary in this context. Peter Cannon-Brookes once interviewed all the surviving members of Ramsden's workshop:

The results were very revealing. On the one side Omar Ramsden ... evolved a highly distinctive style of silver and jewelry which is immediately recognizable, but on the other hand it became evident from interviewing his craftsmen and constantly cross-checking that his personal intervention in individual pieces was minimal. One employee executed his drawings, to Ramsden's instructions, for submission by Ramsden to clients; another modelled the elements for casting in silver, under Ramsden's general supervision; a third undertook the repoussé work; another made the famous hammer marks on silver blanks spun in Sheffield, etc. ... Omar Ramsden thus imposed his personality on the range of productions which proudly bear the engraved signature 'OMAR RAMSDEN ME FECIT'.[76]

Epoiesen, likewise, could presumably encompass the range between hands-on manufacture and commercial workshop practice of this kind. The complexities of the working practices of Attic silversmiths and their relationship with their colleagues in the potteries are, however, beyond reasonable conjecture.[77]

If ceramic were after all to be a secondary rather than a primary source, conveying in a 'haphazard' and 'contradictory' manner the kind of information widely thought to be first-hand and reliable, then a certain caution would be necessary with regard to the evidence it supplied. It would be risky, for example, to assume that *kalos*-names recorded on pots are sure guides to the prosopography of ancient Athens. They *might* be, but unless there is independent support, it is best to leave them to one side. Similarly, if the names of craftsmen which occur on pots are for the most part those of silversmiths and their designers, it would be fruitless, in the absence of much decorated Attic silverware, to attempt to penetrate the 'fog-bank' and to use the evidence of inscriptions on ceramic to fine-tune the Attic silver-manufacturing industry, still less to use it to elucidate the world of the 'vase-painter', to which it is largely irrelevant.

'SOTADES'

It is a fundamental point in the methodology of attribution that 'hands' are identified starting from a core of 'signed' works.[78] It is always assumed in vase scholarship that all 'signed' works are by the same individual, whether as 'painter' (*egrapsen*) or as 'potter' (*epoiesen*). But not only is there the problem of 'Douris' and the 'Triptolemos Painter', but it is also clear that in at least one other instance a supposed individual's 'signature' varies from pot to pot. The 'signatures' of the 'potter' Sotades appear on nine different

[76] Cannon-Brookes (1983), 127.
[77] For a useful list of known Athenian potteries, see Arafat and Morgan (1989), 342.

[78] Chippindale and Gill (1993) in response to C. Morris (1993).

Athenian clay vessels which include cups, a *kantharos*, *phialai*, and *rhyta*.[79]
It has been thought that these 'signatures' represent the work of one man,[80]
but to date there has been no detailed study of the handwriting. This is
surprising given that it has been noted—as recently as 1990—that 'the
alphabet varies, and it is difficult to be sure of the hand'.[81] It has been assumed
that if the same name appears, it must be the same person. Yet in the case
of Sotades, there are two different techniques for applying the 'signatures':
six are incised[82] and three are painted.[83] There is similar variety in the letter
forms, the form of the 'signatures' and even in the style of decoration. The
following is a list of pots 'signed' by Sotades:

α	London D6, from Athens	[ΣΟΤ]ΑΔΕΣΠΟΙΕΣΕΝ	Painted
β	London D5, from Athens	[ΣΟΤ]ΑΔΕΣ (special A)	Painted
γ	Once Goluchow, Czartoryski	ΣΟΤΑΔΕΣ ΕΠΟΙ	Painted
δ	Boston 98.886, from Athens	ΣΟ[ΤΑΔΕΣ]Ε[ΠΟΙΕ	Incised
ε	London D8, from Athens	ΣΟΤΑΔΕΣ ΕΠΟΙΕ	Incised
ζ	Villa Giulia, fr., from Vulci	ΣΩΤΑΔΗΣ ΕΠΟΙΗΣΕΝ	Incised
η	Louvre CA 1526, fr., from Capua	ΣΟΤ[ΑΔΕΣ]ΕΠ[ΟΙΕΣΕΝ]	Incised
θ	Boston 21.2286, from Meroe, Nubia	ΣΟΤΑΔΗΣ ΕΠΟΙΗΣΕΝ	Incised
ι	Louvre CA 3825, probably from Egypt	ΣΟΤΑΔΕΣ ΕΠΟΙΕ	Incised

Some of this variation may be what can be expected within the work of
a single individual. The orthography of Shakespeare's signature, for example,
is notoriously varied over time. Four of the Sotadean 'signatures' come from
pots which are generally believed to have formed a single grave-group and
which first appeared on the antiquities market in the 1890s (α, β, δ, ε), but
belief in the unity of the group ought to be tempered by the fact that objects
that have passed through the antiquities market might be supplied with false
provenances.[84] In addition to the signed pieces, there were also unsigned
items in the group which included two *mastoi*[85] and two stemless cups.[86]
The core group of four shows several variations. Two (α, β) have painted
signatures whereas two have incised (δ, ε). Those outside the grave-group
also include painted and incised inscriptions. Within the grave-group there
are three forms of 'signature'. All bear the name Sotades. One has ΕΠΟΙΕΣΕΝ
(α), one has ΕΠΟΙΕ (ε), and one does not have a verb (β); one is unclear
(δ). Of these three variants only one of the forms is found outside the
group, that of ΕΠΟΙΕ (γ, ι). Within the group there is little variation in letter
form, although there are three types of A: horizontal cross-bar (α), a slanting

[79] Beazley (1963) 772–3; (1971) 416.

[80] e.g. Cohen (1991), 80 (with earlier bibliography).

[81] Immerwahr (1990), 104.

[82] Items δ, ε, ζ, η, θ, and ι in Beazley's list: Beazley (1963), 772.

[83] Items α, β, and γ: Beazley (1963), 772. For the purposes of this study we have assumed that these signatures were applied in antiquity.

[84] Muscarella (1977*a*), (1977*b*), (1979); cf. Johns and Potter (1985); Gill and Chippindale (1993).

[85] London D9, D10: Beazley (1963), 773, 1 and 2.

[86] Brussels A 890 and 891: Beazley (1963), 771, nos. 1 and 2.

cross-bar (ε), and a special form (β). Outside the grave-group only the slanting cross-bar is found (γ, ζ, θ, ι). The special form is quite unusual and finds a parallel on a head *kantharos* attributed to the 'Syriskos Painter'.[87] Two types of Π are found within the grave-group: with equal-length vertical bars (ε), and with a short right-hand vertical (α). Only the latter form is found outside the grave-group (γ, ζ, η, θ, ι). Finally, the decoration of two of the pieces from the grave-group are attributed to the hand of the 'Sotades Painter' (α, β) and two are unattributed (δ, ε). Outside the group one piece is attributed to the 'Sotades Painter' (γ), one 'recalls Sotadean' work (ι), one 'cannot be said to have any connection with the Sotades painter' (θ), and two are unattributed (ζ, η).

It could be, of course, that the 'signatures'[88] on these Sotadean pots are atypical and do not relate to any signing pattern that may exist on other Greek pots, but until detailed analyses of artisans' handwriting are carried out doubts must persist. In the case of Sotades, it has already been suggested that the 'special formality' of his incised work may be intended to evoke inscriptions on metal vessels,[89] and we concur. We would, however, be tempted to go further, and see the extant pots as evocations in ceramic of the kind of vessel originally made in nobler and more costly materials by a Sotadean metalworking concern.

'PENTHESILEANS'

We stated earlier that there may be circumstances in which it might be useful to group individual hands of pot-painters together. Although fine-tuning of the traditional kind is scientifically unprofitable, it may be possible to adopt a 'broad-brush' approach to Beazley's lists, and use them to throw light in very general terms on the output of silversmiths working for aristocratic patrons. One such approach might go as follows:

Beazley isolated a large group of pottery vessels, mostly cups, which he attributed to a workshop within which he considered the 'Penthesilea Painter' to have been the 'chief figure'. Hundreds of pieces (more than 800 in 1944,[90] double that number in 1963,[91] and more since) have been attributed to the 'Penthesileans'. The artisans employed in this workshop, whose output spanned the middle decades of the fifth century, and perhaps as late as the 420s, indulged in working practices that fell little short of mass-production; 'It was evidently not very uncommon for one painter to pass a cup on to his neighbour when it was half-finished, and thus add a little

---

[87] Immerwahr (1990), 133 n. 5.
[88] Note that Martin Robertson now prefers to avoid the term 'signature' when referring to this particular pattern of words on pots: Robertson (1992), *passim.*

[89] Cohen (1991), 82.
[90] Beazley (1944), 111.
[91] Beazley (1963), 877–971.

variety to mass-products which often stood in need of it.'[92] One major theme runs through the output of the 'Penthesileans', namely pictures of boys in their early teens, nearly all of whom are distinguished by a peculiarly sugary expression. Nearly 20 per cent of the vessels in Beazley's 1963 list of 'Penthesileans' include paintings of boys. In 1918, Beazley characterized the output of the workshop as 'numerous . . . Many of them are not without merit: even in the worst, you may sometimes find here a graceful turn of the body, there a pretty inclination of the head: but on the whole they present a dreary spectacle of talent commercialized.'[93]

If the next stage of the argument looks somewhat rickety, we apologize, but it is far less so than is the argumentation behind many of the claims made by some students of Greek ceramics. It does, however, depend on premises which are themselves incapable of objective proof. The first of these is that there were very many of Parrhasius' *graphides* available in the fifth century; that this is a reasonable hypothesis is clear from the fact that *multa vestigia* were still extant in Pliny's day. Then there is the issue of the chronology of Parrhasius' career. The evidence is ambivalent; some suggesting that he was active in the 450s (when the Athena Promachos was probably made),[94] some apparently attesting to artistic activity in the fourth century.[95] But if Parrhasius was active during the second half of the fifth century, it is possible that his artistry lies behind the pictures of boys. It is not simply that his skill in line-drawing[96] may lie behind the slick output of the 'Penthesileans', but that he is recorded as having painted 'two boys in whom is seen the self-confidence and simplicity of their age'[97]—which recalls the appearance and demeanour of the boys who appear in their hundreds on the pottery cups. If the talent that was thus commercialized were that of Parrhasius, it would also account for the existence among the output of the 'Penthesileans' of other subjects recorded among the *œuvre* of Parrhasius. The noteworthy cup in Ferrara—'the largest of red-figure cups' according to Beazley in 1963[98]—includes two themes we know Parrhasius to have treated: Theseus[99] and the Quarrel between Ajax and Odysseus.[100] Its extraordinary size, moreover, recalls that of the 'Heracliot' cup which Parrhasius designed for Mys.[101] Then, the 'Penthesilean workshop' was unusual in that it per-

---

[92] Beazley (1944), 111.

[93] Beazley (1918), 131.

[94] Meiggs (1972), 94–5.

[95] For the issues involved, see Robertson (1975), 411–12, who discounts the 4th-c. thesis.

[96] Quint. 12. 10. 4: '[Parrhasius] examinasse subtilius linias traditur;' cf. Pliny, *NH* 35. 67.

[97] Pliny, *NH* 35. 70: 'et pueros duos in quibus spectatur securitas et aetatis simplicitas'. This is not the only recorded painting of a boy by Parrhasius: cf. ibid.: 'a priest and a boy' 'sacerdotem adstante puero'.

[98] Beazley (1963), 882.35 (on Ferrara 44885, from T. 18 C VP).

[99] Plut. *Thes.* 4; *Mor.* 346a; Pliny, *NH* 35. 69. Cf. the cups listed at Beazley (1963), 880. 13–15; 965. 1.

[100] Pliny, *NH* 35. 71.

[101] Ath. 12. 782b. The composition of the Amazonomachy scene in the large cup in Munich (2688; Beazley (1963), 879, no. 1) has been said with sound common sense to 'have better suited a rectangle than a circle, which does not mean that it was copied from a frieze or a panel, though it clearly follows the style of composition which we associate with major painting': Boardman (1989), 38.

sisted in the depiction of raunchy scenes[102] (comparatively rare on painted pots of the period; restraint was more the norm in contrast to what had gone before).[103] It may be relevant that Parrhasius 'cheered himself up' by painting *minoribus tabellis libidines*—'dirty pictures on small wooden panels'[104]— panels of a kind that recall the *tabulae* on which Parrhasius' *graphides* were preserved.

This is one case for which slight documentation exists. For most workshops in the Athenian potteries, however, it is impossible even to speculate as to who were the personalities behind the decorative schemes they put on their products. Pot-painters will presumably have taught apprentices how to go about their tasks: preparing the clay, throwing pots on the wheel, applying ornament, firing, and marketing the finished vessels. So much is obvious; but what needs to be added to the conventional view is that there was a constant input of new material from outside the craft of pottery. It is among the designs for high-value silverware that we are probably to look for the sources of artistic inspiration, and not among the pots—or the potters—themselves.

What needs to be questioned is the kind of analysis that proceeds: 'Kleophrades like other artists did not attain his full development all at once. We may believe that he began life as an apprentice to Euthymides, for a number of vases which seem to be early works of Kleophrades bear a great resemblance to the work of Euthymides;'[105] (rather, perhaps, both pot decorators made use of the same set of designs). Or: 'the Eucharides-master . . . learnt his craft from the master who painted the Nikoxenos pelike in St Petersburg;'[106] (ditto).[107] This approach became a model for subsequent research, and it is now not uncommon for scholars to write about 'careers' of 'vase-painters', enumerating the likely influences to which they were subjected.[108] Nearly all of these supposed influences are ceramic, and when they are not, the 'artist' is supposed to have left his 'studio' and found inspiration in major mural paintings. Outside influences arriving in the workshop in the form of silversmiths' redundant drawings would, however, account both for apparent allusions to monumental painting (the same individuals might be responsible for both genres), and for the phenomenon that 'some artists develop slowly, and their early work gives little promise of a splendid prime;

---

[102] e.g. Beazley (1963), 897. 116; 923. 29; 931. 2; 971 (Munich *oinochoe*).

[103] What K. Schauenburg once called 'eine Zivilisierung, eine gewisse Verbürgerlichung' had occurred: (1973), 1.

[104] Pliny, *NH* 35. 71; cf. Parrhasius' obscene panel painting of Meleager and Atalanta which Tiberius was later to keep in his bedroom: Suet. *Tib.* 44.

[105] Beazley (1910), 39.

[106] Beazley (1911–12), 232.

[107] Cf. Balzano (1913), 11: 'One imagines a

teacher, then a second teacher with a following of pupils, forming a school . . .'.

[108] e.g. Guy (1981), 10: 'The Triptolemos Painter served his apprenticeship together with Douris, possibly a few years his senior, in the workshop of Euphronios'; ibid. 11: 'The Triptolemos Painter . . . ended his days . . . in the Brygan workshop alongside artists of the next generation, early classical followers such as the Stieglitz Painters, and the Sabouroff and Villa Giulia Painters whose styles he may have had a hand in forming.'

others reveal their quality at once'.[109] The subjects represented on pots would thus be less the products of artists' whims (or 'vigour' or 'wilfulness')[110] but rather a reflection of fashions and tastes in the world catered to by the silversmith. It is also unprofitable, as John Elsner has shown,[111] to use the subject matter on pots in order to determine the tastes of the 'artist' or the potter; to speak, for example, of a 'bourgeois painter with . . . his absurd interest in furniture, plenishing and accoutrement';[112] to write that 'the Rycroft Painter had a strong feeling for nature . . . his painting can also show that he was a man very conscious of his manhood';[113] or to claim that '[Charinos] is most sensitive to the patterning of surface. Underlying structure attracts him less than it does the potters of the Early Ram and Brygan Classes'[114] is to indulge a 'peculiar facility for deduction' further than the evidence allows.

REPRESENTATIONS OF VASES

Mention was made above of the likelihood that pot-painters might depart from the designs they found in silversmiths' designs. Such an explanation might help resolve an impasse that has arisen over the interpretation of the Caputi hydria in Milan (Fig. 6.5),[115] on the shoulder of which is represented an idealized workshop taken by some to be a pottery, with vase-painters at work and being rewarded with wreaths by Athena and Victories;[116] and by others to be a representation of a metalworker's establishment.[117] There are problems with both interpretations: the scene 'is certainly not an average day in the Mannerist Workshop', and *kantharoi* (the most prominent vessels in the scene) are totally absent in the known output of the pottery from which the Caputi hydria emanated.[118] The details of the vessels being decorated: the fluting on the high-handled jug, the handles of the volute-craters, the mouldings on the calyx-crater, the size and slenderness of the *kantharoi*, might, however, all be held to indicate metalwork.[119] And yet, the craftsmen (and woman) are quite clearly painting, with brushes in their hands, and pots of liquid by their sides. For once, the answer may lie in the middle ground: a genre of representations of metalworking establishments seems here to have been adapted to show a highly idealized pottery.[120]

The vessels represented in banquet scenes are frequently discussed in

[109] Beazley (1944), 119.
[110] Beazley (1918), 97.
[111] Elsner (1990), who equates Beazley's approach with that of Sherlock Holmes.
[112] Beazley (1928), 38.
[113] Holmberg (1992), 10.
[114] Guy (1981), 5.
[115] Milan, Torno Collection; Beazley (1963), 571; Green (1961); Noble (1988), 205–6, for references.

[116] Beazley (1944), 93–5; Noble (1965), 54–55; Thompson (1984), 9–10.
[117] e.g. Green (1961).
[118] Beazley (1944), 95.
[119] Green (1961), 74 has a useful list of representations of vessels on pots which are clearly metallic.
[120] Something similar may have occurred on the cup fragments in Athens, Acropolis Museum 166 (Beazley (1944), pls. 1, 2–3), where a potter's wheel has been introduced into a forge, complete with hammers and tongs.

FIG. 6.5   Attic red-figure hydria. Workshop scene. Private collection, Milan.

exclusively ceramic terms, but again it is open to question as to whether pottery or metal is in fact represented. Without excluding the possibility that pots might sometimes be shown, it is again more likely, given the great difference in price between ceramic and precious metal (in the order of 1 : 1,000 in the case of silver, and 1 : 10,000 for gold),[121] that objects of great value would be shown before those which might cost only a couple of drachmas at most.[122] After all, the kind of people likely to attend an aristocratic symposium tended to conduct their business in *minae*,[123] and the use of plate was not unknown among the rich in both Greece and Etruria.[124]

A related question is the nature of the vessels shown in wall-paintings and in sculptured reliefs. The point at issue is neatly encapsulated in the scholarship relating to the Tomba dei Rilievi at Cerveteri. The walls of this fourth-century tomb are decorated with a vast array of *realia*—armour, ropes, satchels, tools, spits, animals, jugs, and drinking-cups—realistically modelled

[121] See above, p. 99.
[122] Cf. pp. 85–8, above.
[123] See ch. 2.
[124] See chs. 2 and 3.

in stucco; many of them still retain their original colours. Excellent photographs have recently been published in a detailed monograph, and the nature of the materials represented subjected to fresh enquiry.[125] The handle of a sword is white to indicate ivory,[126] the blade of a knife is blue-black for iron,[127] and shields are yellow in colour, clearly evoking bronze.[128] One of the jugs is well preserved and still has its yellow surface; it too is thought of as intended to be bronze. There are two drinking-cups, both basically of the same blue-black colour as the knife blade, though one carries additional red and white decoration. Rather than being thought of as metal (though not iron, but silver), these objects have universally been interpreted as pottery,[129] of a kind that sold for next to nothing in antiquity. It is reasonably certain that whoever had the Tomba dei Rilievi constructed belonged to a level of society that regularly used plate, and it is likely that the cups are renderings in coloured stucco of silverware rather than of clay. Their function would thus be analogous to that of the much more numerous pottery surrogates found in tombs in Etruria.

But if the cups in the Cerveteri reliefs evoke silverware, what of the decorated vessels represented in Etruscan wall-paintings? These too are usually interpreted as painted pottery vessels,[130] a view which is perpetuated in the name of the Tomb of the Painted Vases at Tarquinia. But in truth, there is no way to demonstrate whether or not such objects are metal or ceramic; whether the pictures in the Tomba dei Vasi Dipinti represent black-figure or silver-figure amphoras and cups, or whether a column-crater in the Tomba della Nave (also at Tarquinia)[131] is a red-figure pot or a gold-figure vase. Once again, it is all to easy to become embroiled in a dissatisfying game of 'Yes it is, no it isn't'; but once again, it is possible to cut the Gordian knot of argumentation by looking at the larger picture. We might recall the immense booty captured from Tarquinia's neighbours Pyrgi and Caere in 384 BC: 1,000 talents from the sanctuary at the port and 500 from the city.[132] If it is agreed that Athenian aristocrats used plate when entertaining guests,[133] then it is unlikely that their opposite numbers in Etruria—who, if the charge of piracy laid against them was true, knew a thing or two about material values—would have done otherwise. Even after the days of real Etruscan wealth were over, the Etruscans' use of precious metal for dining was a literary *topos*.[134]

Even the presence of undecorated vessels in Etruscan frescoes is open to

[125] Blanck and Proietti (1986).
[126] Ibid. 46–7, pl. 25a.
[127] Ibid. 40, pl. 20a.
[128] Ibid. 48.
[129] Ibid. 21, 34–5, pls. 15c and 18.
[130] Most recently by Spivey (1991), 135–8.
[131] Moretti (1962), 42–3, figs. 12–13.
[132] Diod. 15. 14. 3–4. More than £15,000,000 in movable wealth at the rate of exchange envisaged in Chapter 2: pp. 34–5, above.
[133] On which see p. 38, n. 47, above.
[134] Spivey (1991), 135. For a less thoughtful discussion of Diodorus, see Heurgon (1961), 240, for whom only pottery and bronze vessels are represented in frescoes, a view for which he positivistically finds support in the nature of the surviving grave goods.

widely differing interpretations. A set of vessels on a table in the Tomba del Orco is said by one scholar to be 'gold vases . . . [which] produce an impression of fabulous opulence';[135] for another they are '*kitsch* vases that g[i]ve the illusion of richness'.[136] Much clearly depends upon the tastes of the critic. The Tomba dei Vasi Dipinti was discovered in 1867, at a period when (as we saw in Chapter 1), Greek painted pottery was considered to have been extremely costly and a luxury import into Etruria. It was thus natural to assume that the decorated amphoras and cups were ceramic vessels, without considering the possibility that they may have been intended to represent objects of real intrinsic value. A belief that the vessels in question were ceramic doubtless also led to one amphora being deprived by the nineteenth-century draughtsman (Louis Schulz) of its handle finials (visible in photographs: Fig. 6.6),[137] features which do not occur in pottery, but which may be metallic. Other vessels shown in the Tomba dei Vasi Dipinti are generally acknowledged to be of metal: the crater on the table, the cups being carried by some of the symposiasts, and the strainer and ladle in the hands of a servant. With the exception of a white cup (which could be of ivory)[138] their yellow colour indicates either bronze, gilded bronze,[139] or gold. In fact, the supposedly painted pots in the Tomba dei Vasi Dipinti seem in no way to differ from the 'inlaid metal vessel' on a table in the frieze of the Tomba dei Bighe at Tarquinia.[140] If such tables are indeed *kylikeia* or sideboards, as has been suggested, and if a *kylikeion* constituted 'an extra status symbol, a symbol of aristocratic abundance and wealth',[141] pottery is unlikely to have made its appearance in such a context. We should not expect to see a *kylikeion* bearing surrogates of a kind proper to the dead, but out of place among live aristocrats who were famous in their day for 'abundance and wealth', as well as for the ruthless way in which they might on occasion obtain it.

CONTINUITY

The interrelationships of form and colour between classical pottery and work in metal or ivory discussed in Chapter 5 had a long tradition behind them. They were, however, part of a continuum which can be observed over

---

[135] Pallottino (1952), 114.
[136] van der Meer (1984), 303.
[137] Photograph: Weege (1921), pl. 68 (whence Fig. 6.6). For the much-reproduced line drawing (which frequently departs from the original), see *Mon. Inst.* 9 (1870), pl. 13. For Schulz's original watercolour sketches, see *Pittura etrusca* (1986), 28, 61, pl. 15. More accurate (but less well publicized) drawings exist in Copenhagen, which do include the 'metallic' finials: Moltesen and Weber-Lehmann (1991), 93–5.

[138] Helbig (1870), 9, took it for silver, but cf. the white, and presumably ivory, sword handle in the Tomba dei Rilievi, and the ivory drinking-vessels from the Barberini Tomb at Praeneste: Aubet (1970), pls. 26–9.
[139] Helbig (1870), 9, 12, 72.
[140] Poulsen (1927), 189; illustrated in Poulsen (1922), fig. 15.
[141] van der Meer (1984), 304.

FIG. 6.6 'Tomba dei Vasi Dipinti', detail. Vessels on a table. (After Weege (1921), pl. 68.)

centuries, and certainly beyond the Roman period. The 'essential unity' of the most common kind of Roman fine pottery, the tableware that is 'generally red in colour and with a fine clay coating known variously as a glaze, gloss or slip' has been underlined by Kevin Greene.[142] Whether in the form of Arretine, Samian, Terra Sigillata, North African Slip Ware or Colour-coated Ware, such pottery was widespread throughout the Mediterranean and beyond from the first century BC to the Byzantine period. It is generally acknowledged to derive from the tradition of Greek pottery which, however, generally had a black rather than a red surface coating. The change, so far as Italy was concerned, took place in the mid-first century BC,[143] and Greene has suggested that it was 'determined by taste rather than technology'.[144] In fact, the change may have been due in part to technological (or economic) reasons,[145] and in part to a change in the nature of the tableware of the rich

[142] Greene (1986), 158.
[143] Morel (1965); Schindler (1967), 64–6.
[144] Greene (1986), 158.
[145] See below, pp. 178–80.

that occurred at Rome soon after Lucullus and Pompey's Eastern victories. Lucullus, who celebrated a triumph in 63 BC, 'was the first to introduce luxury to Rome';[146] and gold vessels of the kind that have been preserved from this period suggest—if only faintly—what such luxury encompassed.[147] Silver had been the norm on Roman tables before the first century BC (and the amount strictly limited by law); the amount of silver increased, and gold began to appear—albeit at first in the households of such as the rapacious C. Verres, who spent his period of office as propraetor of Sicily expropriating silver *emblemata* which he would have remounted on gold vessels.[148] Verres' retirement was spent in Southern Gaul, where he was eventually proscribed by Antony (in 43 BC), who coveted the precious objects he had purloined from Sicily. If Roman black wares, which often have a metallic slip, are to be equated with silver vessels,[149] then it is not impossible that the colour of red wares was also a gesture in the direction of precious metal; if so, of gold.[150] This will be explored further in the next section. Seen against the background of other Roman pottery fabrics which clearly evoke other materials, the suggestion is not that remarkable. Some Roman pottery was marbled,[151] anticipating Josiah Wedgwood's renderings of hardstone vessels mounted in ormulu.[152] And some, which bore a green vitreous glaze outside, and a yellow one inside, was made in evocation of bronzework.[153] Pliny states that 'the greater part of mankind uses earthenware vessels',[154] but devoted only one chapter of his *Natural History* to pottery. Fine pottery will not have appeared on the tables of the rich,[155] still less have been regarded as a luxury item.[156]

As in the case of Etruscan 'added red', or Corinthian or South Italian red-figure, different kinds of Roman pottery have long been thought to have imitated other ceramic wares, rather than being much influenced by work in other media. In reality, while technical details of the potter's craft may well have passed from one centre to another, the vessels that were made will usually have evoked the plate made locally for rich households or sanctuaries. Gold- and silversmiths' designs, moulds, and plaster casts probably played a

[146] Ath. 6. 274 f.; cf. 12. 543a.

[147] Marshall (1911), 383, pl. 73 (no. 3168); *Harewood* (1965); *Béhague* (1987), Lot 53.

[148] Cic. *Verr.* 2. 4. 24.

[149] Simpson (1957), 30; Vickers, Impey, and Allan (1986), text to pl. 29; M. H. Crawford (1987), 38.

[150] And probably not 'brass': Crawford (1987), 38: 'it was not simply the shapes of metal wares that ceramic wares attempted to imitate; for these were coloured to give an even stronger impression of silver or brass'.

[151] Simpson (1957), 29; F. F. Jones (1950), 183–4.

[152] e.g. Starr and Starr (1982).

[153] Loeschke 1909, 190 n. 1; (1928), 75; Pinkwart (1972), 140; Gabelmann (1974), 266; (1979); Vickers (1985a), 121. Contrast Hill (1969), 83: 'Nobody has been foolish enough to suggest that green vitreous glaze outside and yellow within, as it occurs on Roman cups of Cicero's time, was imitation of dirty and clean bronze, so let me not start here on such a false scent!' Hochuli-Gysel (1977) unaccountably states that such vessels imitate *silver*; cf. Gabelmann (1979).

[154] Fulford (1986), 154.

[155] Ibid. 155.

[156] Ibid. 159, criticizing Garbsch (1982), who called *terra sigillata* the 'Luxusgeschirr' of the Roman world.

major role.[157] In neither the Greek nor Roman worlds will this have been done with any intention of deceit; the potter simply followed norms created elsewhere.

'RUDDY GOLD'

The use of red on pots was probably but a gesture in the direction of gold, for the vessels in question would never have appeared side-by-side in a context where close comparisons could be made. In the case of Roman pottery, fine red tableware will probably have been made for people who had only heard about gold vessels, or who only saw them from a distance at festivals. The notion of 'ruddy gold' was a commonplace in the Near East, Greece, and Rome for pure metal. At Old Babylonian Mari, we hear of the director of the palace workshops commissioning a 'drinking vessel of red gold'.[158] Then an Assyrian instructs his servant: 'Buy half a pound of red gold of very fine quality with my silver.'[159] Theognis writes of 'refined gold, ruddy (ἐρυθρόν) to look upon',[160] and for Pliny, 'fire serves as a test of [gold's] goodness, making it assume a similar red hue (*rubeat*) and itself becomes the colour of fire',[161] (although this may equally well refer to the behaviour of gold when red-hot).[162] But in any case, the semantic range of ἐρυθρός/red is very wide, comparable with that of μέλας, which encompassed everything between 'gun-metal grey' and 'black',[163] and it is unremarkable that a similarly wide range of hues—from yellow, through orange to red—was adopted for the decoration of the ceramic analogues of goldware. Recent scientific analysis of the red surface coloration of some Egyptian gold objects established that they were the result of 'tarnish films' of a kind that frequently occurs, although 'it seems probable that numerous other examples once existed that have been lost through cleaning',[164] and whoever made a recent forgery of a Roman lamp in 'soft "buttery" gold of very high purity' thought fit to add a 'reddish patina'.[165] 'Tarnish films' may provide the solution to the problem, for just as silver vessels might be left patinated in antiquity, the same might well have been true of gold, especially if the Homeric practice of cleaning precious metal with sulphur continued in use.[166] It is a pity that so little has survived—the three known early Roman

---

[157] Richter (1950); Reeder (1974).

[158] Dalley (1984), 59.

[159] Ichisar (1981), 228. Cf. the footstool covered with 'ruddy gold'; hoes of 'ruddy gold'; wood covered with 34 talents of 'ruddy gold'; an incense altar of 'ruddy gold': Luckenbill (1926–7), 2, nos. 601, 674, 761B, 883, 1001.

[160] Theognis 449.

[161] Pliny, *NH* 33. 19. 59.

[162] See e.g. White (1974), 47.

[163] Dürbeck (1977), 121–3, 151–68.

[164] Frantz and Schorsch (1990), 133, 147–8 (where examples of uncleaned 'bright red' gold are cited: from the Royal Cemetery at Ur; from 'among the trappings from a warrior's burial of the sixth century BC, believed to be from northern Greece' in Baltimore; and on the late Hallstatt gold from Hochdorf in Stuttgart; add the Scythian gold, Basilov (1989), 29).

[165] Content (1992), 262–3, no. 311.

[166] On which see p. 127, above.

imperial vessels were found in the sea, and have been thoroughly cleaned since, so that any 'ruddiness' has disappeared. But a gold jug from the Oxus treasure,[167] though cleaned, has traces of red colour on the foot, and a larger patch inside, very similar to the colour of Samian ware.

HELLENISTIC POTTERY

A similar change in the colour of common tableware took place further east at an earlier period. Black mould-made pottery gave way to red-ware in many centres in the eastern Mediterranean, apparently between 150 and 125 BC;[168] and mould-made pottery had in turn replaced red-figure ware around 320 BC.[169] Such pottery is universally—and rightly—held to be derived from metalwork.[170] If the colour, as well as the shape and decoration, of this kind of pottery depended for its inspiration on that of metalwork, there is a likely explanation. The characteristic forms of pottery made at Athens and elsewhere after Alexander's conquests were rather different from those that had existed before. The mould-made, handle-less bowls decorated in relief that became the norm, doubtless reflected Near Eastern dining practices adopted after the incorporation of the Achaemenid empire into the Greek world. At Athens, the characteristic colour of local mould-made pottery continued to be black: one category of bowls 'are covered with the black glaze familiar from Attic pottery of earlier periods',[171] but are clearly closely based on 'bowls of precious metal'.[172] In wealthier centres elsewhere in the Hellenistic world immense quantities of orangey-red tableware began to be produced. That this may reflect the profusion of gold vessels owned by private individuals in what was now the Greek world[173] is suggested by the change in the character of temple inventories after the third quarter of the fourth century. Before this time, most objects listed are of silver or silver-gilt; thereafter they are mostly of solid gold.[174] The Hellenistic vessels illustrated in Fig. 6.7 may help to clarify the point at issue here. The absolutely plain one is of silver, and is dark grey in colour; the other two have rudimentary moulded decoration, and are orangey-red. The silver bowl supposedly comes from Afghanistan, while the pottery bowls are from Nughri and Ghabagatch in

[167] London, British Museum WA 123918, Dalton (1964), no. 17. We are grateful to Terence Mitchell for allowing us to study this piece.

[168] e.g. Weinberg (1988), 'the change-over from the black-glazed, or red-slipped, wares [seems to have taken place] within the third quarter of the second century BC.'

[169] R. M. Cook (1972), 186.

[170] e.g. Robert (1890), 5: 'die Modelle Originalarbeiten griechischer Toreuten aus Silber waren'; Courby (1922), 169 ff.; Hausmann (1959), 50–1; Kopcke (1964), 25; Ebert (1978), 127; Siebert (1980), 55, 74; Salomonson (1982),

164–73; Rotroff (1982), 6; Barr-Sharrar (1982), 123; Moltesen (1983), 32–53; Weinberg (1988); Hayes (1991).

[171] Rotroff (1982), 14.

[172] Ibid. 6.

[173] Cf. the many thousands of talents of gold and silver taken by Alexander from Susa, Ecbatana, Pasargadae, and Persepolis (Cameron (1948), 10–11; Callataÿ (1989)).

[174] Contrast e.g. the 5th- and 4th-c. Acropolis inventories with Delian treasury accounts of the 3rd c. BC: *IDélos*, 298, 313, 320.

F I G. 6.7   Silver bowl, from Afghanistan, and red-glazed pottery bowls, from Nughri and Ghabagatch, N. Syria. Ashmolean Museum, Oxford AN 1984.129, 1914.778 and 779.

north Syria.[175] A pottery analogue of the silver bowl would doubtless be in black gloss,[176] and the precious metal equivalents of the red-ware bowls would have been of gold.[177] These will have been the ceramic analogues of the gold vessels attested in the sources for the period.

Little attention has been paid in the past, however, as to quite why the basic colour of fine ceramics in the Eastern Mediterranean should have changed from black to red, to be followed in Italy some decades later. If a technological explanation were to be sought, the argument might go like this: in making black wares, pots would first be fired red, before a reducing atmosphere was introduced into the kiln, thus making them turn black. A final oxidizing stage then caused those parts that were intended to be red (figure decoration, or the undersides of many black-glazed vessels) to become rubified.[178] If potters dropped the last two stages, not only might there have been economies of fuel, but the manufacturing process could be carried out more quickly, and with fewer risks of misfiring. If so, it would seem that at some time in the third quarter of the second century BC, potters in some Near Eastern centres began to see the advantages of evoking a nobler material

[175] Ashmolean Museum, Oxford AN 1984.129 (silver bowl); 1914.778–9. Vickers, Impey, and Allan (1986), pl. 28.

[176] Cf. the recent discussion of a Hellenistic black-glossed conical pottery bowl in Columbia, Missouri, for which parallels in silver, bronze, and red-gloss pottery from a wide area have been noted: Weinberg (1988).

[177] Gold vessels are attested for the period, e.g. Jos. *AJ* 13. 8. 2: 'Gold and silver cups', spices, and

'bulls with their horns gilded' were sent as placatory gifts to Antiochus VII when he was besieging Jerusalem in 136 BC. See further, Vickers (1994).

[178] For the procedure, see Tite, Bimson, and Freestone (1982). Cf. F. F. Jones (1950), 154: 'The results of an insufficiently reduced oven were known long before the Hellenistic period and red could be produced if desired; at the time when black-glaze was preferred, care was apparently taken to ensure a successful blackening.'

than silver with considerably less outlay of fuel, time, and effort. At this level, we would readily see potter influencing potter.

THE WIDER CONTEXT

(*a*) *China*

The phenomenon of potters following metalworkers is not restricted to the western end of the Eurasian land-mass, nor did it cease to occur in the West with the decline of the classical world. Well-documented examples are known in, for example, ancient and medieval China and in the Islamic world, and in both cases, the evocation of precious metals plays a prominent part. Scholars working in these areas have, moreover, been more willing than their classical colleagues to admit ceramic evidence in the reconstruction of lost metal prototypes.[179] The main evidence for metalwork in China in *c*.2000 BC is 'indirect, taking the form of pottery skeuomorphs (pottery copies of metal vessels)'.[180] The repertoire of pottery shapes of the Qijia culture of Gansu province 'shows a pervasive influence from vessels of hammered metal', which can be best illustrated in the shape known as *he* (Fig. 6.8). Here, 'the pottery jug . . . was copied to the last detail from a wrought-metal vessel . . . In the metal prototype the tubular spout would have been rolled from sheet metal and attached with solder or an adhesive, and the handle would have been riveted to a rectangular tab hammered out from the edge of the cover. In the pottery version the tab and even its pair of rivets are faithfully copied.'[181] The wrought metal vessels of which such pots were copies have in turn been seen as the forerunners of the earliest Chinese cast bronze vessels.[182]

But the study of early Chinese metallurgy has drawn attention to certain differences between the products of Chinese craftsmen and those of the Near East in the Bronze Age. Most Chinese metalwork of the Shang, Zhou, and Han dynasties (*c*.1700 BC–AD 220) was cast in moulds, but although both lost-wax and section moulding was known in the Near East from an early date, hammered work was the norm for vessels there. This difference has been put down to economic causes: a relative shortage of metal led to the use of smithying techniques in the West, whereas in China metal was in abundant supply, allowing its use in the more wasteful casting process.[183] Another, presumably related, difference is that bronze was the material of choice in China at this period, while gold and silver 'which must always favor economical techniques' were little used.[184] It is this difference in favoured materials which must have led to the prevalence of different techniques. Cast bronze ritual vessels were at the top of the material hierarchy, but were

[179] e.g. Medley (1972); Rawson (1982), 1984; Allan (1976–7); Vickers, Impey, and Allan (1986).
[180] Bagley (1987), 15.
[181] Ibid.
[182] Huber (1983), 207.
[183] Bagley (1987), 17.
[184] Ibid.

FIG. 6.8 Bronze *he*.
Qijia culture, Gansu
province, China.
Shanghai Museum.
(After Chǔgoku
rekidai tōjiten (*Tokyo:
Asahi Shimbunsha and
Seibu Bijutsukan*
(1984), no. 4.))

frequently copied in clay for deposition in tombs. These pottery versions
reproduce features peculiar to bronze casting, which are foreign to ceramic.[185]
They were also frequently made with clays and glazes that imitated the
patina of bronze.[186]

The collapse of the Han empire led to an erosion of the repertoire of
bronze shapes. Social changes led to the introduction of foreign silverware,
in the form of wine bowls, ewers, and dishes. The Western origins of a silver-
gilt ewer found in a sixth-century AD tomb of the Northern Zhou dynasty

---

[185] Rawson (1989), 276.

[186] Leach (1972), 38, pls. 35–6; Tregear (1986),
175; Rawson (1989), 287.

FIG. 6.9   (*Left*) Silver-gilt ewer, from Ningxia Guyuan, China. (After *Wenwu* 1985.11.)
FIG. 6.10   (*Right*) Pottery ewer, from Ji Xian, northern Hebei, China. (After Rawson (1991)).

at Ningxia Guyuan (Fig. 6.9)[187] are clear: the beading is familiar from Hellenistic and Roman silver, the form has parallels in late Roman and Parthian work in precious metal,[188] while the figure decoration has obvious classical forebears. The majority of the imports were probably made in Central Asia,[189] and the earliest finds of foreign metalwork have been found in northern and western China, at the eastern end of the Silk Route.[190] Such silver vessels were taken up by Chinese élites with enthusiasm and they provided a basis for local schools of silversmithing. Since only the rich could afford gold and silver, and few of them placed precious metal in the tomb, a secondary industry to provide pottery versions for daily or funerary use came into being.[191] A ceramic ewer from Ji Xian in northern Hebei (Fig. 6.10) shows

[187] Rawson (1990), 279–80, fig. 4; (1991), 144–5, fig. 6.
[188] e.g. Mundell Mango (1990*a*), 70, fig. 1; Harper (1978), 60–7.
[189] Rawson (1991), 150 n. 2.
[190] Rawson (1989), 279; (1991), 144.
[191] Rawson (1989), 279; (1991), 139.

the kind of local response that was made presumably first in silver, then in clay, to foreign silverware. In contrast to earlier times such vessels, being inherently more precious, were largely made from beaten sheet metal, with only parts such as handles and feet cast in moulds. In this respect, they are similar to classical Greek silverware.

The Chinese repertory of both silver and ceramic shapes was transformed by these developments. New decorative motifs were employed on silverware of the Tang dynasty (AD 618–906), but they come from local sources as well as foreign.[192] Many sets of silver vessels for wine-drinking parties have survived in hoards, and a few in tombs.[193] The funerary record includes both lead-glazed[194] and fine white wares whose forms are made in clear imitation of precious metal.[195] Features that are natural in sheet metal, but less readily attainable in fine clay, allow the inference that silver lies behind the ceramic.[196] The fact that the reception of foreign silverware had occurred overland from Central Asia, and not as the result of maritime trade, will account for the difference between the surface treatment of some Chinese ceramic analogues of silverware and that prevalent in the Mediterranean area. It was the 'fine gleaming surfaces of silver' that was reproduced in the glazed white clays of porcelain wares employed from the sixth century AD onwards,[197] rather than the dusky surface of patinated silver, which informed the black glaze of the Greek wares discussed elsewhere in this book.[198] A comparison of a silver dish, ewer, and wine-cup from a hoard of the ninth/ tenth century said to have been found in Shaanxi province (Fig. 6.11) with similar Ding-ware porcelain vessels from a tomb of AD 900 and now in the Zhejiang Province Museum (Fig. 6.12)[199] shows how close the parallels are. As with Greek pottery, it is indeed the case that 'the history of certain ceramic types has . . . to be considered as developing in response to a standard set by silver'.[200]

One category of porcelain vessels was distinguished by the addition of gold or silver bindings on their rims. This procedure had precedents in other media, such as jade, and was clearly intended to enrich the material used. In the case of some vessels, such as Ding-ware cups, the firing technique meant that the rims were bare of glaze, and binding would serve to cover the rough edge. The procedure would also enhance the value of the goods, and raise

---

[192] Forbes, Kernan, and Wilkins (1975), 16–17; Rawson (1982); W. Watson (1986), 164.

[193] Rawson (1986).

[194] W. Watson (1986).

[195] Cf. O. Impey in Vickers, Impey, and Allan (1986), introduction: 'Continual attempts were made by the Tang Emperors to restrict the burial of precious materials. It was nevertheless an essential part of burial practice to place containers in the tomb, and so ceramic vessels were used for this purpose'; similar considerations probably applied in ancient Greece and Etruria.

[196] Rawson (1989), 287 lists the following char-

acteristics of ceramic that have their origins in metalwork: 'stepped handles on ewers, rolled spouts, flanged and knobbed lids, indented metal sides, faceted vessel sides, everted lips, angled bodies, high footrings, flat rims with rolled lips, lobed and lotus-shaped rims, lobed and lotus-shaped vessel sides'.

[197] Ibid. 287–8.

[198] Paradoxically, it was the development of the Chinese coal industry that brought clays suitable for porcelain to hand; in the raw state such carbon-rich clays are black: ibid. 284.

[199] Cf. Rawson (1986), 45, figs. 8–9.

[200] Ibid. 44.

FIG. 6.11   Silver dish, ewer, and wine-cup, from Shaanxi province, China. British Museum.

them in the hierarchy of materials. Similar considerations will have gone into the occasional adornment of painted Greek pottery with small amounts of gold. Most of these wares have come from tombs, and were presumably intended to make an impression on bystanders at a funeral. The same principle of value-enhancement, combined with the concealment of a defect, can be observed on two Attic pottery cups found in a Celtic grave at Klein Aspergle in southern Germany. They were broken in antiquity and the repair covered with plaques of gold.[201]

Unlike much Greek pottery, porcelain seems to have been a high-status commodity, made to meet the requirements of a large wealthy class in an age when there was probably not enough silver to satisfy demand.[202] The status of the potter too, was relatively high, at least within the hierarchy of crafts; in the tenth century it was only a little below workers in jade and lacquer.[203]

[201] Kimmig (1987), 259–60; but the cups from Klein Aspergle are scarcely objects which had been 'ordered directly' from Athens (p. 259); see too Böhr (1987).

[202] Rawson (1989), 284.
[203] Tregear (1986), 178.

FIG. 6.12   Ding-ware porcelain vessels, from the tomb of Qian Kuan. Zhejiang Province Museum.

Later, in the Ming period, porcelain might be listed in domestic inventories (though the 15,000 porcelain bowls belonging to Yan Song, Grand Secretary 1542–62, were unitemized, while his 3,185 gold vessels, his 367 gold vessels studded with gems, and his 1,649 silver vessels were individually described as to weight and decoration), and in the 1580s the banquets served to successful examination candidates and their examiners were eaten from porcelain.[204] Bribes and presents, however, were customarily in the form of gold or silver vessels.[205] Most old Chinese gold and silver will have been melted down in the ordinary course of events,[206] while the surviving porcelain and earthenware has led to a somewhat unbalanced picture of Chinese material culture,[207] that is only now being remedied.

One development that may have important ramifications for the study of Greek material culture is the realization by students of Chinese art that the porcelain figures made in the *blanc-de-chine* of Dehua in Quanzhou province, and which first appear around 1600, were made in imitation of the ivory carvings that began to be made in the neighbouring province of Zhangzhou a few years earlier. The eighteenth-century porcelain statuette of Guan di, the god of war, in Fig. 6.13 provides a typical example. The potter works within norms created by craftsmen working in the medium of ivory carving. Later, the glaze on some nineteenth-century *blanc-de-chine* was made to resemble more closely the colour of ivory.[208] Some of the ramifications for

[204] Clunas (1986), 85–6.
[205] Ibid. 86.
[206] See Forbes, Kernan, and Wilkins (1975), 23.

[207] Cf. Clunas (1986), 86. For J. D. Beazley and Oriental antiquities, see Ashmole (1970), 459.
[208] Gilman (1984). For Roman period clay skeuomorphs of ivory in India, see Vickers (1994).

FIG. 6.13 Porcelain *blanc-de-chine* statuette of Guan di, eighteenth century. Ashmolean Museum, Oxford EA 1956.3282. Ingram gift.

Greek terracotta statuettes (which often carry a white slip) will be discussed below.[209]

(*b*) *Islam*

The presence of lavish gold and silver revetments and furnishings in the Ka'ba at Mecca, or in the Dome of the Rock in Jerusalem, shows that there cannot have been a very strong resistance to silver in Islamic religious

[209] See pp. 200–2, below.

circles,[210] despite the slogan recorded as·early as 735–8: 'He who drinks from a silver vessel will have Hellfire gurgling in his belly.'[211] It was rather the close association between precious metal and alcohol-drinking which led to the proscription of gold and silver in many Islamic societies. By the same token, it was a love of wine among royalty and military aristocracies, especially in Iran and Turkey, that led to the manufacture of gold and silver vessels.[212] These are frequently mentioned in chronicles, inventories, and literary sources, but—as so often—very few actually survive.

The lacunae in the archaeological record relating to Islamic plate have been filled by means of arguments based on imitative work in ceramic and bronze. Thus the Sāmānid rulers of north-east Iran and Transoxania controlled the most productive silver mines in the Islamic world in the tenth century, but no silver vessels are known. A comparison of surviving ceramic shapes and decoration with those of Islamic silverware made in other centres has, however, made it possible to envision, for example, Sāmānid 'epigraphic-ware', 'vessels which are among the most majestic achievements of the Islamic potter' as silver surrogates, imitating either lost prototypes or made at a time when economic conditions led to the flow of bullion east to Tang China and west to Scandinavia. Either way, the bold, black calligraphy on a white ground will have evoked niello inlay upon light-coloured silver.[213]

The manufacture of inlaid base-metal vessels, of which large numbers still survive, has been held either to be another way of countering the effects of a silver famine suffered by the Islamic world in the eleventh and twelfth centuries,[214] or to be a downmarket evocation of silverware made for the court and the leading members of the military aristocracy.[215] Irrespective of the merits of either argument, gold and silver forms and decorative schemes were ultimately imitated by potters. Lustre ware is thus now held to imitate either gold[216] or inlaid bronze or brass ware,[217] and—one of many such comparisons that could be made—a ceramic jug made in Syria or the Jazīra in the fourteenth century [Fig. 6.14] 'copies in its shape, in its flattened handle form, in its torus moulding and in the vertical emphasis of its neck decoration, a form of inlaid metal jug [Fig. 6.15] common in the region at this period.'[218]

When these issues were discussed at the 'Pots and Pans' colloquium held in Oxford in 1985 to examine 'the dependence of the potter's craft on that of the gold- and silversmith', the potter Alan Caiger-Smith made a distinction

---

[210] Melikian-Chirvani (1986), 89–94.
[211] Juynboll (1986), 110.
[212] Melikian-Chirvani (1986), 95–100; Rogers (1986).
[213] Raby (1986).
[214] Allan (1976–7); (1982); (1986); in Vickers, Impey, and Allan (1986), introduction; O. Watson (1986).
[215] Melikian-Chirvani (1986).

[216] According to Sarre (1925), 32, relief ware with monochrome lustre imitated gold, in order to get around the religious prohibition; cf. Raby (1986), 183 n. 14; Allan, in Vickers, Impey, and Allan (1986), introduction.
[217] O. Watson (1986). Contrast Vallance (1909), who was outspoken in his rejection of any connection between lustre ware and metalwork.
[218] Allan (1986), 64, 68, figs. 8–9.

FIG. 6.14   Underglaze-painted pottery jug, Jazīra. Fourteenth century. Ashmolean Museum, Oxford EA 1978.1658.

between ceramics that were replicas in a cheaper material and those which were a reinterpretation of a recognized metal form. 'Instances of really close dependence turned out to be surprisingly elusive', but Attic pottery was one of the few categories that was considered to be closely derived from work in precious metal.[219] It was this aspect of Greek ceramics that offended the late Bernard Leach; he believed that classical Greek pottery was 'conceived

[219] Caiger-Smith (1986), 213.

FIG. 6.15   High-tin bronze jug inlaid with silver. Jazīra. Fourteenth century. Nuhad Es-Said Collection, no. 10 (after Allan (1982)).

coldly and without reference to its material and to the organic growth of spinning clay shaped by human hands' and was aware of its 'metallic' nature.[220] Leach's judgement deserves respect in this context. So too does an idea put forward in the 1920s, but neglected since. The theoretical basis of L. D. Caskey's *The Geometry of Greek Vases* (1922) in which the complex design of the forms of Greek painted pottery is emphasized, may be some-

---

[220] Leach (1976), 235–6.

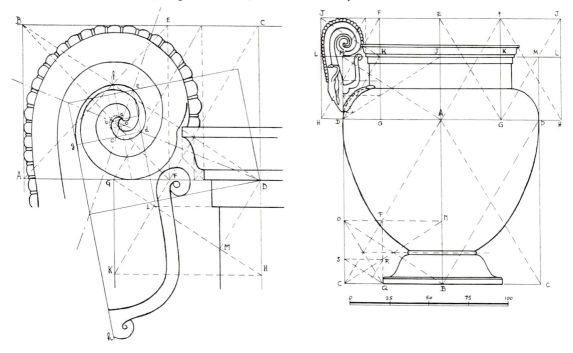

FIG. 6.16 The underlying mathematics of the design of the Vix crater. (After Loret (1961), 55, 52.)

what 'fanciful',[221] but it is considerably less so if the geometry of metal vessels is taken into account.[222] C. Loret has amply demonstrated the complex mathematics involved in the design of the bronze Vix crater (Fig. 6.16),[223] and it will have been careful design of this order which the Greek potter emulated.

[221] R. M. Cook (1972), 355. See too, Hambidge (1920).
[222] Contrast Boardman (1974), 184: 'Where these studies imply a knowledge of geometry far beyond the wit of any ancient potter they can be ignored without more ado.'
[223] Loret (1961), 49–56.

7 The Way Forward

A REASSESSMENT of the availability of gold and silver plate in the ancient world—and in particular at Athens—clearly has implications for other aspects of Greek material culture. Gold and silver vessels were in widespread use among élites in antiquity. They were used in the home, they were dedicated to the gods, but they were only very occasionally disposed of in the grave.

In many ways plate in antiquity played the role that is frequently assigned in modern scholarship to fine figure-decorated pottery. In this context, it is often claimed that potters and pot-painters mixed with élites, that potters could grow rich enough to make lavish dedications, and that merchants could make large profits from the trade in Attic pottery. The evidence for these claims does not stand up to close examination, as has been argued in earlier chapters. If the case presented here is correct, it should no longer be possible to think of the Athenian pottery industry as ever having been 'a major economic force' in the ancient world.[1] Nor can painted pots, which characteristically sold for obols rather than *minae*, ever have been considered works of art in their own right in the eyes of ancient consumers. They do, however, serve to illustrate the range and nature of the kind of objects that the ancients may well have admired (for attested admiration is usually restricted to objects of either great size or of intrinsic value—or both), and their study, if properly conducted, can greatly assist in understanding ancient society. We take this to be the aim of any student of the past.

CERAMIC STUDIES AFTER BEAZLEY

While the accident of survival may have brought about an unreal assessment of the role of painted pottery in antiquity, we have every sympathy with those who regard it as illuminating the development of Western Art.[2] Where we differ is in regarding decorated ceramic as a close reflection of work in media where creative artists might be active, rather than being the medium for that creativity itself. But however fine the decoration of the pottery may seem to us today, there is no evidence to suggest that ceramic was ever regarded as a serious artistic medium in antiquity, and other explanations

---

[1] Shapiro (1989) 5; for a useful corrective, see Arafat (1992), 218.

[2] Robertson (1992); Gill and Vickers (1990), 26; cf. Gill (1993).

need to be found to account for the high standards consistently achieved by potters and pot-painters. Mary Beard has observed that nothing can be said about the painters and potters of the 'vases' that cannot be said about the pots themselves,[3] and we concur.

A salutary parallel to the position that regards Greek figure-decorated pots as Art (with a capital 'A') is to be found in the situation that prevails in the context of the Aegean Bronze Age and the marble sculpture of the Cyclades. Here, the 'elegant simplicity' of Cycladic sculpture coincides with (some) modern tastes,[4] and the modern interest in them in many ways parallels eighteenth-century 'Vasomania' before that particular bubble burst. In both instances, the desire to possess a Cycladic figurine or an 'Etruscan vase' has led to the wholesale destruction of their archaeological contexts. In the case of Cycladic sculpture, recent estimates suggest that less than 10 per cent of the entire corpus of marble figures come from known archaeological findspots.[5] There are in addition certain intellectual consequences for Cycladic archaeology, arising from the fact that figures which were once grouped by archaeological context (e.g. Spedos type)[6] are now named after their present proprietors (e.g. the Bastis or Goulandris Masters).[7] Yet even these attributions are insecure, in that the 'works' of some 'Masters' may be the creation of modern forgers who have taken advantage of the loss of provenance of so many 'orphaned' figures.[8] The fact that nothing could be easier to forge may not be unrelated. The upshot has been that while Cycladic figurines have taught us that modern taste may let us enjoy the simple forms of Cycladic Bronze Age sculpture, it is also the case that modern taste may lead us far from the truth about the Bronze Age Cyclades.

On the classical Greek front, we accept that Beazley's 'achievement'[9] was to classify tens of thousands of Attic (and other) types of figure-decorated pots, but it is not a necessary corollary to believe that Greek painted pottery was ever considered to be an especially desirable commodity in antiquity. Now that we live in a post-Beazley age, it is appropriate that scholars should be seeking new ways of studying the important evidence that is undoubtedly provided by Greek ceramics. But without Beazley's eye (and in the absence of his strict ethical code with regard to the art market), attribution studies become less worthy of respect.[10] Sale catalogues of Greek vases—and they are never pots in these contexts—can sometimes list several attributions by different scholars; and it is only natural in such circumstances that the 'painter'

---

[3] Beard (1991), 17.
[4] For a recent discussion see Renfrew (1991).
[5] Chippindale and Gill (1993).
[6] Renfrew (1969).
[7] Getz-Preziosi (1987).
[8] The problems with Getz-Preziosi's methodology, as well as the issue of forgeries corrupting the corpus, are dealt with in detail by Gill and Chippindale (1993). For the problems of attribution studies in prehistory, see C. Morris (1993).
[9] Beard (1991), 16.
[10] Cf. Robertson (1989*b*), p. xii.

who will attract the highest price might be given the greatest prominence.[11] Not surprisingly such attribution studies are now widely thought to be out of place in scholarly circles, whatever lingering respect they may retain in the eyes of dealers and their academic retainers. The recognition that gold and silver plate was the material of preference among the élites of the Greek world ought to dislodge painted pottery from its previously privileged position. And once it is more widely realized that the study of Greek pottery is largely conducted in an intellectual vacuum which has little point of contact with the values of the ancient world, there should be a decline in the extent to which Etruscan (and other) cemeteries are looted in order to supply museums and collectors—and behind them the market-makers and ancient-art consultants—with works of 'Art'.

We are reliably informed (by a former ancient-art consultant) that one consequence of our thesis is that some North American collectors are now questioning the wisdom of acquiring painted pottery, since the field is so controversial (and nothing puts off collectors as much as controversy: they want their investments to be secure and not subject to the vagaries of scholarship). Our opposition to the machinations of the antiquities trade is shared by the Beazley Archive at Oxford which has recently distanced itself from antiquities dealers and auction-houses by refusing to supply assistance with attributions. Any opposition to the view that Greek pottery did not possess an exalted position in antiquity should now be judged against the background of a market whose supporters are afraid of losing possible financial and material benefits.

A NEW AGENDA FOR THE STUDY OF GREEK POTTERY

The main thrust of our thesis concerns the role of plate and of other luxury goods in the Greek world, but if our arguments are valid, there are certain ramifications in other areas. If Greek pottery can no longer be viewed as a major art form—except from a twentieth-century position—what might the agenda for vasology and other ancient ceramic studies usefully be? Clearly there needs to be a reappraisal of the way in which the extant material culture of the ancient world is handled. Scholars need to understand the implications of the positivist fallacy for their area of research; less use should perhaps be made of 'negative evidence', at least until due consideration has been given to the wider picture. We do not, however, want to throw out the baby with the bath water. Beazley's framework of attributions can be an important starting-point for research on Greek pottery. The fact that Attic

[11] This was most apparent in the recent catalogues of the Athena Fund II sale: It is no secret that these pots belonged to the family that had, ironically, attempted to corner the world market in silver. See p. 34, above.

pottery can be found from Portugal to Palestine, from the Crimea to Cyrenaica, means that a discussion of the ceramic evidence could usefully play a part in the debates about the supply of large urban populations.[12] If, as the evidence from numerous shipwrecks suggests, fine painted pottery was neither a major nor a valuable component in trade, its distribution patterns may nevertheless help to pin-point areas which were directly or indirectly in contact with Athens or other centres of ceramic production. Quantification of finds might suggest places which had direct trading links with the Piraeus. An obvious example is Spina on the Po delta, where vast quantities of Attic pottery have been found. It is clear from Beazley's attributions that the known output of some pot-painters, especially in the fourth century, is confined to Spina. How far does this reflect directional trade or specialization of Athenian potters? What were the archaeologically invisible cargoes travelling in either direction? Such questions may have been overlooked in the past because many of these pots do not fall into the category of Art but rather into what has been described as 'hackwork'.[13] The cemeteries around Spina badly need a study which will consider the individual elements of the tomb-groups.[14] Here, if anywhere, it is possible to identify several pots decorated by the same hand and all coming from the same tomb; this 'attribution' could then be applied to other material from the cemetery to investigate which tombs are roughly contemporary.

The study of commercial graffiti is not unrelated.[15] The scratches and markings on the undersides of Greek—not just Attic—pottery provide one of the major insights into the commercial organization of one part of urban life. These trademarks provide us with information about the ethnic backgrounds of those carrying the pots in their holds—for example, Etruscans, Ionians, Phoenicians—as well as the size, composition, and value of the batches. They can, moreover, inform us about the names given to individual shapes. If the short inscriptions have been correctly interpreted as the abbreviated names of shippers or agents, it should be possible to reconstruct patterns of trading. It is also clear that some of Beazley's 'hands' group conveniently with some of these ligatured names. This could be used to dispel the notion of a second-hand market in Greek pottery,[16] if the graffiti show that groups of Attic pots were leaving the Ceramicus, being shipped by a specific individual to, say, Etruria. The idea of a second-hand market for pottery arose because some Attic pots which had scenes appropriate only to an Attic audience, or *kalos*-names which would be irrelevant outside the circle of the Attic élite, were found outside Athens. It was thus suggested

---

[12] Gill (1991).

[13] Robertson (1991), 4.

[14] Beazley's own study of material from Spina might be a useful starting-point: see his paper in Beazley (1989), 60–5.

[15] Lists may be found in Johnston (1979). For some of the implications see Gill (1991).

[16] Webster (1972), xiii; cf. Robertson (1991), 8, who thinks that 'there does seem to be evidence that such a [sc. second-hand] trade existed'.

that pots were made for specific symposia and afterwards sold off; the individual pots would then appear in Etruscan tombs.[17] The study of commercial graffiti does not appear to support such a view, for if—for the sake of argument—the pots were being sold haphazardly after major symposia, we might expect a wide range of commercial graffiti to be applied to the pottery as it was exported. Yet it is clear that there are distinct clusters of pots attributed to a single 'painter' which have the same commercial mark; the pots were clearly leaving the workshop together, were marked together, and presumably were exported together.

Attribution studies may also help when discussing the plain wares produced alongside the figure-decorated pottery at Athens.[18] It is certainly possible to classify Attic black-glossed wares along these lines.[19] Pots which share similar potting features may be placed in 'classes'.[20] Thus it is possible to define mugs of, say, the 'Class of Oxford 1927.66' where the feet of all the mugs are nicked off from the body and the sides are reserved.[21] This potting feature may in turn be linked to the decorators of figured pots, namely Beazley's 'Douris' and 'Painter of Philadelphia 2449'. Another class may be that of stemmed dishes of the 'Class of Cambridge GR.57–1890' which are characterized by a reserved concave moulding on the underneath of their bowls.[22]

Decoration as well as potting features may help to define a class of plain ware. For example, the *phialai* of the 'Olbia Class' are frequently decorated with coral red, as well as sharing the feature of ribbed bodies.[23] Some black-glossed stemless cups of this delicate class have a prominent cone on their underside. Both this potting feature, as well as the scheme of stamped and impressed decoration, allow these pieces to be placed in the same workshop which produced red-figured stemless cups attributed to Beazley's 'Amphitrite Painter' and 'Carlsruhe Painter'.[24] The workshops of these plain vessels may, however, be identified through the use of shared stamps.[25] It may thus be possible to build up profiles of workshops producing, for example, mugs, *kantharoi*, and *amphoriskoi*; occasionally it is possible to show that the same stamp was used on different types of objects. Indeed the use of stamps on some red-figured vessels allows precise links between the plain and the figured material coming from the same workshops.[26] Such workshop identification

[17] Webster (1972), xiii, and cf. p. 104, above.

[18] Robertson (1991), 8: 'It is evident that these black vessels [sc. black-glossed] were produced in the same workshops from which red-figured pieces also issued, so that the grouping of red-figured by painters, and the relations between those painters, has a direct value for this study'.

[19] Gill (1986); cf. Sparkes and Talcott (1970) for earlier work in this area.

[20] Cf. Robertson (1989b), p. xvi: '"Class" . . . refers to vases put together for likeness in potter-work'.

[21] Gill (1986), 60–1.

[22] Ibid. 155–6.

[23] Ibid. 124–5. These may in turn be linked to stemless cups decorated in coral red, the 'Class of Agora P10359': ibid. 99–102.

[24] Ibid. 111–20.

[25] See Corbett (1955); Gill (1984); (1990c).

[26] For the appearance of stamps on red-figured pottery, see Ure (1936); (1944). Her work may now be extended into the black-glossed material: see Gill (1986), 111–20.

makes it possible to judge whether or not there was directional trade. For example, Brian Shefton has noted the apparent 'popularity' of thick-walled Castulo cups in the Iberian peninsula,[27] and *amphoriskoi* decorated with what may be a silphium plant are commonly found in Southern Italy and Sicily.

This economic aspect of Greek pottery must be linked to a contextual one. For those merely interested in 'vases' as works of art, the findspot is of relatively little importance.[28] Yet how are we to understand the objects—and their imagery—if we ignore the contexts in which these pots were found? The surfacing of Greek pottery in sale catalogues in Europe and North America may disguise the widespread looting of tombs, mostly in Italy. Yet the frequently undamaged condition of the pots themselves attests to their having been placed carefully in the ground in antiquity, only to be carefully disinterred by *tombaroli* in more recent times. Such destruction of the archaeological context is perhaps of little concern to those who are more interested in questions of attribution; the same sub-Morellian principles can still be applied whether or not there is a context. Yet for those who want to understand Greek painted pottery in its original context, the loss of such valuable information must be of some concern.

An encouraging development is the attempt to understand Athenian painted pottery within the context of Etruria,[29] which is after all, where much of it has been found. It is right to stress the funerary aspect of the pottery, for it is in the tomb that the images of Athenian black-and red-figured pots interact with Etruscan funerary iconography. So much of the pottery placed in the tomb is sympotic in character: cups, jugs, *psykteres*, craters, amphoras, *stamnoi*, and so on. Some of the ceramic iconography is sympotic. The final resting-place for the pots is also intended to evoke a space where the deceased continue in an eternal banquet. Reclining banqueters decorate the walls of the Tomba delle Bighe at Tarquinia; they are entertained by male flute-players, and in the pediment of the tomb, a large crater, flanked by two boys carrying jugs, dominates the proceedings. In the Tomba degli Rilievi at Cerveteri, the niches for the corpses are cut as *klinai* at the symposium. Terracotta and stone images of the deceased often make them out to be reclining as if for the banquet. Thus placing an Athenian sympotic pottery vessel in the tomb—whether or not the vessel was also decorated with scenes of the symposium—helped to create a dignified (but not overly expensive) setting for a place where the dead were able to banquet for eternity.

Such an iconographical approach can be expanded. If Etruscan tombs can

---

[27] Shefton (1982).

[28] We agree with Vitelli (1992), 551 that the 'failure' of modern vase specialists 'to comment on how Greek vases get to the art market and the mantelpiece, their avoidance of the subject of looting and its effects on our potential under-standing of the past is, at best, highly irresponsible'. Our own position on the present-day market in antiquities is stated in Gill and Chippindale (1993); Vickers (1992c), 246.

[29] Spivey (1991).

be decorated with scenes of, for example, hunting or athletics, then Athenian pottery with those scenes would complement the iconography of the tomb-paintings. What the unscientific disturbance of these contexts has done is to remove the data which might have allowed a better understanding of the range of images with which the Etruscan dead were buried. Greek painted pottery could also play an important further role in the funerary rites of the Etruscans. We might imagine that these pots arrived at and were placed in the tomb as part of the funeral ceremony. The presence of images relating to the symposium, athletics, or the hunt on sympotic vessels would themselves help to make a statement about the deceased and funerary beliefs. In such a context the image and the viewer are the important things; the 'painter' or 'potter' are almost irrelevant. This was not a parade of works by the 'Amasis Painter' or 'Euphronios'; this was a parade of images relating to death. Such an interpretation might also help to explain why the 'best' Greek pots are found in Etruria.[30] A 'hack' piece might prove to be inappropriate in a funerary procession; the visual image had to be striking.

The more the Etruscan context of pots is emphasized, the more questions arise with regard to certain ideas about political iconography. If there was only a limited second-hand market in Greek painted pottery, then presumably most pottery found in the tombs of Etruria was exported directly. One set of theories concerns the appearance of Heracles and Theseus and the fortunes of tyranny and democracy in Athens. For example, the 'Exekias' amphora in the Vatican Museum showing Ajax and Achilles playing dice has been taken to be a warning to the viewers to be on their guard against tyrants.[31] The argument is that when Pisistratus entered Attica the Athenians were either asleep or playing dice, and thus there was no opposition. Yet such an interpretation has to show that the historical source, namely Herodotus, is accurate and that this particular story was current at the time.[32] Yet how can an Athenian amphora, safely buried alongside an Etruscan corpse hundreds of miles from Athens, attempt to convey a political message to the Athenians? It could only have done so if it can be demonstrated without question that this particular pot was displayed and used over a long period of time in the houses of those in Athens who loved democracy and were opposed to tyranny. (A bronze vessel decorated with silver figures might have been used back in Athens, but that is another story . . .) The same contextual problem also faces those who wish to use the imagery of Greek pottery to provide information about nationalization and defeminization.[33]

It is pleasant to report that some scholars working from a structuralist position have begun to take account of our thesis. For example, Herbert

---

[30] Cf. Vitelli (1992), 101; for a dismissive approach, see Boardman (1991), 101.

[31] Boardman (1972).

[32] For methodological objections to Boardman's approach see Osborne (1983–4).

[33] e.g. Keuls (1984).

Hoffmann has started to discuss the iconology of figure-decorated pottery in the light of substitute offerings placed within a religious or funerary context.[34] We would, however, still wish to distance ourselves, if only slightly, from other recent structuralist work on the imagery of Greek painted pottery.[35] It seems to us that not enough care has been taken to identify the viewers of these images. On gold-figured silver vessels would the images have been meant for women in the women's quarters of the Greek house? Were these images viewed and discussed within the context of a symposium? Although we think that much has been discovered through a structuralist approach, we feel that there is room for a more sophisticated model.

We also welcome the way that our work has helped to refocus the debate about context.[36] Ian Morris has attempted to explore our thesis by examining the presence of white-ground *lekythoi* in both inhumation and cremation burials at Athens.[37] His study uses forty-six graves from two cemeteries (Ceramicus and Syndagma Square)[38] but we wonder if this is an adequate sample of a city which at the time in question may have had a population of a quarter of a million.[39] Although Morris's initial results suggest that there is no link between rite (i.e. cremation, inhumation) and type of vessel (in this case, the *lekythos*) selected for inclusion in the grave, he endorses our main point, 'that when the Athenians put pottery in their graves it was not because they valued it more highly than silver or gold'.[40] Again the debate has returned to whether or not 'silver and gold were regularly used by the rich'[41] and how far down the social scale precious metals were in regular use.[42] Further contextual work by those engaged in the study of cemeteries in Attica and Etruria may well throw further light on this area, but we do not feel that the results so far significantly challenge our central thesis.

Religious sanctuaries are an important source of Greek ceramics. Excavations in both major and minor Greek sanctuaries, some urban, some rural, have yielded large quantities of pottery, some of which was Athenian and figure-decorated. Fragments from Naucratis in Egypt are inscribed with the names of the various Greek deities in whose temples they were dedicated. At Athens, quantities of pots were recovered from the fills within the Acropolis walls, as well as fragments which had fallen over the cliff edge. Likewise the fill under the later temple of Aphaia on the island of Aegina contained large numbers of pots which presumably had been dedicated in the sanctuary.

[34] Hoffmann (1985–6); (1988); (1989).
[35] e.g. Bérard *et al.* (1989); Lissarague (1990); Beard (1991).
[36] Wright (1993).
[37] I. Morris (1992), 108–27.
[38] Ibid. 112. The figures he uses are based on percentages and disguise the actual numbers.
[39] Garnsey (1988), 123.
[40] I. Morris (1992), 118. We do not understand J. C. Wright (1993) or C. J. Smith (1993) who believe that Morris has refuted the case for pottery being a poor relative of gold and silver.
[41] I. Morris (1992), 124.
[42] Ibid. 127.

We may assume that in the last two cases pots were buried as offerings which had been dedicated to the deity but were no longer for display. There may be large numbers of pots, but it seems that they dominate the archaeological record of a Greek sanctuary simply because they were not the type of object worth stealing. Occasionally items of value *are* found, but this does not make the pots any more valuable. A wide range of costly dedications are attested in literary and epigraphic sources. The presence of cheap pottery in addition to these suggests that they may have been the equivalent of *ex voto* candles in modern sanctuaries (and the range of prices of the latter, at 5p to 50p, is apparently similar to that of pots in antiquity).[43] But there is clearly room for much further research here, taking into account the differential survival patterns of different categories of material as well as the types of images that were felt appropriate for offerings dedicated to the gods.

Pottery is also found in domestic contexts, but it is important to recall that excavated dwellings have usually been stripped of most of their recyclable contents, even the tiles from roofs. The problem facing the archaeologist is to determine what sort of family lived in a given building. Were they members of the élite or not? We have already noted how the presence of red-figured pottery in Attic dwellings has been taken to indicate the high status of the family that owned it,[44] but matters might not be quite so straightforward. Outside Attica, large (and stratified) quantities of Attic red-figured pottery have been found in houses at Euesperides in Cyrenaica, but even though the findspots of much of the pottery are known, it is not yet clear which houses in the city were those of the local élite. The finds are currently undergoing study.[45] Similar doubts arise from the profusion of Attic pottery found in recent years in domestic contexts in northern Italy: at Forcello, Bagnolo S. Vito (near Mantua),[46] at Marzobotto,[47] and Case Vandelli, Modena.[48] Olynthus might also benefit from a renewed examination. Such studies should resolve the question as to whether or not the view that Greek pottery might be used in life by élites is a valid one.

We have concentrated on painted pottery from Greek and Etruscan contexts. A further useful line of enquiry might be to look with fresh eyes at societies living on the periphery who received such objects. Greek pottery is occasionally found in ostensibly wealthy burials in north-west Europe, in Thrace and Scythia. Although the intrinsic value of such items will have been minimal in antiquity, their precise role is not without interest. Did they serve as surrogates, as they did in Greece and Italy, or were they somehow valued

---

[43] On which, see pp. 85–8, above.

[44] See above, pp. 102–3.

[45] Cf. Vickers, Gill, and Economou (forthcoming).

[46] de Marinis (1986), 140–63 (House R 18); (1991), 249, 251–6.

[47] De Maria, Mansuelli, Sassatelli, and Vitali (1978), 63, 69, 71, 74, 97–8, 112, 117; Pairault, Massa, and Vallet (1978), 137, 139, 146, 153–4, 156–7.

[48] Malnati (1988). We owe these references to Christoph Reusser.

for their exotic nature? Who used Greek pottery and why are questions which require more attention than they have received in the past. This is especially the case now that it is abundantly clear that painted pots are no longer to be envisaged in the hands of rich Greeks and Etruscans at their symposia.

GREEK TERRACOTTA SCULPTURE—
A FRESH FIELD OF RESEARCH

Much remains to be done in the area of skeuomorphism, for once it is realized that a great deal of what has survived from classical antiquity owed its shape and decoration to work first done in other media, there is plenty to be investigated. An obvious candidate for further research is the work of the coroplast. Greek terracotta statuettes, especially those found in graves, are frequently covered with a white slip. In the light of what was said in earlier chapters about the slip on white-ground *lekythoi* probably being an evocation of ivory, and *blanc-de-chine* statuettes being made as cheap versions of ivory figurines,[49] it is possible that many Greek terracottas were made as cheap surrogates for far more costly ivory objects that would not normally have been placed in the tomb. Ivory, together with gold, represented the acme of Greek sculptural production on a large scale; and while few small ivory figurines have survived, there are sufficient hints in the shapes and dimensions of some terracotta statuettes to suggest that they depended upon work in the more precious material.

A characteristic form of terracotta statuette in the Hellenistic period is the draped dancer with a twisted pose; the whole composition fitting into a curved, elongated, conical form. Many such statuettes have, or had, a white slip, and it is not too difficult to envisage an ivory original, carved from the pointed end of a curved tusk (Fig. 7.1). The twisted poses of many of these figures recall those of ivory Virgins of the Middle Ages, whose 'swaying stance' was forced upon the ivory worker by his medium.[50] Cheaper versions of these exist in wood and stone (Fig. 7.2), which repeat the curve as a gesture in the direction of the more costly material.

It is interesting to note that the largest of the known terracotta dancers come from an area that was closest to a major source of ivory.[51] It has been something of a puzzle as to why the (white) Hellenistic statuettes from tombs in Sicily are twice as large as their equivalents in Cyrenaica;[52] derivation from ivory would solve the problem, in that the best ivory would have been

---

[49] See pp. 149–51 and 185–6, above.
[50] Gaborit-Chopin (1972); Tudor-Craig (1987), 98–101.

[51] Cf. Hermipp. *PCG* 63.15: 'Libya supplies ivory in plenty for trade'.
[52] Burn (forthcoming).

FIG. 7.1   Hellenistic terracotta statuette of a dancer, from Cyrenaica. British Museum, Inv. GR 1856.10.1.43.

traded with the richer community. Similarly, the low stumps on which some Cyrenaican figurines stand, and which have also been the subject of speculation,[53] may owe their form to work in ivory. Although no ivory figurines of dancers have survived, there is a well-known ivory representation of a hunchbacked dwarf in the British Museum,[54] a motif that frequently occurs among Hellenistic terracottas and bronzes. The perishable nature of ivory will have led to the disappearance of nearly everything made from the substance in Graeco-Roman antiquity, but its status with respect to clay is clear from the declaration of Apollonius of Tyana to the effect that he 'would prefer to find an image of gold and ivory in a small shrine, than a big shrine with nothing but a rubbishy terracotta thing in it'.[55] Although most people today would reject Apollonius' criticism of clay, the relationship in antiquity between terracotta figurines and ivory is clear. There is a fruitful field of research here for someone to take up.

[53] Ibid.   [54] Vickers (1987*b*), 47.   [55] Philostr. *VA* 5. 22.

FIG. 7.2 *Virgin and Child*,
School of Andrea Pisano. Marble.
Oxford, Ashmolean Museum WA
B.1270; D.1348.

NEW AVENUES IN THE STUDY OF PRECIOUS METAL

If the study of Greek ceramics can be put on a sensible footing, much good
will be done. But the main purpose of this book has been to reinsert gold
and silver plate into the general picture of antiquity. Precious metals had a
central role to play, and in the case of Athenian silverware, an informative
role so far as local ceramic products were concerned. Ancient values were
rather different from enlightened modern ones, for reasons we have examined at considerable length, and if progress is to be made in understanding
the past, this harsh fact needs to be taken on board. Most ancient historians

are used to viewing the classical world in this light, but archaeologists have tended to idealize life in ancient Greece so that the life of the aristocrat and the craftsman have been confused. The existence of a hierarchy of materials is either ignored, or if recognized, rejected. It should not need to be spelt out that in the eyes of everyone in antiquity gold took precedence over silver, silver over bronze, and bronze over glass and ceramic. The prices of both the raw materials and of finished articles bear this out. No matter how skilful the craftsman in lesser materials might have been, he could not 'buck the system' by means of his artistry alone.

The intrinsic value of the materials used in its manufacture has inevitably meant that nearly all ancient plate has gone into the melting-pot. That there are more pieces of Athenian silverware than there are, say, surviving gold vessels from the early Roman empire is due to the unHellenic burial practices of the lands to the north of Greece, as well as to the fact that plate was regularly melted down to be remade when fashions changed, when it was worn, or when it was looted. An area where more research needs to be done is in determining quite how much the charge for making gold and silver plate might have been. The evidence is slight, and difficult to control, and the amount of metal that might be lost in working is usually unknown. The few attempts that have been made to assess such costs in classical Greek times have been inevitably speculative, and appear to be on the high side compared with what is known from the Roman period. Thus U. Koehler once estimated the cost of making gold crowns in the fourth century BC at between $2\frac{1}{2}$ and 6 per cent of the sum available,[56] and David Lewis the manufacturing cost of a gold *phiale* in 434/3 BC at $6\frac{2}{3}$ per cent.[57] A rare case of such costs being given in detail is to be found in Diocletian's price edict, where there were two grades of workmanship specified for work in gold. 'Simple' workmanship added 0.83 per cent and 'subtle' 1.3 per cent. The three grades of workmanship specified for silver added 5 per cent, 2.5 per cent, and 1.25 per cent.[58] These figures suggest that calculations regarding earlier plate may require revision.

Temple inventories contain great quantities of unexploited material, as David Lewis has already noted.[59] Tullia Linders, Sarah Aleshire, and Diane Harris have begun to exploit the riches, both literal and scholarly, to be found in them, but much remains to be done. When the Delian indices are eventually published[60] it will be possible to make considerable progress in elucidating the contents of one of the Greek world's major shrines. New discoveries of surviving plate are made almost annually, and they can contribute to our understanding both of ancient patronage and of metalworking

---

[56] Koehler (1878), 225–6.
[57] Lewis (1968), 108.
[58] Rea (1986), 79.

[59] Lewis (1986).
[60] Only one volume has appeared to date: Tréheux (1992); others are in preparation.

practices. It is becoming standard procedure for plate and jewellery to be published with their weights, but there are still some regrettable exceptions. The underlying metrology of gold and silver enables us to approach the world of the patron and craftsman in a way that is impossible in ceramic studies, but in a way that is wholly in keeping with ancient material values. If, moreover, Greek standards of craftsmanship were high in the medium of ceramic, this will have been because standards were set by workers in other, nobler, materials.

References

Age of Neo-classicism (1972), Council of Europe Exhibition (London).

Albizzati, C. (1916), 'Two Ivory Fragments of a Statue of Athena', *JHS* 36: 372–402, pls. 8–9.

Aldrovandi, U. (1648), *Musaeum Metallicum in Libros iiii Distributum* (Bonn).

Aleshire, S. (1989), *The Athenian Asklepieion: The People, their Dedications, and the Inventories* (Amsterdam).

Allan, J. W. (1976–7), 'Silver: The Key to Bronze in Early Islamic Iran', *Kunst des Orients*, 11: 5–21.

—— (1982), *Islamic Metalwork: Nuhad Es-Said Collection* (London).

—— (1986), 'The Survival of Precious and Base Metal Objects from the Medieval Islamic World', in Vickers (1986*a*), 57–70.

Alsop, J. (1982), *The Rare Art Traditions: The History of Art Collecting and its Linked Phenomena Wherever These Have Appeared* (London).

Amaury-Duval, P. (1829), 'Notice sur la vie et les ouvrages de M. le baron Vivant Denon', in *Monuments des arts du dessin chez les peuples tant anciens que modernes* (Paris).

Amiran, R. (1984), 'The Silver Goblet from Tell El-Far'ah (N) and its Pottery Imitations', in *Festschrift Rëuben R. Hecht* (Jerusalem) 115–18.

Ampolo, C. (1984), 'Le richezze dei Selinuntini: Tucidide VI 20, 4 e l'iscrizione del Tempio G di Selinunte', *PdP* 39: 81–9.

Amyx, D. A. (1958), 'The Attic Stelai, 3. Vases and Other Containers', *Hesperia*, 27: 163–310.

Andronicos, M. (1984), *Vergina, the Royal Tombs and the Ancient City* (Athens).

Anon. (1910), 'Copper', *Encyclopaedia Britannica*, 11th edn., 7. 102–10.

Arafat, K. W. (1992), review of Shapiro (1989), in *JHS* 112: 217–19.

Arafat, K., and Morgan, C. (1989), 'Pots and Potters in Athens and Corinth: A Review', *OJA* 8: 311–46.

Artamonov, M. (1966), *Richesses des tombeaux scythes* (Prague and St Petersburg).

Ashbee, C. R. (1909), *Modern English Silverwork* (London).

Ashmole, B. (1970), 'Sir John Beazley, 1885–1970', *PBA* 56: 443–61.

—— (1972), *Architect and Sculptor in Classical Greece* (New York).

Ashmolean *Summary Guide* (1951), *Ashmolean Museum, Department of Antiquities: Summary Guide* (Oxford).

Aubet, M. E. (1970), *Los marfiles orientalizantes de Praeneste* (Barcelona).

Bacon, F. (1922), *New Atlantis, a Worke Unfinished* (London, 1627), in *Francis Bacon, Selections*, eds. P. E. and E. F. Matheson (Oxford).

Bagley, R. W. (1987), *Shang Ritual Bronzes in the Arthur M. Sackler Collections* (Washington, DC and Cambridge, Mass.).

Balzano, V. (1913), 'Peasant Art in the Abruzzi', in *Peasant Art in Italy, Special Autumn Number of the Studio*, 9–16.

Baratte, F. (1986), *Le Trésor d'orfèvrerie romaine de Boscoreale* (Paris).

—— (1988) (ed.), *Argenterie romaine et byzantine: Actes de la Table Ronde, Paris 11–13 octobre 1983* (Paris).

—— and Painter, K. (1989) (eds.), *Trésors d'orfèvrerie gallo-romains* (Paris).

—— Le Bot-Helly, A., Helly, B., Depassiot, M.-C., and Langlet, V. (1990), *Le Trésor de la place Camille-Jouffray à Vienne* (*Gallia*, suppl. 50).

Barnett, R. D. (1954), 'Fine Ivory Work', in Singer, Holmyard, and Hall (1954), i. 663–83.

—— (1982), *Ancient Ivories in the Middle East* (*Qedem, Monographs of the Institute of Archaeology, Hebrew University of Jerusalem*, 14) (Jerusalem).

Barr-Sharrar, B. (1982), 'Macedonian Metal Vases in Perspective: Some Observations on Context and Tradition', *Studies in the History of Art*, 10: 124–40.

Basilov, V. N. (1989), *Nomads of Eurasia*. Exhibition catalogue (Los Angeles).

Baudrillart, H. (1878), *Histoire du luxe privé et public depuis l'antiquité à nos jours* (2 vols., Paris).

Baxendall, M. (1972), *Painting and Experience in Fifteenth-Century Italy* (Oxford).

Bazant, J. (1981), 'Homerian Gold and Athenian Pottery', in *Studies on the Use and Decoration of Athenian Vases* (Prague), 4–12.

Beard, M. (1986), 'Signed against Unsigned', *Times Literary Supplement* (12 Sept.), 1013.

—— (1991), 'Adopting an Approach', in Rasmussen and Spivey (1991), 12–35.

Beaucamp-Markowsky, B. (1985), *Porzellandosen des 18. Jahrhunderts* (Fribourg–Munich).

Beazley Gifts (1966), Ashmolean Museum, *Select Exhibition of Sir John and Lady Beazley's Gifts, 1912–1966* (London).

Beazley, J. D. (1910), 'Kleophrades', *JHS* 30: 38–68, pls. 1–9.

—— (1911), 'The Master of the Berlin Amphora', *JHS* 31: 276–95.

—— (1911–12), 'The Master of the Eucharides Stamnos in Copenhagen', *BSA* 18: 217–33, pls. 10–15.

—— (1918), *Attic Red-Figured Vases in American Museums* (Cambridge, Mass.).

—— (1927–8), 'Aryballos', *BSA* 29: 187–215.

—— (1928), *Greek Vases in Poland* (Oxford).

—— (1931), 'Amasea', *JHS* 51: 256–85.

—— (1931–2), 'Groups of Mid-Sixth-Century Black-Figure', *BSA* 32: 1–22.

—— (1938), *Attic White Lekythoi* (Oxford).

—— (1944), 'Potter and Painter in Ancient Athens', *PBA* 30: 87–125, pls. 1–8.

—— (1945), 'The Brygos Tomb at Capua', *AJA* 49: 153–8.

—— (1947), *Etruscan Vase-Painting* (Oxford).

—— (1956), *Attic Black-Figure Vase-Painters* (Oxford).

—— (1961), 'An Amphora by the Berlin Painter', *AK* 4: 49–67.

—— (1963), *Attic Red-Figure Vase-Painters* (2nd edn., Oxford).

—— (1971), *Paralipomena* (Oxford).

—— (1989), in D. C. Kurtz (ed.), *Greek Vases: Lectures by J. D. Beazley* (Oxford).

—— and Ashmole, B. (1932), *Greek Sculpture and Painting to the End of the Hellenistic Period* (Cambridge).

Becker, W. A. (1874), *Charicles, or Illustrations of the Private Life of the Ancient Greeks* (4th edn., London).

Beger, L. (1699), *Thesauri regii et electoralis Brandenburgici volumen tertium: continens antiquorum numismatum et gemmarum, quae Cimelarchio Regio-Electorali Brandenburgico nupe acessere, rariora: ut supellectilem antiquariam uberrimam, id est statuas, Thoraces, Clypeos, Imagines tam Deorum, quam Regum et Illustrium: Item Vasa & Instrumenta varia, eaque inter, fibulas, lampades, urnas: quorum pleraque cum Museo Belloriano, quaedam & aliunde coemta sunt* (Berlin).

Béhague (1987), *Antiquités et objets d'art: Collection de Martine, Comtesse de Béhague* (Sotheby Monte Carlo, 5 December).

Behalova, V. (1970), 'Die Villa Karma von Adolf Loos', *Alte und moderne Kunst*, 113: 11–19.

Bérard, *et al.* (1989), *A City of Images: Iconography and Society in Ancient Greece* (Princeton, NJ).

Berenson, B. (1968), *Italian Pictures of the Renaissance: Central Italian and North Italian Schools* (New York).

Berghaus P., *et al.* (1983) (eds.), *Exhibition Catalogue, Der Archäologe: Graphische Bildnisse aus dem Porträtarchiv Diepenbroick* (Münster).

Best, J. G. P., and de Vries, N. M. W. (1989) (eds.), *Thracians and Mycenaeans: Proceedings of the Fourth International Congress of Thracology, Rotterdam, 24–26 September 1984* (Leiden).

Bioul, A.-C. (1983–4), 'Une oenochoé attique à figures rouges de Bruxelles: Scène quotidienne ou rituelle?', *Bulletin de l'Institut Historique Belge de Rome*, 53–4: 5–39.

Birch, S. (1858), *History of Ancient Pottery: Egyptian, Assyrian, Greek, Etruscan and Roman* (London; 2nd edn.: 1873).

Bittel, K., and Behrends, R.-H. (1981) (eds.), *Die Kelten in Baden-Württemberg* (Stuttgart).

Bivar, A. D. H. (1985), 'Achaemenid Coins, Weights and Measures', *in Cambridge History of Iran*, 2: 610–49.

Blanck, H., and Proietti, G. (1986), *La Tomba dei Rilievi* (*Studi di archeologia pubblicati dalla soprintendenza archeologica per l'Etruria meridionale*, 1).

Blegen, C. (1963), *Troy and the Trojans* (London).

Blinkenberg, C. (1941), *Lindos 2: Inscriptions* (Berlin and Copenhagen).

Blümel, C. (1953), *Griechische Bildhauer an der Arbeit* (Berlin).

Blümner, H. (1875–87), *Technologie und Terminologie der Gewerbe und Künste bei Griechen und Römern* (4 vols., Leipzig).

—— (1905), 'Elfenbein', *RE* 5: 2356–66.

Boardman, J. (1972), 'Herakles, Peisistratos and Sons', *RA* 57–72.

—— (1973), *Greek Art* (2nd edn., London).

—— (1975), *Athenian Red Figure Vases: The Archaic Period* (London).

—— (1978), *Greek Sculpture: The Archaic Period* (London).

—— (1980*a*), *The Greeks Overseas: Their Early Colonies and Trade* (London).

—— (1980*b*), 'The Castle Ashby Vases', *Christie Catalogue* (2 July), 11–12.

—— (1981), 'Epiktetos II R. I. P.', *AA*: 329–31.

—— (1987), 'Silver is White', *RA* 279–95.

Boardman, J. (1988*a*), 'Trade in Greek Decorated Pottery', *OJA* 7: 27–33.

—— (1988*b*), 'The Trade Figures', *OJA* 7: 371–3.

—— (1988*c*) (ed.), *Cambridge Ancient History*, Plates to vol. 4, new edn. (Cambridge).

—— (1989), *Athenian Red Figure Vases: The Classical Period* (London).

—— (1991), 'The Sixth-Century Potters and Painters of Athens and their Public', in Rasmussen and Spivey (1991), 79–102.

Boeckh, A. (1842), *The Public Economy of Athens*, 2nd edn. (London).

Boegehold, A. L. (1985), 'The Time of the Amasis Painter', in Bothmer (1985), 15–32.

Böhr, E. (1987), 'Die griechischen Schalen', in W. Kimmig (ed.), *Das Kleinaspergle* (Stuttgart), 176–90.

Bol, P. C. (1985), *Antike Bronze Technik: Kunst und Handwerk antiker Erzbilder* (Munich).

Bookidis, N. (1990), 'Ritual Dining in the Sanctuary of Demeter and Kore at Corinth: Some Questions', in Murray (1990), 86–94.

Boraiko, A. A., and Ward, F. (1981), 'Silver: A Mineral of Excellent Nature', *National Geographic Magazine*, 160: 280–313.

Borsi, F. (1985) (ed.), *Fortuna degli Etruschi* (Florence).

Bothmer, D. von. (1962–3*a*), 'Painted Greek Vases', *BMMA* NS 21: 1–11.

—— (1962–3*b*), 'A Gold Libation Bowl', *BMMA* NS 21: 154–66.

—— (1981), 'Les Trésors de l'orfèvrerie de la Grèce orientale au Metropolitan Museum de New York', *Comptes-rendus de l'Académie des Inscriptions*, 194–207.

—— (1983), 'Notes on Collectors of Vases', in Tompkins (1983), 37–44.

—— (1984), 'A Greek and Roman Treasury', *BMMA* 42/1.

—— (1985) (ed.), *The Amasis Painter and his World: Vase-Painting in Sixth-Century BC Athens* (Malibu, Calif., New York, and London).

—— (1987), 'Euphronios and Memnon? Observations on a Red-Figured Fragment', *Metropolitan Museum Journal*, 22: 5–11.

—— (1992), 'The Subject Matter of Euphronios', in Denoyelle (1992), 13–32.

Böttiger, K. A. (1797–1800) (ed.), *Griechische Vasengemälde* (3 vols., Weimar and Magdeburg).

Bourdieu, P. (1979), *La Distinction: Critique sociale du jugement* (Paris).

Bowra, C. M. (1960), 'Euripides' Epinician for Alcibiades', *Historia*, 9: 68–79.

Brandon, V. (1913), *Goethe's Hermann and Dorothea* (London).

Briggs, A. (1962), *William Morris: Selected Writings and Designs* (Harmondsworth).

Brijder, H. A. G. (1983), *Siana Cups I and Komast Cups* (Allard Pierson Series, 4; Amsterdam).

—— (1984) (ed.), *Ancient Greek and Related Pottery* (Allard Pierson Series, 5; Amsterdam).

—— (1988), 'The Shapes of Etruscan Bronze Kantharoi from the Seventh Century BC and the Earliest Attic Black-Figure', *BABesch*. 63: 103–14.

British Museum (1976), *Thracian Treasures from Bulgaria*, exhibition catalogue (London).

Brongniart, A., and Riocreux, D. (1845), *Description méthodique du Musée Céramique de la Manufacture Royale de Porcelaine de Sèvres* (Paris).

Browne, T. (1658), *Hydriotaphia, Urne-buriall* (London).

Bruneau, P. (1975), 'Situation méthodologique de l'histoire de l'art antique', *Antiquité classique*, 44: 425–87.

Brunn, C. (1988), 'Einführung', in R. W. Gassen (ed.), *Attische Keramik: Schwarzfigurige Gefässe aus dem Besitz des Martin von Wagner-Museums der Universität Würzburg* (Ludwigshafen), 10–21.

Buchner, G. (1979), 'Early Orientalizing: Aspects of the Euboean Connection', in D. and F. R. Ridgway (eds.), *Italy before the Romans: The Iron Age, Orientalizing and Etruscan Periods* (London), 129–44.

Burn, A. R. (1960), *The Lyric Age of Greece* (London).

Burn, L. (1991), 'Vase-Painting in Fifth-Century Athens, ii. Red Figure and White Ground of the Later Fifth Century', in Rasmussen and Spivey (1991), 118–30.

—— (forthcoming), 'Hellenistic Terracotta Figurines of Cyrenaica: Greek Influences and Local Inspirations', in J. M. Reynolds (ed.), *Proceedings of the Cyrenaican Symposium, Cambridge 1993*.

Busch, H., and Lohse, B. (1959), *Wunderwelt der Schreine: Meisterwerke mittelalterlicher Goldschmiedekunst* (Frankfurt).

Buschor, E. (1914), *Griechische Vasenmalerei* (Munich).

Butler, A. J. (1884), *The Ancient Coptic Churches of Egypt* (2 vols., Oxford).

Butler, E. M. (1958), *The Tyranny of Greece over Germany* (2nd edn., Boston).

Cahn, H. A. (1960), 'Die Gewichte der Goldgefässe', *AK* 3: 27.

Caiger-Smith, A. (1973), *Tin-Glaze Pottery in Europe and the Islamic World* (London).

—— (1986), 'Notes on the Colloquium on Ceramics and Metalware, Oxford, March 1985', in Vickers (1986), 213–16.

Calder, W. M. III (1963), *The Inscription from Temple G at Selinus* (Durham, NC).

Callataÿ, F. de (1989), 'Des trésors royaux achéménides aux monnayages d'Alexandre: Espèces immobilisées et espèces circulantes?', *Actes du Colloque sur l'or dans l'empire achéménide, Bordeaux, March 1989, REA* 91: 259–73.

Cameron, G. C. (1948), *Persepolis Treasury Tablets* (Chicago).

Camp, J. M. (1982), 'Drought and Famine in the 4th century BC', in *Studies in Athenian Architecture, Sculpture and Topography presented to H. A. Thompson* (*Hesperia*, suppl. 20), 9–17.

Canino, Prince of (1831), 'Note on Etruscan Vases Found on his Estate', *Archaeologia*, 23: 260–76.

Cannon-Brookes, P. (1983), 'Sir Peter Paul Rubens & Co.', *The Ringling Museum of Art Journal*, 1: 124–9.

Carradice, I. (1987) (ed.), *Coinage and Administration in the Athenian and Persian Empires* (The Ninth Oxford Symposium on Coinage and Monetary History: BAR International Series, 343: Oxford).

Carter, P. A. (1977), *The Creation of Tomorrow: Fifty Years of Magazine Science Fiction* (New York).

Cartledge, P. (1983), '"Trade and Politics" Revisited: Archaic Greece', in Garnsey, Hopkins, and Whittaker (1983), 1–15.

Caskey, L. D. (1922), *The Geometry of Greek Vases* (Boston).

—— and Beazley, J. D. (1931–63), *Attic Vase Paintings in the Museum of Fine Arts, Boston* (Oxford).

Caylus, Comte de (1752–67), *Recueil d'antiquités égyptiennes, étrusques, grecques, romaines et gauloises* (7 vols., Paris).

Chamberlin, R. (1983), *Loot! The Heritage of Plunder* (London).

Chambers, M. H., Gallucci, R., and Spanos, P. (1990), 'Athens' Alliance with Egesta in the Year of Antiphon', *ZPE* 83: 38–63.

Charles, R. (1964), *Continental Porcelain of the Eighteenth Century* (London).

Chatelain, J. (1973), *Dominique Vivant Denon et le Louvre de Napoléon* (Paris).

Cherici, A. (1991), 'Granai o arnie? Considerazioni su una classe fittile attica tra IX e VII sec. a. C.', *Rend. Linc.* 44: 215–30, pls. 1–9.

Childe, V. G. (1924), 'A Gold Vase of Early Helladic Type', *JHS* 35: 196.

—— (1944), *Progress and Archaeology* (London).

—— (1956), *Piecing Together the Past: The Interpretation of Archaeological Data* (London).

Chippindale, C., and Gill, D. W. J. (1993), Discussion of C. Morris (1993), in *Cambridge Archaeological Journal*, 3: 57–8.

Clairmont, C. W. (1970), *Gravestone and Epigram: Greek Memorials from the Archaic and Classical Period* (Mainz).

Clark, A. J. (1981), 'The Earliest Known Chous by the Amasis Painter', *Metropolitan Museum Journal*, 15: 35–51.

Clark, G. (1986), *Symbols of Excellence: Precious Materials as Expressions of Status* (Cambridge).

Clark, R. J. (1972), *The Arts and Crafts Movement in America 1876–1916* (Princeton, NJ).

Clifford, T., and Mallet, J. V. G. (1976), 'Battista Franco as a Designer for Maiolica', *Burlington Magazine*, 118: 387–410.

Clunas, C. (1986), 'Some Literary Evidence for Gold and Silver Vessels in the Ming Period (1368–1644)', in Vickers (1986*a*), 83–8.

Coarelli, F. (1975) (ed.), *Etruscan Cities* (London).

Cohen, B. (1978), *Attic Bilingual Vases and their Painters* (New York).

—— (1989), 'Oddities of Very Early Red-Figure and a New Fragment at the Getty', in *Occasional Papers on Antiquities*, 5. *Greek Vases in the J. Paul Getty Museum*, 4: 73–82.

—— (1991), 'The Literate Potter: A Tradition of Incised Signatures on Attic Vases', *Metropolitan Museum Journal*, 26: 49–95.

Coldstream, J. N. (1968), *Greek Geometric Pottery* (London).

Collins, J. (1983), *The Omega Workshops* (London).

Conophagos, C. E. (1980), *Le Laurium antique et la technique grecque de la production de l'argent* (Athens).

Constantine, D. (1984), *Early Greek Travellers and the Hellenic Ideal* (Cambridge).

Content, D. J. (1992), *Gold and Silver Auction, 2. Ancient to Renaissance* (Singapore).

Cook, B. F. (1962–3), 'Aristaios', *BMMA* NS 21: 31–6.

—— (1989) (ed.), *The Rogozen Treasure: Papers of the Anglo-Bulgarian Conference, 12 March 1987* (London).

Cook, J. M. (1983), *The Persian Empire* (London).

Cook, R. M. (1937), 'The Date of the Hesiodic Shield', *Classical Quarterly*, 31: 204–14.

—— (1959), 'Die Bedeutung der bemalten Keramik für den griechischen Handel', *JdI* 74: 118–23.

—— (1971), '"Epoiesen" on Greek Vases', *JHS* 91: 137–8.

—— (1972), *Greek Painted Pottery* (2nd edn., London).

—— (1987), '"Artful Crafts": A Commentary', *JHS* 107: 169–71.

Cooper, E. (1981), *A History of World Pottery* (2nd edn., London).

Coral Gables Junior Women's Club (1980), *The Children's Guide to Miami* (2nd edn., Coral Gables, Fla.).

Corbett, P. E. (1949), 'Attic Pottery of the Later Fifth Century from the Athenian Agora', *Hesperia*, 18: 298–345.

—— (1955), 'Palmette Stamps from an Attic Black-Glaze Workshop', *Hesperia*, 24: 172–86.

—— (1965), 'Preliminary Sketches in Greek Vase-painting', *JHS* 85: 16–28.

Courby, F. (1922), *Les Vases grecs à reliefs* (Paris).

Cox, W. E. (1946), *Chinese Ivory Sculpture* (New York).

Craddock, P. T. (1977), 'The Composition of the Copper Alloys Used by the Greek, Etruscan and Roman Civilisations, 2. The Archaic, Classical and Hellenistic Greeks', *Journal of Archaeological Science*, 4: 103–23.

—— (1983), 'A Roman Silver Mirror Discovered in the British Museum: A Note on its Composition', *Antiquaries Journal*, 63: 131–2.

Crawford, M. H. (1987), 'Tableware for Trimalchio', in J. North, M. H. Crawford and T. Cornell (eds.), *Art and Production in the Age of the Caesars* (Milan), 37–44.

Crawford, O. G. S. (1953), *Archaeology in the Field* (London).

Cristofani, M. (1970), '*Kotyle* d'argento dal Circolo degi Avori di Marsigliana d'Albegna', *Studi Etruschi*, 38: 271–80, pls. 24–7.

—— (1985) (ed.), *Civiltà degli etruschi* (Milan).

Crow, C. (1937), *400 Million Customers* (London).

Curtius, F. (1903), *Ernst Curtius. Ein Lebensbild in Briefen* (Berlin).

Dalley, S. (1984), *Mari and Karana: Two Old Babylonian Cities* (London).

—— (1985), 'Foreign Chariotry and Cavalry in the Armies of Tiglath-Pileser III and Sargon II', *Iraq*, 47: 31–48.

Dalton, O. M. (1964), *The Treasure of the Oxus with other Examples of Early Oriental Metal-Work* (3rd edn., London).

Danov, C., and Ivanov, T. (1980), *Antique Tombs in Bulgaria* (Sofia).

Daremberg, C., and Saglio, E. (1877–1910), *Dictionnaire des antiquités grecques et romaines d'après les textes et les monuments* (5 vols.; Paris).

Davies, J. K. (1971), *Athenian Propertied Families 600–300 BC* (Oxford).

Davis, E. N. (1974), 'The Vapheio Cups: One Minoan and One Mycenaean?', *Art Bulletin*, 56: 472–87.

—— (1977), *The Vapheio Cups and Aegean Gold and Silver Ware* (New York and London).

Delmaire, R. (1988), 'Les Largesses impériales et l'emission d'argenterie du ive au vi^e siècle', in Baratte (1988), 113–22.

De Maria, S., Mansuelli, G. A., Sassatelli, G., and Vitali, D. (1978), 'Marzabotto (Bologna). Scavi nelle città etrusca di Misano (campagne 1969–74)', *NSc*: 57–130.

De Marinis, R. C. (1985), 'L'abitato etrusco del Forcello di Bagnolo S. Vito', in De Marinis, *Gli Etruschi a nord del Po*, 1 (Mantua), 140–63.

—— (1991), 'La stratigrafia dell'abitato etrusco del Forcello di Bagnolo S. Vito e i rapporti cronologici con le culture dell'area circumalpina', *Archeologia classica*, 43: 237–59.

Dennis, G. (1848), *Cities and Cemeteries of Etruria* (2nd edn.: 1878; 3rd edn.: 1883, London). The first edition reprinted in the Everyman series in 1907.

—— (1864), *A Handbook for Travellers in Sicily* (London).

—— (1985), *The Cities and Cemeteries of Etruria* (Abridged edition, ed. P. Hemphill; Princeton, NJ).

Denoyelle, M. (1992*a*) (ed.), *Euphronios peintre: Actes de la journée d'étude organisée par l'École du Louvre et le département des Antiquités grecques étrusques et romaines du musée du Louvre 10 octobre 1990*.

—— (1992*b*), 'Autour du cratère en calice Louvre G 110, signé par Euphronios', in Denoyelle (1992*a*), 47–60.

Diderot, D. (1875–7), *Œuvres complètes* (20 vols., Paris).

Diepolder, H., and Rehm, W. (1952–7), *Johann Joachim Winckelmann, Briefe* (4 vols., Berlin).

Dimitrov, D. P. (1949), 'Trouvailles funéraires de Dalboki, arr. de Stara-Zagora', *Fouilles et recherches du Musée National Bulgare*, NS 4: 207–47.

Disney, J. (1849), *Museum Disneianum, being a Description of a Collection of Ancient Marbles in the Possession of John Disney, Esq., F.R.S., F.S.A., at the Hyde, near Ingatestone*, 2nd edn., Part 3. *A Description of a Collection of Various Ancient Fictile Vases* (London).

Dodd, E. C. (1961), *Byzantine Silver Stamps* (Washington, DC).

Dodwell, C. R. (1982), *Anglo-Saxon Art: A New Perspective* (Manchester).

Dover, K. J. (1968), *Lysias and the Corpus Lysiacum* (Berkeley, Calif., and Los Angeles).

Driver, G. R. (1957), *Aramaic Documents of the Fifth Century* BC (Oxford).

Duncker, A. (1882) (ed.), *Denkmal Johann Winckelmann's: Eine ungekronte Preisschrift J. G. Herder's aus dem Jahre 1778* (Kassel).

Dürbeck, H. (1977), *Zur Charakteristik der griechischen Farbenzeichnungen* (Bonn).

Ebert, J. (1978), 'Ein Homerischer Ilias-Aithiopis-Becher im Robertinum zu Halle an der Saale', *Wissenschaftliche Zeitschrift der Universität Halle*, 27: 123–32.

Eddy, S. (1977), 'The Gold in the Athena Parthenos', *AJA* 81: 107–11.

Edmundson, C. N. (1982), 'Onesippos' Herm', *Studies in Attic Epigraphy, History and Topography presented to Eugene Vanderpool* (*Hesperia*, suppl. 19), 48–55.

Ehrenberg, V. (1951), *The People of Aristophanes* (Oxford).

—— (1973), *From Solon to Socrates* (2nd edn., London).

Eiseman, C. J. (1979*a*), *The Porticello Shipwreck: A Mediterranean Merchant Vessel of 415–385 BC* (Ann Arbor, Mich.).

—— (1979*b*), 'The Porticello Shipwreck: Lead Isotope Data', *International Journal of Nautical Archaeology*, 8: 339–340.

—— (1980), 'Greek Lead: Ingots from a Shipwreck Raise Questions about Metal Trade in Classical Times', *Expedition*, 22(2): 41–7.

Eiseman, C. J., and Ridgway, B. S. (1987), *The Porticello Shipwreck: A Mediterranean Merchant Vessel of 415–385 BC* (College Station, Texas).

Eisman, M. M. (1974), 'A Further Note on Epoiesen Signatures', *JHS* 94: 172.

Eiwanger, J. (1989), 'Talanton, Ein bronzezeitlicher Goldstandard zwischen Ägäis und Mitteleuropa', *Germania*, 67: 443–62.

Elferink, L. J. (1934), *Lekythos: Archäologische, sprachliche und religionsgeschichtliche Untersuchungen* (Amsterdam).

Elsner, J. (1990), 'Significant Details: Systems, Certainties and the Art-Historian as Detective', *Antiquity*, 64: 950–2.

Engelmann, H. (1980), *Die Inschriften von Ephesos*, 4 (Bonn).

—— (1987), '"Wie nie Euphronios"', *ZPE*, 129–34.

Epstein, I. (1938), *The Babylonian Talmud: Shabbath* (London).

Erbse, H. (1961), *Geschichte der Textüberlieferung der antiken und mittelalterlichen Literatur* (Zurich).

Eriksen, S. (1974), *Early Neo-Classicism in France* (London).

Evans, A. J. (1884), *The Ashmolean Museum as a Home of Archaeology in Oxford* (Oxford).

—— (1891), 'Syracusan "Medallions" and their Engravers in the Light of Recent Finds', *NC* 3rd ser., 11: 205–324.

—— (1921–36), *The Palace of Minos at Knossos* (4 vols., London).

Evans, U. R. (1960), *The Corrosion and Oxidation of Metals: Scientific Principles and Practical Applications* (New York).

Fallers, L. A. (1967), 'A Note on the "Trickle Effect"', in R. Bendix and S. M. Lipset (eds.), *Class, Status and Power* (2nd edn., London), 402–4.

Farrar, Lady (1973) (ed.), *Letters of Josiah Wedgwood* (2nd impression, 3 vols.; Manchester).

Fehervari, G., and Safadi, Y. H. (1981), *1400 Years of Islamic Art: A Descriptive Catalogue* (London).

Filow, B. D. (1934), *Die Grabhügelnekropole bei Duvanli in Südbulgarien* (Sofia).

Finer, A., and Savage, G. (1965) (eds.), *The Selected Letters of Josiah Wedgwood* (New York).

Finlay, G. (1857), *Greece under the Romans: A Historical View of the Conditions of the Greek Nation AD175–AD717* (2nd edn., Edinburgh).

Finley, M. I. (1960) (ed.), *Slavery in Classical Antiquity: Views and Controversies* (Cambridge).

—— (1985), *Ancient History: Evidence and Models* (London).

Firenze (1971), Exhibition catalogue, *Nuove letture di monumenti etruschi* (Florence).

Fitton, J. Lesley (1992) (ed.), *Proceedings of the British Museum Classical Colloquium 1991: Ivory in Greece and the Eastern Mediterranean from the Bronze Age to the Hellenistic Period* (London).

Forbes, H. A. C., Kernan, J. D., and Wilkins, R. S. (1975), *Chinese Export Silver 1785 to 1885* (Milton, Mass.).

Fortnum, C. D. E. (1873), *A Descriptive Catalogue of the Maiolica in the South Kensington Museum* (London).

Foster, K. P. (1989), 'Translations into Clay: Inspiration and Imitation in Minoan Pottery', in McGovern and Notis (1989), 31–44.

Fothergill, B. (1969), *Sir William Hamilton, Envoy Extraordinary* (London).

Frakiiskii klad (1986), Exhibition catalogue, *Frakiiskii klad iz Rogozena* (Pushkin Museum, Moscow).

Francis, E. D. (1990), *Image and Idea in Fifth-Century Greece: Art and Literature after the Persian Wars* (London).

François, A., and Braun, E. (1849), *Le dipinture di Clizia sopra vaso chiusino d'Ergotimo* (Rome). Reprinted in Marzi (1981*a*), 65–83.

Frantz, J. H., and Schorsch, D. (1990), 'Egyptian Red Gold', *Archeomaterials*, 4: 133–52.

Frederiksen, M. (1979), 'The Etruscans in Campania', in Ridgway and Serra Ridgway (1979), 277–311.

—— (1984), in N. Purcell (ed.), *Campania* (London).

Frel, J. (1973), *Panathenaic Prize Amphoras* (Athens).

Frost, F. J. (1980), *Plutarch's Themistocles: A Historical Commentary* (Princeton, NJ).

Fulford, M. G. (1983), 'Pottery and the Economy of Carthage and its Hinterland', *Opus*, 2: 5–14.

—— (1986), 'Pottery and Precious Metals in the Roman World', in Vickers (1986*a*), 153–60.

—— (1987), 'Economic Interdependence among Urban Communities of the Roman Mediterranean', *World Archaeology*, 19(1): 58–75.

Gabelmann, H. (1974), 'Zur hellenistisch-römischen Bleiglasurkeramik in Kleinasien', *JdI* 89: 260–307.

—— (1979), Review of Hochuli-Gysel (1977), *Gnomon*, 51: 679.

Gaborit, J.-R. (1984), in Exposition Hôtel de la Monnaie, *Diderot et l'Art de Boucher à David. Les Salons: 1759–1781* (Paris).

Gaborit-Chopin, D. (1972), 'La Vierge à l'enfant d'ivoire de la Sainte Chapelle', *Bulletin Monumental*, 130: 213–24.

Galanina, L., and Grach, N. (1986), *Scythian Art: The Legacy of the Scythian World: Mid-7th to 3rd Century BC* (St Petersburg).

Gale, N. H., and Stos-Gale, Z. (1981*a*), 'Lead and Silver in the Ancient Aegean', *Scientific American*, 204: 176–192.

—— (1981*b*), 'Cycladic Lead and Silver Metallurgy', *BSA* 76: 169–224, pls. 33–40.

—— Gentner, W., and Wagner, G. A. (1980), 'Mineralogical and Geographical Sources of Archaic Greek Coinage', in D. M. Metcalf and W. A. Oddy, *Metallurgy in Numismatics*, 1 (London), 3–49.

Garbsch, J. (1982), *Terra sigillata: Ein Weltreich im Spiegel seines Luxusgeschirrs* (Munich).

Gardner, E. A. (1897), *A Catalogue of the Greek Vases in the Fitzwilliam Museum, Cambridge* (Cambridge).

Gardner, P. (1893), *Catalogue of the Greek Vases in the Ashmolean Museum* (Oxford).

Gargiulo, R. (1843), *Cenni sulla maniera di rinvenire i vasi fittili italo-greci* (2nd edn., Naples).

Garnsey, P. (1988), *Famine and Food Supply in the Graeco-Roman World: Responses to Risk and Crisis* (Cambridge).

—— Hopkins, K., and Whittaker, C. R. (1983) (eds.), *Trade in the Ancient Economy* (London).

Gatz, B. (1967), *Weltalter, goldene Zeit und sinnverwandte Vorstellungen* (Spudasmata, 16) (Hildesheim).

Gauthier, P. (1985), *Les Cités grecques et leurs bienfaiteurs* (Paris).

Gerhard, E. (1831), *Rapporto intorno i vasi volcenti* (Rome).

Getz-Preziosi, P. (1987), *Sculptors of the Cyclades: Individual and Tradition in the Third Millennium* BC (Ann Arbor, Mich.).

Gibbon, E. (1896–1900), *Decline and Fall of the Roman Empire* (ed. J. B. Bury; 7 vols.; London).

Gill, D. W. J. (1984), 'The Workshops of the Attic Bolsal', in Brijder (1984), 102–6.

—— (1986a), 'Classical Greek Fictile Imitations of Precious Metal Vases', in Vickers (1986a), 9–30.

—— (1986b), 'Attic Black-Glazed Pottery in the Fifth Century B.C.: Workshops and Export' (Oxford: D.Phil. diss.).

—— (1987a), 'METRU.MENECE: An Etruscan Painted Inscription on a Mid-Fifth-Century BC Red-Figure Cup from Populonia', *Antiquity*, 61: 82–7.

—— (1987b), 'The Date of the Porticello Shipwreck: Some Observations on the Attic Bolsals', *International Journal of Nautical Archaeology*, 16: 31–33.

—— (1987c), 'An Attic Lamp in Reggio: The Largest Batch Notation outside Athens', *OJA* 6: 212–15.

—— (1988a), ' "Trade in Greek Decorated Pottery": Some Corrections', *OJA* 7: 369–70.

—— (1988b), 'The Distribution of Greek Vases and Long Distance Trade', in J. Christiansen and T. Melander (eds.), *Proceedings of the 3rd Symposium on Ancient Greek and Related Pottery, Copenhagen, 1987* (Copenhagen), 175–85.

—— (1988c), 'Expressions of Wealth: Greek Art and Society', *Antiquity*, 62: 735–43.

—— (1988d), 'Luxury Vases', *Omnibus*, 15: 10–12.

—— (1990a), ' "Ancient Fictile Vases" from the Disney Collection', *Journal of the History of Collections*, 2: 227–31.

—— (1990b), 'A One-Mina *Phiale* from Kozani', *AJA* 94: 625.

—— (1990c), 'Stamped Palmettes and an Attic Black-Glazed Oinochoe', *OJA* 9: 369–72.

—— (1991), 'Pots and Trade: Spacefillers or *Objets d'art*?' *JHS* 111: 29–47.

—— (1992), 'The Ivory Trade', in Fitton (1992), 233–7.

—— (1993), 'Art and Vases *vs*. Craft and Pots', *Antiquity*, 67: 452–5.

—— and Chippindale, C. (1993), 'Material and Intellectual Consequences of Esteem for Cycladic Figures', *AJA* 97: 601–59.

—— and Vickers, M. (1989), 'Pots and Kettles', *RA* 297–30.

—— (1990), 'Reflected Glory: Pottery and Precious Metal in Classical Greece', *JdI* 105: 1–30.

Gillis, C. (1991–2), 'All That Glitters is Not Gold', *Medelhavsmuseet Bulletin*, 26–7: 24–32.

Gilman, D. (1984), in British Museum Exhibition Catalogue, *Chinese Ivories from the Shang to the Qing* (London).

Giovannini, A. (1990), 'Le Parthenon, le trésor d'Athéna et le tribut des alliés', *Historia*, 39: 129–48.

Giudice, P. (1977), 'Osservazioni sul commercio dei vasi attici in Etruria e in Sicilia: Su una lekythos del pittore della Gigantomachia con l'inscrizione "LASA SA" ', *Cronache di Archeologia*, 18: 1–10.

Goethe, J. W. (1817 (1964)), in H. von Einern and E. Trunz (eds.), *Italienische Reise* (Hamburger Ausgabe, 6th edn., 14 vols.; Hamburg).

Gold der Thraker (1979), *Gold der Thraker: Archäologische Schätze aus Bulgarien* (Mainz).

Gold vom Kuban (1989), *Gold und Kunsthandwerk vom antiken Kuban* (Stuttgart).

Goldthwaite R. A. (1989), 'The Economic and Social World of Italian Renaissance Maiolica', *Renaissance Quarterly*, 42: 1–32.

Gollan, B. A. (1982), *Ancient Athenian Pottery: Craft and Art* (St Lucia, Queensland).

Gombrich, E. (1979), *The Sense of Order* (London).

Gonzalez-Palacios, A. (1984), *Il Tempio del Gusto: Le arti decorativi in Italia fra classicismo e barocco. Roma e il Regno delle Due Sicilie* (Milan).

Goodman, M. (1983), *State and Society in Roman Galilee, AD 132–212* (Totowa, NJ).

Gorbunova, K. S. (1971), 'Engraved Silver Kylikes from the Semibratny Barrows', *Kultura e iskusstvo antichnogo mira*, 18–38 and 123.

Gould, J. (1991), 'Give and Take in Herodotus', *The Fifteenth J. L. Myres Memorial Lecture* (Oxford).

Grach, N. (1985), *Antichnoe khudozhestbennoe serebro* (St Petersburg).

Grandjean, S. (1957), 'Une création mi-royale mi-impériale de la manufacture de Sèvres', *Cahiers de la céramique*, 8: 180–4.

Gras, M. (1985), *Trafics tyrrhéniens archaïques* (Rome).

Gray, Mrs Hamilton (1843), *Tour to the Sepulchres of Etruria in 1839* (London).

Grayson, C. H. (1975), 'Greek Weighing' (D.Phil. thesis, Oxford).

Green, J. R. (1961), 'The Caputi Hydria', *JHS* 81: 73–5, pls. 6–7.

—— (1972), 'Oinochoe', *BICS* 19: 1–16, pls. 1–5.

Green, T. (1985), *The New World of Gold: The Inside Story of the Mines, the Markets, the Politics, the Investors* (2nd edn., London).

Greene, K. (1986), *The Archaeology of the Roman Economy* (London).

Greenfield, J. C. (1985), 'The Meaning of *TKWNH*', in A. Kort and S. Morschauser (eds.), *Biblical and Related Studies Presented to Samuel Iwry* (Winona Lake, Ind.), 81–5.

Greifenhagen, A. (1978), 'Griechische Vasen auf Bildern des 19. Jahrhunderts', *Sitzungsberichte der Heidelberger Akademie der Wissenschaften*.

Griener, P. (1992), *Le antichità etrusche greche e romane 1766–1776 di Pierre Hugues d'Hancarville: La pubblicazione delle ceramiche antiche della prima collezione Hamilton* (Rome).

Griffin, J. (1976), 'Augustan Poetry and the Life of Luxury', *JRS* 66: 87–105.

Griffin, L. (1988), *Clarice Cliff: The Bizarre Affair* (London).

Griffith, J. G. (1988), *Festinat Senex: Essays in Greek and Latin Literature and Archaeology* (Oxford).

Guarducci, M. (1961), 'Epigraphical Appendix', in G. M. A. Richter, *The Archaic Gravestones of Attica* (London), 155–72.

Guide (1929), *A Guide to the Select Greek and Latin Inscriptions Exhibited in the Department of Greek and Roman Antiquities in the British Museum* (London).

Gulick, C. B. (1927–41), *Athenaeus: The Deipnosophists* (Loeb Classical Library; London and Cambridge, Mass.).

Gunn, B. (1943), 'Notes on the Naukratis Stela', *Journal of Egyptian Archaeology*, 29: 55–9.

Guth, P. (1958), 'La Laiterie de Rambouillet', *Connaissance des arts*, 75 (May): 74–81, esp. 78.

Guy, J. R. (1981), 'A Ram's Head Rhyton Signed by Charinos', *Arts in Virginia*, 21(2): 2–15.

—— (1983), 'Herakles and Philoctetes', in Lissarague and Thelamon (1983), 151–2.

Guzzo, P. G. (1973), 'Coppe ioniche in bronzo', *Mélanges de l'École Française de Rome, Antiquité*, 85: 55–64.

Hakluyt, R. (1904), *The Discovery of Muscovy* (London).

Hambidge, J. (1920), *Dynamic Symmetry: The Greek Vase* (New Haven, Conn.).

Hamilton, W. (1791–5), *Collection of Engravings from Ancient Vases mostly of pure Greek Workmanship discovered in sepulchres in the kingdom of the Two Sicilies, but chiefly in the neighbourhood of Naples during the course of the years MDCCLXXXIX and MDCCLXXXX now in the possession of Sir W^m. Hamilton, his Britannic Maiestaty's Envoy Extr.^y and Plenipotentiary at the Court of Naples, with remarks on each vase by the collector* (3 vols.; Naples).

—— (1800–3), *Pitture de' vasi antichi posseduti da sua Eccellenza il Sig. Cav. Hamilton* (Florence).

Hampe, R., and Simon, E. (1981), *The Birth of Greek Art from the Mycenaean to the Archaic Period* (London).

Hancarville, P. d' (1766[1767]–76), *Collection of Etruscan, Greek and Roman Antiquities from the Cabinet of the Hon. W. Hamilton, His Britannick Majesty's Envoy Extraordinary and Plenipotentiary at the Court of Naples* (4 vols., Naples).

—— (1785–8), *Antiquités étrusques, grecques et romaines, ou les beaux vases étrusques, grecs et romains, et les peintures rendues avec les couleurs qui leur sont propres, gravées par F. A. David avec leurs explications, par d'Hancarville* (5 vols., Paris).

Harewood (1965), *Catalogue of a Highly Important Roman Gold Vase. The Property of the Earl of Harewood* (Christie's, 23 June).

Harper, P. (1978), *The Royal Hunter* (New York).

Harris, D. (1988), 'Nikokrates of Kolonos, Metalworker', *Hesperia*, 57: 329–37.

Hartt, F. (1958), *Giulio Romano* (New Haven, Conn.).

Harvey, F. D. (1976), 'Sostratos of Aegina', *PdP* 31: 206–14.

Hasebroek, J. (1933), *Trade and Politics in Ancient Greece* (London).

Haskell, F. (1963), *Patrons and Painters: A Study in the Relations between Italian Art and Society in the Age of the Baroque* (London).

—— (1987), 'The Baron d'Hancarville: An Adventurer and Art Historian in Eighteenth-Century Europe', in *Past and Present in Art and Taste*, 30–45 (New Haven, Conn. and London).

Hastings, M. (1979), *Bomber Command* (London).

Hatcher, J., and Barker, T. C. (1974), *A History of British Pewter* (London).

Hausmann, U. (1959), *Hellenistische Reliefbecher* (Stuttgart).

Havens, G. R. (1946) (ed.), *Jean-Jacques Rousseau: Discours sur les sciences et les arts* (New York).

Haverkamp-Begemann, E. (1975), *Corpus Rubenianum Ludwig Burchard. 10. The Achilles Series* (London).

Hawes, H. B. (1908), *Gournia: Vasiliki and Other Prehistoric Sites on the Isthmus of Hyperia, Crete* (Philadelphia).

Hayes, J. W. (1984), *Greek and Italian Black-Gloss Wares and Related Wares in the Royal Ontario Museum: A Catalogue* (Toronto).

—— (1991), 'Fine Wares in the Hellenistic World', in Rasmussen and Spivey (1991), 182–202.

Hayward, J. F. (1952), *Viennese Porcelain of the Du Paquier Period* (London).

—— (1959), *Huguenot Silver in England 1688–1727* (London).

—— (1970), 'Ottavio Strada and the Goldsmith's Designs of Giulio Romano', *Burlington Magazine*, 112: 10–14.

—— (1976), *Virtuoso Goldsmiths and the Triumph of Mannerism 1540–1620* (London).

Heckscher, W. S. (1962*a*), *Goethe and Weimar* (Durham, NH).

—— (1962*b*), 'Goethe im Banne der Sinnbilder: Ein Beitrage zur Emblematik', *Jahrbuch der Hamburger Kunstsammlungen*, 7: 35–56.

—— (1966/7), '"Sturm und Drang": Conjectures on the Origin of a Phrase', *Simiolus*, 1: 95–106.

—— (1981), 'Pearls from a Dungheap: Andrea Alciati's Offensive Emblem, "Adversus naturam peccantes"', in M. Marasch and C. F. Sandler (eds.), *Art the Ape of Nature, H. W. Janson Festschrift*, New York, 291–311.

Heinrich, D. (1985), 'The Contemporary Relevance of Hegel's Aesthetics', in M. Inwood (ed.), *Oxford Readings in Philosophy: Hegel* (Oxford), 199–207.

Helbig, W. (1870), 'Dipinti Tarquiniesi', *Bulletino del Instituto*, 42: 5–74.

Hemelrijk, J. (1985), *Schalen en scherven, een kijkje in de keuken* (*Verenining van Vrienden Allard Pierson Museum Amsterdam Mededelingenblad*, 34) (Amsterdam).

—— (1991), 'A Closer Look at the Potter', in Rasmussen and Spivey (1991), 232–56.

Henry, A. (1992), 'Through a Laser Beam Darkly: Space Age Technology and the Egesta Decree (*IG* 1³. 11)' *ZPE* 91: 137–46.

Herman, G. (1987), *Ritualised Friendship and the Greek City* (Cambridge).

Hernmarck, C. (1977), *The Art of the European Silversmith 1430–1830* (London).

Herrero, C. (1992), 'Los tapices', in *Tapices y armaduras del renacimiento: Joyas de las colecciones reales* (Barcelona and Madrid), 25–98.

Heurgon, J. (1961), *La Vie quotidienne chez les Étrusques* (Paris).

Hill, D. K. (1947), 'The Technique of Greek Metal Vases and its Bearing on Vase Forms in Metal and Pottery', *AJA* 51: 248–56.

—— (1969), 'Bronze Working', in C. Roebuck (ed.), *The Muses at Work, Arts, Crafts and Professions in Ancient Greece and Rome* (Cambridge, Mass.), 60–83.

His, E. (1886), *Dessins d'ornements de Hans Holbein* (Paris).

Hitzl, K. (1982), *Die Entstehung und Entwicklung des Volutenkraters von den frühesten Anfängen bis zur Ausprägung des kanonischen Stils in der attish schwarz-figurigen Vasenmalerei* (Frankfurt and Bern).

Hobhouse, H. (1985), *Seeds of Change: Five Plants that Transformed Mankind* (London).

Hochuli-Gysel, A. (1977), *Kleinasiatische glasierte Reliefkeramik (50 v. Chr.–50 n. Chr.), und ihre oberitalischen Nachahmungen* (Bern).

Hoffmann, H. (1961), 'The Persian Origin of the Attic Rhyta', *AK* 4: 21–26, pls. 8–12.

—— (1979), 'In the Wake of Beazley: Prolegomena to an Anthropological Study of Greek Vase-Painting', *Hephaistos*, 1: 61–70.

—— (1985/6), 'Iconography and Iconology', *Hephaistos*, 7/8: 61–6.

—— (1988), 'Why Did the Greeks Need Imagery? An Anthropological Approach to the Study of Greek Vase Painting', *Hephaistos*, 9: 143–62.

—— (1989), 'Rhyta and Kantharoi in Greek Ritual', *Greek Vases in the J. Paul Getty Museum*, 4: 131–66.

Holm, A. (1894–7), *The History of Greece from its Commencement to the Close of the Independence of the Greek Nation* (4 vols., London).

Holmberg, E. J. (1992), *On the Rycroft Painter and Other Athenian Black-Figure Vase-Painters with a Feeling for Nature* (Jonsered).

Holquist, M. (1971), 'How to Play Utopia: Some Brief Notes on the Distinctive-ness of Utopian Fiction', *Yale French Studies*, 41: 106–23.

Honour, H. (1971), *Goldsmiths and Silversmiths* (London).

Hood, S. (1978), *The Arts in Prehistoric Greece* (Harmondsworth).

Hopkins, K. (1980), 'Taxes and Trade in the Roman Empire 200 BC–AD 400', *JRS* 70: 101–25.

—— (1983), 'Introduction', in P. Garnsey, K. Hopkins, and C. R. Whittaker (eds.), *Trade in the Ancient Economy* (London), pp. ix–xxv.

Hornblower, S. (1987), *Thucydides* (London).

Houser, C. (1982), 'The Riace Marina Bronze Statues, Classical or Classicizing?', *Source: Notes in the History of Art*, 1(3): 5–11.

Howard, S. (1985), 'The Steel Pen and the Modern Line of Beauty', *Technology and Culture*, 26: 785–98.

Huber, L. G. F. (1983), 'The Relationship of the Painted Pottery and Lung-shan Cultures', in D. N. Keightley (ed.), *The Origins of Chinese Civilisation* (Berkeley, Calif., and Los Angeles), 177–216.

Hudeczek, E. (1972–5), 'Theseus und die Tyrannenmörder', *Jahreshefte des Österreichischen Archäologischen Instituts*, 50: 134–49.

Hughes, D., and Parsons, P. J. (1984), 'Against Philosophers', *Oxyrhynchus Papyri*, 52: 55–61, no. 3659.

Huygen, W., and Poortvliet, R. (1977), *Gnomes* (London).

Ichisar, M. (1981), *Les Archives cappadociennes du marchand Imdilum* (Paris).

Immerwahr, H. R. (1990), *The Attic Script* (Oxford).

Iongh, M. L. de (1982), 'Twee gouden bokalen door Louis en Philippe Metayer', *Bulletin van het Rijksmuseum*, 30: 115–31.

Irwin, D. (1972), 'The Industrial Revolution and the Dissemination of Neo-Classical Taste', *Studies in Voltaire and the Eighteenth Century*, 113: 1087–98.

—— (1976), 'Industry Plunders Antiquity', *Apollo*, 96: 288–97.

Isager, S., and Hansen, M. H. (1975), *Aspects of Athenian Society in the Fourth Century BC* (Odense).

Jacob, A. (1892), 'Ebur', in Daremberg and Saglio (1877–1910), 2: 444–9.

Jacobsthal, P. (1927), *Ornamente griechischer Vasen* (Berlin).

Jacquemart, A. (1873), *Histoire de la céramique* (Paris).

—— (1874), *History of the Ceramic Art* (London).

Jaennicke, F. (1879), *Grundriss der Keramik* (Stuttgart).

Jahn, O. (1854), *Beschreibung der Vasen König Ludwigs in der Pinakothek zu München* (Munich).

—— and Michaelis, A. (1901), *Arx Athenarum* (Bonn).

Javakliashvili, A., and Abramishvili, G. (1986), *Jewellery and Metalwork in the Museums of Georgia* (London).

Jeffery, L. H. (1961), *Local Scripts of Archaic Greece* (Oxford).

Jenkins, I. (1988), 'Adam Buck and the Vogue for Greek Vases', *Burlington Magazine*, 130: 448–57.

Joffroy, R. (1954), *Le Trésor de Vix (Côte d'Or)* (Paris).

Johns, C. M., and Potter, T. W. (1985), 'The Canterbury Late Roman Treasure', *AJ* 65: 312–52.

Johnson, S. (1825), *Works* (Oxford).

Johnston, A. W. (1972), 'The Rehabilitation of Sostratos', *PdP* 27: 416–23.

—— (1978), 'Some Non-Greek Ghosts', *BICS* 25: 79–84.

—— (1979), *Trademarks on Greek Vases* (Warminster).

—— (1988), 'Amasis and the Vase Trade', in M. True (ed.), *Papers on the Amasis Painter and his World* (Malibu, Calif.), 125–9.

Jones, A. H. M. (1957), *Athenian Democracy* (Oxford).

—— (1960), 'Slavery in the Ancient World', in Finley (1960), 1–16.

—— (1964), *The Later Roman Empire 284–602: A Social, Economic and Administrative Survey* (3 vols., Oxford).

Jones, F. F. (1950), 'The Pottery', in H. Goldman (ed.), *Excavations at Gözlü Kule, Tarsus*, 1 (Princeton, NJ).

Jones, J. E. (1984–5), 'Laurion: Agrileza, 1977–83: Excavations at a Silver-Mine Site', *AR* 31: 106–23.

—— Sackett, L. H., and Graham, A. J. (1962), 'The Dema House in Attica', *BSA* 57: 75–114.

—— (1973), 'An Attic Country House below the Cave of Pan at Vari', *BSA* 68: 355–452.

Jones, R. (1986), *Greek and Cypriot Pottery: A Review of Scientific Studies* (Athens).

Jörg, C. J. A. (1982), *Porcelain and the Dutch China Trade* (The Hague).

Juynboll, G. H. A. (1986), 'The Attitude towards Gold and Silver in Early Islam', in Vickers (1986a), 107–16.

Kaeser, B. (1987), 'Attische Massamphora', *Münchner Jahrbuch der bildenden Kunst*, 3rd series, 38: 228–31.

'Katalog' (1986), 'Katalog na Rogozenskoto sakrovishte', *Izkustvo* 36(6) (Sofia).

Kalicz, N. (1963), *Die péceler (Badener) Kultur und Anatolien* (Budapest).

Kathirithamby-Wells, J. (1977), *The British West Sumatran Presidency 1760–1785: Problems of Early Colonial Enterprise* (Kuala Lumpur).

Keightley, D. N. (1983), *The Origins of Chinese Civilization* (Berkeley, Calif., and Los Angeles).

Kent, R. G. (1950), *Old Persian Grammar, Texts, Lexicon* (New Haven, Conn.).

Keudell, E. von and Deetjen, W. (1931), *Goethe als Benutzer der Weimarer Bibliothek* (Weimar).

Keuls, E. (1984), 'Patriotic Propaganda and Counter-Cultural Protest in Athens as Evidenced by Vase Painting', in Brijder (1984), 256–9.

Keynes, J. M. (1931), 'The Economic Possibilities for our Grandchildren', in *Essays in Persuasion* (London), 358–73.

Kimmig, W. (1987), 'Klein Aspergle', in J.-P. Mohan, A. Doval, and C. Eluère (eds.), *Trésors des princes celtes* (Paris), 255–64.

Knigge, U. (1976), *Der Südhügel* (*Kerameikos: Ergebnisse der Ausgrabungen*, 9) (Berlin).

—— and Willemsen, F. (1964), 'Ausgrabungen im Kerameikos 1963, 2. Die Höhe östlich des Querweges', *ADelt.* 19, Chron. 42–6.

Knoepfler, D. (1988) (ed.), *Comptes et inventaires dans la cité grecque* (Neuchâtel).

Koehler, U. (1878), 'Aus der Finanzverwaltung Lykurgs', *Hermes*, 5: 223–7.

Kopcke, G. (1964), 'Golddekorierte attische Schwarzfirniskeramik des vierten Jahrhunderts v. Chr.', *Athenische Mitteilungen*, 79: 22–84.

Koumanoudes, S. N., and Miller, S. G. (1971), '*Inscriptiones Graecae* II², 1477 and 3046 Rediscovered', *Hesperia*, 40: 448–57.

Kourou, N. (1985), 'Musical Processions in Early Greek Art: Their Oriental and Cypriot Models', in Πρακτικὰ Β΄ Διεθνούς Κυπριολογικού Συνεδρίου 1: 415–22.

Kraay, C. M. (1977), 'The Asyut Hoard: Some Comments on Chronology', *NC* 137: 189–98.

—— and Emeleus, V. M. (1962), *The Composition of Greek Silver Coins: Analysis by Neutron Activation* (Oxford).

—— and Jenkins, G. K. (1968) (eds.), *Essays in Greek Coinage presented to Stanley Robinson* (Oxford).

Krauskopf, I. (1984), 'Terrakotta-Imitationen der Bronzekannen der Form Beazley VI in Athen, Westgriechenland und Etruria', in Brijder (1984), 83–7.

Krzyszkowska, O. (1990), *Classical Handbook*, 3. *Ivory and Related Materials* (*Bulletin of the Institute of Classical Studies*, 59) (London).

Kubaschewski, O., and Hopkins, B. E. (1962), *Oxidation of Metals and Alloys*, 2nd edn. (London).

Kunze, E. (1958), 'Helme', *Bericht über die Ausgrabungen in Olympia*, 6: 118–51.

Kurtz, D. C. (1975), *Athenian White Lekythoi* (Oxford).

—— (1985), 'Beazley and the Connoisseurship of Greek Vases', *Occasional Papers on Antiquities, 3. Greek Vases in the J. Paul Getty Museum*, 237–50.

—— (1988), 'Mistress and Maid', *Annali del Dipartimento di Studi del mondo classico e del Mediterraneo antico del Istituto Universitario Orientale, Sezione di Archeologia e Storia Antica*, 10: 141–9, pls. 22–4.

—— and Boardman, J. (1971), *Greek Burial Customs* (London).

La Borde, A. de. (1813–28), *Collection de vases grecs de Mr le Comte de Lamberg* (2 vols., Paris).

La Niece, S. (1983), 'Niello, an Historical and Technical Survey', *Antiquaries Journal*, 63: 278–97.

Lacau, P. (1956), 'L'Or dans l'architecture égyptienne', *Annales du Service*, 53: 221–50.

Lach, D. (1970), *Asia in the Making of Europe*, 2. *A Century of Wonder*, 1. *The Visual Arts* (Chicago and London).

Laffineur, R. (1986), *Amanthonte* III, Testimonia, 3 (Paris).

Lamb, W. (1931–2), 'Antissa', *BSA* 32: 41–67, pls. 17–25.

—— (1932), 'Grey Wares from Lesbos', *JHS* 52: 1–12, pl. 1.

Lamberg, Maximilian Joseph, Count (1774), *Le Mémorial d'un mondain*. 'Au Cap Corse'.

Lane, A. (1963), *Greek Pottery* (2nd edn., London).

Lang, M. (1970), 'Weights', *OCD*² (Oxford), 1138.

Langlotz, E. (1920), *Zur Zeitbestimmung der strengrotfigurigen Vasenmalerei und der gleichzeitigen Plastik* (Leipzig).

Leach, B. (1961), 'Belief and Hope', in Arts Council exhibition catalogue, *Bernard Leach: Fifty Years a Potter* (London).

—— (1976), *A Potter's Book* (new edn., London).

Lelièvre, P. (1942), *Vivant Denon, Directeur des Beaux-Arts de Napoléon* (Paris).

Levy, P. (1979), *Moore: G. E. Moore and the Cambridge Apostles* (London).

Lewis, C. (1939), *Self-Portrait Taken from the Letters and Journals of Charles Ricketts, R. A.* (London).

Lewis, D. M. (1966), 'After the Profanation of the Mysteries', *Ancient Society and Institutions: Studies presented to Victor Ehrenberg* (Oxford), 177–92.

—— (1968), 'New Evidence for the Gold-silver Ratio', in Kraay and Jenkins (1968), 105–10.

—— (1986), 'Temple Inventories in Ancient Greece', in Vickers (1986a), 71–81.

—— (1987), 'The Athenian Coinage Decree', in Carradice (1987), 53–63.

Lezzi-Hafter, A. (1983), 'Mänadengelage und Götterliebe in Malibu: Zu einem Komplex attischer rotfiguriger Fragmente aus Etrurien im J. Paul Getty Museum', *Occasional Papers on Antiquities*, 1: 85–114.

Lightbown, R. W. (1979), 'Ex-votos in Gold and Silver: A Forgotten Art', *Burlington Magazine*, 121: 353–9.

Linders, T. (1975), *The Treasurers of the Other Gods in Athens and their Functions* (Meisenheim).

—— (1987), 'Gods, Gifts, Society', *Boreas*, 15: 115–22 (Uppsala).

—— (1988), 'The Purpose of Inventories: A Close Reading of the Delian Inventories of the Independence', in Knoepfler (1988), 37–47.

—— (1989–90), 'The Melting Down of Discarded Metal Offerings in Greek Sanctuaries', *Scienze dell'antichità: Storia archeologia antropologia*, 3–4: 281–5.

—— (1992a), 'Fallen Money and Broken Crowns—or When is a Coin Not a Coin?', in *Florilegium Numismaticum. Studia in honorem U. Westermark edita* (Stockholm).

—— (1992b), 'Inscriptions and Orality', *Symbolae Osloenses*, 67: 27–40.

Linfert, A. (1977), 'Zwei Versuche über antiken Witz und Esprit', *Rivista di archeologia*, 1: 19–22.

Lipking, L. (1970), *The Ordering of the Arts in Eighteenth-Century England* (Princeton, NJ).

Lissarague, F. (1987), *Un flot d'images: Une esthétique du banquet grec* (Paris).

—— (1990), *The Aesthetics of the Greek Banquet, Images of Wine and Ritual* (Princeton, NJ).

—— and Thelamon, F. (1983) (eds.), *Image et céramique grecque: Actes du colloque de Rouen 25–26 novembre 1982* (Rouen).

Littman, R. J. (1970), 'The Loves of Alcibiades', *Transactions of the American Philological Association*, 101: 263–76.

Lloyd, S. (1956), *Early Anatolia: The Archaeology of Asia Minor before the Greeks* (Harmondsworth).

Loeschke, S. (1909), 'Keramische Funde in Haltern', *Mitteilungen der Altertumskommission für Westfalen*, 5: 101–322.

—— (1928), 'Römische Gefässe aus Bronze, Glas und Ton im Provinzialmuseum Trier', *Trierer Zeitschrift*, 3: 69–81, pls. 1–7.

Loos, A. (1962), *Sämtliche Schriften* (Vienna).

Lordkipanidze, O. (1971), 'La Civilisation de l'ancienne Colchide aux Vᵉ–IVᵉ siècles à la lumière des plus récentes découvertes archéologiques', *RA* 259–88.

Loret, C. (1961), 'Le Cratère de Vix et le nombre d'or', *Bulletin de la société archéologique du Châtillonnais*, 4th series, 2: 49–56.

Lorimer, H. L. (1936), 'Gold and Ivory in Greek Mythology', in *Greek Poetry and Life: Essays Presented to Gilbert Murray* (Oxford), 14–33.

Luckenbill, D. D. (1926–7), *Ancient Records of Assyria and Babylonia* (2 vols., Chicago).

Lunsingh Scheurleer, C. (1926), 'Grieksch steenen vaatwerk', *BABesch.* 1: 7–10.

Lyons, C. (1992), 'The Museo Mastrilli and the Culture of Collecting in Naples, 1700–1755', *Journal of the History of Collections*, 4: 1–26.

McGovern, P. E., and Notis, M. D. (1989) (eds.), *Cross-Craft and Cross-Cultural Interactions in Ceramics (Ceramics and Civilization*, 4), (Westerville, Oh.).

McGrail, S. (1989), 'The Shipment of Traded Goods and of Ballast in Antiquity', *OJA* 8: 353–8.

McKendrick, N., Brewer, J., and Plumb, J. H. (1982), *The Birth of a Consumer Society: The Commercialization of Eighteenth Century England* (London).

MacSween, A., and Burgess, C. (1984), *Au temps de Stonehenge: La Grande Bretagne et l'Europe du nord-ouest au néolithique récent et l'âge du bronze ancien* (Tournai).

Maginnis, H. B. J. (1990), 'The Role of Perceptual Learning in Connoisseurship: Morelli, Berenson and Beyond', *Art History*, 13: 104–17.

Maiuri, A. (1953), *Roman Painting* (New York).

Mallowan, M., and Davies, L. G. (1970), *Ivories in Assyrian Style (Ivories from Nimrud (1949–63), 2)* (London).

Malnati, L. (1988), 'Lo scavo di una fattoria etrusca a Baggiovara—Località Case Vandelli', in A. Cardarelli, I. Pulini, and C. Zanasi (eds.), *Modena dagli origini all'anno Mille: Studi di archeologia e storia*. Exhibition catalogue (Modena), 262–71.

Mango, C., Vickers, M., and Francis, E. D. (1992), 'The Palace of Lausus at Constantinople and its Collection of Ancient Statues', *Journal of the History of Collections*, 4: 89–98.

Markoe, G. (1985), *Phoenician Bronze and Silver Bowls from Cyprus and the Mediterranean* (Berkeley, Calif.).

Marshall, F. W. (1911), *Catalogue of the Jewellery, Greek, Etruscan and Roman, in the Department of Antiquities, British Museum* (London).

Marsilli, P. (1982), 'La ceramica faentina nei suoi rapporti col potere pubblico', *Faenza*, 69: 159–66.

Martelli, M. (1985), 'I luoghi e i prodotti dello scambio', in Cristofani (1985), 175–81.

Marzi, M. G. (1981*a*), 'La pubblicazione, l'esposizione e la prima fortuna del cratere', in *Materiali* (1981), 51–84.

Marzi, M. G. (1981*b*), 'La scoperta', in *Materiali* (1981), 27–50.

Maskell, A. O. (1911), 'Ivory', in *Encyclopedia Britannica*, 11th edn., 15: 92–9.

Masson, M. E., and Pugacenova, G. A. (1982), *The Parthian Rhytons of Nisa* (Florence).

Massoul, M. (1934), *Corpus Vasorum Antiquorum, Musée National de Sèvres* (Paris).

Masterpieces (1981), *Masterpieces of Russian Culture and Art: The Hermitage, Leningrad* (Moscow).

Matchabeli, K. (1983), *Argenterie de l'ancienne Géorgie* (Tbilisi).

Materiali (1977 (1981)), *Materiali per servire alla storia del vaso François* (*Bollettino d'Arte*, serie speciale, 1).

Mat-Hasquin, M. (1981), *Voltaire et l'antiquité grecque* (*Studies on Voltaire and the Eighteenth Century*, 197) (Oxford).

Mathias, P. (1959), *The Brewing Industry in England* (Cambridge).

Matthäus, H. (1985), *Metallgefässe und Gefässuntersätze der Bronzezeit, der geometrischen und archaischen Periode auf Cypern* (Prähistorische Bronzefunde 2/8) (Munich).

—— (1989), 'Mykenai, der mittlere Donauraum während des Hadjúsámson-Horizontes und der Schatz von Valcitran', in Best and de Vries (1989), 86–105.

Mattingly, D. J. (1988), 'Oil for Export? A Comparison of Libyan, Spanish and Tunisian Olive Oil Production in the Roman Empire', *Journal of Roman Archaeology*, 1: 33–56.

Mattingly, H. B. (1987), 'The Athenian Coinage Decree and the Assertion of Empire', in Carradice (1987), 65–71.

Maxmin, J. (1972), 'Euphronios *epoiesen*: Portrait of the Artist as a Presbyopic Potter', *GR* 21: 178–80.

Mayo, M. E. (1982), *The Art of South Italy: Vases from Magna Graecia* (Richmond, Va.).

—— (1983), 'Collecting Ancient Art: An Historical Perspective', in Tompkins (1983), 25–35.

Medley, M. (1972), *Metalwork and Chinese Ceramics* (London).

Mee, C. B., Gill, D. W. J., Forbes, H. A., and Foxhall, L. (1991), 'Rural Settlement Change in the Methana Peninsula, Greece', in G. Barker and J. Lloyd (eds.), *Roman Landscape: Archaeological Survey in the Mediterranean* (Archaeological Monographs of the British School at Rome, 2) (London), 223–32.

Meer, L. van der (1984), 'Kylikeia in Etruscan Tomb Painting', in Brijder (1984), 298–304.

Meiggs, R. (1972), *The Athenian Empire* (Oxford).

—— and Lewis, D. M. (1969), *A Selection of Greek Historical Inscriptions to the End of the Fifth Century BC* (Oxford).

Melikian-Chirvani, A. S. (1986), 'Silver in Islamic Iran: The Evidence from Literature and Epigraphy', in Vickers (1986*a*), 89–106.

Mellinghoff, F. (1968), 'Materialkopie bei den Griechen', *Museum Folkwang Essen Mitteilungen*, 2: 56–65.

Mellor, E. (1950), *Education through Experience in the Infant School Years* (Oxford).

Melville, A. (1983), *Gnomes and Gardens* (London).

Melville-Jones, J. R. (1979), 'Darics at Delphi', *Revue belge de Numismatique*, 125: 25–36.

Mertens, J. R. (1975), 'A White Lekythos in the Getty Museum', *J. Paul Getty Museum Journal*, 2: 27–36.

Meteyard, E. (1865–6), *The Life of Josiah Wedgwood from his Private Correspondence and Private Papers* (2 vols., London).

Metzler, D. (1983–4), 'J. J. Winckelmann (1717–1768)', *Hephaistos*, 5–6: 7–17.

Michea, E. (1933), 'Le "Voyage en Italie" de Goethe devant l'opinion européenne', *Études Italiennes*, NS 3: 103–13.

Michel, C. (1900), *Recueil d'inscriptions grecques* (Paris).

Millard, A. R. (1988), 'King Solomon's Gold: Biblical Records in the Light of Antiquity', *The Society for Mesopotamian Studies, Bulletin*, 15: 5–11.

—— (1989), 'Does the Bible Exaggerate King Solomon's Golden Wealth?', *Biblical Archaeology Review*, 15: 20–31, 34.

Miller, M. C. (1989), 'Peacocks and *tryphe* in Classical Athens', *Archaeological News*, 15: 1–10.

Millin, A. L. (1808–10), *Peintures de vases antiques vulgairement appelés étrusques* (2 vols., Paris).

Millingen, J. (1817), *Peintures de vases antiques de la collection de Sir John Coghill Bart* (Rome).

—— (1822–6), *Ancient Unedited Monuments: Painted Greek Vases* (2 vols., London).

Milne, M. J. (1945), 'A Prize for Woolworking', *AJA* 49: 528–33.

Mingazzini, P. (1971), *Catalogo dei vasi della collezione Augusto Castellani* (Rome).

Mintz, S. W. (1985), *Sweetness and Power: The Place of Sugar in Modern History* (New York).

Mitchell, S. (1983), 'Cornish Tin, Iulius Caesar, and the Invasion of Britain', in C. Deroux (ed.), *Studies in Latin Literature and Roman History* (Collection Latomus, 180) (Brussels).

Mitford, T. B. (1963), 'Akestor, King of Paphos', *BICS* 10: 27–30, pls. 4–7.

Mittlmeier, W. (1977), *Die Neue Pinakothek in München 1843–1854, Planung, Baugeschichte und Fresken* (Munich).

Moderne Vergangenheit 1800–1900 (1981), Künstlerthaus (Vienna).

Moltesen, M. (1983), 'Solvtoj i ler', *Meddelelser fra Ny Carlsberg Glyptotek*, 39: 32–53.

—— (1991), 'A Group of Late-Etruscan Silver-Imitating Vases', *Meddelelser fra Ny Carlsberg Glyptotek*, 47: 435–44.

—— and Weber-Lehmann, C. (1991), *Catalogue of the Copies of Etruscan Tomb Paintings in the Ny Carlsberg Glyptotek* (Copenhagen).

Montfaucon, B. de (1719–24), *L'Antiquité expliquée* (10 vols., Paris).

Moon, W. G. (1979), *Greek Vase-Painting in Midwestern Collections* (Chicago).

—— (1983) (ed.), *Ancient Greek Art and Iconography* (Madison, Wis.).

Moore, M. B. (1971), 'Horses on Black-Figure Vases of the Archaic Period, ca. 620–480 BC (Diss., New York University).

Moorey, P. R. S. (1988), 'The Technique of Gold-Figure Decoration on Achaemenid Silver Vessels and its Antecedents', *Iranica Antiqua*, 23: 231–46.

Morel, J.-P. (1965), *Céramique à vernis noir du Forum romain et du Palatin* (Mélanges d'archéologie et d'histoire. Suppléments 3) (Paris).

—— (1981), *Céramique campanienne: Les Formes*, Bibliothèque des Écoles françaises d'Athènes et de Rome (Paris), 244.

Morel, J.-P. (1983), 'La Céramique comme indice du commerce antique (réalités et interprétations)', in Garnsey, Hopkins, and Whittaker (1983), 66–74.

Moretti, M. (1962), *La Tomba della Nave a Tarquinia* (Milan).

Morley, H. (1852), *Palissy the Potter. The Life of Bernard Palissy of Saintes, his Labours and Discoveries in Art and Science; with an Outline of his Philosophical Doctrines* (London).

Morris, C. (1993), 'Hands Up for the Individual! The Role of Attribution Studies in Aegean Prehistory', *Cambridge Archaeological Journal*, 3: 41–66.

Morris, I. (1987), *Burial and Ancient Society: The Rise of the Greek City-State* (Cambridge).

—— (1992), *Death-Ritual and Social Structure in Classical Antiquity* (Cambridge).

Morris, S. (1986), Review of Bothmer (1985), *AJA* 90: 360–1.

Morris, W. (1890), *News from Nowhere*, in Briggs (1962), 183–301.

Münzen und Medaillen (1986), *Auktion*, 70 (Basle).

Mundell Mango, M. (1986), *Silver from Early Byzantium: The Kaper Karaon and Related Treasures* (Baltimore).

—— (1988), 'The Origins of the Syrian Ecclesiastical Silver Treasures of the Sixth–Seventh Centuries', in Barratte (1988), 163–84.

—— (1990*a*), 'Der Seuso-Schatzfund: Ein Ensemble westlichen und östlichen Kunstschaffens', *Antike Welt*, 21: 70–88.

—— (1990*b*), 'The Uses of Liturgical Silver, 4th–7th Centuries', in R. Morris (ed.), *Church and People in Byzantium* (Birmingham).

—— (forthcoming), 'The Monetary Value of Silver Furniture Revetments and Objects in Early Byzantine Church Treasures', in S. Boyd, M. Mundell Mango, and G. Vikan (eds.), *Ecclesiastical Silver Plate in Sixth-Century Byzantium* (Washington, DC).

Mureddu, P. (1972), 'Χρυσεῖα a Pithecussai', *PdP* 27: 407–9.

Murray, A. S. (1892), *Handbook of Greek Archaeology* (London).

Murray, O. (1980), *Early Greece* (London).

—— (1982), 'Symposium and Männerbund', *Concilium Eirene*, 16: 94–112.

—— (1983), 'The Greek Symposium in History', in E. Gabba (ed.), *Tria Cordia. Scritti in honore di Arnaldo Momigliano* (257–72).

—— (1990) (ed.), *Sympotica: A Symposium on the* Symposion (Oxford).

Muscarella, O. W. (1977*a*), '"Ziwiye" and Ziwiye: The Forgery of a Provenience', *Journal of Field Archaeology*, 4: 197–219.

—— (1977*b*), 'Unexcavated Objects and Ancient Near Eastern Art', in L. D. Levine and T. Cuyler Young (eds.), *Mountains and Lowlands: Essays in the Archaeology of Greater Mesopotamia* (Malibu, Calif.), 153–208.

—— (1979), 'Excavated and Unexcavated Achaemenian Art', in D. Schmandt-Besserat (ed.), *Ancient Persia: The Art of an Empire*, Invited Lectures on the Middle East at the University of Texas at Austin (Malibu, Calif.), 4: 23–42, pls. 5–19.

Naylor, G. (1971), *The Arts and Crafts Movement: A Study of its Sources, Ideals and Influence on Design Theory* (London).

Neumann, G. (1977), 'Zu einigen Beischriften auf Münchner Vasen', *AA* 39–41.

New Thracian Treasure (1986), Exhibition catalogue, *The New Thracian Treasure from Rogozen, Bulgaria* (British Museum, London).

Niebuhr, B. G. (1838), *Lebensnachrichten über Barthold Georg Niebuhr* (3 vols., Hamburg).

Noble, J. V. (1988), *The Technique of Painted Attic Pottery*, 2nd edn. (New York).

Noe, S. P. (1956), 'Two Hoards of Persian Sigloi', *Numismatic Notes and Monographs*, 136: 1–44.

Non, V. de (1788), *Voyage en Sicile, par M. de Non, Gentilhomme ordinaire du Roi, et de l'Académie royale de peinture et sculpture* (Paris).

Norton, L. (1967), *Historical Memoirs of the Duc de Saint-Simon* (London).

Nowinski, J. (1970), *Baron Dominique Vivant Denon (1747–1825)* (Rutherford).

Oakley, J. H. (1990), *The Phiale Painter* (Mainz).

O'Connor, S. (1992), review of Krzyszkowska (1990), in *Antiquity*, 66: 270–1.

Oddy, W. A. (1988), 'The Gilding of Roman Silver Plate', in Baratte (1988), 9–25.

—— La Niece, S., Curtis, J. E., and Meeks, N. D. (1981), 'Diffusion-Bonding as a Method of Gilding in Antiquity', *MASCA Journal*, 1: 238–41.

Oliver, A. Jr. (1977), *Silver for the Gods: 800 Years of Greek and Roman Silver* (Toledo, Oh.).

Oliver, P., Davies, I., and Bentley, I. (1981) (eds.), *Dunroamin: The Suburban Semi and its Enemies* (London).

Olson, G., and Thordemann, B. (1951), 'The Cleaning of Silver Objects', *Museums Journal*, 50: 250–2.

Olympia Catalogue (1972), *100 Jahre deutsche Ausgrabung in Olympia* (Munich).

Oman, C. (1961), *The English Silver in the Kremlin, 1557–1663* (London).

O'Reilly, S., Taylor, J., and Atterbury, P. (1984), *Artist Potters Now: A Touring and Selling Exhibition of Contemporary Ceramics Made by Potters Working in Britain Today* (Oxford).

Osborne, R. (1983/4), 'The Myth of Propaganda and the Propaganda of Myth', *Hephaistos*, 5–6: 61–70.

—— (1985), *Demos: The Discovery of Classical Attika* (Cambridge).

—— (1987a), *Classical Landscape with Figures: The Ancient Greek City and its Countryside* (London).

—— (1987b), 'The Viewing and Obscuring of the Parthenon Frieze', *JHS* 107: 98–105.

—— (1988), 'Death Revisited; Death Revised: The Death of the Artist in Archaic and Classical Greece', *Art History*, 11: 1–16.

—— (1991), 'Whose Image and Superscription is This?' *Arion*, 1: 255–75.

Ostwald, M. (1986), *From Popular Sovereignty to the Sovereignty of Law: Law, Society and Politics in Fifth-Century Athens* (Berkeley, Calif., and Los Angeles).

Overbeck, J. (1868), *Die Antike Schriftquellen zur Geschichte der bildenden Künste bei den Griechen* (Leipzig).

Owen, D. I. (1970), 'Picking up the Pieces: The Salvage Excavations of a Looted Fifth Century BC Shipwreck in the Straits of Messina', *Expedition*, 13(1): 24–9.

—— (1971), 'Excavating a Classical Shipwreck', *Archaeology*, 24: 118–29.

Oxe, A., and Comfort, H. (1968), *Corpus Vasorum Arretinorum* (Bonn).

Oxford Arts Club (1928), *Drawings and Photographs of Greek Vase-Paintings by Professor and Mrs J. D. Beazley* (Oxford).

Padgett, J. M. (1991), 'Phineus and the Boreads on a Pelike by the Nausicaa Painter', *Journal of the Museum of Fine Arts, Boston*, 3: 15–33.

Page, D. L. (1981), *Further Greek Epigrams* (Cambridge).

Painter, K. (1988), 'Roman Silver Hoards: Ownership and Status', in Baratte (1988), 97–112.

Pairault Massa, F.-H., and Vallet, G. (1978), 'Marzabotto (Bologna). Rapport préliminaire sur six ans de recherches (1971–76) dans l'insula VIII (Brizio) = V, 3', *NSc* 1978: 131–58.

Pallottino, M. (1952), *Etruscan Painting* (Geneva).

Panofka, T. (1834), *Antiques du cabinet du Comte de Portalès-Gorgier* (Paris).

Pape, M. (1975), *Griechische Kunstwerke aus Kriegsbeute und ihre öffentliche Aufstellung in Rom* (Diss., Hamburg).

Parabeni, E. (1966), 'Triptolemos, pittore di', *Enciclopedia dell'arte antica*, 7 (Rome).

Parker, A. J. (1984), 'Shipwrecks and Ancient Trade in the Mediterranean', *Archaeological Review from Cambridge*, 3(2): 99–112.

—— (1990), 'Classical Antiquity: The Maritime Dimension', *Antiquity*, 64: 335–46.

Parker, R. (1983), *Miasma: Pollution and Purification in Early Greek Religion* (Oxford).

Pascal, R. (1973), *From Naturalism to Expressionism* (London).

Pater, W. (1895), *Greek Studies* (London).

Paul, E. (1982), *Antike Keramik: Entdeckung und Erforschung bemalter Tongefässe in Griechenland und Italien* (Leipzig).

Payne, H. (1931), *Necrocorinthia* (Oxford).

Pazaurek, G. E. (1912), *Guter und Schlechter Geschmack im Kunstgewerbe* (Stuttgart and Berlin).

Peacock, D. P. S. (1982), *Pottery in the Roman World: An Ethnoarchaeological Approach* (London and New York).

Penniman, T. K. (1952), *Pictures of Ivory and Other Animal Teeth, Bone and Antler* (Pitt Rivers Museum Occasional Papers on Technology, 5).

Peredolskaya, A. A. (1945), 'Les Dessins sur ivoire du Tumulus Koul-Oba', *Trudy otdela istorii iskusstva i kul'tury antichnogo mira*, 1: 69–83, pls. 1–6.

Pevsner, N. (1937), *An Enquiry into Industrial Art in England* (London).

Pharmakowsky, B. (1910), 'Archäologische Funde im Jahre 1909: Russland', *AA* 178–234.

Pijl-Ketel, C. L. van der (1982) (ed.), *The Ceramic Load of the Witte Leeuw (1613)* (Amsterdam).

Pinelli, P., and Wasowicz, A. (1986), *Musée du Louvre: Catalogue des bois et stucs grecs et romains provenant de Kertch* (Paris).

Pinkwart, D. (1972), 'Hellenistisch-römische Bleiglasurkeramik aus Pergamon', *Pergamenische Forschungen*, 1: 140–63.

Pittura etrusca (1986), *Pittura etrusca: Disegni e documenti del XIX secolo dall'archivio dell'Istituto Archeologico Germanico* (*Studi di archeologia pubblicati dalla soprintendenza archeologica per l'Etruria meridionale*, 2) (Rome).

Platnauer, M. (1921), 'Greek Colour Perception', *Classical Quarterly*, 15: 153–62.

Plenderleith, H. J., and Werner, A. E. A. (1971), *The Conservation of Antiquities and Works of Art* (2nd edn., London).

Plumier, C. (1701), *L'Art de tourner toutes sortes de choses* (Lyon).

Podlecki, A. J. (1975), *The Life of Themistocles* (Montreal).

Politi, R. (1826), *Illustrazione della pittura di un vaso greco-siculo rappresentante Nemesi trovato nell'antica Agrigento nel'Aprile del MDCCCXXV ed acquistato da S. E. il Marchese delle Favare, Ministro Segretario di Stato, Luogotenente Generale in Sicilia, scritta, e dedicata allo stesso da Raffaello Politi pittore, ed architetto siracusano* (Palermo).

Pollen, J. H. (1879), *Gold and Silver* (London).

Pollitt, J. J. (1986), *Art in the Hellenistic Age* (Cambridge).

Pope, M. (1988), 'Thucydides and Democracy', *Historia*, 37: 276–96.

Pottier, E. (1905), *Douris et les peintres des vases grecs* (2nd edn., Paris).

Poulsen, F. (1922), *Etruscan Tomb Paintings: Their Subjects and Significance* (Oxford).

—— (1927), *Das Helbig Museum der Ny Carlsberg Glyptotek* (Copenhagen).

Price, M. J. (1968), 'Early Greek Bronze Coinage', in Kraay and Jenkins (1968), 90–104.

—— and Waggoner, N. (1975), *Archaic Greek Silver Coinage: The 'Asyut' Hoard* (London).

Priestley, M. (1965), *Going Abroad* (London).

Pritchard, J. B. (1969), *Ancient Near Eastern Texts Relating to the Old Testament* (3rd edn., Princeton, NJ).

Pritchett, W. K. (1956), 'The Attic Stelai, 2', *Hesperia*, 25: 178–317.

—— (1971), *Ancient Greek Military Practices*, 1 (*The Greek Art of War*, 1) (Berkeley Calif., and Los Angeles).

Prochorov, V. (1880), *Bolgarskiya raskopki bliz' Eski-zagr'i* (St Petersburg).

Pucci, G. (1985), 'Per una storia del lusso nella cultura materiale fra repubblica e alto impero', *Index*, 13: 573–87.

Raby, J. (1986), 'Looking for Silver in Clay: A New Perspective on Sāmānid Ceramics', in Vickers (1986*a*), 179–203.

Raby, J., and Vickers, M. (1986), 'Puritanism and Positivism', in Vickers (1986*a*), 217–23.

Ramage, N. H. (1987), 'Initial letters in Sir William Hamilton's "Collection of Antiquities"', *Burlington Magazine*, 129: 446–56.

—— (1990*a*), 'Sir William Hamilton as Collector, Exporter and Dealer: The Acquisition and Dispersal of his Collections', *AJA* 94: 469–80.

—— (1990*b*), 'Wedgwood and Sir William Hamilton: Their Personal and Artistic Relationship', in *Thirty-Fifth Annual Wedgwood International Seminar, May 2, 3, 4 and 5, 1990: The Consumer Revolution in 18th Century English Pottery* (Birmingham, Ala.), 71–90.

—— (1991), 'The Publication Dates of Sir William Hamilton's Four Volumes', *Ars Ceramica*, 8: 35.

Rasmussen, T. B. (1979), *Bucchero Pottery from Southern Etruria* (Cambridge).

—— and Spivey, N. (1991) (eds.), *Looking at Greek Vases* (Cambridge).

Raubitschek, A. E. (1949), *Dedications from the Athenian Akropolis* (Cambridge, Mass.).

Rawson, J. (1982), *The Ornament on Chinese Silver of the Tang Dynasty (AD 618–906)*, (British Museum Occasional Paper, no. 40) (London).

—— (1984), 'Song Silver and its Connexions with Ceramics', *Apollo*, 120: 18–23.

—— (1986), 'Tombs or Hoards: The Survival of Chinese Silver of the Tang and

Song Periods, Seventh to Thirteenth Centuries AD', in Vickers (1986*a*), 31–56.

—— (1989), 'Chinese Silver and its Influence on Porcelain Development', in McGovern and Notis (1989), 275–300.

—— (1991), 'Central Asian Silver and its Influence on Chinese Ceramics', *Bulletin of the Asia Institute*, NS 5: 139–51.

Rea, J. (1986), 'P.Oxy. XLIII 31321 and Goldsmiths' Pay', *ZPE* 62: 79–80.

Reeder, E. D. (1974), 'Clay Impressions from Attic Metalwork' (Diss., Princeton).

Regter, W. (forthcoming), *Bucchero Pottery from Veii*. (Amsterdam).

Reitlinger, G. (1961–70), *The Economics of Taste* (3 vols., London).

Renfrew, C. (1967), 'Cycladic Metallurgy and the Aegean Early Bronze Age', *AJA* 71: 1–20.

—— (1969), 'The Development and Chronology of the Early Cycladic Figurines', *AJA* 73: 1–32.

—— (1972), *The Emergence of Civilisation: The Cyclades and the Aegean in the Third Millennium* BC (London).

—— (1991), *The Cycladic Spirit: Masterpieces from the Nicholas P. Goulandris Collection* (London).

Rhodes, D. E. (1973), *Dennis of Etruria: The Life of George Dennis* (London).

Rice, E. E. (1983), *The Grand Procession of Ptolemy Philadelphus* (Oxford).

—— (1986), 'The Date of the Rhodian Sculptors of the Laocoon and Sperlonga Sculptures', *AJA* 90: 209.

Richter, G. (1972), *Kitsch-Lexicon von A bis Z* (Gütersloh).

Richter, G. M. A. (1904–5), 'The Distribution of Attic Vases: A Study of the Home Market', *BSA* 11: 224–42.

—— (1916), 'Hellenistic and Roman Glazed Vases', *BMMA* 11: 64–8.

—— (1923), *The Craft of Athenian Pottery* (New Haven, Conn.).

—— (1931), 'A Stand by Kleitias and an Athenian Jug', *BMMA* 26: 289–94.

—— (1937*a*), 'A Greek Bronze Hydria', *BMMA* 32: 255–9.

—— (1937*b*), 'A Greek Bronze Hydria in the Metropolitan Museum', *AJA* 41: 532–8.

—— (1941), 'A Greek Silver Phiale in the Metropolitan Museum, and the Light it Throws on Greek Embossed Metalwork (*toreutice*), of the Fifth Century BC and on the "Calene" Phialai Mesomphalai of the Hellenistic Period', *AJA* 65: 363–89.

—— (1946), *Attic Red-Figured Vases: A Survey*. (Second edn., 1958; New Haven, Conn.).

—— (1950), 'Greek Fifth Century Silverware and Later Imitations', *AJA* 54: 357–70.

—— (1965), Review of Beazley (1963), *AJA* 69: 74–6.

—— and Hall, L. F. (1936), *Red-Figured Athenian Vases in the Metropolitan Museum of Art* (New Haven, Conn.).

Richter, P., and Ricardo, I. (1980), *Voltaire* (Boston).

Ridgway, B. (1967), 'The Bronze Apollo from Piombino in the Louvre', *Antike Plastik*, 7: 43–75.

Ridgway, D. (1973), 'The First Western Greeks: Campanian Coasts and Southern Etruria', in C. Hawkes and S. Hawkes (eds.), *Greeks, Celts and Romans* (London), 5–38.

—— (1973–4), 'Archaeology in Central Italy and Etruria 1968–73', *AR* 20: 42–59.

—— (1989), 'James Byres and the Ancient State of Italy: Unpublished Documents in Edinburgh', *Istituto Nazionale di Studi Etruschi e Italici*, Atti del secondo congresso internazionale etrusco (Firenze, 26 Maggio–2 Giugno 1985), 213–29.

—— (1992), *The First Western Greeks* (Cambridge).

—— and Serra Ridgway, F. de (1979) (eds.), *Italy Before the Romans: The Iron Age, Orientalizing and Etruscan Periods* (London).

Ritchie, C. I. A. (1969), *Ivory Carving* (London).

Robert, C. (1890), 'Homerische Becher', *Berliner Winckelmanns-programm*, 50: 1–96.

Roberts, S. R. (1978), *The Attic Pyxis* (Chicago).

Robertson, M. (1959), *Greek Painting* (Geneva).

—— (1965), 'Attic Red-Figure Vase-Painters', *JHS* 85: 90–101.

—— (1972), '"Epoiesen" on Greek Vases: Other Considerations', *JHS* 92: 180–3.

—— (1973), 'A Vignette by the Amasis Painter', *Antike Kunst*, Beiheft 9: 81–4, pl. 29.

—— (1975), *A History of Greek Art* (Cambridge).

—— (1976), 'Beazley and After', *Münchner Jahrbuch der Bildenden Kunst*, 27: 29–46.

—— (1981), 'Euphronios at the Getty', *J. Paul Getty Museum Journal*, 9: 23–34.

—— (1985), 'Beazley and Attic Vase Painting', in D. C. Kurtz (ed.), *Beazley and Oxford* (Oxford), 19–30.

—— (1987), 'The State of Attic Vase-Painting in the Mid-Sixth Century', in M. True (ed.), *Papers on the Amasis Painter and his World* (Malibu, Calif.), 13–28.

—— (1988*a*), 'The State of Attic Vase-Painting in the Mid-Sixth Century', in *Papers on the Amasis Painter and his World* (Malibu, Calif.), 13–28.

—— (1988*b*), 'Vase Painting', in Exhibition Catalogue, *The Human Figure in Early Greek Art* (Washington, DC), 37–40.

—— (1989*a*), 'Bernard Ashmole', *PBA* 75: 313–28.

—— (1989*b*), 'Beazley's Use of Terms', in *Beazley Addenda. Additional References to ABV, ARV² & Paralipomena*, compiled by T. H. Carpenter (2nd edn., Oxford).

—— (1991), 'Adopting an Approach', in Rasmusssen and Spivey (1991), 1–12.

—— (1992), *The Art of Vase-Painting in Classical Athens* (Cambridge).

—— (forthcoming), 'Attic Vase-Painting: Beazley's Work and its Effect on the Subject'.

Robinson, E. G. D. (1990), 'Between Greek and Native: The Xenon Group', in J.-P. Descœudres (ed.), *Greek Colonists and Native Populations* (Oxford), 251–65, pls. 28–9.

Robinson, E. S. G. (1958), 'The Beginnings of Archaemenid Coinage', *NC* 6th ser. 18: 187–93.

Robinson, D. M. (1933), *Mosaics, Vases, and Lamps of Olynthus found in 1928 and 1931. Excavations at Olynthus*, 5 (Baltimore).

Robson-Scott, W. D. (1981), *The Younger Goethe and the Visual Arts* (Cambridge).

Rodinis, G. T. (1977), *Dominique Vivant Denon: I Fiordalisi, il beretto frigio, la sfinge* (Florence).

Rodríguez-Almeida, E. (1984), *Il monte Testaccio: Ambiente, storia, materiali* (Rome).

Rogers, M. (1986), 'Plate and its Substitutes in Ottoman Inventories', in Vickers (1986*a*), 117–36.

Rolle, R., and Walls, G. (1989), *The World of the Scythians* (London).

Rombai, L. (1980) (ed.), *I Medici e lo stato senese 1555–1609: Storia e territorio* (Rome).

Ronsard, P. de (1967), 'Le Verre', in *Les œuvres de Pierre de Ronsard*, ed. I. Silver, vol. 4 (Chicago).

Rosati, R. (1974), 'I ceramisti nella società ateniese del VI secolo a.C.', *Atti della Accademia delle Scienze dell'Istituto di Bologna, Classe di Scienze Morali*, 62: 178–201.

—— (1976–7), 'La nozione di "proprietà dell' officina" e l'epoiesen nei vasi attici', *Atti della Accademia delle Scienze dell'Istituto di Bologna, Classe di Scienze Morali*, 65: 45–73.

Rosenberg, M. (1924), *Niello, 1, Bis zum Jahre 1000 nach Chr.* (Frankfurt).

Ross, L. (1863), *Erinnerungen und Mittheilungen aus Griechenland* (Berlin).

Rotroff, S. I. (1982), *Hellenistic Pottery: Athenian and Imported Moldmade Bowls* (*Agora*, 22) (Princeton, NJ).

—— and Oakley, J. H. (1992), Debris from a Public Dining Place in the Athenian Agora (*Hesperia*, Suppl. 25).

Ruskin, J. (1903–12), *The Works*, eds. E. T. Cook and A. Wedderburn (The Library Edition), 39 vols. (London).

Russell, D. A. (1966), 'On Reading Plutarch's Lives', *Greece and Rome*, 13: 139–54.

Rykwert, J. (1980), *The First Moderns: The Architects of the Eighteenth Century*, (Cambridge, Mass.).

—— (1982), *The Necessity of Artifice* (London).

Saint-Aubyn, F. (1987) (ed.), *Ivory: A History and Collector's Guide* (London).

Saint-Non, Abbé de (1781–6), *Voyage pittoresque: Ou description des royaumes de Naples et de Sicile* (5 vols., Paris).

Saint-Simon, Duc de (1984), *Mémoires (1707–10)* (Paris).

Salet, F. (1973), 'Introduction', in Exhibition Catalogue, *Masterpieces of Tapestry from the Fourteenth to the Sixteenth Century* (New York), 11–23.

Salomonson, J. W. (1982), 'Der hellenistische Töpfer als Toreut', *BABesch.* 57: 164–73.

Salter, S. (1982), 'The Perils of Being Simple', *New Scientist*, 25 February, 495–7.

Sanctis, F. de (1814) (ed.), *Pitture de' vasi antichi cavate dalla collezione del sig. cav. Hamilton, edizione romana, tradotta e pubblicata da Francesco de Sanctis* (Rome).

Sarre, F. (1925), *Die Keramik von Samarra* (Berlin).

Savignoni, L. (1897), 'Di un bronzetto arcaico dell'acropoli di Atene e di una classe di tripodi di tipo greco-orientale', *Monumenti antichi*, 7: 277–375.

Sayce, A. H. (1883), *The Ancient Empires of the East: Herodotos I–III* (London).

Schachel, R. L. (1970), 'Adolf Loos, Amerika und die Antike', *Alte und moderne Kunst*, 113: 6–10.

Schachermeyr, F. (1955), *Die ältesten Kulturen Griechenlands* (Stuttgart).

Schafer, E. H. (1963), *The Golden Peaches of Samarkand: A Study of T'ang Exotics* (Berkeley, Calif., and Los Angeles).

Schama, S. (1987), *The Embarrassment of Riches: An Interpretation of Dutch Culture in the Golden Age* (New York).

Schauenburg, K. (1973), 'Silene beim Symposion', *JdI* 88: 1–26.

Schefold, K. (1931), 'Attische Silberschale', *Römische Mitteilungen*, 46: 119–29.

Scheibler, I. (1983), *Griechische Töpferkunst, Herstellung, Handel und Gebrauch der antiken Tongefässe* (Munich).

Schiering, W. (1967), *Griechische Tongefässe: Gestalt, Bestimmung und Formwandel* (Berlin).

Schindler, M. (1967), *Die 'schwarze Sigillata' des Magdalensberges* (Klagenfurt).

Schlaifer, R. (1936 (1960)), 'Greek Theories of Slavery from Homer to Aristotle', *HSCP* 47: 165–204 (reprinted in Finley (1960), 93–132).

Schmidt, M. (1980), 'Zu Amazonomachiedarstellungen des Berliner Malers und des Euphronios', in *Taenia, Festschrift für R. Hampe* (Mainz), 153–72, pls. 37–41.

—— (1982), 'Etruscan Grave Group. Etruscan Bucchero Kyathos', in H. Bloesch (ed.), *Greek Vases from the Hirschmann Collection* (Zurich), 40–1.

Schmitt, R. (1983), 'Achaemenid Dynasty', *Encyclopedia Iranica*, 1/4: 414–26 (London).

Schmitt-Pantel, P. (1985), 'Banquet et cité grecque: Quelques questions suscitées par le recherches récentes', *Mélanges de l'École française de Rome: Antiquité*, 97, 135–58.

—— (1992), *La Cité au banquet: histoire des repas publics dans les cités grecques* (Collection de l'École française de Rome, 157).

Schnapp, A. (1990), 'De l'idolâtrie des Grecs au figurisme des lumières', in *Rencontres de l'École du Louvre: L'Idolâtrie*, 69–80.

—— (1991), 'La pratica del collezionismo e le sue consequenze nell storia dell'antichità: il Cavaliere d'Hancarville,' in *La Grecia antica. Mito e simbolo per l'età della Grande Rivoluzione: Genesi e crisi di un modello nella cultura del settecento* (Milan).

Schneider, L. A. (1975), *Zur sozialen Bedeutung der archaischen Korenstatuen* (Hamburger Beiträge zur Archäologie, Beiheft 2).

Schneider-Hermann, G. (1962), 'Apulische Schalengriffe verschiedener Formen', *BABesch*. 37: 40–51.

Schuchardt, C. (1848), *Goethe's Kunstsammlungen* (3 vols., Jena).

Scott, L. (1954), 'Pottery' in Singer, Holmyard, and Hall (1954), 376–412.

Scott, W. B. (1874), 'Jacquemart's Ceramic Art', *Portfolio*, 5: 40–4.

Scribner, H. S. (1937), *A Catalogue of the Spang Collection of Greek and Italian Vases and Etruscan Urns in the Carnegie Museum* (Pittsburgh).

The Search for Alexander: An Exhibition (1980), edited by N. Yalouris, M. Andronikos, K. Rhomiopoulou, A. Herrmann, and C. Vermeule (New York).

Semper, G. (1863–79), *Der Stil* (Munich).

Serra Rafols, J. de C. (1941), 'El poblado ibérico del Castellet de Banyoles (Tivissa—Bajo Ebro)', *Ampurias*, 3: 15–34.

—— (1964–5), 'La destrucción del poblado ibérico del Castellet de Banyoles de Tivissa (Bajo Ebro)', *Ampurias*, 26–7: 105–17.

Shapiro, H. A. (1981*a*), 'Courtship Scenes in Attic Vase-Painting', *AJA* 85: 132–43.

—— (1981*b*), *Art, Myth and Culture: Greek Vases from Southern Collections* (New Orleans).

—— (1989), *Art and Cult under the Tyrants in Athens* (Mainz).

Shefton, B. B. (1967), 'Attisches Meisterwerk und etruskische Kopie', in *Die Griechische Vase*, 529–37, pls. 86–87.1 (Rostock).

—— (1971), 'Persian Gold and Attic Black Glaze, Achaemenid Influences on Attic Pottery of the 5th and 4th Centuries BC', *9th International Congress of Classical Archaeology, Damascus 11–20 October 1969*, 109–11.

—— (1982), 'Greeks and Greek Imports in the South of the Iberian Peninsula: The Archaeological Evidence', in H. G. Niemeyer (ed.), *Phönizier im Westen* (Madrider Beiträge 8) (Mainz), 337–70.

Sherratt, A. G. (1987), Review of B. Otto, *Die verzierte Keramik der Sesklo- und Diminikultur Thessaliens* in *Classical Review*, 37: 320–1.

—— and Taylor, T. (1989), 'Metal Vessels in Bronze Age Europe and the Context of Vulchetrun', in Best and de Vries (1989), 106–33.

Sherratt, S., and Sherratt, A. G. (1993), 'The Growth of the Mediterranean Economy in the Early 1st Millennium BC', *World Archaeology*, 24: 361–78.

Siebert, G. (1980), 'Les Bols à relief: Une industrie d'art de l'époque hellénistique', in *Céramiques hellénistiques et romaines* (Centre de recherches d'histoire ancienne, 36 (= Annales littéraires de l'Université de Besançon, 242), 53–83.

Simpson, G. (1957), 'Metallic Black Slip Vases from Central Gaul with Applied and Moulded Decoration', *Antiquaries Journal*, 37: 29–42, pls. 13–14.

Singer, C., Holmyard, E. J., and Hall, A. R. (1954), *A History of Technology*, 1 (Oxford).

Slavin, A. J. (1976), 'The American Principle from More to Locke', in F. Chiapelli (ed.), *First Images of America* (Berkeley, Calif., and Los Angeles), 139–64.

Smith, C. H. (1899), *The Forman Collection: Catalogue of the Egyptian, Greek and Roman Antiquities* (London).

Smith, C. J. (1993), Review of Morris (1992), in *Antiquity*, 67: 464–5.

Smith, H. R. W. (1944), *The Hearst Hydria: An Attic Footnote to Corinthian History* (Berkeley, Calif., and Los Angeles).

Smyth, J. (1821), *The Practice of the Customs in the Entry, Examination and Delivery of Goods* (2nd edn., London).

Snodgrass, A. M. (1980), *Archaic Greece: The Age of Experiment* (London).

Sokolowski, F. (1969), *Lois sacrées des cités grecques* (Paris).

Sourvinou-Inwood, C. (1979), *Theseus as Son and Stepson* (London).

Spätantike Catalogue (1978), *Spätantike und früh-byzantinische Silbergefässe aus der Staatlichen Ermitage Leningrad* (Berlin).

Spalding, K. (1968) (ed.), *J. W. Goethe, Hermann und Dorothea* (London).

Sparkes, B. A., and Talcott, L. (1958), *Pots and Pans of Classical Athens* (Agora Picture Book, 1) (Princeton, NJ).

—— (1970), *Black and Plain Pottery of the 6th, 5th and 4th Centuries BC* (*Athenian Agora*, 12) (Princeton, NJ).

Spence, I. (1988), 'The Athenian Hippeis in the Fifth and Fourth Centuries BC' (Ph.D. thesis, University of London).

—— (forthcoming), 'The Cost of Cavalry Service in Classical Athens', in *State, Citizen, and Military Obligations in Ancient Greece* (London).

Spivey, N. (1991), 'Greek Vases in Etruria', in Rasmussen and Spivey (1991), 131–50.

Spours, J. (1988), *Art Deco Tableware: British Domestic Ceramics 1925–1939* (London).

Stadter, P. (1989), *A Commentary on Plutarch's* Pericles (Chapel Hill and London).

Stähler, K. (1985) (ed.), *Apulien, Kulturberührungen in griechischer Zeit: Antiken der Sammlung G.-St.* (Münster).

Starr, B., and Starr, L. (1982), 'Variegated: Mimicry of Stone', in L. S. Rakow and G. Tropper (eds.), *Wedgwood Specialities* (New York), 12–19.

Ste Croix, G. E. M. de (1981), *The Class Struggle in the Ancient Greek World: From the Archaic Age to the Arab Conquests* (London).

Stephani, L. (1881), 'Erklärung einiger Kunstwerke der Kaiserlichen Ermitage', Supplement to *Compte-Rendu*, 5–138.

Stevens, G. P., and Paton, J. M. (1927), *The Erechtheum* (Cambridge, Mass.).

Stewart, A. F. (1977), 'To Entertain an Emperor: Sperlonga, Laokoon, and Tiberius at the Dinner-Table', *JRS* 67: 76–91.

—— (1979), *Attika: Studies in Athenian Sculpture of the Hellenistic Age* (London).

—— (1983), 'Stesichoros and the François Vase', in Moon (1983), 53–74.

Stibbe, C. M. (1972), *Lakonische Vasenmaler des sechsten Jhdts v. Chr.* (Amsterdam).

Stone, J. (1965), *English Silver of the Eighteenth Century* (London).

Stratford, N. (1984), 'Metalwork', in Exhibition Catalogue, *English Romanesque Art 1066–1200* (Hayward Gallery, London), 232–6.

Stroheker, K. F. (1958), *Dionysios I. Gestalt und Geschichte des Tyrannen von Syrakus* (Wiesbaden).

Strong, D. E. (1966), *Greek and Roman Gold and Silver Plate* (London).

Swinburne, H. (1785–7), *Voyage dans les Deux-Siciles* (2 vols., Paris).

Themelis, P. G. (1983), *Delphi: The Archaeological Site and the Museum* (Athens).

Θησαυροί (1979), Exhibition Catalogue, Θησαυροί τῆς ἀρχαίας Μακεδονίας (Thessaloniki).

Thompson, D. B. (1939), '*Mater caelaturae*: Impressions from Ancient Metalwork', *Hesperia*, 8: 385–16.

Thompson, H. A. (1940), 'A Golden Nike from the Athenian Agora', in *Athenian Studies Presented to William Scott Ferguson* (*HSCP*, suppl. vol. 1), 183–210.

—— (1984), 'The Athenian Vase-Painters and their Neighbors', in P. M. Rice (ed.), *Pots and Potters: Current Approaches in Ceramic Archaeology* (Institute of Archaeology, University of California, Los Angeles, Monograph 24), 7–19.

—— and Wycherley, R. E. (1972), *The Agora of Athens: The History, Shape and Uses of an Ancient City Center* (*Athenian Agora*, 14) (Princeton, NJ).

Thracian Treasures (1976), British Museum, *Thracian Treasures from Bulgaria* (London).

Thrakische Silberschatz (n.d.), *Der Thrakische Silberschatz aus Rogosen Bulgarien*. Exhibition Catalogue, Hamburg (n. pl).

Tite, M. S., Bimson, M., and Freestone, I. C. (1982), 'An Examination of the High Gloss Surface Finishes on Greek Attic and Roman Samian Wares', *Archaeometry*, 24: 117–26.

Tognarini, I. (1980), 'La questione del ferro nella Toscana del XVI secolo', in L. Rombai (1980), 239–61.

Tomlinson, R. A. (1969), 'Perachora: The Remains outside the Two Sanctuaries', *BSA* 64: 155–258.

—— (1970), 'Ancient Macedonian Symposia', *Symposium 'Ancient Macedonia', August 1968* (Thessaloniki), 308–15.

—— (1980), 'Two Notes on Possible *Hestiatoria*', *BSA* 75: 221–8.

Tompkins, J. F. (1983) (ed.), *Wealth of the Ancient World: The Nelson Bunker Hunt and William Herbert Hunt Collections* (Fort Worth, Tex.).

Toynbee, J. M. C., and Painter, K. S. (1986), 'Silver Picture Plates of Late Antiquity', *Archaeologia*, 108: 15–65, pls. 7–30.

Toynbee, Mrs Paget (1903–5) (ed.), *Horace Walpole, Letters* (16 vols., Oxford).

Trachsler, W. (1966), 'The Influence of Metalworking on Prehistoric Pottery: Some Observations on Iron Age Pottery in the Alpine Region', in F. R. Matson (ed.), *Ceramics and Man* (London), 140–57.

Tregear, M. (1986), 'Tenth Century Yue Ware and Silver and Gold', in Vickers (1986*a*), 175–8.

Tréheux, J. (1991), 'Retour à Imbros et à Samothrace', *Hellènika Symmikta, Histoire, archéologie, épigraphie* (Études d'archéologie classique, 7) (Nancy).

—— (1992), *Inscriptions de Délos, Index I* (Paris).

Trevelyan, H. (1941), *Goethe and the Greeks* (Cambridge).

Tripp, D. E. (1986), 'Coinage', in L. Bonfante (ed.), *Etruscan Life and Afterlife: A Handbook of Etruscan Studies* (Detroit), 202–14.

Tsetskhladze, G. (forthcoming), 'A Note on the Silver Phiale from Phasis', *OJA* 13 (1994).

Tudor-Craig, P. (1987), 'Late Middle Ages', in Saint Aubyn (1987), 94–107.

Turner, P. (1965), *Thomas More, Utopia* (Harmondsworth).

Ure, P. N. (1936), 'Red Figure Cups with Incised and Stamped Decoration 1', *JHS* 56: 205–15.

—— (1944), 'Red Figure Cups with Incised and Stamped Decoration 2', *JHS* 64: 67–77.

—— (1954), *Corpus Vasorum Antiquorum*, University of Reading (London).

Vallance, A. (1909), 'Hispano-Moresque Lustre Ware', *Studio*, 47: 14–20.

Vaulina, M., and Wasovicz, A. (1974), *Bois grecs et romains de l'Ermitage* (Wroclaw).

Venedikov, I., and Gerassimov, T. (1973), *Thrakische Kunst* (Vienna and Munich).

Verheyen, E. (1985) (ed.), *William S. Heckscher, Art and Literature: Studies in Relationship* (Saecula Spiritualia, 17) (Baden-Baden).

Vermeule, C. C. III (1974), *Greek and Roman Sculpture in Gold and Silver* (Boston).

—— (1977), *Greek Sculpture and Roman Taste: The Purpose and Setting of Graeco-Roman Art in Italy and the Greek Imperial East* (Ann Arbor, Mich.).

Vespucci, A. [1505/6] (1893), *The First Four Voyages* [Florence] (London).

Vessberg, O. (1941), *Studien zur Kunstgeschichte der römischen Republik* (Lund and Leipzig).

Vestergaard, T., and Schroder, K. (1985), *The Language of Advertising* (Oxford).

Vickers, M. (1978), *Greek Vases* (Oxford).

—— (1979), *Scythian Treasures in Oxford* (Oxford).

—— (1983*a*), 'Les Vases peintes: Image ou mirage?', in Lissarague and Thelamon (1983), 29–44.

—— (1983*b*), 'Arthur Evans, Sicily and Greek Vases in Oxford', *Apollo*, 117: 276–9.

—— (1984), 'The Influence of Exotic Materials on Attic White-ground Pottery', in Brijder (1984), 88–97.

—— (1984 (1988)), 'Demus' Gold *Phiale* (Lysias 19.25)', *American Journal of Ancient History*, 9: 48–53.

—— (1985*a*), 'Artful Crafts: The Influence of Metalwork on Athenian Painted Pottery', *JHS* 105: 108–28.

—— (1985*b*), 'Early Greek Coinage: A Reassessment', *NC* 145: 1–44.

—— (1985–6), 'Imaginary Etruscans: Changing Perceptions of Etruria since the Fifteenth Century', *Hephaistos*, 7/8: 153–68, pls. 1–5.

—— (1986*a*) (ed.), *Pots and Pans: Proceedings of the Colloquium on Precious Metal and Ceramics in the Muslim, Chinese and Graeco-Roman Worlds* (Oxford Studies in Islamic Art, 3) (Oxford).

—— (1986*b*), 'Silver, Copper and Ceramics in Ancient Athens', in Vickers (1986*a*), 137–51.

—— (1987*a*), 'Value and Simplicity: Eighteenth Century Taste and the Study of Greek Vases', *Past and Present*, 116: 98–137.

—— (1987*b*), 'Early Civilizations', in Saint Aubyn (1987), 32–49.

—— (1989*a*), 'The Cultural Context of Ancient Greek Ceramics: An Essay in Skeuomorphism', in McGovern and Notis (1989), 45–64.

—— (1989*b*), 'Persian Gold on the Athenian Acropolis', *Actes du Colloque sur l'or dans l'empire achéménide, Bordeaux, March 1989. REA* 91: 249–57.

—— (1990*a*), 'Golden Greece: Relative Values, Minae and Temple Inventories', *AJA* 94: 613–25.

—— (1990*b*), 'The Impoverishment of the Past: The Case of Classical Greece', *Antiquity*, 64: 455–63.

—— (1992*a*), 'The Metrology of Gold and Silver Plate in Classical Greece', *Boreas* 21: 53–71 (Uppsala).

—— (1992*b*), 'Phidias' Zeus and its *fortuna*', in Fitton (1992), 217–25.

—— (1992*c*), 'Recent Acquisitions of Greek and Etruscan Antiquities by the Ashmolean Museum, Oxford 1981–90', *JHS* 112: 246–8, pls. 7–8.

—— (1993), 'Early Silver, 3000 BC–1000 AD', in *Sotheby's Concise Encyclopedia of Silver* (London), 15–33.

—— (1994), 'Nabataea, India, Gaul and Carthage: Reflections on Hellenistic and Roman Gold and Red Gloss Pottery', *AJA* 98: 231–48.

—— (forthcoming), 'The Greek Pottery Vases from Gela in Oxford: Their Place in History and the History of Art', *Atti del Convegno internazionale sulla ceramica greca* (Catania).

—— Gill, D. W. J., and Economou, M. (forthcoming), 'Euesperides, the Rescue of an Excavation', in J. M. Reynolds (ed.), *Proceedings of the Cyrenaican Symposium, Cambridge 1993*.

—— Impey, O., and Allan, J. (1986), *From Silver to Ceramic* (Oxford).

Vischer, R. (1965), *Das einfache Leben: Wort- und motiv-geschichtliche Untersuchungen zu einem Wertbegriff der antiken Literatur* (Gottingen).

Vitelli, K. (1992), 'Pots *vs.* Vases', *Antiquity*, 66: 550–3.

Vitto, F. (1986), 'Potters and Pottery Manufacture in Roman Palestine', *University of London, Institute of Archaeology Bulletin*, 23: 47–64.

Vittori, O. (1979), 'Pliny the Elder on Gilding: A New Interpretation of his Comments', *Gold Bulletin*, 12(1): 35–9.

Voltaire (1767), *Les Scythes* (Paris).

Vocotopoulou, J. (1986) to 'Η Υδρία της Αίνειας', in Αμητός. Τιμητικός τόμος για τον Καθηγετή Μ. Ανδρόνικο (Thessaloniki), 157–69.

Vulic, N. (1930), 'Das neue Grab von Trebenischte', *AA* 276–99.

Walberg, G. (1976), 'Kamares: A Study of the Character of Palatial Middle Minoan Pottery', *Boreas*, 8: 34–9 (Uppsala).

Walters, H. B., and Birch, S. (1905), *History of Ancient Pottery, Greek, Etruscan and Roman* (London).

Wasovicz, A. (1966), *Obróbka drewna w starozytnej Grecji* (Wroclaw).

Watkin, D. (1968), *Thomas Hope 1769–1831 and the Neo-Classical Idea* (London).

—— (1977), *Morality and Architecture* (Oxford).

Watson, F. (1977), 'Mentmore and its Art Collections', *Mentmore*, 2 (Sotheby Catalogue, 18–23 May), pp. x–xi.

Watson, H. (1988), *Collecting Clarice Cliff* (London).

Watson, O. (1986), 'Pottery and Metal Shapes in Persia in the 12th and 13th Centuries', in Vickers (1986*a*), 205–12.

Watson, W. (1986), Precious Metal—Its Influence on Tang Earthenware', in Vickers (1986*a*), 161–75.

Weber, T. (1983), *Bronzekannen. Studien zu ausgewählten archaischen und klassischen Oinochoenformen aus Metall in Griechenland und Etruria* (Frankfurt and Bern).

—— (1990), 'Etruskisches Bronzegerät in Syrien', *AA* 435–48.

Webster, T. B. L. (1972), *Potter and Patron in Ancient Athens* (London).

Wedgwood, J. (1790), *Description abregée du vase de Barberini, maintenant vase de Portland, et de la méthode que l'on a suivie pour un* [sic] *former les bas-reliefs* (London).

Weege, F. (1921), *Etruskische Malerei* (Halle).

Wegner, M. (1944), *Goethes Anschauung antiker Kunst* (Berlin).

Weinberg, S. S. (1969), 'A Gold Sauceboat in the Israel Museum', *AK* 12: 3–8.

—— (1988), 'A Syro-Palestinian Bowl Type', *Muse*, 22: 64–74.

Wentworth-Shields, P. (1976), *Clarice Cliff* (London).

West, M. L. (1984), *Carmina Anacreonta* (Leipzig).

Westhoff-Krummacher, H. (1980), *Porzellan des Bürgertums—englisches und deutsches Steingut und seine Beziehungen zu Westfalen* (Münster).

White, P. T. (1974), 'The Eternal Treasure: Gold', *National Geographic*, 145(1): 1–51.

Wiesehöfer, J. (1980), 'Die "Freunde" und "Wohltäter" des Grosskönigs', *Studia Iranica*, 9: 7–21.

Willemsen, F. (1968), 'Die Ausgrabungen im Kerameikos 1966', *Archaiologikon Deltion*, 23/2. 1: 24–32.

Williams, D. (1985), *Greek Vases* (London).

Williamson, G. C. (1938), *The Book of Ivory* (London).

Winckelmann, J. J. (1755), *Gedanken über die Nachahmung der griechischen Werke in der Malerei und Bildhauerkunst* (Friederichstadt).

—— (1764), *Geschichte der Kunst des Altertums* (2 vols., Dresden).

Winckelmann, W. (1909), *Edle Einfalt und Stille Grösse* (Berlin).

Wiseman, D. J. (1956), *Chronicles of the Chaldaean Kings (626–556 BC), in the British Museum* (London).

Wittkower, R. and M. (1963), *Born Under Saturn. The Character and Conduct of Artists: Documentary Evidence from Antiquity to the French Revolution* (London).

Wolf, E. R. (1982), *Europe and the People without History* (Berkeley, Calif., and Los Angeles).

Woolley, L. (1953), *A Forgotten Kingdom; being a Record of the Results Obtained from the Excavation of Two Mounds, Atchana and Al Mina, in the Turkish Hatay* (Harmondsworth).

Wornum, R. N. (1851), 'The Exhibition as an Essay in Taste', in *The Art Journal Illustrated Catalogue of the Great Exhibition*, i***–xxii*** [*sic*] (London).

Wranglén, G. (1985), *An Introduction to Corrosion and Protection of Metals* (London).

Wright, F. A. (1923), *The Arts in Greece: Three Essays* (London).

Wright, J. C. (1993), Review of Morris (1992), in *Bryn Mawr Classical Review*, Electronic Edition.

Wycherley, R. E. (1976), 'Rhodes', in *The Princeton Encyclopedia of Classical Sites* (Princeton, NJ), 755–8.

—— (1978), *The Stones of Athens* (Princeton, NJ).

Young, J. J. (1879), *The Ceramic Art* (London).

Young, R. S. (1951), 'An Industrial District of Ancient Athens', *Hesperia*, 20: 135–288.

Züchner, W. (1950–1), 'Von Toreuten und Töpfern', *JdI* 65–6: 175–205.

Index of Sources

INSCRIPTIONS AND PAPYRI

General Index

Acknowledgements

Oxford University Press wishes to thank the following for permission to reproduce the illustrations:

Museo Arqueologico, Barcelona (Fig. 5.9); The Trustees of the British Museum (Figs 6.11, 7.1); Museum of Fine Arts, Boston (Fig. 3.2) The Bulgarian Committee for Culture (Frontispiece, Fig. 2.6); The Museum of Oriental Art, Moscow (Fig. 2.3); The Metropolitan Museum, New York (Fig. 2.4); Département des Antiquités grecques, étrusques et romaines, Musée du Louvre, Paris (Fig. 6.2); The Committee of the Ashmolean Library, Oxford (Figs. 1.2, 1.3, 1.4, 1.5, 1.6, 1.8); The Visitors of the Ashmolean Museum, Oxford (Figs. 1.1, 2.1, 2.5, 4.2, 4.3, 4.4, 5.1, 5.2, 5.3, 5.4, 5.6, 5.7, 5.8, 5.10, 5.12, 5.13, 5.16, 5.17, 5.18, 5.19, 5.21, 5.25, 5.28, 5.29, 5.30, 5.31, 5.32, 5.34, 6.1, 6.3, 6.4, 6.7, 6.13, 6.14, 6.15); Dr Jessica Rawson (Fig. 6.11); The Hermitage Museum, St Petersburg (Figs. 2.5, 3.1, 3.2, 5.20); Archives, Manufacture Nationale de Sèvres (Fig. 1.9); Michael Vickers (Figs. 5.22, 5.23, 5.24); The Trustees of the Wedgwood Museum, Barlaston, Staffordshire (Fig. 1.7). Chapter 1 first appeared in *Past and Present* 116 (1987), and is reprinted, with minor changes, by kind permission of the editors.